P9-DCO-531

Thinking About Women

THINKING ABOUT
WOMEN
Sociological and Feminist Perspectives

Margaret L. Andersen
University of Delaware, Newark

Macmillan Publishing Co., Inc.
New York

Collier Macmillan Publishers
London

Copyright © 1983, Macmillan Publishing Co., Inc.

Printed in the United States of America

All rights reserved. No part of this book may be reproduced or transmitted in any form or by any means, electronic or mechanical, including photocopying, recording, or any information storage and retrieval system, without permission in writing from the Publisher.

Macmillan Publishing Co., Inc.
866 Third Avenue, New York, New York 10022

Collier Macmillan Canada, Inc.

Library of Congress Cataloging in Publication Data

Andersen, Margaret L.

  Thinking about women.
  Bibliography: p.
  Includes index.
  1. Women—United States—Social conditions.
2. Feminism—United States. 3. Social institutions
—United States. 4. Social change. I. Title.
HQ1426.A6825 1983   305.4′2′0973   82-14030
ISBN 0-02-303370-3

Printing: 4 5 6 7 8   Year: 5 6 7 8 9 0

ISBN   0-02-303370-3

PS1875

For my Grandmother,

Sybil R. Wangberg

PREFACE

Thinking About Women introduces students to the contemporary research and theoretical perspectives which observe and explain the sociological character of women's lives in American society. The idea for this book emerged from my dissatisfaction with textbooks on sex roles and gender that take primarily a social-psychological view and that also ignore theoretical issues about gender relations. Since I began teaching courses on the sociology of sex roles in the early 1970s, a rich and intellectually exciting literature has developed among feminist scholars. In the most recent years, this scholarship has not only contributed new research insights, but it has also initiated theoretical discussions that make women's lives central to the basic concepts and perspectives of sociological thinking.

The sociological perspective is one that roots the experience of individuals and social groups in the social organization of the society in which they live. But much of the sociological theory and research has been flawed because it has largely overlooked women's roles in society and the way in which gender influences social organization. Like other major sociological categories—class and race—gender influences who we will become in society, what resources will be available to us, and how we are defined by others. The wealth of research that has emerged from feminist analysis of sociological issues shows how gender shapes our personalities, skills, and self-concepts, organizes the social institutions in which we live, and influences the distribution of wealth, power, and privilege.

Hopefully, this book will sensitize students to the position of women in American society and will give them the intellectual tools with which to comprehend women's experience. The sociological perspective is particularly significant to feminist thought because it ties individual experience to the social organization of society. Although this book is not intended to help students find personal solutions to collective problems, it does show how individual experiences are created and transformed through social, political, and economic institutions. Feminist scholarship helps explain the structure of these institutions, and is also a means of dispersing this knowledge to promote liberating social changes for women and for men.

Part One of *Thinking About Women* introduces the sociological perspective and the emergence of feminist thinking in sociology. Chapter 1 is a discussion of feminist perspectives in sociology and it outlines the criticisms that the feminist movement has brought to traditional sociological study. Chapters 2 and 3 focus on the most immediately experienced levels of gender relations—human biology and the individual in society. Chapter 2 reviews biological issues about gender and its relationship to culture and social structure. Chapter 3 examines sex role socialization, which is the process by which social expectations about gender are developed.

Part Two studies the significance of gender in contemporary social institutions. Institutions are established and organized patterns of values, norms, roles, and status that develop around some of the basic functions of a society. The persistence of these social institutions defines the social structure in which we live and also makes each society distinct. Chapter 4 discusses women and economic institutions; Chapter 5 is an analysis of women and the family; Chapter 6 examines issues surrounding women, reproduction, and health care; and Chapter 7 discusses women, crime, and social deviance.

Part Three reviews feminist theoretical perspectives and the origins of feminist thought. The ideas we form about women and gender, although they are subjective in character, have their origins in objective social systems. The dynamic relationship between social structure and consciousness is such that one must understand social change as involving both changes in consciousness and objective social conditions. Chapter 8 discusses the social construction of ideas about women and gender, especially as they are created in the public media and in academic knowledge. Chapters 9 and 10 review feminist theory and its implications for social change. These chapters are also organized according to the dialogue that has emerged between liberal and radical perspectives in feminist and social theory.

In developing research and theory on gender relations in society, feminist scholars do not mean merely to create another abstract category for sociological analysis. Like race and class, the social organization of gender has specific social, economic, and political consequences for women, as well as for men. Feminist studies in sociology are not intended to construct abstract empirical analyses of gender, nor to develop grand theories that have no relevance to the lives of actual human beings (Mills 1959). While concept-building and observational studies are necessary in constructing accurate feminist accounts of social life, their purpose is the transformation of gender relations and the society in which we live. Thus, complete accounts of social life must explain the experiences of all women. Just as male-centered sociological studies are biased by their omission of women, so are feminist studies flawed when they are based only on the experiences of white, middle-class, and heterosexual women. Throughout this book, the questions must be asked, "Is this true for nonwhite women and lesbian women?" and "How is their experience similar to and different from other women?" Because feminist analysis seeks to understand the commonalities and the differences in women's experiences, sound feminist scholarship must entail an understanding of race, class, and heterosexual relations. Although this book may not stand up completely to the challenge, I hope that it does contribute to feminist scholars' growing analysis.

Many people have contributed to the development of this book. Their ideas about women and their encouragement and support for this project have been invaluable to me. Many provided thoughtful reviews of earlier drafts of this book and many worked long hours typing and editing the manuscript. I see it as a measure of the success of the women's movement that this project has been accomplished with the help of such a strong network of women friends and colleagues and the lively and interdisciplinary community of feminist scholars who are working to transform the academic disciplines.

In particular, I thank Peggy Phelan, Valerie Hans, Gloria Hull, Jerry Turkel, Leslie Goldstein, Tricia Farris, Caryn Horwitz, Jan DeAmicis, Patty Klausner, and Marion Palley for discussing numerous parts of this book with me and providing careful reviews of my work. I also thank the members of Sociologists for Women in Society for sharing their criticisms of this book with me and for the many stimulating discussions we have had. Although many of my students remain unnamed here, they have stimulated the creation of much of this book, both through their enthusiasm for the material and their questioning about the issues involved. I appreciate the timely support of a Grant-in-Aid from the Dean of the College of Arts and Science at the University of Delaware.

I thank Gaye Tuchman, Anne Pottieger, and the anonymous reviewers who provided valuable criticisms on earlier drafts of the manuscript. I especially appreciated the assistance of Rachel Kahn-Hut whose excellent editorial work provided careful criticism of the substance of the book, at the same time that she gave excellent advice for the book's style and organization with an emphasis on clarity for readers. Ken Scott, my editor, deserves special thanks because he is a superb editor with great academic integrity and an encouraging attitude. And, without the ongoing support of a group of wonderful, hardworking, and grossly underpaid women, this work would never have been published; I thank Carol Anderson, Marie Gregg, Claire Blessing, Sylvia Knight, Fran Price, and Shirley Anderson for typing this manuscript and for their generous assistance during the two years of writing this book.

Although I have no wife to thank for her constant support, attention to detail, and undying loyalty, I do express my thanks to friends who, in their own ways, helped me complete this book. Time and time again I faced the problem of expressing my ideas with confidence and clarity while retaining the intellectual doubts and questions that are essential to the development of ideas. The very act of writing brings authenticity to what we think and there were many times when maintaining the balance between doubting and knowing would not have been possible without the support of some very special friends. Especially, I want to thank Lewis Killian and Michael Lewis for teaching me the value of sociological thinking and the necessity for creating a humanistic approach to the study of social problems. There is no one who has contributed so enormously to my feminist thinking as Sandra Harding. Her friendship, wisdom, and intellectual challenge have kept me working when it seemed impossible. I thank her deeply for her careful reading of my work, her work as a coteacher, and her persistent passion for feminist theory. Linda Hall and Jane Bennett have shown me the value of women's lives in a way that no academic study could, and I thank them for the support they provided throughout the time I was working on this book. Also, I thank Jane, whose meticulous attention to detail made order of a chaotic bibliography. And, in more ways than I could show in print, I thank Richard Rosenfeld for his patience, humanity, and humility and for keeping the home fires burning.

Margaret Andersen

C O N T E N T S

Thinking About Women

PART ONE

WOMEN'S LIVES AND THE SOCIOLOGICAL PERSPECTIVE

C H A P T E R

1

SOCIOLOGICAL AND FEMINIST PERSPECTIVES

INTRODUCTION

In the ordinary course of our daily lives, we are surrounded by evidence of the position of women in American society. In the checkout lane at the grocery store, most of the cashiers are women; the managers and baggers, men. Where children are playing, there is usually a woman nearby. In bars, men touch women more often, more aggressively, and in more different places than happens when women touch men. Gender differences can even be seen between men and women who cross the street against the light. As one student observed, men not only cross against the light more often than do women, but, when they do, they walk without hesitating and with a steady gait. Women, on the other hand, are more likely to pause, laugh, and then run.

Each of these examples reveals patterns of sex role behavior; yet, much of the time, these patterns go unnoticed. So deeply are they embedded in the minds of both men and women that, unless they become a problem, we are hardly aware of them. We take these patterns of everyday life for granted, and they become part of the natural landscape that surrounds us in the social world.

This book studies patterns of behavior and social organization as they are influenced by gender relations. Only recently, because of the influence of feminism, have sociologists begun to study gender as a sociological issue. As sociologists began to look more carefully at gender in society, they often had to change some of their previous assumptions about the roles of women and the ways in which gender relations were organized in society. Consequently, new studies about gender roles and women's status have transformed sociological perspectives on society and the position of men and women within it. In this book, we will see how sociological and feminist perspectives inform us about women's lives, and we will review some of the recent research and theory that scholars have produced in studying that experience.

First, this chapter will discuss feminism and its influence on sociological thinking. The chapter will introduce students to some of the basic premises of the sociological perspective and will discuss the meaning of feminism and its pertinence to sociological study. As we will see, the rebirth of feminism in the 1960s has caused us to reconsider much of what we thought we knew about women and men in society. Thus, the influence of feminism on sociological thinking has been considerable and has raised new questions about the social organization of gender relations, the possibilities for social change, and the relationship of social change to academic knowledge. This first chapter introduces these issues and discusses the emergence of feminist perspectives in sociology and its related disciplines. We will begin by discussing feminism and the sociological perspective.

FEMINISM AND THE SOCIOLOGICAL PERSPECTIVE

As already noted, patterns in gender relations are found throughout society, although much of the time, these patterns remain invisible to us. But at some point, we may start to notice them. Perhaps at school we see that most of the professors are men and that, among students, men are more outspoken in class. Or perhaps at work we notice that women are concentrated in the lowest-level jobs and are sometimes treated as if they were not even there. Or it may occur to us one night as we are walking through city streets that the bright lights shining in the night skyline represent the thousands of women—many of them black, Hispanic, or Asian—who clean the corporate suites and offices for organizations that are dominated by white men.

Recognizing these events as indications of the status of women helps us see inequities in the experience of men and women in society. Once we begin to recognize these patterns, we are often astounded at how pervasive they are. And, as the unequal status of women becomes more apparent, we might feel overwhelmed by the vast extent of a problem we never acknowledged before. What we see might become troubling, and we may find it difficult to imagine ways in which these long-standing inequities can be changed. But, once we start to question the position of women in society, we will want to know more and will begin to ask questions such as: What exactly is the status of women in society? How did things become this way?, How can we change the inequalities that women experience?

When we first ask such questions, we sometimes have to rely on already existing explanations of people's experience in society. But much of the time, what is already known makes little sense of women's lives. Think of a student who wants to know why so few (if any) women artists are shown in the material for an introductory art history course. The student reads in the textbook, "The fountainhead of creativity lies in the imagination, which manifests itself in the projection of images. . . . Man also possesses creative powers in his own right, and in turn creates his gods, his ideas, his ideals, his arts, in his own human image. . . . Art, then, is the language in images by which man communicates his ideas, his conceptions of himself, his fellowmen, and his universe" (Fleming 1974:1).

If there are no women artists shown in the course or the book, does this mean that women have no imagination, no creativity? Why are women absent from the collections of great art? Is the "universal" only the experience that is shared by men? What does this introduction to art history tell us about the experience of women who were creative and who wanted to express their creativity through the arts?

Adrienne Rich (1976), a feminist poet, suggests that simply asking "What is life like for women?" will create a new awareness of the situation of women in society and history. This questioning, in part, is what the feminist movement has encouraged in most of the academic disciplines. With whatever question we begin, whether it is "Why are there no great women artists?" (Nochlin 1971) or "Why is it that women clean the offices and men manage them?," by virtue of asking, we are creating new questions and new issues for investigation. These questions, then, form the basis for emerging feminist theory, and it is this process of questioning that gives birth to the sociological and feminist imagination.

The sociological imagination was first described by C. Wright Mills (1916–1962), an eminent sociologist and radical in his time. Mills's radicalism is founded, in part, on his passionate belief that the task of sociology is to understand the relations between individuals and the society in which they live. Furthermore, he argued that sociological understanding must be used in the reconstruction of more just social institutions. Except for the masculine references in his language, his words still provide a compelling argument that sociology must make sense of the experience of women and men as they exist in contemporary society. He writes:

Nowadays men often feel that their private lives are a series of traps. They sense that within their everyday world, they cannot overcome their troubles, and, in this feeling, they are often quite correct. What ordinary men are directly aware of and what they try to do are bounded by the private orbits in which they live; . . . The sociological imagination enables its possessor to understand the larger historical scene in terms of its meaning for the inner life and external career of a variety of individuals. . . . The first fruit of this imagination—and the first lesson of the social science that embodies it—is the idea that the individual can understand his experience and gauge his fate only by locating himself within his period, that he can know his chances in life only by becoming aware of those of all individuals in his circumstances. (Mills 1959:3–5)

Mills's ideas are strikingly parallel to the feminist argument that women can see how their private experience is rooted in social conditions by discovering their shared experience with other women. In fact, Mills professes that the central task of sociology is to understand personal biography and social structure and the relations between the two. His argument is best illustrated in the distinction he makes between personal troubles and social issues.

Troubles are those that are located in the personal experience of an individual. They are privately felt, and they involve only those persons and events in an individual's immediate surroundings. Public issues are events that originate beyond one's immediate experience, even though they are still felt there. Public issues involve the structure of social institutions and their historical development. Mills's own example is that of marriage. He says, "Inside a marriage a man and a woman may experience personal troubles, but when the divorce rate during the first four years of marriage is 250 out of every 1,000 attempts, this is an indication of a structural issue having to do with the institutions of marriage and the family and other institutions that bear upon them" (1959:9). Mills's point is that events that are felt as personal troubles often have their origins in the public issues that emerge from specific historical and social conditions.

Another example is that of a woman who is beaten by her husband. She experiences deep personal trouble, and perhaps her situation appears to her as unique or as only a private problem between herself and her husband. But when others in the society have the same experience, then a public issue is found. Common patterns in the experiences of battered wives reveal that wife beating is more than just a private matter. It has its origins in complex social institutions that define women's place as in the home, as subordinate to their husbands, and as dependent upon men. In this sense, wife beating is both a personal trouble and a public issue. As Mills would conclude, it is then a subject for the sociological imagination. For feminists, this junction between personal experience and the social organization of gender roles is also a starting point for analysis.

The relationship between personal troubles and public issues reveals an essential premise of the sociological perspective—that individual life is situated in specific social and historical environments. These environments condition not only what our experience is but also how we think about it. This premise is also basic to feminist perspectives on society and women's and men's experiences within it. Although, as this book will show, feminism encompasses a variety of perspectives, one basic premise of feminist thought is that women's experience emerges from the social, political, and economic structure of society. Both feminists and sociologists recognize that individuals are caught up in the social institutions of their time. This insight forms the beginning of sociological and feminist perspectives on social life.

Feminist perspectives in sociology were formulated only recently when women (and some men) in the profession of sociology began applying the tools of sociological analysis to their understanding of the position of women in society. Many questions that form the crux of the sociological imagination have now been revised by feminist scholars in trying to comprehend women's experience.

For example, C. Wright Mills identified a series of questions that have been consistently asked by sociologists. They include: What is the structure of this particular society as a whole? How does it differ from other varieties of social order? Where does this society stand in human history, and what are the mechanics by which it is changing? What types of men and women now prevail in this society and in this period (1959:6–7)?

Feminist investigations of these questions have revealed, as a beginning, that the structure of American society is one of inequality between women and men. Although women constitute over 40 percent of the total labor force, they earn fifty-nine cents for every dollar earned by men. And if we include housework in the definition of productive work, these women, in fact, work longer hours every week than full-time employed men (Hartmann 1981). Worldwide, a United Nations study shows that women are one third of the world labor force and do most of the unpaid work. But women receive only 10 percent of the world's income and own less than 1 percent of the world's property (United Nations Commission on the Status of Women 1980; cited in Leghorn and Parker 1981:4–5).

Yet, the inequality of women is not an inevitable fact; studies of a variety of societies indicate that women's status varies cross-culturally and over time. We learn from cross-cultural and historical research that women's role in society is one of great diversity, even though there are many commonalities from society to society. For instance, not all societies see women as powerless citizens, and in some societies women exercise more control over reproduction and production than in others. These varieties of social organization show us that women's role is not innate and, therefore, is subject to social change. Feminist scholars believe that study of the differences and similarities in women's experiences can lead us to new directions for social change and liberation.

Feminist studies have also revealed the varieties of women and men who exist within our own society. They have done so by rediscovering groups of women who are rendered invisible by studies that concentrate only on the experiences and perspectives of dominant groups. Thus, feminism recognizes the experience of black, Hispanic, Asian, and native American women as unique, founded in the intersection of racism and sexism. Feminist studies also require us to include the experiences of lesbian women in our analysis of how society is organized and how groups within society are socially controlled. Therefore, the feminist perspective brings issues of racism, class, and lesbian oppression to our analysis of gender relations, and it causes us to consider all of the varieties in women's experience that occur in this society.

Moreover, feminist perspectives also change the way we see men in the world, because traditional studies see men in terms of what they ought to be, not necessarily what they are or even what they want to be. As feminist scholars have studied men's lives, they find that, although men benefit from institutionalized power and privilege, they, too, are subjected to sexist cultural expectations of masculinity that affect their emotions, identities, and social roles (Pleck and Brannon 1978).

In sum, in considering old sociological questions, feminists have discovered new facts about society that emerge from documenting patterns of gender inequality and from studying the experiences of all women within the society. Feminist research in sociology has unmasked the biases in conventional studies and has shown how these studies result in inadequate accounts of the lives of both women and men. And as the feminist dialogue with sociology has developed, scholars have begun to explain the emergence and persistence of gender inequality and sex roles.

Yet, it is important to point out that, just as there is no single sociological interpretation of complex social issues, there is no single feminist perspective. Within feminist thought, different assumptions and observations lead to a rich and varied analysis of the position of women in society. There are some basic premises that feminists share, as we will see, but feminist explanations of women's experience are the subject of scholarly as well as political debate.

Feminism begins with the premise that women's and men's positions in society are the result of social, not natural, factors. The meaning of feminism has been developed and understood in different ways, but it begins with the idea that social institutions and social attitudes are the basis of women's position in society. Furthermore, feminism takes women's interests and perspectives as not inferior to those of men, believing that where women are treated as inferior citizens, then liberating social changes on their behalf can and should be made. Thus, feminism is both a way of thinking and a way of acting, and the union of action and thought is central to feminist programs for social change. Although feminists would not necessarily argue that women should be like men, they do believe that women's experiences and perspectives are as valuable as those of men. Moreover, feminism makes women's interests central to all movements for liberating social change.

FEMINIST SCHOLARSHIP AND SOCIAL CHANGE

The reemergence of feminism in the 1960s signaled the beginning of a decade in which social changes in women's roles would extend to every area of life, ranging from the workplace and the courts to religion, the arts, and the private dynamics of family life. Within American society, the feminist movement has made significant changes in the ways men's and women's roles are defined and the ways in which they think of each other. At the individual level, many women, as well as many men, have questioned their traditional social roles and the beliefs about themselves that they have acquired. And in institutions such as the family and work, new practices and policies have transformed male and female behavior. These individual and social changes reveal the impact of feminism upon our daily lives and the structure of our society.

These changes in the fabric of American society show that feminism is one of the most significant social movements of modern times. Its impact has been made not only on the individual and collective lives of people but also on the way we think and on how knowledge about our society is developed and used. The effects of feminism can be found both in the societal changes it has generated and in the transformations in social thought and scholarship it has inspired.

The women's liberation movement began in the late 1960s in a climate of political activism and criticism of traditional societal institutions and policies. The civil rights movement, the anti-Vietnam War movement, and the student movements of the 1960s focused attention on issues of the inequality of economic and social resources, on the need for a realignment of power in the society, on the inhumane character of war and our national policies, and on the need to establish political and civil rights for all social groups.

For women who participated in these movements, a new political consciousness was born as they used the analysis of oppression being created in these movements to comprehend their own experience. Frequently, they observed contradictions between the analysis of equality and liberation developed in these movements and the existence within these movements of the same sexist attitudes and behaviors that were demonstrated in the society at large. These movements generated an analysis by women of their oppression as women (Evans 1979). Moreover, the movements provided black and white women with opportunities to use and develop skills in political organizing and consciousness raising.

At the same time, structural changes in the employment and education of white, middle-class women fostered a sense of contradiction, or relative deprivation, among them. More white, middle-class women were working than ever before. They were also becoming better educated because post-World War II expansion in higher education had created new opportunities for men and women of the white middle class. Yet, in spite of their educational backgrounds, most of these women still found themselves isolated in the family or trapped in sex-segregated jobs where they earned less and had less chance for advancement than their male counterparts. Thus, relative to their training and their aspirations for success, these women were deprived of an equal share of the social and economic resources of society. To the extent that they received such resources, their status remained one of dependence upon men if they were married or poverty if they were not.

For black women, as well as other minority women, the disadvantages imposed by sexism are added to those already incurred by racism. Although the middle-class bias of the white women's movement has alienated many black women, black women clearly see the effects of sexism in their own experiences. Even with the gains resulting from the civil rights movement, black women have remained in sex-segregated jobs, thus fostering feminist perspectives among them (Lewis 1977). Now many black women have a stronger tendency to identify with the principles of feminism than do white women even though they perceive the women's liberation movement as being primarily for white women (Hemmons 1980).

Thus, from the start, modern feminism had its origins in the experiences of both well-educated, white, middle-class women and minority women. Moreover, feminism emerged in a political context that drew connections between the experience of women and those of other oppressed groups. Yet, differences between white women and women of color have created both tensions and bonds within the women's movement, and this fact has important implications for the race and class analyses needed in feminist theory and feminist programs for change. The problem of racism within the women's movement remains critical; however, the feminist movement is one of the few movements today in which an analysis of racism is tied to an analysis of sexism and a critical challenge is posed to the public and private institutions in which sexism and racism flourish.

The origins of modern feminism among educated women also draw attention to the university system and the knowledge about society that it imparts. During the 1960s, the university became a symbol and a representative of the American power elite. Universities were criticized for their complicity in the Vietnam War and charged with racist and sexist practices—both in their treatment of social groups and in the knowledge they generated about them. Thus, the impact of feminism has been felt not only in the society at large but also within the academic world, where scholars and activists have criticized existing scholarship for not understanding oppressed groups and for not generating public policy that would meet their needs.

The feminist criticism of traditional scholarship involves the purpose, content, and method of academic studies (Westkott 1979). With regard to purpose, feminists share with radical sociologists the idea that the purpose of knowledge must be social change (Flacks and Turkel 1978). Feminist inquiry takes human emancipation as the goal of social-scientific study and claims that knowledge must be used in the construction of more egalitarian societies—ones in which both women and men are freed from sexist and other forms of oppression. Feminists have different visions of what an egalitarian society would look like, some solutions being more radical than others. But all feminists insist upon a political and academic ethic that sees social change as part of the purpose of academic knowledge.

Not only do feminists see that academic inquiry must be tied to social change, but their critique of traditional scholarship is focused on problems in the content and method of traditional scholarly work. Feminists assert that what is known by scholarly study must make sense of women's experience. Traditional social thought and scholarship, based largely on the lives of men, have not provided such an account. As a result, feminism has begun to transform academic knowledge and the theories and research on which it rests.

Since the resurgence of feminism in the 1960s, there has been a dramatic outpouring of studies and theories about women in society. These studies have questioned the assumptions and biases of existing work in almost every field, including science, the humanities, and the social sciences (Carroll 1976; Hubbard 1979; Jaquette 1976; Jusenius 1976; Kolodny 1976; Millman and Kanter 1975; Parlee 1975; Pierce 1975; Reiter 1975). Women working in different fields soon discovered that much of what stood for knowledge in their disciplines was either overtly sexist or ignored women altogether. Often, academic women found that they had more in common with each other than they did with the men in their disciplines. As they began to study what their disciplines said about women, they forged new ideas that were critical of the preestablished thinking in traditional disciplines and that fostered interdisciplinary women's studies. Feminist reconstructions of academic scholarship have now touched every discipline and have resulted in major changes in the assumptions, theoretical frameworks, and research data upon which the disciplines rest.

At first, revisions within the disciplines took an "add-women-and-stir" approach (Smith 1974). This method recognized the presence of women in the world but only added them to preexisting analytical frameworks. For example, in sociology, scholars began to include sex as a variable in research designs, comparing, for instance, men's and women's income (Suter and Miller 1973) or showing differences in the socialization patterns of boys and girls (Hochschild 1973). In the field of history, this approach took the form of studying the contributions of notable women to history—labeled the "women worthies" approach by historian Gerda Lerner (1976). Other fields, too, began to recognize women by incorporating women's issues into the established procedures and analyses of the discipline. In philosophy, women's issues such as abortion and equal rights were scrutinized by philosophical analysis (Gould and Wartosky 1976); political scientists documented the political participation of women (Boals 1975); anthropologists looked at women's roles in the societies they studied (Reiter 1975); and psychologists investigated the development and effects of sex role stereotyping (Bem and Bem 1971).

The add-and-stir method of studying women was valuable for discovering women's experience and moving women from an invisible to a visible location in social science research. But ultimately, it has proven inadequate as an approach, for it still accepts male-centered models as the proper form of analysis and seeks to find out how many women fit into these perspectives. More often than not, feminist scholars have determined that because women's experience is unlike that of men, then traditional models of social life do not reveal women's situations; therefore, more revisions are necessary.

One of the best examples in sociology comes from considering the issue of housework. Although feminists have encouraged us to think of housework as work, it does not fit neatly into the frameworks sociologists use to study work. For example, one's occupation usually provides a good measure of one's social status. But because status is also derived from income and because housework is unpaid labor, the status of housewives is difficult to evaluate. Moreover, sociologists usually distinguish work from leisure, although this distinction is not so clear in the case of housework. Would we, for example, consider mothering a child to be work or leisure? Child care certainly contains many of the features of work, including a schedule, routinization of tasks, and physical exertion, but it also includes elements of leisure, such as reading a story or walking to a park. Moreover, it would be difficult to compare the emotional commitment of a mother to that involved in other forms of labor.

These examples show how asking sociological questions from a woman-centered perspective necessarily transforms traditional models of sociological inquiry. Examples from other disciplines as well show that, when women's experiences are taken seriously, new methods and perspectives must be established. For example, in history, feminist scholars have criticized the "women worthies" approach for recognizing only women who meet male standards for eminence in history. Although it is important to recognize the contributions of prominent women in history, these women stand out because they are deviant. They do not represent the experience of the majority of women in their time. In their transformations of historical scholarship, feminist historians have shown how even the periods used to define time frameworks in history are based on men's achievements and men's activities (Lerner 1976). The Renaissance, for example, is typically depicted as a progressive age that encouraged humanism and creativity. Yet, for women, the Renaissance was a time of increased domestication of bourgeois wives and intensified persecution of witches—most of whom were single peasant women. To see the Renaissance from a woman-centered perspective is to see that this is a period marked by increased restriction of the powers of women (Kelly-Gadol 1976), not the era of creativity and humanism that male-based studies have defined.

Similarly, in the area of psychological development, feminists are revising models of development that have been based on male experience. Gilligan's (1979) work on moral development shows how theories of moral development have taken male experience as the norm and then measured female experience against it. In fact, as Gilligan shows, women's moral development follows a different path than men's, women's orientation toward morality being more contextual than that of men. In other words, women make moral judgments based on their assessments of conflicting responsibilities in a given situation, whereas men are more likely to make moral decisions based on their judgments of competing rights and abstract principles. Gilligan's point is not only to show that men and women have different conceptions of morality, but also that the male model has been taken by psychologists to be the universal standard by which both men and women are evaluated.

The purpose here is to see how scholarly models have been derived from the particular experiences of men and then used as the universal standards against which women's experiences have been judged. In all of these fields, with men's experience as the standard, women can only appear incomplete, inadequate, or invisible. The add-and-stir method does not explain women's experience because it assumes that such experience has no legitimacy of its own. For this reason, feminist scholarship, in taking a woman-centered perspective, has had to revise existing research frameworks. And in so doing, feminist scholars are discovering new questions and new perspectives that emerge from studying the female world (Bernard 1981).

Feminist scholarship begins by documenting women's experience and observing the patterns found in looking at gender as a category of social experience. Some of these studies use existing research techniques in the disciplines and aim to correct the mistakes and omissions of earlier work. This approach has yielded volumes of new research that detail patterns of behavior such as the sex role socialization of children (Frieze et al. 1978), earning differentials between men and women (Lloyd 1975), male-female social interaction patterns (Henley and Freeman 1979), and patterns of female crime (Datesman and Scarpitti 1980), to name a few. These studies are valuable because they provide the factual basis for new investigations. But more substantially, feminist perspectives have brought new issues to scholarly research by challenging the presuppositions of classical scholarship. We will now look in more detail at the nature of these revisions in sociology.

THE FEMINIST CRITIQUE OF SOCIOLOGY

The method of sociological inquiry is defined as empirical study, meaning that the objects of sociological investigation are events that can be observed in the social world. The sociologist observes social events, discovers their patterns, and formulates concepts and theories that interpret relationships among them. An important point about empirical studies is that, when the theories that explain observed events no longer make sense of what is observed or when one's observations change, then revisions are necessary. A central point in feminist criticism of sociological work is that conventional theories have not made sense of women's experience and, therefore, must be revised.

Sociology is also a discipline that claims social improvement as part of its goal. The history of sociology as a discipline is related to the search for humanitarian social change, and most sociologists believe that sociology should contribute to the improvement of social life. They differ in how to produce this change—some emphasizing gradual improvement through existing governmental and political channels and others believing that only radical social change can solve contemporary social problems. But regardless of their differences, sociologists believe that the purpose of sociological investigation is to generate improved social policy and, consequently, social change.

So, although feminists agree with the basic empirical, theoretical, and practical goals of sociology, they argue that, in practice, sociology has not been true to its claims. Women have been ignored in the content of sociological research, and their experience and consciousness have been absent from the theoretical paradigms that guide sociological thinking.

A review essay by Millman and Kanter (1975), two feminist sociologists, provides six major points that highlight the feminist critique of sociology. They include:

1. Conventional topics studied by sociologists lead us to ignore issues that would further illuminate women's lives.
2. Sociology, by focusing on public roles and behaviors, ignores the areas where women's experience is more likely revealed.
3. Sociology tends to depict society as a single generalizable entity.
4. Gender is seldom considered by sociologists to be a significant factor that influences behavior.
5. Sociology focuses on the status quo, thus giving it a conservative bias.
6. Conventional sociological methodologies are likely to elicit only certain kinds of information, most notably the kind that is least likely to reveal new data.

The first point states that sociologists have focused on topics and concepts that implicitly bias the study of women. For example, sociologists tend to see social behavior as rational and goal-oriented—an assumption that, from the outset, takes male behavior as the norm. Throughout sociological work, there is an emphasis on conceptual dichotomies such as community and association, Gemeinschaft and Gesellschaft, or expressive and instrumental action. In these dichotomies, the rationalized forms of interaction (association, Gesellschaft, and instrumental action) are seen as indicative of modern social structures. Other forms of interaction (community, Gemeinschaft, and expressive action) are often considered to be of secondary interest or assumed to be relics of past traditions. Implicitly, the argument is made in sociological analysis that these forms of interaction either disappear in modern society or are restricted to the primary world of the family—that is, the world of women. In addition to treating the world of women as unimportant or secondary, this perspective creates a sociological picture of the world as more rational than it is, and it glosses over the emotions that human beings feel in their confrontations with the world (Hochschild 1975). In sum, this perspective in sociology projects the traditionally masculine trait of rationality onto the sociological accounts that men have created of the social world.

The second point made by Millman and Kanter is that sociology has focused on public and official roles and behaviors as the foremost subjects of inquiry. Again, by dividing emotional from intellectual life, conventional sociology tends to ignore the private realms of existence. This fact has particular significance for women's studies because of the fact that women have traditionally been relegated to the private realms of social structure. Even in their public role, women do emotional work, meaning that they provide personal services, negotiate social relations between people, and are often responsible for the kinds of jobs that are people-oriented. Thus, emotional work is considered to be women's work (Chodorow, 1978), and sociologists who ignore the areas of life where emotional work is most obviously performed also ignore much of the social activity of women. Secretaries, housewives, nurses, and maids all work in ways that bridge public and private life. To restrict the study of women to their contributions to public life is to overlook a major part of women's contributions to society. By rethinking the assumed dichotomy between public and private life, feminists have concluded that conventional sociology has constructed an inaccurate account of the lives, feelings, and thoughts of women and men.

Third, Millman and Kanter argue that sociology tends to depict society as if it were a single entity. They write, "Sociology often assumes a 'single society' with respect to men and women, in which generalizations can be made about all participants, yet men and women may actually inhabit different social worlds, and these must be taken into account" (1975:xiii). Evidence for their assertion recurs in the sociological literature, as study after study makes conclusions about the society based on investigations in which all of the research subjects are male.

Blau and Duncan's classic study, *The American Occupational Structure* (1967), is a case in point. The research is based on a "national" sample of 20,000 men, and the study concludes that social mobility is "simply a function of education and social origins and there are no further conditions that affect the mobility chances of the various educational groups" (159). Had this study included a sample of women, it is highly unlikely that a similar conclusion would have been reached. Even more recently, it is common to find sociologists publishing studies of social stratification in which blacks and women are omitted from the analysis because they make the data too complex (Kalleberg and Griffin 1980).

Another example of generalization founded in male experience comes from a widely used introductory textbook that defines the American cultural mainstream as "the conviction that every individual should struggle to rise in the status system, to 'get ahead,' to succeed. As a result, the acquisition of material goods, economic independence, and symbols of prestige is a goal that we as a people hold very high" (DeFleur, D'Antonio, and Nelson 1977:107). Again, one wonders if the same conclusion would hold if the universal "we" specifically included women. The claim that the American mainstream is represented by the culture of white men assumes that white men's experience is the universal form of social life in this society. This conclusion is true only if we assume that the world of women and of racial and ethnic minorities is either nonexistent, uninteresting, or trivial and dull. Implicitly, sociological research has assumed that the world of women can be subsumed under the world of men. Research showing that women use language differently from men (McConnell-Ginet 1978), that black adolescent girls develop unique definitions of womanhood (Ladner 1971), or that lesbian couples are freer from restrictive roles than heterosexual couples (Tanner 1978) belies such an assumption.

Millman and Kanter's fourth point is that, in sociological work, gender is seldom considered to be a factor that influences social behavior. They point out that the sex distribution of social groups is often assumed to be irrelevant to social behavior and, secondly, that when a group is all-male, then it is assumed to be gender neutral. Feminist studies show the falsehood of such a claim, as in Kanter's (1977) work on formal organizations. Kanter shows that the experience of women in corporations is greatly influenced by the proportion of women in the company. Women, as well as other minorities, become tokens in predominantly white male settings. Those in the majority, in the presence of token members, exaggerate the dominant culture, isolate the token outsiders, and constantly remind tokens of their difference. As proportions by gender shift, so do the social experiences of both sexes.

The fifth point of feminist criticism is that sociology is implicitly a conservative discipline because of its tendency to explain the status quo. From its origin, the central problem of sociological inquiry has been the question, "How is social order possible?" Although much of sociological inquiry has emerged from studying the conflicts and contradictions in social life, there is also a strong interest in the persistence of behavioral patterns and the mechanisms of social stability. The focus on norms, roles, and stability emphasizes the status quo, whereas feminists argue that sociology must provide the foundation for social transformation and the liberation of oppressed groups.

Finally, Millman and Kanter make the point that conventional sociological methodologies are likely to elicit only certain kinds of information. The methods that sociologists use may blind them to certain views of the world. For example, the frequently used questionnaire method provides research subjects with responses that have been preestablished by the researcher. This method tends to impose the researcher's ideas upon the persons being studied. An alternative strategy, and one that Millman and Kanter suggest, is to encourage researchers to let subjects speak for themselves. By hearing subjects speak in their own words, sociologists are more likely to discover new ideas rather than to reinforce their old ones.

In sum, feminist perspectives in sociology are critical of frameworks that are derived solely from male experience or that merely recapitulate traditional perspectives on the social relations of the sexes. In revising traditional work, feminist scholars are creating a new sociology, one that intends to represent better the experience of women and men in the world and to make a stronger contribution to policies for social change.

Feminist perspectives in sociology have opened up a new discourse and encouraged scholars to observe social relations of the sexes without the blinders that have been encouraged by earlier work. By providing a new discourse, feminists would argue that we are improving sociological methods because we are more aware of observations and ideas that have hitherto gone unnoticed. Millman and Kanter aptly describe this process through their rewriting of a classic parable:

Everyone knows the story about the Emperor and his fine clothes: although the townspeople persuaded themselves that the Emperor was elegantly costumed, a child, possessing an unspoiled vision, showed the citizenry that the Emporor was really naked. The story instructs us about one of our basic sociological premises: that reality is subjective, or, rather, subject to social definition. The story also reminds us that collective delusions can be undone by introducing fresh perspectives. Movements of social liberation are like the story in this respect: they make it possible for people to see the world in an enlarged perspective because they remove the covers and blinders that obscure knowledge and observation. In the last decade no social movement has had a more startling or consequential impact on the way people see and act in the world than the women's movement. Like the onlookers in the Emperor's parade, we can see and plainly speak about things that have always been there, but that formerly were unacknowledged. Indeed, today it is impossible to escape noticing features of social life that were invisible only ten years ago. (1975:vii)

Seeing without the blinders of earlier perspectives will not reveal ultimate truths about social life any more than will other forms of social thought. And the feminist critique of knowledge does not offer final solutions to the problems experienced by women or men in contemporary society. But it has dramatically shown how little we know and what distorted information we have about at least one-half of the human population, and it casts doubt upon what we know about the other half. Also, the feminist critique emphasizes that what we have known in the past is tied to the perspectives and interests of dominant groups. The insights feminist thought provides and the self-criticism it encourages have created a new challenge for scholars who are committed to new visions of the future. Perspectives in feminist thought and the research those perspectives have generated form the substance of this book.

C H A P T E R 2

SEX, BIOLOGY, AND CULTURE

INTRODUCTION

On a train between New York and Philadelphia, two men, strangers to each other, board, take adjoining seats, introduce themselves as stockbrokers, and begin exchanging "hot tips" on the rising returns on investments in nuclear storage companies. After discovering that they were graduates of the same college and had frequented the same college bars, their talk turns to their personal lives. One is returning to his suburban home, where his wife and four children (three girls and a boy) are waiting. The other, single, is returning to his center city townhouse, where for $600 a month he receives maid and laundry service, a telephone answering service, private security, and so "doesn't need a wife"! But he adds, "it must be nice having children. You know, I've got a friend with two children—girls. He wanted sons and told his wife when their second daughter was born that she had delivered two losers. She told him it was his fault—he had given an X chromosome, not a Y, so it was he who was responsible for the loss!"

The two men laugh, talk about the family's "misfortune," and go on to talk about their theories on the determination of sex. With an attitude of certainty and authority on the topic, both present their opinions. One believes that whether a man contributes an X or a Y chromosome is a question of heredity; some men, he says, are more likely to produce sons than others. The second man says that he disagrees because he has heard about some research in Sweden, "where they know all about sex," and that the male chromosome is related to tension. He claims, "tense men push harder, and that makes the strong Y chromosome come out!"

The men's dialogue reveals several interesting issues pertinent to a discussion of biology and sex differences. The men are correct that genetic sex is determined by the pairing of XX (female) or XY (male) sex chromosomes. And it is the paternal chromosome (either an X or a Y) that determines the sex of the offspring. (The mother always contributes an X chromosome.) But their explanation of what determines the male's genetic contribution is wrong even though it shows that social attitudes about sex and gender infiltrate popular and scientific explanations of sex differences.

This chapter discusses sex differences and their relationship to human culture and society. Throughout the chapter, we will see that both scientific and popular discussions of biological sex differences have been distorted by cultural assumptions about appropriate forms of male-female behavior. This chapter begins with a discussion of the biological determination of sex and is followed by a chapter showing how sex differences emerge from the social environment in which they develop.

For feminists, the discussion of biological sex differences is critical because women's anatomy has been seen as determining their destiny. The conservative belief that psychological and social differences between the sexes are determined by biological differences has been used to argue that women's status in society is both natural and unchangeable (Jaggar and Struhl 1978). But as we have seen, feminist perspectives begin with the understanding of women's status as socially, not biologically, rooted. Thus, a discussion of the relationship between biology and culture is central to feminist interpretations of the social relations between the sexes.

This chapter will show that human biology and culture are intricately intertwined, making any claims about the biological determination of sex differences not only politically suspect but unscientific. However, scientific discussions of sex differences have themselves been produced under sexist conditions. Thus, assumptions have often appeared in scientific research and theory that distort our understanding of sex and gender in society. Feminist revisions of scientific work have tried to produce more accurate descriptions and explanations of biological events that are important to understanding the relationship of the sexes in society.

BIOLOGICAL SEX AND SOCIOLOGICAL GENDER

The biological sex of a person is established at the moment of conception and is elaborated during the period of fetal development in the womb. During conception, each parent contributes 23 chromosomes to the fertilized egg, for a total of 46 or 23 chomosomal pairs. One of these pairs determines the sex of the offspring; these are called the *sex chromosomes*. Under normal conditions, the sex chromosomes consist of an X from the mother's egg and an X or a Y from the father's sperm. Genetically, normal girls have a pair of X chromosomes (designated 46, XX), and normal boys have the chromosomal pair XY (designated 46, XY). Because the sex chromosome from the ovum is always an X, the chromosome carried by the father's sperm (either an X or a Y) determines the sex of the child.

Despite what the strangers on the train may believe, there is no evidence that Y chromosomes are stronger than Xs. In fact, the XY male chromosome pair forms a link that is less viable in genetic coding than is the XX female pair. This fact accounts, in part, for the greater vulnerability of male fetuses in the womb and may contribute to higher prenatal and early childhood mortality rates for males (Harrison 1978). Moreover, the 23 paternal chromosomes (including the X or Y sex chromosome) are selected randomly when the sperm is formed (Hoyenga and Hoyenga 1979), thus giving little credence to the idea that the sex of the offspring is somehow determined by the father's behavior during sexual intercourse.

Following fertilization of the egg, the sex chromosomes of the fetus determine whether ovaries or testes will develop. With the Y chromosome present, the fetal gonads differentiate into male sexual organs in about the sixth week of gestation; without the Y chromosome, the gonads begin development as an ovary in about the tenth week of gestation. With the development of fetal gonads, sex differentiation becomes a function of the sex hormones. In the case of males, androgen is secreted by the testes (in about the third month of development), causing further differentiation of the internal and, later, external male sex organs. In the absence of androgen hormones, female sex organs develop (Hoyenga and Hoyenga 1979; Lambert 1978).

Although this process describes the determination of genetic sex under normal circumstances, cases of chromosomal abnormalities do occur that result in biologically mixed or incomplete sex characteristics. Studies of these cases reveal the complex relationship between genetic and biological sex and the social definition of *male* and *female*. Two such conditions, Turner's syndrome and Klinefelter's syndrome, result from sex chromosomal abnormalities. Turner's syndrome is a condition occurring when the fetus has only one X (and no Y) chromosome present. Physically, the child is female in appearance, although she is genetically incomplete. Typically, Turner's syndrome individuals have the physical abnormalities of shortness (four to five feet tall), malformation of the nails, feet, and fingers, and cardiac difficulties. Although Turner's syndrome females are typically infertile, researchers have reported that their social behavior displays exaggerated feminine traits compared to that of other girls matched for age, IQ, race, and socioeconomic background (Money and Ehrhardt 1972). Turner's females show greater interest in feminine dress, have stronger preferences for dolls, and daydream more about marriage and motherhood. The appearance of these socially feminine traits among genetically incomplete females indicates that complete genetic status as a female is not necessary to produce socially feminine results (Hoyenga and Hoyenga 1979).

In another chromosomal abnormality, Klinefelter's syndrome, persons may be born with extra X chromosomes (47, XXY or 48, XXXY). Genetically, they have both the male (XY) and female (XX) chromosomal patterns and thus have ambiguous sex characteristics. Klinefelter's individuals are male in external appearance, although they show low levels of testosterone, the male sex hormone. Typically, they show breast enlargement and have small penises. Although they appear to be men, Klinefelter's individuals are frequently confused about their gender identity. Klinefelter's syndrome has often been associated with mental retardation (Hoyenga and Hoyenga 1979), although patterns of intelligence do vary among these individuals, with some showing very high IQs. Researchers have concluded that it is unclear to what extent the behavioral effects of Klinefelter's syndrome are caused by genetic problems, by abnormalities in brain activity, and by societal reactions to persons exhibiting the physical appearance of the syndrome (Hoyenga and Hoyenga 1979).

The research on genetic abnormalities associated with the sex chromosomes reveals a complex interplay among genetic, physical, and behavioral traits. Although statistically very few individuals are born with these abnormalities, the cases in which they do occur reveal much about the normal evolution of gender identity. It is useful to distinguish biological sex from gender identity, because they are often confused in discussions of sex differences.

The concept of *gender* refers specifically to socially learned behavior and expectations that are associated with members of a biological sex category. Gender is an acquired identity; biological sex usually is not. *Biological sex* refers to the genetic and physical sexual identity of the person. The distinction between sex and gender is important because it underscores the fact that social identities emerge from conditions other than biological categories. Moreover, as the following discussion of hermaphroditism will show, gender identities emerge even when the biological sex is unclear. These illustrations demonstrate the power of socially learned gender identities not only in unusual situations but also in situations in which biological sex is consistent with acquired gender roles.

Hermaphroditism is "a condition of prenatal origin in which embryonic and/or fetal differentiation of the reproductive system fails to reach completion as either entirely female or entirely male" (Money and Ehrhardt 1972:5). Normally, during fetal development, fetal gonads produce sex hormones that, in turn, produce the internal and external sex organs (Hoyenga and Hoyenga 1979; Lambert 1978). In the case of hermaphroditism, babies are born with their sexual anatomy improperly differentiated; thus, they may look either ambiguous or incomplete.

In one example of hermaphroditism, a genetic male was born with a tiny penis (one centimeter long) and no urinary canal. At age seventeen months, the child was reclassified as a girl. She was given a new name, hairdo, and clothing. Shortly after the sex reassignment, the parents noticed a change in the older brother's treatment of her. Before the sex reassignment, he had treated his "brother" roughly; now he was very protective and gentle toward his new "sister." By age three, the daughter had developed clearly feminine interests. "For Christmas, she wanted glass slippers, so that she could go to the ball like Cinderella, and a doll. The parents were delighted. The girl continued to receive typically girlish toys from her parents. She continued more and more to show feminine interests, as in helping her mother" (Money and Ehrhardt 1972:125).

Hermaphroditism has been studied along with other cases of biologically ambiguous sex in which sex reassignment produces a person whose gender identity is different from his or her sex identity. One such case involves a male identical twin who, at the age of seven months, during a routine circumcision by electrocautery, had his penis burned off by a too powerful electrical current. The entire tissues of the penis died and sloughed off; the parents were advised to change the sex of their child to female. At age seventeen months, the sex transformation was begun and the child was given a new name, hairstyle, and clothing; at twenty-one months, reconstruction of the genitals was surgically initiated, to be followed by vaginoplasty (construction of the vagina) when the body was full-grown. Meanwhile, the child's pubertal growth and feminization were regulated by estrogen therapy. In this case, the genetic sex of the child remained intact (XY = male), even though her physical sex was indistinguishable from that of genetic females. The researchers in this case point out that social transformations in gender identity are a necessary part of the process of sex reassignment. The child's parents were carefully advised on her social development, and the researchers observed their socialization practices. They dressed the child in pink, frilly, feminine clothes, and her mother encouraged her to be tidy.

One incident aptly shows how different the parents' social expectations are for their genetically identical but now differently gendered children. The mother reports of her son, "One time I caught him—he went out and he took a leak in my flower garden in the front yard, you know. He was quite happy with himself. And I just didn't do anything. I just couldn't. I started laughing and told Daddy about it." About the daughter, she said, "I've never had a problem with her. She did once when she was little, she took off her panties and threw them over the fence. And she didn't have no panties on. But I just, I gave her a little swat on the rear, and I told her that nice little girls didn't do that, and she should keep her panties on. . . . And she didn't take them off after that" (Money and Ehrhardt 1972:120). It is little wonder that, as the mother put it, "one thing that really amazes me is that she is so feminine" (Money and Ehrhardt 1972:119).

These studies demonstrate that biological sex alone does not determine gender identity. In fact, one's social gender can be different from one's genetic sex. Arguments that reduce the issue of gender to biological phenomena not only ignore the social processes associated with gender identity but also oversimplify the interdependent influence of biology and culture.

SEX DIFFERENCES: NATURE OR NURTURE?

Controversy about the relative effects of nature versus nurture has been plentiful in the social science literature for years. This discussion has special significance for the study of sex and gender because differences between men and women have often been attributed to biological differences between the sexes. A review of the biological and sociological literature will show that it is most reasonable at this point to conclude that there is complex interdependence between biological and social systems. This section will review the interdependence of biological and social factors that influence sex differences and will discuss problems in the argument that biological facts themselves cause differences in the social relations of the sexes.

Beginning with genetic structure, human life involves the interplay of biology and culture. Geneticists distinguish between *single-gene traits* (those controlled by a single gene) and *polygenetic traits* (those controlled by multiple genes). Single-gene traits include characteristics such as blood type and albinism; they are known to be discontinuous traits. In other words, single-gene traits vary qualitatively from each other; polygenetic traits (such as height, hair color, skin pigment, sex) show continuous and quantitative variation. Polygenetic traits occur along a continuum, and thus vary in degree but not kind. Furthermore, polygenetic traits are known to interact with the environment in which they exist. *Genotype* refers to inherited genetic characteristics; *phenotype* refers to external appearance and results from the combined expression of the genes as they interact with each other *and* with the environment in which the person lives. The phenotype usually differs from the genotype, depending upon the total genetic structure and the environmental context. Thus, even genetic traits are known to interact with the environment in which they exist.

Sex differences that do appear between males and females are known as *sexually dimorphic traits*. These are traits that occur in different frequencies among male and female populations. For example, color blindness is a sexually dimorphic trait that is found more often in men than in women. But most sexually dimorphic traits are distributed widely throughout both male and female populations. They are dimorphic primarily because there is a significant difference between the two populations, not usually because a sexually dimorphic trait appears in one sex.

Statistical measures of the variation of a trait within a given population represent the degree to which the population deviates from the typical case. Most sex differences are distributed widely throughout the population, leaving a wide range of variation on any given trait appearing among men or among women. Body weight provides a good example. On the average, men weigh more than women, but weight differences among women and among men far exceed the average weight difference between men and women as populations. Moreover, a sex difference may be found when comparing male and female populations as a whole, but it may not be found when comparing any given male-female pair.

The point is that the variability within gender is usually larger than the mean difference between genders. Sexually dimorphic traits are so labeled because they are found in different frequencies in men and women. Referring to Figure 2-1, we can see that in a given set of frequency distributions, there may be a substantial degree of overlap between the two populations. Usually, sexually dimorphic traits represent quantitative, not qualitative, differences between the sexes, and because sexually dimorphic traits may include social as well as biological traits, we may find many traits that have environmental causes. Body size, again, provides a good example. Although men are, on the average, larger than women, body size is known to be influenced by diet and physical activity. These factors, in turn, may be influenced by culture, as well as by social class, race, and gender. Explanations of sex differences that ignore these factors distort our understanding of the nature of sexual dimorphism and the significance of observed differences between the sexes.

It is interesting to note that research has found very few consistent sex differences, although discussions of male-female traits almost always emphasize traits that are different instead of similar in men and women. Simply put, the vast majority of human traits are shared by both men and women. Because knowing a person's biological sex does not provide a very accurate prediction of his or her behavior, we have to wonder why biological differences are so often claimed as explaining inequality between the sexes (Lambert 1978; Reid 1975).

Although there may be a general biological basis for human societies, human biology sets extremely broad limits for behavior. Most of us vastly underuse our biological capacities, including both motor skills and cognitive ability. Yet, differences between the sexes have often been attributed to their biological origins, thereby giving the impression that

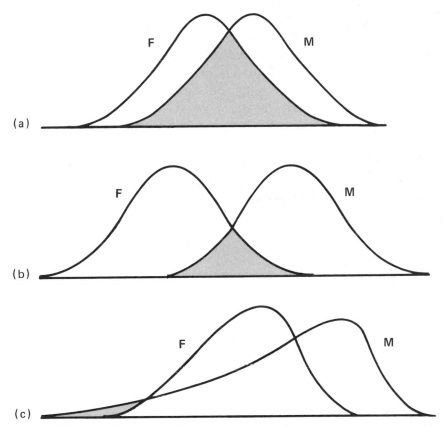

Figure 2-1. Hypothetical distribution of sexually dimorphic traits. Glockenspiel counts eye blinks in 18,346 infants on the third day of life and discovers that on the average the males blink .415 times more often than the females. She reports this difference as "statistically significant." If the distribution of eyeblink frequencies were charted, any one of the situations illustrated could be found: (a) There may be a large overlap of cases; (b) there may be a small overlap of cases; (c) there may be cases of males who blink less frequently than females. Probability statistics are such that any of these situations is often possible. Glockenspiel's notes on the amount of variation in the samples could be one clue to identifying the underlying distribution. Also, because the difference is "statistically significant," it is not necessarily "socially significant." That is for the reader to decide. [Redrawn with permission from Clarice Stasz Stoll, *Female and Male.* (Dubuque, Iowa: William C. Brown Co., 1978), p. 20.]

nature is more significant than nurture in determining our social identities and social positions. An argument that reduces a complex event or process (such as social identity) to a single monolithic cause (such as the form of one's genitals) is called a *reductionist argument*. A related form of argument is known as *determinism*. Determinist arguments are those that assume that a given condition (such as the presence of a penis) inevitably determines a particular event (such as male aggression). Arguments about the biological inferiority of women are usually both reductionist and determinist in that they explain sex differences in the social world as the natural and inevitable consequence of the singular fact of women's biological nature.

Determinist and reductionist arguments are closely related and can be made in any number of forms, including psychological, economic, and cultural contexts. But biological determinism and reductionism have been especially rampant in the discussion of sex differences, and they have been the basis for conservative views about the proper role for women in society. Consider, for example, the following argument taken from Steven Goldberg's book, *The Inevitability of Patriarchy:*

We are assuming . . . that there are no differences between men and women except in the hormonal system that renders the man more aggressive. This alone would explain patriarchy, male dominance, and male attainment of high-status roles, for the male hormonal system gives an insuperable "head start" toward attaining those roles which any society associates with leadership or high status as long as the roles are not ones which males are biologically incapable of filling. . . . One need merely consider the result of a society's not socializing women away from competitions with men, from its not directing girls toward roles women are more capable of playing than are men. . . . No doubt some women would be aggressive enough to succeed in competitions with men and there would be considerably more women in high-status positions than there are now. But most women would lose in such competitive struggles with men (because men have the aggression advantage) and so most women would be forced to live in adult lives as failures in areas in which the society had wanted them to succeed. (1974:104–107)

Goldberg's book is a good example (although a bad piece of scholarship) of biological reductionism and determinism, and his argument that anatomy is destiny is a familiar one. He makes several assumptions pertinent to a discussion of sex differences, all of which need close examination. First, his argument is determinist because he sees biological differences alone as explaining the complex systems of patriarchy, male dominance, and male attainment—systems that feminists would say involve a wide array of social, psychological, historical, economic, and political as well as cultural factors. Goldberg seems to assume that patriarchy is compatible with the biological needs of all men, and yet, clearly, not all men are equally aggressive, nor do they participate equally in patriarchal systems of power. His argument leaves him with no explanation of race and class inequality (even among men) except to rely on biological claims alleging the innate inferiority of racial groups and lower social classes. We can see from this example how racism and sexism are parallel arguments, each resting on faulty biological claims. Moreover, Goldberg assumes that aggressive differences between men and women are universal—a fact that simply does not stand up to the cross-cultural evidence (Mead 1949). *What does new work in Mead say?*

But because it is a common argument, let us examine Goldberg's fundamental premise that hormonal differences are the basis for different levels of aggression between men and women. Many biologists have studied the association between the hormone testosterone and aggressive behavior, and their conclusions reveal important issues in the association between biological factors and social behavior.

To begin with, both males and females have measurable quantities of the three major sex hormones—estrogen, progestin, and testosterone. Hormonal sex differences are causes by differences in the levels of production and concentration of each, not in their presence or absence per se. The greater production of testosterone in males is due to stimulation by the testes, whereas in females, the ovaries secrete additional estrogens and progestins. Before puberty, however, there are few or no sex differences in the quantity of sex hormones in each gender; at this time, all of the sex hormones are at very low levels. If high levels of testosterone were needed to produce aggression, then we would expect to see little difference in aggressive behavior between prepubescent boys and girls. However, much research shows that boys are more aggressive at an early age, thereby contradicting the implications of biologically determinist arguments.

Similarly, following menopause, women actually have lower levels of estradol (the major estrogen) and progesterone (the major progestin) than do men of the same age (Hawkins and Oakey 1974; Hoyenga and Hoyenga 1979; Tea, et al., 1975). Because there is no empirical evidence that older men are more feminine than older women, we must doubt the conclusion that hormonal differences explain differences in the behavior of the sexes.

Research on human males shows that changes in testosterone levels do not consistently predict changes in aggressive behavior (Hoyenga and Hoyenga 1979). Some studies find small correlations between the level of testosterone and aggressive behavior, but correlations show only association, not cause. Although there may be a slight tendency for aggression and testosterone to vary together, "this does not mean that testosterone caused aggression or dominance; the reverse could just as well be true" (Hoyenga and Hoyenga 1979:139). In fact, much of the research on hormones and aggression shows that experiential factors (such as stress, fatigue, or fear) may have a greater effect on hormonal production than hormones have on behavior (Hoyenga and Hoyenga 1979). This finding raises the important consideration that culture can influence biological processes just as much as, if not more than, biological processes influence culture.

In sum, reductionist arguments do not account for the complexities of an issue such as human aggression. And they certainly do not explain the wide variation found in patterns of aggression even among men or among women. Biologically reductionist arguments rest on the assumption that differences between the sexes are natural and thus are not subject to change. Yet, on further consideration, it is, in fact, quite difficult to distinguish between the natural and the social. Cultural attitudes themselves influence what we think of as natural, because what is considered natural is usually believed to be unchangeable.

Throughout Western history, allegedly natural differences have been summoned to explain the inequality of women and of racial and cultural minorities. The assertion that their oppression is caused by biological inferiority is an overtly racist and sexist claim. When we carefully examine supposedly natural relations between the sexes, we discover that what is perceived as natural has an ideological basis. An *ideology* is a belief system that seems to justify the status quo. By labeling something as natural, we make it appear to be a phenomenon that is not influenced by human behavior. The falsehood of such a claim is easily seen when we recognize that what is considered natural in one time or place is often considered odd or deviant in another. Take, for example, the issue of lesbianism.

Typically, we are told (implicitly and explicitly) that women's primary sexual orientation is naturally directed toward men. If we are heterosexual, we might never question that claim. But if we view the claim from the perspective of lesbian women's experience, we are likely to think otherwise. The belief that heterosexuality is the only natural form of sexual expression is rooted in a cultural framework that defines heterosexuality as compulsory and homosexuality as deviant or pathological (Rich 1980). Although it may at first seem odd to think of heterosexuality as a compulsory institution, the social sanctions brought against women who do not couple with men show how heterosexuality is maintained through social control. Even if women remain single and couple with no one, they are ridiculed and ostracized. If they love other women, they are seen as deviant or sexually pathological. In addition, lesbian women and gay men are subjected to legal sanctions that deny their basic civil rights, and they are often subjected to overt acts of violence and personal harm.

In fact, human sexual expression takes a variety of forms, and restricting legitimate sex only to heterosexual (and often coercive) relations between men and women is an example of social control. Yet, the belief that heterosexuality is the only natural way of expressing sexuality keeps us blind to other possibilities for human life. In the end, claims about the allegedly natural character of sex differences and female sexuality are important mechanisms for the social control of women.

The formation of human society and the character of persons living within it are complex processes that involve both biological and social causes. Explanations that reduce human life simply to nature or nurture are unlikely to reveal the complex dynamics produced by the interdependence of biology and culture. Moreover, the physical and social aspects of the human environment exert profound influences on human life, both socially and biologically. Because human beings are essentially adaptive creatures, they continuously respond and change within their environments. Any argument that reduces the complexity of human life to its biological basis alone makes the fallacious assumption that biology sets an inevitable course for human social and physical development. Vast recorded differences among human cultures demonstrate the inadequacy of such an argument and challenge the assumption that biology somehow sets predetermined limits on the expression of human skill and ability. And in fact, the evolution of human society shows that the adaptation in interaction with the social and physical environment is an essential process in the development of human life and society.

THE SEXES IN HUMAN EVOLUTION

The evolution of human life is said to have begun about 5 million years ago in the forests and savannahs of eastern Africa. Although the earliest hominid (prehuman, bipedal primate mammals) groups vastly differed from *Homo sapiens* today, the transformations that occurred in these early species provide several clues to the role of gender in the evolution of human society.

Because of the lack of fossil records for this early period, evolutionary theorists have constructed their evidence from observations of living chimpanzee populations; these groups represent the kind of population from which human beings have evolved. Studies of primates reveal that humans are closely related in genetic structure and biochemical makeup to some primate species. The genes of humans and chimpanzees are 99 percent identical, and studies on blood proteins and DNA show remarkable commonalities between chimpanzees and humans (Tanner and Zihlman 1976). For this reason, chimpanzee behavior has provided an opportunity to observe some of the rudimentary forms of social organization and behavior from which humans have likely evolved.

Primates engage in a variety of social behaviors, the specifics of which vary from species to species. But chimpanzees hunt, gather, and share food, feed and groom their offspring, make tools, and develop systems of social organization. Male and female chimpanzees develop patterns of sociability and engage in extensive gestural and nonverbal communication. In most primate species, maternal involvement with offspring exceeds paternal care, but in some species the reverse is true. In the South American titi monkey, for example, males carry the infant except when it is nursing.

Studies of the evolution from primates to humans show that changes in behavioral patterns and, eventually, in morphology (structure) occurred as new environments were encountered. As early hominids moved in search of food, they adopted new physical and social forms to cope with the new environments they found.

The transition from ape to human began when ape populations moved from the forests to the more open savannahs of eastern Africa. As these groups moved to different regions, new patterns of food gathering emerged that, over time, influenced the bipedal locomotion of the species and led to the creation of tools, new defense patterns, flexible systems of food sharing, and new patterns of communication and social organization (Tanner and Zihlman 1976). New methods of acquiring food and a reduction in competition with other populations also created an environmental basis for major transformations and adaptations in the species.

The role of females in the evolution of human society is critical. Females were most often responsible for the survival of offspring; they invested more time than males in gathering food and tending the young. Among the earliest ancestors, *Australopithecus,* plant foods gathered by women provided a higher proportion of caloric intake than was obtainable through the hunting of meat (Zihlman 1978). As feminist scholars have reexamined the archaeological record, they have found that the importance of meat in early human diets has been exaggerated, in part because bone matter is more durable than vegetative matter and leaves a more obvious record. But recent research shows that females have an equally important (in fact, central) role in the evolution of innovative skills and social organization, in spite of the fact that Western anthropologists have traditionally cast evolutionary theory and the anthropological record in terms of "man the great hunter" and "woman the silent gatherer."

The transition from *Australopithecus to Homo erectus* is believed to have occurred 1.8 to 1.2 million years ago. Fossil records show the transition to involve a slight increase in body size, increased cranial capacity, and an increased ratio of brain to body size. Evidence of stone tools from this period shows signs of human workmanship, marking the introduction of human creativity. The increased mental capacity of humans makes social learning possible, thus introducing a capability to remember larger home terrains. Between 1 million and 500,000 years ago, populations of *Homo erectus* had spread from southern and eastern Africa to northern Asia and Europe. More regular use of cave shelters and constructed huts increased cooperative food sharing because dependent children could remain in the hands of caretakers while mothers assisted in the gathering of food. By the time of the evolution of *Homo sapiens,* between 100,000 and 200,000 years ago, the brain had expanded to nearly its present size. Along with that adaptation, complex communicative, technical, and conceptual skills evolved, forming the basis for what we would now call human culture.

Throughout the evolution of human society, flexibility and cooperation between males and females were essential for human survival. As early hominid groups found new food sources, predators, and environmental hazards, the key to their survival was the invention of new patterns of social cooperation. Females did not merely benefit from the inventions of males; they were central actors in the adaptations leading to human life (Zihlman 1978; Zihlman and Tanner 1976).

food / sharing

As primary caretakers of new members of the population, females developed food-sharing networks and systems of communication to train the young and protect them from environmental hazards. The reproductive and socialization tasks for which the women were responsible did not exclude them from the fabric of society but instead made their role fundamental to the emergence of human groups. As these

shared / child / care

early groups developed home bases in caves and huts, it is likely that systems of shared child care emerged. Dependent children could remain with adult caretakers while their mothers gathered food. In fact, it is suggested that "the sharing of child care beyond the immediate kin group may have been a further step toward building networks within a larger community that shared food and defended itself against predators and cooperated for survival in the harsh environment of this colder world" (Zihlman 1978:17).

The evolutionary record reveals three essential points. First, females

(1) have an essential and central role in the making of human society. In addition to developing food-sharing systems and networks for child care, women probably invented basketry, weaving, and pottery. And as the feminist writer Dorothy Dinnerstein has suggested, "receptacles in which to store food are by no means a trivial cultural achievement. They extend the time scale on which life can be lived, changing food gathering from a hand-to-mouth activity to one that refers to the future and whose results can be experienced with reference to the past" (1976:22).

(2) Second, it is clear from the evolutionary record that human society emerges from the complex interaction of biological and environmental conditions. Human beings developed as they adapted to environmental conditions. As environmental conditions changed, adaptations in human life were made. This point should serve as a reminder not only of the past from which we come, but also of the need for flexible human arrangements in the present and future that we face.

(3) Third, discussions of the evolutionary record have been heavily biased by gender-laden assumptions about the proper roles of males and females. Scientific analyses and anthropological descriptions of human societies often reflect patriarchal values, showing how contemporary culture distorts our view of the past. For example, the evolutionary record has been filled with descriptions of "dominance hierarchies" or

"male competition for female sexual favors"—descriptions that tell us more about the values of the observer than the actual conditions of earlier human groups.

Despite the seeming importance of cooperative arrangements in the evolution of human society, most discussions of human evolution have ignored or belittled the role of women in the origins of human society. Projecting their own cultural bias onto the past, evolutionary theories have left the impression that "only men evolved" (Hubbard 1979) and that women played a passive role in the care of offspring and the nurturance of their kin. This problem of the projection of social values onto scientific research has been endemic in discussion of sex, biology, and culture and thus warrants further examination.

SEXISM, SCIENCE, AND SOCIETY

Scientific explanations are generally thought to be objective accounts that are uninfluenced by the values and interests of scientific thinkers. Thus, science has the image of being value-neutral and true to the facts. Objectivity in science is depicted as stemming from the calculated distance between the observer and the observed. In the scientific framework, personal characteristics of scientific observers are not expected to influence their results.

Yet, the world of science is overwhelmingly male—a fact that is well documented in studies revealing the small proportion of women in virtually every scientific field (Aldrich 1978). It is therefore possible that science carries a distinctively masculine tone—one that values objective separation from the objects of research and, yet, is nonetheless gendered in the descriptions it offers and the explanations it creates (Keller 1978).

In considering gender, we can find numerous examples showing that the ideals of scientific objectivity have, in fact, not been met in reaching specific research conclusions. Note, for example, the description of the experimental scientific method offered by Francis Bacon, one of the sixteenth-century founders of modern scientific thought:

For you have but to follow and as it were hound nature in her wanderings, and you will be able when you like to lead and drive her afterward to the same

place again. . . . Neither ought a man to make scruple of entering and pene-
trating into those holes and corners, when the inquisition of truth is his whole
object. (Cited in Harding 1983:22)

The emergence of modern science is founded upon an image of rational
man as conquering the passions of nature, which is depicted as female.
Consider Machiavelli's famed quotation regarding fortune:

fortune is a woman and it is necessary if you wish to master her to conquer her
by force; and it can be seen that she lets herself be overcome by the bold rather
than by those who proceed coldly, and therefore like a woman, she is always a
friend to the young because they are less cautious, fiercer, and master her with
greater audacity. (From *The Prince;* cited in Harding 1983)

Such depictions of science and nature might be dismissed as old-fash-
ioned ramblings of patriarchal days gone by, except for the fact that
gendered descriptions of biological phenomena continue to appear in
scientific texts. One of the best examples comes from Alice Rossi's
description of the way in which male fantasies of sexual power have
been projected onto descriptions of biological reproduction. Rossi
writes:

A good starting place to observe such fantasy is the initial coming together of
sperm and ovum. Ever since Leewenhoek first saw sperm under the microscope,
great significance has been attached to the fact that sperm are equipped with
motile flagella, and it was assumed that the locomotive ability of the sperm
fully explained their journey from the vagina through the cervix and uterus to
the oviduct for the encounter with the ovum. . . . Rorvik (1971) describes the
seven-inch journey through the birth canal and womb to the waiting egg as
equivalent to a 500-mile upstream swim for a salmon and comments with
admiration that they often make the hazardous journey in under an
hour,"more than earning their title as the most powerful and rapid living creatures on earth." The image is clear: powerful active sperm and a passive ovum
awaiting its arrival and penetration, male sexual imagery structuring the very
act of conception. (1977:16–17)

In fact, as Rossi points out, uterine contractions, stimulated by the
release of the hormone oxytocin, propel the sperm through the female
system so that "completely inert substances such as dead sperm and
even particles of India ink reach the oviducts as rapidly as live sperm
do" (Rossi 1977:17).

Particularly when scientists are observing events that are connected to our social lives, it is easy for their descriptions to become contaminated by social assumptions about gender roles. This does not mean that these investigators are dishonest or engaged in conscious delusion, but only that our social values can easily be projected onto the observations, descriptions, and explanations that we make (Hubbard 1979). If we are unconscious of those values, as has often been the case with gender bias, then we will have created descriptions of the world that merely reproduce what we take for granted. Thus, to produce truly objective knowledge of the social world requires knowing the social conditions in which science is produced and seeing how those conditions are reflected in scientific conclusions. In the case of scientific discussions of sex differences and sexuality, the problem has sometimes been a semantic one: The language in which ideas are communicated has been gender-biased. But in addition to eliminating sexist language, more substantive changes have been necessary, particularly when scientific thought has served ideological purposes that reflect its attempts to justify the status quo.

Sociologists use the concept of *ideology* to refer to systems of belief that distort reality so as to justify and maintain the status quo (Mannheim 1936). Biological explanations of gender inequality are a case in point. It is interesting to note that biologically determinist arguments tend to flourish in times of political conservatism, when powerful groups are working to maintain their own advantages. In such a setting, claims to scientific truth lend legitimacy and scientific authority to beliefs that otherwise would have a clear political bias.

In the history of social thought, Social Darwinism is a good example. Social Darwinism emerged at the turn of the twentieth century during a time of rapid expansion of capitalist wealth together with extensive exploitation of immigrant and racial minorities (Hofstadter 1959; Rossi 1977; Schwendinger and Schwendinger 1974). Capitalists such as John D. Rockefeller were inspired by Social Darwinism—a doctrine that claimed that only the most fit would survive and rise to the top. Such a belief justified their own accumulation of wealth while fostering the racist belief that those who failed did so out of biological inferiority. Rockefeller declared in a Sunday school address:

The growth of a large business is merely survival of the fittest. . . . The American Beauty rose can be produced in the splendor and fragrance which bring cheer to its beholder only by sacrificing the early birds which grew up around it. This is not an evil tendency in business. It is merely the working out of a law of nature and a law of God. (Ghent 1902:29)

Social Darwinism justified the emergence of capitalism by claiming it to be the result of natural laws over which man has no control. Clearly, Rockefeller's arguments rested on both racist and class-bound claims. Similarly, analyses that explain gender inequality as naturally arising from differences between the sexes are an ideological defense of patriarchal privilege. They justify the rule of men over women while at the same time distorting women's actual experience, both in a biological and a social sense. When these distortions become part of the scientific record, then science clearly is serving an ideological purpose.

Freud's theory of the double orgasm is a case in point. Freud's argument, and one that was widely believed until very recently, was that women have two kinds of orgasm—clitoral and vaginal. Clitoral orgasm, in Freud's view, was less "mature." He maintained that adult women should transfer their center of orgasm to the vagina, where male penetration made their sexual response complete. Freud's theory of the double orgasm has no basis in fact. The center of female sexuality is the clitoris; female orgasm is achieved through stimulation of the clitoris, whether or not accompanied by vaginal penetration (Masters and Johnson 1966). But, for nearly a century, the myth of the double orgasm led women to believe that they were frigid—unable to produce a mature sexual response. During this period, psychiatrists (most of whom were male) reported frigidity as the single most common reason for women to seek clinical therapy (Chesler 1972). In fact, the emphasis on male penetration meant that most women were not sexually satisfied in heterosexual relations because sexual intercourse and the ideology that buttressed it served male interests. This fact, in turn, supported the attitude that women needed men for sexually mature relationships, even though, as recent research shows, women have higher rates of orgasm when they masturbate, have sex with another woman, or engage in cunnilingus (English 1980). One study, in fact, reports higher rates of orgasm for female virgins (through mutual masturbation and cunnilingus) than for coitally experienced females (Sorenson 1973; cited in Rossi and Rossi 1977).

The assumption that women need men to achieve a mature sexual response is related to the larger issue that women are dependent on men for their sexual, emotional, social, and economic well-being. This assumption not only legitimates "compulsory heterosexuality" as an institution (Rich 1980) but denigrates women's relationships with other women and subjects them to continued domination by men.

In sum, feminist research has unraveled the way that gender bias has infiltrated the scientific record. Feminist revisions have not only cast a new light on old assumptions about sex and biology but have shown how many of the "truths" alleged by scientific study merely reflect the interests of a male-dominated society. Feminist revisions in science aim for a more objective perspective by recognizing the interplay between scientific knowledge and the social systems in which it is produced. This perspective shows that culture influences the production of knowledge while at the same time (as the concluding section will show) affecting actual biological processes.

CONCLUSION: THE INTERACTION OF BIOLOGY AND CULTURE

It is easy to think of biological events as unaffected by the intervention of cultural systems. Yet, as scholars have discovered, the natural and social worlds often overlap. Events that we think of as physiological processes—such as aging, illness, and reproduction—are heavily influenced by the social-cultural systems in which they occur. This fact has particular significance for feminist studies because it demonstrates the inadequacies of explanations of sex differences that rest upon biological explanations alone.

Consider, for example, the biological process of aging—clearly one that is universal, inevitable, and based on human physiology. Research shows that how long one lives is strongly influenced by one's gender. Life expectancy is shorter for men (71.1 years in 1980) than for women (76.3 years), and males have higher accidental death rates (in both childhood and adulthood) than do women. Men also have higher suicide and homicide rates than do women (Hess and Markson 1980). Some research has shown that men with personalities marked by ambition, single-mindedness, and devotion to work are more prone to heart attacks than others (Friedman and Rosenman 1974). In fact, the risks associated with traditionally masculine roles are so great that one psychologist has called masculinity a "lethal role" (Jourard, 1974).

But even the physiological changes associated with aging are greatly affected by the social context in which aging occurs. Nutrition, for example, affects the biological health of aging persons, but social factors such as living alone or in an institution are known to affect dietary habits, as are factors such as income, cultural preferences for food, and exercise. Aging is also aggravated by stress—a condition generated by a variety of social and psychological difficulties.

For women, the aging process has its own strains. In a society in which women are valued for their youth and beauty, aging becomes a difficult social and psychological experience. Birthday cards that joke about women deteriorating after age twenty-nine and commercials for creams that "hide your aging spots" tell American women that they should be ashamed of growing old. It should be no surprise, then, that a biological process such as menopause becomes a difficult psychological experience. Research shows that menopause produces more anxiety and more depression in cultures that are less supportive of women as they age (Bart 1979; Clay 1977; Hess and Markson 1980; Reitz 1977).

What we learn from looking at the interaction of biology and culture is that cultural beliefs about biological events imbue them with a significance greater than their physiological character. Menstruation, for example, is a universal phenomenon, yet one that in different cultures takes on very different meanings. In many cultures, menstruation is symbolic of the strength of women, and elaborate rituals and rites of passage symbolize that power (Powers 1980). Yet, in other cultures, menstruation is seen as symbolic of defilement, and elaborate practices may be developed to isolate and restrict menstruating women. In the nineteenth century, for example, southeast Asian women could not be employed in the opium industry, for it was believed that, were a menstruating woman nearby, the opium would turn bitter (Delaney, Lupton, and Toth 1976). And, in contemporary American culture, menstruation is depicted as secretive and invisible, as best seen in the advertising industry, which advises menstruating women to keep their "secret" protected, yet to feel confident, secure, and free.

Work on menstrual moods shows, in another context, the interactive effect of culture and biological events (Rossi and Rossi 1977). The Rossis' research studies college-aged men and women who were asked to rate their daily moods over a 40-day period. Women in the sample also noted their first day of menstruation as it occurred during the rating cycle. The Rossis then compared mood ratings as clocked by biological time (measured by phases in the menstrual cycle) and by calendar (or social) time. Surprisingly, the results show that men marked more days per month when they felt "achy" "crampy," and "sick" than did women. But, more to the point, the Rossis' results show that the most significant changes in moods occurred for women according to changes in the calendar week, not their menstrual cycles.

Women were more likely to feel "happy," "loving," and "healthy" on weekends and "depressed," "unhappy," and "sick" on "blue Wednesday." The research also finds no significant elevation of negative moods in the premenstrual phase for women; there was, however, an elevation of positive moods in the ovulatory phase of menstruation and an elevation of negative moods in the luteal phase (days 17–24 in a 28-day menstrual cycle). But, more important than the independent effects of biological and social time, this research finds that moods (especially positive moods) were most strongly affected when biological and social cycles were synchronized (e.g., when ovulation occurred on a weekend).

In another example of the interaction of biology and culture, something once dismissed as an old wives' tale now appears to have scientific validity. It appears that menstrual cycles become synchronized among women who live in close proximity to each other and as close friends (McClintock 1971). Although the explanation for this phenomenon is not yet clear (Comfort 1971), it is likely that *pheromones*—a generic term used to refer to communication by chemical signals—are responsible for synchronization of menstrual cycles. This phenomenon shows how cultural living arrangements can exert an influence on physiological processes such as menstruation.

Such conclusions demonstrate the simplicity of reductionist arguments that trace sex differences to biological causes alone. Research in biology and human evolution points to the extreme difficulty of separating biological from social causes. In an evolutionary sense, the biological basis for human life must be flexible enough to allow for environmental change and adaptation. Moreover, the opinion that sex differences are biologically caused seems to assume that environmental conditions are changeable, whereas biological conditions are not. Research that examines ways in which culture influences biological events shows that this is a false assumption.

The study of human culture shows that there is no fixed correspondence between innate human dispositions (if they exist) and human social forms. Whatever link exists between biology and social life is mediated by the influence of culture. Because culture is symbolic (its meaning is derived from social interaction), it cannot be found in the intrinsic properties of persons or objects. One of the unique characteristics of human societies is their freedom from natural relationships

(Sahlins 1977). For example, even though the act of human reproduction is a physical one, its significance lies as much, if not more, in its social meaning. Moreover, what we reproduce is not just a genetic object, but a human being whose life is part of a system of human groups.

This does not mean that the biological basis for human life is irrelevant or unimportant, but it stresses the mutual and interdependent influence of even biological events. With regard to sex differences, culture exerts a powerful influence on who we are and what we become. In the next chapter, we will study the process by which culture is learned and the ways in which our gender identities are acquired.

SEX ROLE SOCIALIZATION

CULTURE AND GENDER

In the village of Uder, located in the rugged hills of northern Nigeria, lives a population of people who call themselves Birom. When a boy is born here, his umbilical cord is cut with an iron knife used to cut acha— the most valued staple grain of the culture. Traditionally, women were forbidden to grow acha, and even today, the size of a man's acha crop is taken as a measure of his strength and virility. When a girl is born, her umbilical cord is cut with a blade of grass or a bamboo knife. The afterbirth of a boy is placed in a clay pot and put high on a branch of a cottonwood tree; the girl's afterbirth is buried in the soil, usually during a fertility ritual. In the same society, crying in boy infants is regarded as a sign of strength, virility, and lust for life; crying in girls is regarded as indicative of a fretful and complaining personality (Smedley 1974).

To an outsider, these practices may seem unusual and strange. However, if we as outsiders, considered our own cultural practices surrounding birth, they too would seem quite odd. In American culture, baby boys are dressed in blue, girls in pink. Although the origins of this practice are not known, most parents comply with the cultural habit. Some will dress their daughters in blue as well as pink, but it is a rare parent who dresses a boy in pink. Children's names in our culture are also selected according to the masculinity or femininity that they symbolize. A pamphlet distributed to expectant parents by a baby product company gives advice on the selection of the baby' name:

Choosing a suitable name for your new baby is very important. The name you decide on will be much more than just a term of identification. It will, to a degree, be a reflection of how you picture your baby as a grownup. . . . Even though they're lovely names, be careful of names that, at least soundwise, fit both sexes. Examples are Francis (Frances), Jean (Gene), Kerry (Carrie), and Gail (Gale). These are safer used as a middle name with a first name that is unmistakingly masculine or feminine. . . . In the case of boys, parents should beware of giving names that will forever, have a "little-boy" sound, such as Dickie, Bobby, Jimmy, and Billy. (Mead, Johnson and Company 1978:2–3)

In our own culture, we engage in social practices that differentiate boys and girls, and we make assumptions about what are appropriately masculine and feminine names; names are labels that we carry throughout our lives. Girls' names are supposed to be feminine—soft, pretty, and symbolic of goodness, sweetness, and beauty; boys' names are supposed to be masculine—short, harder in tone, and symbolic of strength, determination, and intellect. More diminutive endings are found on girls' than on boys' names (for example, Debbie, Nanette, Jeannie, Anita), implying the lesser status of women. Names also symbolize the homophobia (fear of homosexuality) of our culture, because, especially with boys, parents are advised not to give names that have a feminine tone. Girls' names are sometimes feminized forms of boys' names (such as Roberta, Denise, Carla), but the reverse seldom occurs (Richardson 1981).

When parents take a child home from the hospital, they begin a complex, often unintentional, series of practices that slowly but effectively create the gender of their child. Every human infant is born into a cultural environment. That environment shapes what persons become, what chances in life are available to them, and how they perceive the world in which they live.

This chapter will discuss the process by which persons learn the gender roles that culture defines as appropriate for them. *Socialization* is a term sociologists use to refer to the process by which social roles are learned. Because gender is a significant part of our acquired identity, the learning of gender (or sex roles) through socialization is a primary part of the process of growing up. In this chapter, we will see that socialization goes on throughout life, although it is particularly critical in our early years. We will examine different sources of sex role socialization and study the consequences of sex role socialization for our identities, skills, and relationships. Finally, this chapter will examine some of the theoretical perspectives that have been developed by sociologists and psychologists to explain the socialization process.

Because socialization emerges from its cultural setting, it is important to begin with a brief discussion of the meaning of culture as well as some basic concepts used by sociologists in discussing the socialization process. We will see how important culture and socialization are in understanding gender relations in society, and we will discuss the fact that socialization emerges from the institutional framework of society.

DEFINING CULTURE AND SOCIALIZATION

Culture is defined as "the set of definitions of reality held in common by people who share a distinctive way of life" (Kluckhohn 1962:52). Culture is, in essence, a pattern of expectations about what are appropriate behaviors and beliefs for the members of the society. Thus, culture provides prescriptions for social behavior. Culture tells us what we ought to do, what we ought to think, who we ought to be, and what we ought to expect of others.

The concept of culture explains a great deal to us about variation in human life-styles and human societies. Cultural norms (the expectations that culture provides) vary tremendously from one society to another and, within any given society, from one historical setting to another and among different groups in the society. Cross-cultural studies reveal an immense diversity in human social relations, because human creativity and cultural adaptations to different circumstances create a rich and complex mosaic of the different possibilities for human life.

In every known culture, gender is a major category for the organization of cultural and social relations, although specific cultural expectations vary from society to society. One feature of a culture is that its members come to take cultural patterns for granted. Thus, culture provides its members with tacit knowledge; much of what they believe as true or what they perceive as real is learned to the point where it is no longer questioned. Culture provides a bedrock of assumptions that often go unexamined but that, nonetheless, guide the fundamentals of our behavior and our beliefs.

Gender expectations of a culture are sometimes expressed subtly in social interaction, as, for example, in American culture, where men interrupt women more frequently than women interrupt men (Frieze and Ramsey 1976), where women smile more than do men (Mehrabian 1971), and where men stare at women more than women stare at men (Frieze et al. 1978). At other times, gender expectations are not so subtle, as in the cultural practices of Chinese foot binding, Indian suttee, European witch hunts, and the genital mutilation of women documented in some African countries (Hosken 1979; Jacobsen 1974; Stein 1978; Wong 1974). Within our own culture, such extreme physical practices are also evidenced in the sadistic treatment of women in pornography and in the common surgical practices of face lifts and silicone implants.

In different ways and for a variety of reasons, all cultures use gender as a primary category of social relations. The differences we observe between men and women can be attributed largely to these cultural patterns. Were sex differences determined by biological factors alone, we would not find the vast diversity that exists in gender relations from society to society. Moreover, were sex differences universal in content, we would not observe that masculinity and femininity vary in meaning from one culture to another. Masculinity and femininity, although attached to persons usually by virtue of their biological sex, are cultural ideals. They refer to expectations established by society, not categories that are fixed by one's biological status. The discussion of hermaphroditism in the preceding chapter provides an example of the importance of gender rearing in the creation of gender identity, even where there is an incongruence between biological and social sex type.

The concept of gender as used in the sociological literature refers to the cultural attributes expected of the different sexes. It includes learned social and psychological attributes and is a fundamental category of one's experience. Similar to the social categories established by race and social class, it patterns what others expect of us; it establishes, in large measure, our life chances; and it directs our social relations with others.

Although gender may be based on the fact of one's biological sex, its reference is cultural, not biological. As the previous chapter shows, *biological sex* refers to the genetic and physiological facts of one's sex. Although biological sex usually establishes a pattern of social expectations that create gender, biological sex is not always the same as one's social sex or gender. Similarly, the fact that someone is born female does not mean that she will become stereotypically feminine. Nor does the biological fact of maleness necessarily create a stereotypically masculine man. Femininity and masculinity are cultural concepts and, as such, they have fluctuating expectations, are learned differently by different members of the culture, and are relative to the historical and social settings in which they emerge.

Sociologists use the concept of *social roles* to refer to culturally prescribed expectations, duties, and rights that define the relationship between a person in a particular social position and the other people with whom he or she interacts. For example, to be a mother is a specific social role with a definable set of expectations, rights, and duties. We all occupy multiple roles in society, and we can think of roles as linking individuals to society. It is through social roles that cultural norms are patterned and learned.

Sex roles are those expectations for behavior and attitudes that the culture defines as appropriate for men and women, and *sex role socialization* refers to the process by which sex roles are learned by a society's members. Through sex role socialization, different behaviors and attitudes are encouraged and discouraged in men and women. That is, social expectations about what is properly masculine and feminine are communicated to us through the socialization process. Our family, peers, and teachers, as well as the media, act as agents of the socialization process. Although probably no one of us becomes exactly what the cultural ideal prescribes, our roles in social institutions are conditioned by the gender relations we learn in our social development.

Some persons become more perfectly socialized than others, and sociologists have warned against the idea of seeing humans as totally passive, overly socialized creatures (Wrong 1961). To some extent, we probably all resist the expectations society has of us. Our uniqueness as individuals stems in part from this resistance, as well as from variations in the social experience we have. The idea of sex role socialization does not deny individual differences, but it does point to the common experiences shared by girls as they become women and by boys as they become men. However much we may believe that we were raised in a gender-neutral environment, research and careful observation show how pervasive and generally effective is the process of sex role socialization. Although some of us conform more than others, socialization acts as a powerful system of social control.

This fact can be seen in the argument that sex roles are hazardous to our health. By shaping persons into masculine and feminine types, we may be condemning both sexes to a "one-sided existence" (Tolson 1977). Traditional sex roles deny women access to the public world of power, achievement, and independence. Men, on the other hand, are denied the nurturant, emotive, and other-oriented world of domestic life. In this sense, typical sex roles limit the psychological and social possibilities for human beings.

Particularly among those who conform most fully to sex role expectations, research shows that they may experience negative consequences. For example, women who score as very feminine on personality tests tend to be dissatisfied and anxious and to have low-self-esteem (Bem 1972). Research on depression indicates it to be more frequent and more intense among men and women who are too tightly integrated into social roles. For example, married women are more often depressed than single women, although single men are more depressed than married men (Bernard 1971); *supermothers*—those who overly conform to the maternal role—are more depressed than other women (Bart 1979); housewives are more often depressed than working women, and when they are depressed, they show more impairment in physical and mental functioning than do working women (Weissman and Paykel 1974). Finally, women and men who are rigid in their world outlook tend to experience more depression than others (Weissman and Paykel 1974). If these mental health patterns are any indication of social adjustment, then it indeed appears that sex roles condition our social and psychological well-being.

Feminists have found the study of socialization to be extremely valuable in understanding how we emerge as gendered persons. Although there are some limitations to what we find out by studying sex role socialization (as the concluding section of this chapter will show), socialization is a valuable concept in understanding the way in which cultural expectations about gender are transmitted to the individuals in a society. Because socialization patterns can be easily observed in individual and group experience, the study of socialization is valuable in linking individuals to the society in which they live. It is important to remember that socialization takes place in the context of institutions such as the family, the school, and the mass media. Each of these institutions acts as an agent of the socialization process and, thus, passes on gender expectations that are consistent with institutional needs. The following section examines the process of socialization as it occurs throughout the life cycle. This section will be followed by a discussion of research on socialization as it occurs in selected social institutions.

SOCIALIZATION THROUGHOUT THE LIFE CYCLE

As the introduction to this chapter shows, socialization begins from the moment one is born, but it continues throughout our adult lives even though our gender roles are established very early. Although much of the sex role research has focused on childhood socialization, it is important to remember that socialization is an ongoing process and one that is especially significant when we encounter new roles and new social experience.

Infancy

Beginning in infancy, boys and girls are treated differently. Review of the research on infant socialization shows how quickly gendered expectations become part of our experience. One innovative study asked first-time parents to describe their baby only twenty-four hours after birth. Although physical examination revealed no objective differences between male and female infants, the parents of girls reported their babies to be softer, smaller, and less attentive than did the parents of boys. This study also shows that fathers are more influenced by the child's gender than are mothers. More than mothers, fathers describe their sons as larger, better coordinated, more alert, and stronger than girls; more than mothers, fathers describe their daughters as delicate, weak, and inattentive (Rubin, Provenzano, and Luria 1974).

Research on child-parent interaction does not, however, reveal consistent patterns of sex differences in social interaction between parents and newborns. There is a tendency for parents to elicit motor behavior more from sons than from daughters, but little difference appears by sex in the amount of affectionate contact between mother and infant (Maccoby and Jacklin 1974). Studies find that there are no consistent sex differences in the incidence of separation anxiety among male and female infants, and research findings are mixed on the question of whether girl infants smile and respond more to human faces than do boy infants (Frieze et al. 1978).

Taken together, research on sex differences in infants shows that parents treat their infants differently according to their sex, but that differences in the infants' patterns of behavior are extremely small. One frequently cited study shows that, by age thirteen months, girls are more likely than boys to cling to, look at, and talk to their mothers (Goldberg and Lewis 1969), but attempts to replicate this study have failed to confirm these results (Coates, Anderson, and Hartup 1972; Jacklin, MacCoby, and Dick 1973). However, mothers do tend to touch and talk to infant girls more than infant boys (Kagan and Lewis 1965), and fathers are likely to mock-wrestle with baby sons and to play more gently with baby daughters (Komarovsky 1953).

Because sex differences in human infants are negligible and inconsistent, we cannot draw conclusions about the immediate effect of socialization on baby boys and girls. However, even though these expectations may be subtle and without conscious intent, they are likely to be effective in guiding the later behavior of the child. As the child grows older, gender expectations and, consequently, differences in gender behavior seem to increase. Long before boys and girls reach the age of puberty (when the effect of biological hormones is at its greatest), clear differences in the behavior of each sex appear. Whereas in infants socialization occurs largely as the result of behavior reinforcement, as the child develops, more complex cognitive learning occurs. At this point, sex role expectations become even more marked (Weitzman 1979).

Childhood Play and Games

Research in child development emphasizes the importance of play and games in the maturation of children. Through play, children learn the skills of social interaction, develop cognitive and analytical abilities, and are taught the values and attitudes of their culture. The games that children play have great significance for the child's intellectural, moral, personal, and social development.

George Herbert Mead, a social psychologist and major sociological theorist in the early twentieth century, describes three stages in which socialization occurs: imitation, play, and game. In the imitation stage, infants simply copy the behavior of significant persons in their environment. In the play stage, the child begins "taking the role of the other"—seeing himself or herself from the perspective of another person. Mead argues that taking the role of the other is a cognitive process that permits the child to develop a self-concept. Self-concepts emerge through interacting with other people and from learning to perceive how others see us. The other people most emotionally important to the child (who may be parents, siblings, or other primary caretakers) are, in Mead's term, *significant others.* In the play stage, children learn to take the role of significant others, primarily by practicing their social roles—for example, "playing Mommy" or "playing Daddy."

In the game stage, children are able to do more. Rather than seeing themselves from the perspective of only one significant other at a time, they can play games requiring them to understand how several other people (including more than just significant others) view them simultaneously. Playing baseball, to use Mead's example, involves the roles and expectations of many more people than does "playing Mommy." Eventually, children in the game stage learn to orient themselves not just to significant others but to a *generalized other* as well. The generalized other represents the cultural expectations of the whole social community.

Throughout Mead's analysis of the emergence of the self, he emphasizes the importance of interpretive behavior in the way the child relates to others in the social environment. Early activity, especially through play, locates children's experience in a social environment; therefore, meanings communicated through play help the child organize personal experience into an emerging self. Children's play is then a very significant part of the socialization process.

With regard to sex roles, research reveals the pervasiveness of gender stereotyping as it is learned in early childhood play. Researchers have observed that, compared to girls' rooms, boys' rooms contain toys of more different classes (educational, sports, animals, spatial-temporal objects, depots, military equipmnt, machines, and vehicles) and that boys' toys tend to encourage activities outside of the home. Girls' toys, on the other hand, are both less varied in type and encourage play within the home (Rheingold and Cook 1975). Additionally, Rheingold and Cook find that boys' toys have a greater "competency-eliciting potential" than girls' toys. That is, boys' toys encourage more flexible responses, diverse reactions, and improvisational play.

Moreover, content analyses find that females are underrepresented in the titles, pictures, character roles, and plots of children's literature and that most of these books deal with males (both as persons and as animals) and their adventures (Weitzman et al. 1972). Weitzman writes, "through books, children learn about the world outside their immediate environment; they learn what other boys and girls do, say and feel, and they learn what is expected of children their age. Picture books are especially important to the preschool child because they are often looked at over and over again at a time when children are in the process of developing their own sex role identities" (Weitzman 1979:7). It is significant that preschool books show women's roles as confined to the home and as either cleaning or caring for others, for this is a precursor to the roles women find in their adult lives. The only major exception is in the portrayal of women as fairy godmothers exhibiting power and leadership, although clearly in a mythical setting (Weitzman 1979).

A recent study of children's games adds another dimension to the study of sex roles and play. Lever's (1978) study criticizes Mead for ignoring both sex differences in children's play and the dimension of complexity in the games of boys and girls.

Lever's work is based on observations of fifth-grade children, most of whom in her study are white and middle class. Based on observations in school playgrounds, questionnaires, interviews, and the children's diaries of leisure activities, Lever measured the complexity of boys' and girls' play in six dimensions: role differentiation (how many distinct roles occur in the game), player interdependence (whether the action of one player affects the performance of another), size of the play group, explicitness of goals, number and specificity of rules, and finally, team formation. She distinguishes play from games by noting that play does not involve explicit goals, whereas games tend to have a recognized goal or end point. Also, games tend to be structured by teams that work together toward a common goal; play, although it involves cooperative interaction, is not structured in team relationships.

Lever's findings reveal several patterns in the sex differences of children's play. Girls tend to play, whereas boys interact through games. Girls' games have fewer rules than boys' games and, for girls, the largest category of activity is play involving a single role. The next largest category of play for girls includes games focused on a single central person (e.g., tag), whereas boys play in larger groups and with more complex role differentiation. Lever also finds that girls are more cooperative, whereas boys are more competitive; boys' play and games often include face-to-face competition, whereas girls' competition is more indirect. In terms of game rules, Lever finds that girls are more likely to play games involving repeated ritual (such as jumping rope), whereas boys will follow more elaborate rules. According to Lever, ritualistic play does not exercise physical and mental skills to the extent that rules do because it is repetitive and more passive. Finally, when girls play games with rules, they tend to ignore the rules, whereas boys more rigidly adhere to established principles of play.

Lever concludes that through play and games, boys learn involvement with the generalized other; girls, on the other hand, are more involved with "particular others." Such differences are significant because the dimension of complexity that characterizes children's play also describes the organization of modern industrial societies. Complex societies involve an elaborate division of labor and elaborate differentiation of roles; these societies also are heterogeneous and are organized according to rationalized rules and social structures. Lever concludes that boys' games better prepare them for leadership and organizational skills that are useful both in childhood and in adult life. Her implication is that girls' socialization through games leaves them inadequately prepared to succeed in the complex organization of modern society.

Lever's conclusions imply that girls' experience is deficient because they develop different skills and modes of relating than do boys. However, although to function in a male-dominated society girls may need some of the skills that boys develop, we should be careful not to make the normative judgment that the female world is inferior to the male world. Childhood sex role socialization certainly teaches boys and girls different abilities and different identities. But just as girls may not learn to be rational, competitive, and rule-oriented, so boys may not learn to be nurturing and emotionally expressive.

We must also recognize that Lever's conclusions come from the particular white, middle-class sample that she used. Ladner's (1971) work on black adolescent girls shows us that, in adapting to the conditions of racism and sexism, black girls acquire self-concepts that promote mastery of the world they face. And it is extremely important to remember that not all girls and not all boys grow up in the sex-stereotyped way that a perfect separation of the female and male worlds would imply.

The characteristics associated with masculine and feminine sex stereotypes are those that are valued by dominant social institutions. In reading about the socialization process, it is important to keep in mind that research on socialization may exaggerate the extent to which the sexes are different and, in particular, may primarily reflect the experience of white, middle-class persons—those who are most frequently found as research subjects in these studies.

Nevertheless, research on childhood learning underscores the point that sex role socialization is situated within social institutions that do tend to value masculine, not feminine, traits. Were female-oriented values, such as flexibility, orientation toward others, and cooperation, to be incorporated into dominant social institutions, then we might well produce more gender-balanced boys and girls. As it is, the process of socialization throughout life pushes men and women away from each other so that, by the time they become adults, most are gender-typed. As we grow older, gender roles continue to influence our beliefs, our choices, and our relations with others.

ADULT SOCIALIZATION AND THE AGING PROCESS

As we encounter new experiences throughout our lives, we learn the role expectations associated with our new statuses. Although our gender identity is established relatively early in life, changes in our status in the society—for example, graduation, marriage, or starting a job— bring new expectations for behavior and beliefs. In later chapters, we will see that occupational and family roles carry explicit expectations for men and for women. Here, we will look specifically at the process of aging and the expectations that men and women face as they grow older.

Aging is perhaps the one thing about our lives that is inevitable. Yet, as a social experience, it has different consequences for men and women. Physiologically, the process of aging is similar for both sexes, with the exception of menopause. But social myths surrounding menopause have made it a more difficult process than its physiology alone creates. Physiologically, at menopause the ovaries stop producing 90 percent of their hormones, and following menopause, women become infertile. However, women may be as sexually active as before, and many women report an even more satisfying sex life once they are relieved from the connection between sexuality and childbearing.

Still, social myths portray the menopausal woman as prone to depression and anxiety, lacking sexual interest, and without self-confidence

(Hess and Markson 1980). Yet, research indicates that when these problems exist, they stem from the social devaluation of aging women, not from the physiological process of aging itself (Clay 1977; Collins 1976: Livson 1977; Reitz 1977). In fact, Bart (1979) finds cross-cultural evidence showing that aging is less stressful for women in societies where there is a strong tie to family and kin, not just to a husband; where there are extended, not nuclear, family systems; where there is a positive role for mothers-in-law (rather than the degrading status attached to it in our society); and where there are strong mother-child relationships throughout life. Even in our own society, racial and ethnic groups attach more value to older persons, thereby easing the transition to later life. Although the elderly in black and minority communities experience even greater difficulties with poverty and health than do the white elderly, their valued role in the extended family seems to alleviate some of the stress associated with growing old (Hess and Markson 1980).

Sex differences in the social process of aging can be attributed greatly to the emphasis on youth found in this culture and, in particular, to the association of youth and sexuality in women. Cultural stereotypes portray older men as distinguished, older women as barren. Unlike a man, as a woman ages, she will generally experience a loss of prestige; men gain prestige as they become more established in their careers. The consequences for both are great. Because men draw their self-esteem and their connections to others largely from their jobs, they may find retirement to be an especially stressful period (Bell 1979). Sociologists also point out that because men have learned to be task-oriented rather than person-oriented, they may have difficulty establishing new relationships in retirement or widowhood (Hess and Markson 1980).

For women, on the other hand, the disappearance of their mother role at middle age may be particularly stressful. Women who play this role to its fullest can become depressed and anxious when their children leave home and leave her behind (Bart 1979). Many of these women now find themselves reentering the labor force, either to help support their families (Curric, Dunn, and Fogarty 1980) or as the result of being displaced by divorce or widowhood (Jacobs 1979).

Friendship patterns among the elderly also show some sex differences in experience. Men have a wider circle of friends, but women have more diverse and intense friendships (Hess 1977; Powers and Bultena 1976). Men at all ages are more likely to describe their spouse as their best friend; for these men, the death of their spouse may be even more troubling than for men with other friends. Some researchers report high risks of mental illness and suicide among these men (Bock and Webber 1972). It is also true that women who were especially devoted to their husbands find the death of a spouse to be an especially difficult adjustment (Lopata 1973).

Once past the empty nest syndrome, women generally report more satisfaction and personal freedom in their later years than they had in their earlier life (Hess and Markson 1980; Neugarten 1975). Although aging is a difficult and stressful time for both men and women (and economic pressures contribute to this stress) it seems that aging also relaxes some of the social pressure experienced as a younger person. One study of college students' expectations of their grandparents found, for instance, that images of grandfathers and grandmothers did not appear to be sex-linked (Hess and Markson 1980). In fact, the adjectives used to describe grandparents *(loving, supportive, teacher, generous, concerned)* moved in the direction of female-type nurturant values for both sexes, as images of grandparents seem to become more gender neutral.

The influence of sex role socialization is strong throughout our lives because it is so pervasive in our social relations and our social institutions. In the next section, we will examine the influence of schools on the socialization process because, outside of the family, schools exert the most powerful influence on our early years—those years when gender is first established as a foundation for the rest of our lives.

SOCIALIZATION AND EDUCATION

The socialization process is not restricted to the child's life within the family, although we tend to think of the family as the primary source of one's social values and identity. But socialization is an ongoing process, and when the child leaves the family, other institutions continue the process of sex role learning. In school systems, curriculum material, teachers' different expectations, and the practice of educational tracking combine to encourage girls to learn skills and self-concepts that are different from those of boys.

Beginning with curriculum material, textbooks convey limited images of females that subtly communicate the idea that women are less important than men. Women's roles in history, in the sciences, in social studies, and in literature usually receive only passing notice, leaving the impression that women who contribute to history or knowledge must be quite exceptional (Lerner 1976). The effect is to see women as notable only when they "act like men" or when they stand out as deviant from other women.

Studies of textbooks show that men and women are portrayed in sex-stereotypic roles. Women are represented in far fewer occupations than men, and boys are more often shown as solving problems, displaying aggression, and being physically active (Women on Words and Images 1972). Compared to boys, girls are shown to be more conforming, more engaged in fantasy, and more involved in verbal rather than physical behavior (Child, Potter, and Levine 1960; Richardson 1981). Moreover, the situation does not seem to be improving. A survey of children's readers in 1972 found a five-to-two ratio of boy-centered to girl-centered stories; in 1977, the ratio had increased to seven-to-two (Tavris and Offir 1977). Researchers also found that test items on standard achievement tests show substantial bias by referring more often to males and the male world (Sario, Jacklin, and Tittle 1973).

Studies of teachers' expectations also find gender patterns in the behavior of teachers toward their students. Teachers respond more often to boys than to girls who misbehave (Serbin and O'Leary 1975), thereby calling more attention to them and perhaps encouraging them even further. Boys in school receive more reprimands and physical restraint (Serbin et al. 1973), but they also receive more praise than girls (Meyer and Thompson 1956). Even in progressive schools where there are deliberate attempts to avoid sex role stereotyping, researchers find that teachers subtly communicate gender expectations by, for example, complimenting girls when they wear dresses, but not pants, and seldom commenting on the way boys dress (Joffe 1971).

The skills and self-concepts that boys and girls learn in school will guide their experience beyond the school environment. The sex role messages they receive, both subtle and explicit, forge personalities and abilities that are generally different for boys and for girls. Research in the area of skills development shows the influence of gender on the acquisition of different abilities.

Differences in verbal and mathematical ability between women and men are not fixed because their comparative abilities change over time. Until high school, girls excel at reading, writing, and mathematics (Maccoby 1966); during their high school years, girls' intellectual achievements tend to drop, especially in mathematics (Richardson 1981). Research does show a tendency for girls to have better verbal skills than boys (Fox, Fennema, and Sherman 1977), and it is generally believed that boys have greater mathematical skills than girls. However, researchers point out that there is no consensus about what constitutes math ability (Ernest 1976; Weitzman 1979). Although it is often claimed that boys have better *analytical ability* than girls, the exact referent of this term is unclear. Most studies of analytical ability have focused primarily on spatial perception—one's ability to perceive an object independently of its background. Girls tend to be field dependent, that is, they have more trouble seeing an object independently of its context (Richardson 1981). As many have argued, this is a narrow reference for a term as broad as *analytical ability.*

Girls do show greater ability in verbal reasoning and perception (Sherman and Beck 1979), and the evidence as to whether girls perform differently on quantitative skills such as computation, geometry, and algebra is inconclusive, if not negative (Ernest 1976; Fox, Fennema, and Sherman 1977).

What does appear true is that sex differences in mathematics achievement are largely a function of the number of courses taken (Fox, Fennema, and Sherman 1977) and that, although boys and girls equally report liking math (Ernest 1976), math eventually becomes identified as a male preserve (Weitzman 1979). It seems that the focus of courses is important in conveying the message to girls that they can do well in mathematics. Girls do poorly on word problems that are based on male-typed activities, such as woodworking and guns, but do better when the same logical problems are put in the context of female-typed activities, such as cooking and gardening (Milton, 1958). Also, girls' math skills improve when they are examined by other women (Pederson, Shinedling, and Johnson 1968).

It has been suggested that students do well in math depending upon its perceived usefulness to their future careers (Fennema and Sherman 1977; Hilton and Berglund 1974). This finding suggests that sex differences in intellectual skills do not appear in the absence of societal influence. If girls do better in computation than in abstract reasoning, this may be because of their implicit understanding that computational skills may be more useful to them in their future jobs and roles in the family.

A wealth of research indicates that cultural norms discourage women from excelling at math (Tobias 1978). Critics contend, though, that the attention given to math anxiety among women may be a self-fulfilling prophecy. No one seems too concerned, for instance, about the extent of language anxiety among men, leading us to wonder if the focus on math anxiety is a reflection of the superior status attached to areas that are identified as male skills. Similarly, although research on spatial skills indicates that men tend to have better ability than women "to visually manipulate, locate, and make judgements about the spatial relationships of items in two-or-three-dimensional space" (Frieze et al. 1978:62), these differences do not appear among young children (Maccoby and Jacklin 1974), nor have they been found in cross-cultural studies among non-Western or nonindustrialized people (Berry 1971).

Others also suggest that differences in girls' intellectual abilities can be attributed to their learned "motive to avoid success." Matina Horner's (1972) work on this motive has been widely cited to explain women's lack of success. According to Horner's research, women want to excel, but the conflict caused by the social pressure not to succeed produces ambivalence in women that makes them want to succeed, but not too much. According to Horner, women will try to succeed, but will purposefully fail. However, replications of Horner's research have failed to reproduce her results (Levine and Crumrine 1975), and scholars now conclude that there were serious methodological flaws in her study. Because Horner's conclusions have been widely adopted, her critics have asked why this theory has become so popular. They conclude that this theory is a classic example of blaming the victim, because it blames women's failures on their own, not society's, inadequacies (Levine and Crumrine 1975).

In summary, sex differences in intellectual skills can be explained by the different role expectations placed on men and women in society. Girls, who are expected to be more oriented toward others, do best at skills requiring contextual understanding. They have more facility with verbal reasoning, perhaps because of the expectation that they will be talkers, not thinkers. On the other hand, boys, who are expected to move into scientific and technical professions and to be in a position to manipulate and control their environment, are more likely to learn skills of abstract reasoning and intellectual detachment that allow them to enter such roles. As long as opportunities for success are more limited for women than for men, we can expect girls and boys to learn different skills that are appropriate for the chances that await them.

Yet, we should also remember that socialization is a process by which human beings adapt to their environment. Much of the research on sex roles fails to find consistent sex differences in abilities, in personality, or in how boys and girls relate to others (Frieze et al. 1978). Although sex differences do appear in many cases, the failure of research to predict them consistently speaks to the fluidity of men and women in their confrontations with society. The fact that we do not end up equally feminine or equally masculine attests to the incredible human resilience and flexibility that exist even in the face of powerful processes of social control. In the next section, we will look at socialization as a process of social control—one that, although imperfect, does carefully shape who and what we become.

SOCIALIZATION AS SOCIAL CONTROL

Peter Berger (1963) describes social control as something like a series of concentric circles. At the center is the individual who is surrounded by different levels of control, ranging from subtle—such as learned roles, peer pressure, and ridicule—to overt—such as violence, physical threat, and imprisonment. According to Berger, it is usually not necessary for powerful agents in the society to resort to extreme sanctions because what we think and believe about ourselves usually keep us in line. In this sense, socialization acts as a powerful system of social control.

In the case of sex roles, social control is shown by the pressure we experience to adopt sex-appropriate behaviors. Some argue that these pressures are even more restrictive of boys, at least at the early ages, than they are of girls (Fling and Manosevitz 1972; Hartley 1959). Male roles are more rigidly defined, as witnessed in the more severe social sanctions brought against boys not to be sissies, compared to girls who are thought of as tomboys. For girls, being a tomboy may be a source of mild ridicule, but it appears to be more acceptable (at least until puberty) than being a sissy is for boys. Some researchers explain this finding as the result of male homophobia—fear of being homosexual (Morin and Garfinkle 1978; Sears 1959). According to Pleck, male homophobia acts as a system of social control because it encourages boys and men to act more masculine, as a way of indicating that they are not homosexual. Male homophobia further separates the cultural roles of masculinity and femininity by discouraging men from showing so-called feminine traits, such as caring, nurturing, emotional expression, and gentleness.

Research seems to support Pleck's point. One study that observed boys and girls "playing store" found that boys were more upset than girls by customers who chose sex-inappropriate toys (Ross and Ross 1972). Based on a review of the research on male homophobia, Morin and Garfinkle also conclude that "homophobia thus appears to be functional in the dynamics of maintaining the traditional male role. The fear of being labeled homosexual serves to keep men within the confines of what the culture defines as sex-appropriate behavior, and it interferes with the development of intimacy between men" (1978:41).

These conclusions may be particular to white, middle- and upper-class men, because it may well be that the further one moves into the system (as in joining a corporation or moving into a position of power), the more rigid sex role expectations become. As long as one exists on the margins of society, the more room for sex role deviation there may be. But success in the dominant world often requires conformity, so it is likely that those who benefit most from sexist institutions are the ones who are most likely to uphold them.

At the same time, changes are evident in people's support for modifications in sex role attitudes and behaviors. One experimenter asked college women to select a man and, for an hour, to act in accordance with the ideals of the women's liberation movement. One-quarter of the students said that this action required no change in their behavior, and another 10 percent received positive support from their peers for rejecting the traditional feminine role. Still, a majority of the women reported anger, conflict, surprise, and resistance from their male friends (Weitzman 1979). The conflict encountered when we try to cross or deny the boundaries between the sexes is good evidence of the strength of sex role expectations in our culture.

The pressure to adopt sex-appropriate behavior is evidence that the socialization process controls us in several ways. First, it gives us a definition of ourselves. Second, it defines the external world and our place within it. Third, it provides our definition of others and our relationships with them. And, as we have seen in the preceding section, the socialization process encourages and discourages the acquisition of certain skills by gender.

Socialization helps us establish our definition of ourselves by creating our self-concept (the way we think of ourselves) and self-esteem (the way we evaluate ourselves). Although men are usually stereotyped as more self-confident than women, research does not show this finding to be true. Rather, most personality tests do not reveal sex differences on generalized measures of self-esteem (Frieze et al. 1978; Maccoby and Jacklin 1974). However, studies of achievement-related competence and expectations for success show that women have more negative evaluations of their own abilities and performance and are less likely than men to believe in their future success (Frieze et al 1978; Maccoby and Jacklin 1974). Successful women are more likely than men to attribute their success to luck, not skill whereas successful men do just the opposite (Deaux, White, and Farris 1975). Psychologists interpret these results to mean that women think of themselves as externally controlled, whereas men think of themselves as internally controlled (Tavris and Offir 1977). Women's belief that they are externally controlled is likely a realistic assessment of their situation. Moreover, blacks and women who blame what happens to them on "the system" have higher self-esteem than blacks and women who blame themselves (Tavris and Offir 1977).

Research is inconclusive on the question of whether women are more dependent and emotional and men more independent and aggressive. No consistent differences have been found between women and men on measures of dependent behavior (Maccooy and Jacklin 1974); some suggest that the methods used to study sex differences tend to exaggerate the extent to which masculine and feminine traits are polarized (Cicone and Ruble 1978). However, there is strong support in the research evidence that men are more aggressive (Frieze et al. 1978; Maccoby and Jacklin 1974) and women are more emotional, although problems in interpreting what constitutes emotion remain unresolved (Frieze et al. 1978).

It is important to point out that few of the studies of sex role differences also consider the issue of race differences in sex role development. Consequently, many of the studies of sex differences are race-biased, and their results should not be generalized to all women. The identity development of black, Hispanic, Asian-American, and native American women is complicated by the particular features of their culture and their devaluation by the dominant culture. Yet, contrary to what many believe, research finds that these women maintain positive images of themselves because they rely on their own group's assessment of the dominant white society (Carrington 1980; Myers 1975). Many of the characteristics associated with the feminine stereotype—dependence on men, weakness, and learned helplessness, for example—simply are not typical of minority women who have to rely on themselves and their community for survival.

Research on black women speaks to this point. Although black women are socialized, like white women, to place primary emphasis on nurturing their loved ones (Carrington 1980), black adolescent girls are also socialized to become self-sufficient, to aspire to an education and occupation, to regard work as part of the normal female role, and to be more independent than white girls (Ladner 1971). As one black woman reports, "I never had the image of a nice suburban house surrounded by a white picket fence!" These observations reiterate the point that socialization reflects realistic adaptations to the social and economic environments we face.

Conformity to traditional roles takes its toll upon both males and females. Research on masculinity shows that higher male mortality rates can be attributed to the stress in masculine roles (Journard 1974), whereas for women, expressions of female helplessness and passivity seem to encourage higher rates of mental illness (Chesler 1972). Research also finds that female and male college students with androgynous gender roles (i.e., those who score high on both masculine and feminine traits) have higher self-esteem than students who score either high on one gender type or low on both (Spence, Helmreich, and Stapp 1975). Each of these examples shows how, in spite of the cost, sex role socialization encourages us to behave in sex-appropriate ways.

In addition to creating our self-definitions, socialization controls us by defining the external world and our relationship to it. Girls learn that women's place in the world is in the home, and they therefore, learn early to prefer domestic activities and toys (Maccoby and Jacklin 1974). Several studies indicate that children (both girls and boys) differentiate between "inside" and "outside" activities for men and women. Men are perceived as working in the yard and fixing things, women as staying inside with domestic chores (Fauls and Smith 1956). Again, however, race differences are significant on this point. Black male adolescents expect to have egalitarian roles in marriage (Rooks and King 1973), and black husbands are more accepting of a wife's employment outside the home (Axelson 1970).

Finally, socialization defines others for us and specifies our appropriate relationships to them. Studies of friendship and self-disclosure are indicative of this result. Four factors often used to measure intimacy are the length and amount of time spent together, the degree of self-disclosure to friends, the amount of physical touching involved in the friendship, and whether the friend is someone to consult when making important decisions. The results show that men report more friends than do women, but based on these indices of intimacy, men's friendships are not as close as those of women (Lewis 1978). Also, studies of self-disclosure (how much of one's self is revealed to others) show women to be more self-disclosing than men; both men and women are more likely to direct self-disclosure toward women (Jourard 1974).

In sum, the socialization process creates our definition of who we are, our place in the world, and our relationships to others within it. This chapter now turns to the theoretical perspectives that have been used to study and explain the way in which socialization occurs.

THEORETICAL PERSPECTIVES ON SOCIALIZATION

Three perspectives are used to explain the socialization process. They include identification theory, social learning theory, and cognitive-developmental theory. The first, *identification theory,* sees children as learning gender-appropriate behaviors by identifying with their same-sex parent. This explanation is based on a Freudian psychoanalytic perspective that assumes that children unconsciously model their identities upon the behavior of their parents. Identification theory posits that children learn behaviors, feelings, and attitudes unconsciously; through unconscious learning, children develop motivational systems. The child's identification with the same-sex parent, coupled with the powerful emotion associated with the parent-child relationship, results in an unconscious psychosexual bond that shapes the child's sex role identity.

Empirical evidence to support the perspective of identification theory is, at best, shaky. Because the focus of this theory is on unconscious states of mind, it is impossible to measure directly the internal motivation of the child. Instead, researchers study motives indirectly by examining characteristics of the parents and associating them with behaviors and attitudes of the child. But such associations do not show a causal relationship between the parents' characteristics and the personality tendencies of their child. Because there is no direct way to observe the process of identification, this theory remains largely speculative. Moreover, evidence that children are oriented to same-sex models is inconclusive, casting further doubt upon the validity of identification theory.

More recently, Nancy Chodorow (1978) has developed a theory of gender identity that is related to the perspective of identification theory. Chodorow's work is an explanation of how gender identities emerge from the social organization of parents' roles in society. We will discuss her work in more detail in Chapter 5, but here we can say that she sees the "asymmetrical structure of parenting" (a division of labor in which women "mother" and men do not and in which women's work is devalued) as creating a dynamic of identification in which only girls adopt the personality characteristics associated with mothering. In Chodorow's theory, called *object relations theory,* as boys and girls develop their own identities, they must become psychologically separate from their parents. Boys, who gender-identify with their fathers, form personalities that are more detached from others, because family structures in this society are based largely on the father's absence. Girls, who gender-identify with their mothers, become less detached because the mother's role in the family is one of close attachment to others. Girls' personalities, then, are more focused on attachment behaviors and on orientation to others. Boys, on the other hand, have personalities characterized by repression of their emotional needs and their commitments to others.

Chodorow's work maintains some of the orientation of identification theory in its emphasis on unconscious psychic processes. But it is distinguished from traditional psychoanalytic theory by placing gender identity clearly in the context of the division of labor by gender in work and in the family. The importance of Chodorow's work lies in the connection it makes between gender identity and the structure of the family in Western capitalist societies. But, it is important to point out that, because this family form is not universal, her theory may be highly specific to families based on a traditional division of labor.

A second theoretical perspective on socialization comes from *social learning theory,* which is highly critical of identification theory and the psychoanalytic perspective. These theorists argue that Freud's work was culture bound and, in particular, that it reflects the bias of Western patriarchal societies. The debate over psychoanalysis, from a feminist point of view, has been long and heated, and it will not be repeated here (see Figes 1970; Mitchell 1974; Weisstein 1971). But whereas identification theory rests on the idea of unconscious learning, social learning theory emphasizes the significance of the environment in explaining sex role socialization. Social learning theory is a behaviorist orientation, meaning that it sees social behavior as explained in terms of human responses to the environment. According to behaviorists, appropriate responses are positively rewarded, whereas inappropriate responses are punished. Thus, social learning occurs through an ongoing process of reinforcement from other people (Frieze et al. 1978). Like identification theorists, many social learning theorists believe that children model themselves based on the behaviors and attitudes of same-sex parents. But social learning theorists reject the idea that humans have stable, fixed internal motives (Mischel 1970), suggesting instead that persons "reproduce actions, attitudes or emotional responses exhibited by real-life or symbolic models" (Bandura and Walters 1963:89). From a social learning perspective, behavior is not fixed according to early established patterns; rather, behavior and attitudes change as the situations and expectations in the environment change. Sex role learning, although very significant in childhood, continues throughout life. Thus, one's gender identity is not fixed or permanent except when the social environment continues to reinforce it.

Like identification theory, social learning theory rests on the assumption that children model their behavior according to the roles of same-sex significant others. But social learning theorists posit that emotional identification is not a prerequisite for sex role learning, nor are parents the only significant role models. Consequently, observations of a wide array of sex role images and expectations in the culture serve as reinforcement for sex role modeling. Empirical evidence to support social learning theory comes from the vast amount of research on variations in parental expectations for children of different sexes, stereotypic responses from teachers and peers, and the influence of institutional practices that reinforce sex role stereotypes. One implication of social learning theory is the view expressed by some feminists that women need female role models in positions of leadership and authority to compensate for the learned sense of self that they acquire through traditional socialization practices.

The third theoretical framework used to explain sex role learning is *cognitive-developmental theory*. This theory is based largely on the work of the Swiss psychologist Jean Piaget and, more recently, the psychologist Lawrence Kohlberg (1966). Piaget suggested that people create *schemata*—mental categories that emerge through one's interactions with the social world. These schemata, in turn, are used in the child's subsequent encounters with his or her environment. Thus, the child accommodates and assimilates new information into this existing stock of knowledge. According to Piaget, all children go through a set of distinct stages of cognitive development, so that the developmental process is marked by alternate states of equilibrium and disequilibrium. In other words, as the developing child discovers new information or experiences in the world, he or she must adjust previously existing schemata to fit these new observations. At various points in cognitive development, the child reaches equilibrium because the child's reasoning ability is limited. Most importantly, cognitive-developmental theory emphasizes that the process of social development is one in which the child interacts with the social world through the mediation and active involvement of his or her cognitive abilities.

Kohlberg uses Piaget's perspective to explain the emergence of children's gender identities. According to Kohlberg, children early discover that people are divided into two sexes. Thus, they come to know their own sex, and they categorize others as either male or female. As their own gender identity stabilizes, they also begin to categorize behaviors and objects in the social world as appropriate for one sex or the other. At his point, gender has become an organizing scheme for the developing child, and the child attributes value to the traits and attitudes associated with his or her own sex. Children also begin to believe that gender is an unchanging category. As a result, they model their own behavior on the behaviors of those of the same sex, and they develop a strong emotional attachment to the same-sex parent.

Although Kohlberg's work on gender concepts is similar in part, to identification and social learning theories, there are important differences among the three perspectives. Identification theorists assume that imitation of same-sex persons is motivated by fear—the fear of separation from a psychosexual love object. Cognitive-developmental theorists assume a more positive motivational basis for learning, namely, mastery. In the cognitive-developmental framework, children are actively involved in the construction of their social world. In contrast, both social learning and identification theories assume a more passive view of the child's development. That is, "in contrast to both identification and social-learning theories, cognitive developmentalists assume that the initial emergence of gender as an important social category is the result of the child's cognitive system rather than the result of either psychosexual dynamics or the impact of external models and rewards" (Frieze et al. 1978:120).

Both the social learning and cognitive-developmental perspectives emphasize the role of culture in shaping gender identity. But social learning theorists have a more deterministic view, in that culture is seen as a model and reinforcer for what the child becomes. In the cognitive-developmental framework, the child does more than simply react to the culture. He or she searches for patterns in the culture and actively seeks to structure and organize the conceptions of the world that the culture provides.

The three theories described in the preceding paragraphs have been primarily developed by psychologists, but the cognitive-developmental perspective is related to the sociological perspective called *symbolic interactionism*. This perspective is based heavily on the work of George Herbert Mead, whose work was described in the section on children's play and games. According to the symbolic interactionist perspective, the process of socialization rests on our ability to take the role of the other. That is, we come to see ourselves as others see us. Through a reflective process of envisioning ourselves from the perspective of others, we form our self-concepts. Thus, the self is established as one becomes an object to oneself. Symbolic interactionism emphasizes the human ability to form and understand symbols, for it is through symbolic interpretation that consciousness and, therefore, the self is possible.

Each of these perspectives on sex role socialization shows us how central gender is to the formation of our gender identity. From the day we are born to the day we die, social expectations about our gender confront us in the everyday world. Through the sex role socialization process, these external social expectations become internalized in our self-concepts, and they become identities through which we experience the social world. Thus, socialization is an essential sociological concept, for it describes the process that relates individuals to society.

CONCLUSION: SOCIALIZATION AND THE SEX ROLE PERSPECTIVE

Understanding the influence of socialization on the development of sex roles encourages us to see how sex roles guide our behavior and beliefs. For feminists and sociologists, this recognition is important because it shows us how individual experience reflects the larger society in which we live. Moreover, as feminist consciousness-raising groups have shown, a reexamination of the events in our lives that socialized us in sex-stereotypic ways is a fundamental step in recognizing how we came to be who we are and how we can change. Thus, understanding the socialization process and the emergence of sex roles is a critical part of developing a feminist consciousness and a sociological analysis of gender relations in society.

But there are also a number of limitations in working only from a sex role perspective, and in this concluding section, we will consider some of these issues. In particular, although the socialization process shows how individuals become gendered persons, it does not explain the social structural origins of gender inequality. A perspective on socialization causes us to see that gender expectations have their origins outside the individual, but it does not explain the institutional bases of those origins and, therefore, is not a causal theory of women's status in society.

If we limit our understanding of gender relations to a perspective on sex roles, we tend to downplay the significance of gender in the social-institutional framework of society. To illustrate this point, consider how absurd it would be to explain racism in society in terms of a role perspective. No one uses the term *race roles* to describe patterns of inequality between blacks and whites, although surely it is true that, because of racism, blacks and whites establish expectations of each other. Similarly, to assume that roles are the only appropriate framework for studying gender is to assume that consciousness, not structured inequality, is the sole basis for women's subordination (Lopata and Thorne 1978).

Socialization no doubt occurs, and sex roles are real in the sense that we learn to expect from ourselves what others expect of us. But as a theory of the origin of gender inequality, the sex role perspective has many limitations.

Because the sex role perspective neglects the institutional basis for gender inequality, it tends to explain gender relations exclusively in psychological terms. This does not mean that *sex roles* or *socialzation* are incorrect concepts, merely that, in use, they are sometimes treated in reductionist terms. We have to remember that a *social role* is merely an abstract concept used by sociologists to describe and explain patterns of social behavior. If this concept becomes overglorified, we run the risk of assuming that simply rejecting our social roles will bring social change. Such a perspective underestimates the influence of the institutionalized gender inequality that created the roles. Moreover, the role perspective encourages us to think of men and women as passive vessels into whom a variety of expectations are poured. This concept denies the extent to which people are active agents in their social relations. As such, people are not mere receptacles for social life; rather, they actively participate in and create social change. The sex role perspective may exaggerate the extent to which we become socialized, leading to an over-socialized view of human life.

Finally, the focus on sex roles tends to exaggerate the differences between the sexes because, by definition, its emphasis is on differences, not similarities. In sex role research, sex differences actually get built into research designs. The items on questionnaires, for example, or the factors selected for manipulation in experimental studies necessarily reflect the differences that a researcher wants to test. The end result may be that the research literature on sex roles exaggerates and polarizes masculine and feminine differences (Cicone and Ruble 1978).

Additionally, it has been found that the sex of the researcher is a good predictor of whether sex differences will be found in research studies. Men are more likely to find sex differences than women; thus, research conclusions may subtly reflect the gender biases of the researcher (Eagly and Carli 1981). In other words, if a researcher expects to find sex differences, chances are that the research will reveal this finding.

In conclusion, although a perspective on sex role socialization should inform our analysis of gender relations, it is, by itself, inadequate in explaining the status of women in society. In Part Two of this book, we will examine the institutional structure of gender relations. In particular, we will consider four areas that have had special significance in feminist analyses of women's status—work, the family, health, and crime. Then, in Part Three, we will develop the theoretical perspectives that feminists have used to interpret women's status in society.

PART TWO

GENDER AND SOCIAL INSTITUTIONS

CHAPTER 4

WOMEN, WORK, AND THE ECONOMY

INTRODUCTION

In 1980, the average woman worker earned $11,590; the average man earned $19,712. Among full-time workers, women's earnings were about 60 percent of men's (U.S. Department of Commerce 1981); one-quarter of all women workers were either secretaries, household workers, elementary school teachers, waitresses, or bookkeepers (Blau 1979). Moreover, differences in income appear despite women's qualifications to work, as evidenced by the fact that in 1980 women college graduates earned less ($16,362) than male high school graduates ($19,469). Male college graduates earned $25,849 (U.S. Department of Commerce 1981).

Women's role in economic life has always been underestimated, as well as obscured by social myths about the work that women do. These myths include the idea that women who stay at home as full-time housewives are not working, that women who work for wages are doing it for "pin money," and that women's work is not as valuable as men's. As a result, women's work has not been paid the same as men's, nor has it been as highly valued. And because women's work has been seen as less important than men's, it has not, until recently, been seriously studied.

This chapter will review sociological perspectives on women's work and will describe the contemporary status of women workers. It will also discuss the relationship of the family to the economy by focusing on the issue of housework as a significant part of women's economic role. And finally, this chapter develops a historical overview of changes in women's labor in industrial capitalist societies.

SOCIOLOGICAL PERSPECTIVES ON WORK AND GENDER STRATIFICATION

There are two ways one can approach the issues of gender and work. One is an individualistic perspective; the other is sociological. From an individual point of view, the worker focuses on economic status and job satisfaction. Included are questions such as the following: How can I choose the right job? How can I be successful and earn a good income? How can I find a job that will satisfy my interests? And especially for women, how can I manage having both a career and a family? Additionally, as women enter the labor force, particularly in traditionally male jobs, they might ask, how can I find support for myself and my abilities in a company that is primarily organized for men?

All of these questions are important, and individuals will no doubt ask them at various points in their working lives. But for sociologists, questions about work and the economy have a different focus. Sociologists are concerned with the quality of individual experiences, but they are more likely to ask questions about the social organization of work, gender, and economic relations. From a feminist perspective, the important sociological questions about work are those that examine men and women's experience within the context of gender stratification and the gender division of labor. Therefore, the questions inspired by a feminist and sociological perspective include: What is women's role in the labor force? How do we explain historical change in women's labor force participation? What is the socioeconomic status of women and the households in which they live? What factors influence the economic mobility of women workers? How are gender issues at work complicated by those of race and social class? These questions form the basis for new investigations of the relationships between women's work and the larger economy.

Gender stratification refers to the hierarchical distribution by gender of economic and social resources in a society. All societies are organized around a system for the production and distribution of goods. In addition, most societies are marked by a system of social stratification. Sociologists define *stratification* as the process whereby groups or individuals in a society are located in a hierarchical arrangement on the basis of their differential access to social and economic resources. But sociologists also point out that there is nothing inherent in human nature or inevitable in social organization that requires unequal access to social and economic resources. Were inequality an inevitable result of human nature, stratification patterns would not vary in societies to the extent that they do. Moreover, we would not find egalitarian societies in the record of human history.

But because these differences in stratification are found, sociologists are very interested in the conditions that generate social inequality. Many point out that socioeconomic inequality emerges when there is a surplus of goods available in the society (Blumberg 1978; Marx 1970). Simply put, a surplus of goods creates the possibility that one group of people can appropriate the surplus for themselves. This action forms the initial basis for class systems in which one class controls the resources of other groups in the society.

In most societies, gender is a primary category that stratifies social groups. Women's access to societal rewards is greatly influenced by the degree to which they control the means and forms of social and economic production. In virtually all societies, women's work sustains the economy, although in many societies (such as our own), women's work is either invisible or devalued (Leghorn and Parker 1981). Cross-cultural research shows us that women tend to have the most egalitarian status in societies in which they directly contribute to the production of goods (Blumberg 1978; Leacock 1978). In hunting and gathering societies, for example, women produce most of the food supply. Their status in these societies is relatively equal to that of men, even though a gender division of labor still exists. In agricultural societies, although women continue to be primary producers, their status deteriorates because land, economic surplus, and, subsequently, political power are concentrated in the hands of male rulers.

In preindustrialized societies, women's labor in the home is a vital part of the productive system because it is in the home that goods are produced. Moreover, in these societies, women also have visible roles outside the home, as they distribute their goods in markets or even operate small businesses. As industrialization advances, though, economic production is shifted from the home to the factory, and although working-class and immigrant women hold factory jobs, women's domestic labor becomes both invisible and devalued. In American history, the devaluation of household labor not only results in a loss of status for middle-class women who work at home but also creates a class of the most severely underpaid and socially devalued laborers—black domestic workers (Davis 1981).

We will study the historical evolution of women's labor and social status in more detail in a later section of this chapter. But first, several basic concepts are important in untangling the data on women workers and their place in the American economy. To begin with, women's labor refers simply to the work that women do—both inside and outside of the home. But the labor of all workers is differentially rewarded and has a different relationship to the economic system. Sociologists use the concepts of *class* and *status* to refer to the different place of workers in the economic system and the different value they are perceived as having. As we will see, both of these concepts raise particular conceptual difficulties when we use them to refer to women's role in the economy.

Two different definitions of *class* form two schools of thought among sociologists. First, class can be defined simply in terms of one's access to social and economic resources. Typically, sociologists who think of class this way see stratification as involving a class hierarchy, with the upper class having the greatest access to resources and the middle and lower classes having proportionately less. In this definition, class is most typically measured in terms of one's income or the relative status of one's occupation. *Status* (also called *prestige*) is a related concept, defined as the social value attached to one's position in the stratification system. Typically, status or prestige is associated with one's occupation. Therefore, sociologists who study stratification often measure social class by a combination of variables such as income and occupation.

From a different perspective, one informed by the work of Karl Marx (1818–1883), class is defined in terms of the relationship of groups to the system of production. Marx's theory is concerned with the class system of capitalism and is particular to that economic system. He defines the *capitalist class* as those who own the means of production (i.e., the factories where goods are produced); the *bourgeois class* include those who identify with capitalists and are functionally dependent on them, but who do not own the means of production (e.g., business managers).

The *working class,* or *proletariat,* includes those who sell their labor to the capitalists in return for wages (i.e., laborers). The *lumpenproletariat* are those who have been permanently discarded by the system and, thus, no longer have an economic role (including the permanently unemployed, the mentally ill, and the aged). Marx's concept of class is a dynamic one in that, unlike the more simple hierarchical definition previously described, it assumes an active relationship between the formation of classes and developments in the economic system of capitalism.

Although each of these perspectives has contributed much to sociological research and theory, both have problems when they are applied to women's experience. The two concluding chapters of this book will discuss theoretical perspectives on women's experience in more detail, but for now, it is important to see that both concepts of class are inadequate in understanding women's economic role.

In the case of the first definition, we can see that many women workers (housewives, in particular) have no income. Thus, a measure of their class standing is impossible to derive. Moreover, housework has not been defined as an occupation and, thus, has no clear occupational status. Traditionally, a woman's status and class have been seen as derived from her husband's. There is a certain degree of truth in this belief, because many of us probably think of all members of a family as being of the same class. But there are numerous problems with this assumption as well. How, for instance, would we describe the class position of single women or women who head families with no husband present? Or, in another example, how do we describe the class standing of a women divorced from a middle-class man? Although she may have been considered middle class while married, following her divorce, she may have lost her house, access to her husband's income, her car, and even her own definition of her class position. And how do we define the class position of lesbian women who, although they may earn middle-class incomes, may legally not have the right to own property or maintain custody of their children?

Similarly, in the Marxist concept of class, women also seem to have no place. Although many women do have working-class and bourgeois jobs, the Marxist concept of class does not account for women's domestic labor. Housewives, in the Marxist framework, again become an invisible class of workers who, because they do not produce goods for profit, are eliminated from the otherwise illuminating analysis of the class system that Marx has given us.

Thus, the study of women's labor requires new concepts and theories to describe and analyze the economic role of women in society. Beginning with their criticism of the inadequacies of traditional sociological thought, feminist scholars have begun to develop new modes of analysis that attempt to explain women's place in the stratification system. As we will see in Chapters 9 and 10, the theoretical perspectives of feminist scholars are diverse, but they all stem from the attempt to understand how gender inequality is tied to the social institutions of society.

The next two sections of this chapter detail some of the observations that have been made regarding women's work and economic status and review explanations for such facts as sex differences in earnings. Following these sections on the contemporary status and income of women, we will review the historical development of women's role in capitalist-industrial societies. As we will see, in the contemporary capitalist economy, women make both direct and indirect contributions to economic production. However, because of the interaction of capitalism with male domination, women do not generally control their own labor or the resources they receive. As a result, as contemporary data will show, they have an unequal position in the receipt of social and economic resources.

We should also understand from the beginning that an analysis of gender in the economy cannot be separated from an analysis of the family. The family and the economy are two interconnected institutions, even though prevailing images of the family see it as a separate sphere of activity. The family is discussed in the following chapter, but as this chapter will show, the interconnectedness of the family and the economy is an essential feature of social and economic organization.

THE CONTEMPORARY STATUS OF WOMEN

Social myth has it that women do not work. Yet, in 1981, 52.3 percent of all women were in the paid labor force compared to 77.5 percent of men. Moreover, women's labor force participation has increased over time, notably in the last twenty years. The increase in the number of women workers is especially marked among women with children. Between 1960 and 1975, married women with children under six more than doubled their labor force participation (Almquist 1977). In 1980, 44.9 percent of married women with children under six and a husband present were working; and 53.1 percent of married women with children and no husband present were working. (U.S. Department of Labor 1980). These increases in the number of working mothers mean that whether or not a woman has children is no longer an accurate predictor of whether she will be engaged in paid labor (Almquist 1977).

Public opinion often assumes that women work because of boredom or a search for fulfillment. Although that belief may be true for a small number of women, most women work out of economic necessity. That is, 40.3 percent of the women in the work force are single, divorced, or widowed, and although the majority of working women are married, 45 percent of them are married to men who (based on 1975 data) earn less than $10,000 per year (Schlozman 1979; U.S. Department of Commerce, *Statistical Abstracts of the United States* 1980). Additionally, recent opinion polls show that only 14 percent of American women work primarily because they want something interesting to do. Most women work either to support themselves or their family or to bring in extra money (Roper Organization 1980). This finding is particularly evident when we consider the high number of female-headed households; they constituted one-sixth of all American households in 1981.

Women who work have, in the past, been stereotyped as *career women*—the assumption being that working women are somehow different from other women in the population. Women workers are now younger, better educated, more likely married, and more likely to be minding children than their predecessors. But unlike the social stereotype, women engaged in paid labor closely represent the female population as a whole (Blau 1979).

Black and other minority women are even more likely than white women to be working, although the gap between the two groups is narrowing. In 1980, among women twenty years of age and older, the labor force participation rate for black women was 54.9, for Hispanic women 48.8, and for white women 50.8 (U.S. Department of Labor 1980). The figure for Hispanic women is inflated somewhat by the high percentage of Cuban working women. Because the label *Hispanic* includes Cubans, Puerto Ricans, and Mexican-Americans, the aggregate statistics on Hispanic workers misrepresent the experience of any one of these groups. For example, in 1979, the labor force participation rate of Puerto Rican women in the United States was 35 percent, for Mexican-American women 48 percent, and for Cuban women 55 percent (U.S. Department of Labor 1977). Differences in labor force participation are particularly high between minority and white women working during their prime childbearing years (ages twenty-five to thirty-four). In this group, 65 percent of minority women work, compared to 56 percent of white women (U.S. Department of Labor 1977).

The occupational distribution of women workers shows that most women work in sex-segregated jobs where they receive low wages and low prestige. The U.S. Bureau of the Census uses four categories to describe the occupational distribution of workers: white-collar jobs (including professional-technical workers, managers and administrators, sales workers, and clerical workers); blue-collar workers (craftspersons and kindred workers, operatives, transport workers, and nonfarm laborers); service workers; and farm laborers (see Table 4.1).

Typically, white-collar jobs are seen as more prestigious than blue-collar jobs, although this distinction is a poor one in describing women's work. Although nearly two thirds of women in the labor force are in white-collar jobs, most of these women have clerical positions. Moreover, among women holding professional-technical jobs, the majority are in the traditionally female occupations of school teacher and nurse.

Table 4.1 Occupational Distribution of the Labor Force by Sex and Race (1981)

| | **Percent of Employed Labor Force** | | | |
| | **Males** | | **Females** | |
Major Occupational Group	**White**	**Black and Other**	**White**	**Black and Other**
White-collar workers	44.4	29.6	67.9	52.2
Professional-technical workers	16.3	11.7	17.3	15.4
Managers and administrators	15.5	7.0	7.8	4.1
Sales workers	6.5	2.7	7.3	3.2
Clerical workers	6.1	8.2	35.5	29.5
Blue-collar workers	43.5	51.4	13.0	17.6
Craft and kindred workers	21.1	16.4	1.9	1.5
Operatives, except transport	10.6	15.0	9.1	14.2
Transport equipment operators	5.2	8.5	.7	.7
Nonfarm laborers	6.5	11.5	1.2	1.3
Service workers	8.0	16.4	17.9	29.6
Private household workers	.1	.2	1.8	6.0
Other service workers	8.0	16.2	16.1	23.7
Farm workers	4.1	2.6	1.2	.5
Farmers and farm managers	2.5	.5	.4	.1
Farm laborers and supervisors	1.6	2.1	.8	.5

Source: U.S. Department of Labor, Bureau of Labor Statistics. *Employment and Earnings.* Washington, D.C.: U.S. Government Printing Office, January 1982.

Thus, although a greater proportion of women than men hold professional jobs, men are still more likely to be located in high-prestige and highly paid professional positions. And a substantial number of women workers are found in service work (including, for example, waitresses, maids, and hairdressers), which has been labeled the *pink collar ghetto* (Howe 1977). Therefore, the traditional status distinction between white-collar and blue-collar work is based on the experience of male, not female, workers.

The experience of nonwhite women in the labor force is described as one of double jeopardy, because these women face the inequities of both race and gender. Compared to white women, they are more likely to work in service and blue-collar fields (see Table 4.1). Black women have always been present in the labor force. In fact, they were rarely able to remain in their own homes as housewives. Although they have carried the double burden of wage labor and housework, they did not have the privilege of "feminine weakness and wifely submissiveness" that is associated with white, middle-class housewives (Davis 1981). Because of the necessity to work, black women escaped the psychological damage of isolation found among white, middle-class housewives. As a result, black women are less likely to experience conflict over the choice of family and job than are white women (Epstein 1973), and they do not regard career interests as unfeminine (Ladner 1971).

Mexican-American women are less likely than black and white women to be in the labor force (48 percent are in full-time paid labor). The majority of those who do work are concentrated in clerical, operative, and nonhousehold service occupations (Almquist and Wehrle-Einhorn 1978), and their median income is less than that of any other group except native American women. The proportion of Mexican-American women who are farm laborers (4 percent) is higher than that of any of the other groups, reflecting the large proportion of migrant farm workers in the Southwest who are Mexican-American. This figure, of course, probably vastly underestimates the actual number of women working as migrant laborers who never show up in the government statistics.

Puerto Rican women are heavily concentrated in operative labor; 40 percent of those employed work as operatives. Another 30 percent work in clerical work and 13 percent in service occupations (Almquist and Wehrle-Einhorn 1978). Cuban-American women are more likely to be employed than Mexican-American and Puerto Rican women, in part because of their higher educational level. Still, an extraordinary proportion (43 percent) work as operatives, and smaller proportions than white and other nonwhite women are clerical workers (26 percent), private household workers (1 percent), and nonhousehold service workers (11 percent).

Among native American women, only 35.3 percent are in the labor force. One-quarter are in clerical positions, 26 percent in nonhousehold service, and 19 percent in operative jobs (Almquist and Wehrle-Einhorn 1978). Japanese-American, Filipino-American, and Chinese-American women have an occupational distribution similar to that of white women, although their income is less than that of white women (Almquist and Wehrle-Einhorn 1978).

The experience of minority women workers underscores the complexities of a society that discriminates against women based on their sex, race, and class. In spite of the myth that minority women are highly sought after by employers wanting to meet affirmative action guidelines, their experience in the labor force lags behind that of the white majority (Almquist 1979). Moreover, the situation of minority women reveals that there are no simple feminist solutions to the problems of women and work. Whereas white, middle-class feminists have wanted to get out of the home and into the labor force, many minority women would like not to work. Historically, for instance, all black women worked involuntarily in slavery. Their work experience and their family relationships have to be remembered in this context so that we are careful not to generalize from the experience of white women to all women.

The data on women workers would be incomplete without considering the situation of part-time women workers. These women face problems in the labor market that are particular to their part-time status. Almost half of the women in craft and operative jobs are employed part-time; seven out of ten in service jobs work part-time (Baker 1978). Either because they are unable to find full-time work or because of home responsibilities, these women do not usually get the employee benefits of health insurance, retirement plans, seniority, training, and promotion that are often available to full-time workers. The working conditions for these women are poor and largely subject to the discretion of employers. In the first quarter of 1981, female part-time workers over twenty-five years of age had median earnings of $89 per week; for men, median part-time earnings were $100 per week. Females who maintained their own families had even lower earnings—$84 per week—compared to wives, who earned $91 per week, and husbands, who earned $100 per week (U.S. Department of Labor 1981). And students who work as part-time waitresses or in household service jobs know that the personal whims of an employer can make these jobs both financially insecure and psychologically degrading.

Because the particular situations faced by women in the labor market vary depending on the actual occupation, we will briefly describe the conditions faced by women in a selected sample of jobs. Although these job types are by no means exhaustive of women's occupations, they point to the variety of circumstances that women face in the paid work they do. Moreover, these summaries illustrate the effects of gender in the social and economic organization of work.

Women in the Professions

Women who work in the professions have the advantage of holding the most prestigious and highly paid jobs in the labor market. Yet, women professional workers are a small minority of professionals, even following a decade of reforms in professional training, recruitment, and rewards. In medicine, for example, women constitute 8.6 percent of all doctors (Mandelbaum 1978), although they are now an increasing proportion of medical school students. In 1979, women constituted 12.4 percent of all lawyers, 18.9 percent of life and physical scientists, and only 2.9 percent of engineers (U.S. Department of Commerce, *Statistical Abstracts of the United States* 1980).

Moreover, within the professions, women are concentrated in the lower ranks and in less prestigious specialties (Patterson and Engleberg 1978). In universities, for instance, where women constitute 21 percent of all faculty, they represent only 9 percent of full professors (the top rank), but they are 50 percent of all instructors—positions which are usually one-year, nontenured, and often part-time appointments. In medicine, women are heavily concentrated in the usually less prestigious fields as pediatricians, obstetricians, gynecologists, and general practitioners. Additionally, in universities, medicine, law, and the scientific professions, women tend to earn less than their male colleages (Hornig 1980).

Recent surveys show that women Ph.D.s earn about 23 percent less than men regardless of their field of work, their experience, the nature of their jobs, and the quality of their training (Babco 1981; National Research Council Committee on the Education and Employment of Women in Science and Engineering 1981; Vetter 1981). Moreover, minority Ph.D.s, including both men and women, have lower median salaries than white Ph.D.s, in part because they are disproportionately clustered at the lower ranks (Maxwell 1981). And among Ph.D.s, the unemployment rate of minorities is twice that of nonminorities and is also higher for minority and nonminority women than for white men (Maxwell 1981). And because many believe that women do not advance in the professions because of their family commitments, it is important to note that women lag behind men regardless of their marital status, the presence of children, and whether they are primarily involved in research or teaching.

Clearly, women and minorities who work in the professions do not receive the same objective material rewards as men. But women's work in professional careers is also influenced by more subjective features of professional organizations. Professions are socially organized like communities, and, as such, they involve informal roles and practices, as well as tending toward homogeneity and exclusionary relations (Epstein 1970; Goode 1957). Social control in professional life, as well as access to rewards, typically operates through a sponsorship system that feminists have labeled the *old boy network*. Within the network, social relations with one's peers and mentors can bring access to jobs, promotions, opportunities, and status.

The woman professional who is excluded from the protégé system is likely to find herself at a disadvantage when it comes to professional opportunity. Additionally, the information and colleaguality shared by those in the network are likely to give professional advantage to those who are "in the know." Whether by exclusion or personal choice, women who are not part of the old boy network are likely to find their careers detrimentally affected (Epstein 1970).

This professional culture has encouraged women professionals in most fields to establish alternative networks of support—both for professional advancement and personal encouragement. Groups such as the Association for Women in Science, the Society of Women Engineers, Sociologists for Women in Society, and the Association for Women in Psychology, to name only a few, have flourished in recent years (Briscoe 1978). As both professional networks and local support groups for women professionals, these organizations encourage the development of alternative networks to promote the status of professional women.

Among other women professionals, sex typing is a common phenomenon. That is, many white-collar women (as well as other women workers, as we will see) are employed in occupations where most of the workers are women. Oppenheimer (1968) finds that over half of all working women are in jobs where at least 70 percent of the workers are female. Sociologists use the *sex segregation index* to measure the percentage of women workers who would have to change jobs to match the occupational distribution of women with that of men. Since 1900, the sex segregation index has remained virtually unchanged (Blau 1979; Gross 1968). Additionally, the desegregation of sex-typed jobs has been largely the result of men entering traditionally female fields as librarians, nurses, elementary school teachers, and social workers (Blau 1979). And within all of these fields, women remain concentrated at the lower level positions (Brugh and Beede 1976; Grimm 1978; Potter and Fischel 1977).

Many of these professional jobs can be perceived as extensions of stereotypic female roles. For example, women's work as secretaries, nurses, waitresses, and teachers involves them in helping roles and in roles in which they nurture or socialize their clients. In secretarial and nursing work, women are also bound by the authority of male bosses. Many observers have concluded that even professional work tends to involve women in the negotiation of social relations for others. Thus, nurses who cater to doctors' needs and teachers who nurture their students (and sometimes other colleagues) are engaged in traditional female helping roles.

Women as Clerical Workers

Women comprise about 75 percent of all clerical workers in the United States, and some experts claim that by the end of the century, this proportion will rise to 90 percent (Olesen and Katsuranis 1978). Over the last century, the number of clerical workers has drastically increased, while at the same time their prestige has declined.

Prior to the mechanization of office work by the invention of the typewriter in the late nineteenth century, skills such as shorthand and accounting were male trades, and relatively prestigious trades at that. An 1888 book titled *How to Succeed As a Stenographer or Typewriter* was addressed to men, saying, "There are comparatively few verbatim reporters, and the young shorthand writer who has reached that distinction should consider that it gives him the rank of a scholar and a gentleman" (Baker 1888; cited in Benet 1972:39). Yet, the introduction of mechanized switchboards and typewriters and the corresponding need for new workers brought the rapid introduction of women workers to these jobs. Whereas capitalist owners saved money by tapping the cheap, large female labor market, women workers experienced a decline in the wages and prestige associated with office work.

To this day, the median weekly earnings for women clerical workers are low, especially compared to those of male clericals. In the first quarter of 1981, full-time male clerical workers earned $331 per week; women clerical workers in the same period earned $214 per week (U.S. Department of Labor 1981). A huge supply of women clerical workers are also provided by temporary clerical services, where workers have low wages, little control of their work, minimal social relationships with co-workers, and highly alienated attitudes toward their jobs (Olesen and Katsuranis 1978).

Full-time secretaries, except those who work in large typing pools where work is heavily routinized, are tied to individual and patrimonial relationships with their bosses. Their status is then contingent on that of the boss, whose power may determine their own. Although studies find that secretaries most resent doing personal work for their bosses, bosses expect their secretaries to appreciate and provide nonmaterial rewards such as emotional intimacy, praise, and affection. Moreover, loyalty and devotion to their employer are often the basis for secretaries' rewards at work (Kanter 1977).

Women in Blue-Collar Work

Among blue-collar workers, women have been entering the skilled trades at a rapid rate—faster, in fact, than men in recent years. The number of women in skilled trades doubled between 1960 and 1970 (Blau 1979) and has since continued to increase. Yet, in these jobs, men continue to hold the higher-status and higher-paid positions, as demonstrated by the larger proportion of women employed as operatives rather than skilled craftspersons, compared to men (see Table 4.1). Among craft and kindred workers in 1981, men earned a weekly median income of $353; women earned $239. Among operatives, men earned $289 per week, women $187. And for nonfarm labor, men earned $236 per week, women $192 (U.S. Department of Labor 1981).

In addition, the unemployment rates of women in blue-collar labor exceed those of men.

Women in blue-collar labor also find sex segregation on the job. Even when women are employed in the same occupational category as men, such as machine operators, they tend to be located in different industries. The vast majority of women operatives work in apparel and textile manufacturing, whereas men are more likely employed in steel mills and automobile manufacturing (Baker 1978). Although we should not underestimate the job crises that men in these industries face, women (especially minority women) tend to be isolated in the poorest-quality blue-collar jobs available.

Labor force analysts identify what they call *dual labor markets,* with jobs in the primary labor market having more stability, higher wages, better working conditions, chances for advancement, and due process in the administration of work roles. The secondary labor market, where women are more likely employed, has jobs with low wages, few or no fringe benefits, poor working conditions, high turnover, few chances for advancement, and often arbitrary and capricious supervision (Doeringer and Piore 1971).

Within the secondary labor market, the firms where women are employed have lower capital investments, low profit margins, irregular personnel practices, higher turnover, and lower pay (Baker 1978; Smuts 1959), leaving women more at the mercy of economic fluctuations. Even in the less marginal industries where blue-collar women work, the jobs that women hold tend to have the characteristics of the secondary labor market (e.g., poor wages, poor fringe benefits, and unstable employment). Yet, the steady supply of women workers discourages employers from paying women wages that would be equivalent to men's (Baker 1978).

Moreover, women workers are much less likely to be protected by labor unions. Women's union membership has increased in recent years, although the ratio of unionized women to women in the labor force has declined slightly (Wertheimer and Nelson 1975). And the overall representation of women in union leadership is low. Women constitute one-fifth of all union members, but they hold few top posts in union management. Women who do hold official union posts tend to be found in the position of secretary of secretary-treasurer (Tarr-Whelan 1978; Wertheimer and Nelson 1975). Even unions with a majority female membership have few women officials. For example, the Clothing Workers union with a 75 percent female membership, the Ladies' Garment Workers Union with an 80 percent female membership, and the Electrical Workers' Union with a 40 percent female membership all report only one woman union official each; the Textile Workers, with a 40 percent female membership, have two (Berquist 1974). Moreover, women in service occupations and clerical work tend not to be unionized, leaving them subject to the discretionary practices of individual companies and employers. The significance of union membership for women is evidenced by the fact that the weekly earnings of organized women exceed those of unorganized women by 30 percent; however, the weekly earnings of organized men still exceed those of organized women (U.S. Department of Labor 1980).

Women in Domestic Work

Women who work in domestic labor, both public and private, are among the lowest paid American women workers. In 1980, the median weekly earnings for all service workers was $223 for men and $147 for women (U.S. Department of Labor 1981). Although poorly paid, domestic work is often the only work available for incoming groups of immigrant women, women with little education, and women with little choice of occupation. Public service workers, although poorly paid, at least have the advantage of unionization and more job benefits. But women in private domestic labor are left in the hands of individual employers, who are unlikely to provide health and retirement benefits or paid sick leave. Private household workers often have the advantage of negotiating their own work schedules and, thus, may have greater flexibility than workers in the public sector, but they pay the price in terms of low wages and little job security (Katzman 1978).

In 1979, the hourly earnings of white private household workers averaged $2.13; for black private household workers, the rate was $2.68 per hour. Weekly earnings for full-time private household workers were $80 per week for white women and $110 per week for black women. The surprising reversal in black and white women's earnings are perhaps explained by the fact that 60.2 percent of white private household workers are employed in child care, compared to 10.5 percent of black household workers. Black women are more likely employed as cleaners and servants. These positions account for 73 percent of black private household workers and 30.3 percent of white household workers (Grossman 1980).

Women in Farm and Migrant Labor

Changes in the social and economic organization of farming have radically altered the work of women farm workers. In the 1940s, nearly one-quarter of the U.S. population lived on farms. Now, the farm population is less than 4 percent of the U.S. population (U.S. Department of Commerce, *Statistical Abstracts of the United States* 1980). Small family farms have been particularly hard hit by the development of corporate farming as the average farm has increased in total acreage.

The transformation of farming from a family enterprise to agribusiness has specifically eroded the position of women in farming. Whereas much farm labor was originally performed by women, men now control and operate the technological equipment of farm production. Typically, women's farm work is now described as that of a helpmate; men who have taken over the business and technology of farming work in more sophisticated jobs that bring them higher incomes and more social status. The introduction of more sophisticated farm technology has produced a more complex hierarchy of farm jobs, with women relegated to the botttom. Women receive low wages for assembly-line jobs in farming, whereas the higher wages are given to men who work as operatives and managers (Hacker 1980).

Migrant workers are at the very bottom of the agribusiness ladder, where they face physically demanding jobs, poor working conditions, and extremely low wages. The typical laborer in 1979 received a daily wage of $20.99, but men earned more ($21.88) than women ($19.95). Migrant women, like other women workers, also work a double day—first in farm fields and then in their own families. Research on the family life of migrant laborers shows that the dominant pattern of decision making in migrant families tends to be more egalitarian than we might assume. The same researchers find that women in migrant families tend to be less dependent on their husbands than they might have been within more traditional cultures (Hawkes and Taylor 1975).

This information on women's work shows that most women work in sex-segregated jobs. Women work not only in fewer occupations but also in different occupations than men. Thus, although a majority of both men and women support efforts to strengthen women's status (Roper Organization 1980), solutions such as equal pay for equal work are inadequate because most women do not do the same jobs as men.

Within occupational categories, women earn less than men. For example, women professional and technical workers earn 65 percent of the income of men in that category. Female clerical workers earn 63 percent of male clerical earnings; female sales workers earn 43 percent of male sales earnings; female crafts workers and operatives earn 57 percent of male earnings, and female service workers earn 57 percent of what male service workers earn (Blau 1979).

Women in typically female occupations earn less than women in typically male occupations (Jusenius 1976); therefore, occupational segregation explains a large portion of the wage gap between men and women, both white and black (Chiswick et al. 1975). But a recent survey by the Labor Department also shows that even in jobs where women do the same work as men, they receive substantially less pay (*New York Times,* March 5, 1982). In the following section, we will examine sex differences in earnings and the consequences of low earnings, for women's economic status.

EARNINGS, POVERTY, AND UNEMPLOYMENT

Women's earnings in the labor force overall are about 60 percent of those of men. In 1979 the average weekly wage or salary for full-time white women workers was $187; for white men, it was $306 (U.S. Department of Commerce, *Statistical Abstracts of the United States* 1980). Women of color were further disadvantaged by their racial status. Black women's weekly earnings were $174, compared to $233 for black and other minority men. Hispanic women had a lower income of $156, Hispanic men $226.

Explanations of the wage differentials by sex are varied. Often, public opinion claims that women are paid less than men because their careers are shorter and frequently interrupted by family responsibilities. But this rationale cannot explain the fact that even unmarried women earn less than their male counterparts. The idea that characteristics of women, not gender discrimination, explain wage differentials is called *human capital theory.*

Human capital consists of the things workers can do to make themselves more productive. The assumption of human capital theory is that, in a competitive economic system, wage differences reflect differences in human capital (Stevenson 1978; Stromberg and Harkess 1978). According to this perspective, the quality of labor supplied by men and women varies because of their different patterns of labor force participation (Mincer and Polachek 1974; Polachek 1975). Presumedly high turnover rates, interrupted careers, and shorter participation in the labor force among women lead to their lesser productivity and, therefore, lower wages (Blau and Jusenius 1976). Additionally, human capital theory looks at the investments workers make in their own work (such as education and special skills training) as indicative of the value of different groups.

Critics of human capital theory point to its inadequacies on both empirical and theoretical grounds. First, research shows that women's returns on investment in education do not equal those of men. And within similar occupational levels, women tend to have higher education than men (Stevenson 1975). Moreover, even when women are more highly educated, they receive lower pay than men. Black women are lower paid and have less education than white men, but the percentage differences in pay exceed the percentage differences in education. Other research finds that in occupations employing an equal number of men and women, women still earn 8 to 18 percent less than men, controlling for age, seniority, education, and experience (Rees and Schultz 1970). Other research finds an unexplained wage gap of 38 percent even after controlling for male-female differences in education, occupational status, year-round full-time work, and lifetime work experience (Suter and Miller 1973). And with regard to the question of intermittent work patterns and the effect of work experience on wage differentials, other research finds that prior work experience has a greater effect on wages in some occupations than others; consequently, prior work history does not fully explain the wage gap (Jusenius 1976). Moreover, the causal relationship of work experience and wages is far from clear because low wages encourage many women to leave the labor force for unpaid housework. It is equally likely that women leave work because of low wages as it is that they receive low wages because of interrupted work histories (Stevenson 1975).

The theoretical grounds of the human capital perspective "assume an open, fully competitive market process in which individual characteristics are identified and rewarded according to their societal value" (Horan 1978:536). Status attainment research in sociology reveals several problems with this assumption. Sociological research finds that women are not rewarded for increased social status with higher incomes to the same extent as men (Featherman and Hauser 1976; Treiman and Terrell 1975), nor do women and men with similar occupational prestige have similar incomes or similar authority in the workplace (Featherman and Hauser 1976; Treiman and Terrell 1975; Wolf and Fligstein 1979).

An alternative approach to explaining wage differentials by sex is suggested by *dual labor market analysis*. This perspective sees the labor market as organized around both a primary and a secondary internal market. Disadvantaged groups such as women and minorities are employed primarily in the secondary market, which is less internally structured than the primary market and is characterized by numerous points of entry, short or nonexistent promotion ladders, low wages leading to less worker stability, poor working conditions, little job security, and often arbitrary work rules. The primary labor market, on the other hand, restricts entry to a relatively few low-level entry jobs but is organized around long promotion ladders, worker stability encouraged by high wages, opportunities for advancement, good working conditions, and job security (Blau and Jusenius 1976). The dual labor market perspective causes us to look at the occupational distribution by sex as a major factor in the earnings gap between men and women and leads us to conclude that where people work, not what their individual characteristics are, is a better predictor of income differences (Beck, Horan, and Tolbert 1978). This conclusion seems to be supported by the fact that women tend to earn more in establishments that hire men and women for the same occupation than they earn in establishments that hire women only (McNulty 1967). Whatever the explanation for sex differences in earnings, it is certain that women's low earnings have a number of consequences for their economic well-being.

One consequence is the high incidence of poverty, especially among female-headed households with no man present. In 1980, the median family income for all families was $21,023. Among female-headed households, the median family income was $11,908 for white households, $7,425 for black households, and $7,031 for Hispanic households. In comparison, male-headed households with no woman present have a median income of $18,731 for whites, $12,557 for blacks, and, $13,302 for Hispanic (U.S. Department of Commerce 1981). As shown in Table 4.2, clearly the most prosperous families are white families with both husband and wife present and the wife working. However, as we will see in the following chapter, these families are not typical of the American household of the 1980s.

Table 4.2   Median Income for Families and Individuals, 1980

	White	Black	Hispanic
All families	$21,023		
All families (by race)	$21,904	$12,674	$14,717
Married couples	23,501	18,593	17,361
with wife working	27,238	22,795	21,649
Female-headed households (no husband present)	11,908	7,425	7,031
Male-headed households (no wife present)	18,731	12,557	13,302
Individual,			
All males, $19,173			
All females, $11,591			
All males	19,720	13,875	13,790
All females	11,703	9,887	11,830

Also in 1980, 32.7 percent of all female-headed households lived below the official poverty line ($8,414 in that year). As Table 4.3 shows, the likelihood of a family's being poor is complicated not only by the sex of the head of the household but also by this person's marital and racial status. For example, 25.7 percent of white female-headed households were poor, compared to 49.4 percent of black female-headed households and 51.3 percent of Hispanic female-headed households (U.S. Department of Commerce 1981).

Many of the poor are also older persons—many of them women—who, when they reach age sixty-five, find their lives complicated by poverty, often regardless of their prior economic class. Among white women sixty-five years and older, 30 percent are poor, compared to 24 percent of white males over sixty-five years of age. Among older black women and men, poverty is an even more startling reality; 68 percent of black women and 44 percent of black men over age sixty-five live below the poverty line (Markson and Hess 1980).

Unemployment rates among women also reveal women's disadvantage in the labor force, although unemployment is influenced more by

Table 4.3   Poverty Status of Families and Persons, 1980
(percent below the poverty line, $8,414)

	White	Black	Hispanic
All families	8.0	28.9	23.2
Married couples	5.4	14.0	15.3
Female-headed households (no husband present)	25.7	49.4	51.3
Male-headed households (no wife present)	9.4	17.7	16.0

race than by gender. In 1981, among those twenty years and older, white men had an unemployment rate of 5.7 and minority men 12.3 percent. White women had an unemployment rate of 6.0 percent and black and other minority women 12.6 (U.S. Department of Labor 1982). The Hispanic unemployment rate among those over twenty was 8.8 percent for men and 9.5 percent for women. Again, there are differences among Hispanic groups, with unemployment highest among Puerto Ricans (12.1 percent for men and 10.3 percent for women) and lowest among Cubans (8.1 percent for men and 7.9 percent for women). Mexican-Americans had an unemployment rate of 8.6 percent for men 9.8 percent for women. It should also be pointed out that unemployment has risen steadily since 1981 and that the official statistics on unemployment underrepresent the number of persons who are, in fact, unemployed but do not show up in government figures.

Social myth claims that high unemployment among men is a result of women's entry into the labor force. Research, however, shows that the unemployment rate does not vary directly with changes in women's labor force participation (Scholzman 1979). Moreover, because most women (especially those returning to the labor force) work in sex-segregated jobs, it is hardly reasonable to think that they are taking jobs from men. Women, like men, when unemployed, experience the hardship of economic need, and unemployment is complicated for women by the fact that they are less often eligible for unemployment than men and are less likely to be cushioned by insurance or union benefits (Scholzman 1979).

The effect of the current economic situation on women's work remains to be seen, although demographic projections and a preview of current trends give some indication of what to expect. Future projections indicate that women will continue to enter the labor force; between 1980 and 1995, women will account for two thirds of the growth in the job market (Fullerton 1980). In addition, as the population ages, increases in women's labor force participation will be seen especially in older age groups. By 1990, it is projected that 59.9 percent of women between the ages of forty-five and fifty-four will be in the labor force, compared to 56.3 percent in 1980 for that age group. Among women fifty-four to sixty-four years of age, 42.2 percent are expected to be in the labor force in 1990, compared to 41.6 percent in 1980. For men, labor force participation is expected to decline in both age cohorts by 1990 (Hess and Markson 1980:183).

As women continue to outlive men and as a larger proportion of the population becomes older, more women will be supporting themselves and, perhaps, living in poverty. By the year 2030, when those born in 1965 or earlier will be over sixty-five, 17 percent of the population (compared to 11 percent now) will be sixty-five years of age and over (Hess and Markson 1980:11). By the year 2000, there will be 154 women for every 100 men over sixty-five. Currently, 75 percent of the men over sixty-five are married and live with their spouse; only 37.6 percent of women over sixty-five live with spouses present; these figures are not expected to change (Markson and Hess 1980). Without major changes in the social and economic value placed on older persons in this society, these men and women will likely experience not only increasing impoverishment but also the psychological difficulties of being perceived as socially and economically useless (Markson and Hess 1980; Rosow 1965).

But we do not have to look that far into the future to see increasing difficulties in economic life. American families, and especially American women, are already facing the realities of an economic crisis marked by rising inflation, increased work, and a decline in the standard of living. From 1960 to 1979, median family income rose from $5,620 to $19,684. Yet, despite increases in the absolute dollar amount of median income, when we control for the real value of the dollar, family incomes and the resulting standard of living have declined (Currie, Dunn, and Fogarty 1980). Discretionary income (that is, disposable income minus expenditures for necessities) declined by about 5 percent between 1973 and 1979. Living standards have been maintained only by increased labor. Incomes of families with one earner fell about 7 percent behind the cost of living from 1969 to 1978; those with two earners were about 6 percent above the cost of living (Currie, Dunn and Fogarty 1980).

The consequences of this situation for women are not only their increasing need to work but also the fact that they maintain two jobs— a paid job outside the home and unpaid household labor. For those who can afford it, the tasks of child care and housework are being pushed into the private labor sector—usually other women. The fast-food industry, as well, benefits from the push of this work out of the household. But especially for those who cannot afford outside services, "social speedup" (Currie, Dunn, and Fogarty 1980) results from the decline in leisure and the increased amount of time involved in work (including domestic services). Most of the extra work caused by speedup falls on women who have not been freed from unpaid labor in the home. As we will see in the next section, the amount of time women spend on unpaid household labor has not declined since 1920, when it was first measured (Vanek 1978). The work that women perform as unpaid houseworkers adds a new dimension to a discussion of women, work, and the economy.

THE POLITICAL ECONOMY OF HOUSEWORK

Feminist studies of housework have shown that we cannot conceive of women's work only in terms of paid labor. Because our concept of work has been tied to the idea of paid employment, women's work as housewives has long gone unrecognized as work, even though it is socially and economically necessary. The work that housewives do not only takes care of people's basic needs—food, shelter, and clothing—but also socializes new members of the society. Some argue that housewives' labor benefits employers, too, because housework sustains workers, making it possible for them to return to the labor force (Benston 1969). But social myths about housework show us the contradictions that pervade our images of the work women do in the home. On the one hand, to be a housewife is idealized as a desirable goal for women; at the same time, however, housework is depicted as drudgery and menial labor. Both images obscure the fact that, for most women, housework is time-consuming as well as physically and psychologically demanding.

The glamorous image of the housewife is found in commercials, where women are surrounded by happy families and a wealth of material goods. The housewife in these ads is usually cheerful, buoyant, and smiling, although pathologically obsessed with cleanliness and food. Three-quarters of all television ads using females, in fact, are for products found in the kitchen or bathroom (Dominick and Rauch 1972), clearly giving the image that this is women's place. Still, the use of male "experts" in the voice-overs in these commercials makes it appear that men know best when it comes to household matters. So, although housework is seen as glamorous, housewives are also ridiculed as scatter-brained, lazy, and disorganized. Anyone who has seen comic strip and greeting card depictions of a housewife standing bedraggled with rollers in her hair, an apron around her waist, a broom in her hand, and a cigarette dangling from her mouth has seen one facet of the contemporary myth about housework. The other is that of the lady of leisure whose only concern in life seems to be how clean her husband's shirts are.

The artificial picture these myths create about housework is unsupported by social and economic research. To begin with, the role of the housewife is multidimensional and is experienced by women in different ways (Lopata 1971). Many housewives are overwhelmed by the isolation of their work and by the repetitiveness of their tasks. As a result, many of them experience prolonged depression and anxiety. Betty Friedan's early book, *The Feminine Mystique* (1963), was based on the alienation of middle-class housewives, whose emotional state was such that they could not even identify their anxiety. "The problem that has no name" was, to Friedan, a state of mind in which the alienation of housewives was so pervasive that they experienced only vague anxieties and intense feelings of powerlessness.

But it would be a mistake to see the housewife role as totally oppressive, for many women find this work both creative and autonomous, especially when compared to the jobs most women occupy in the paid labor force. Historians suggest that housework is less alienating than paid labor because it is task-oriented rather than ordered by the timed structures of industrial activity (Thompson 1967). Because women's work at home is oriented to the needs of others and allows for some personal flexibility, many women prefer it to the alienating labor they would likely encounter in the paid labor force.

Sociological studies of housewives confirm this point. Research finds that housewives dislike the monotony and routinization of their work, but they like the autonomy that housework provides (Oakley 1974). Others find that housewives' work as volunteers also provides them with an independent source of satisfaction and personal expression, although their ability to work in these roles is to a large extent dependent on their husbands' affluence (Andersen 1981). These studies of housewives' roles tell us that the role is both complex and fragile. Many housewives will remain satisfied with the work they do and content to have the personal autonomy that this work can bring. Others will find it stultifying and unsatisfying. But in discussing housework, we should remember that although this work is economically necessary and often psychologically burdensome, many black and working-class women see it as a privilege.

Many of these women have never been "just housewives," for they have worked at two jobs to support their families—one job in the paid labor force and the other in the home (Davis 1981). Moreover, even for women in privileged classes, the role of affluent housewife is precariously based on the continued economic and emotional support of their husbands. A sudden death, divorce, or economic need can quickly change even the happiest housewife to an anxious and possibly poor woman who must find a way to support herself and her family.

The emotional experience of housework is, however, only one side of the issue. Whatever the women's response to housework, her work is real, although traditionally it is unrecognized and unpaid. The most detailed pictures of housework have emerged from time-budget studies that record the tasks that make up housework and measure the amount of time used in household labor. These studies show that the contemporary full-time housewife works an average of 57 hours per week on household tasks by preparing and cleaning up after meals, doing laundry, cleaning the house, taking care of children and other family members, shopping, and keeping records (Hartmann 1981). Economists have not agreed on the best way to measure the monetary value of housework, but early estimates put its worth at more than $13,000 per year, based on 1973 figures (Malbin-Glazer 1976).

Housework is organized in the modern economy as a private service, one that women provide for men and children. Housework is organized around a gender division of labor in which women not only do more work than men, but also do different tasks. The gender division of labor in housework is evident when we look at the tasks that different members of the family do. These tasks can be categorized into two types: work internal and work external to the home. The work that men, including male children, do most frequently is largely external—mowing the lawn, carrying out garbage, raking leaves, and some shopping; the work that women and female children do includes washing and drying dishes, preparing meals, cleaning the house, and doing the laundry (Cherrin 1981; Roper Organization 1980). Thus, the gendered character of housework maintains a split between the private sphere of the home as women's world and the public sphere as that of men. Compared to the 57 hours wives report spending per week on housework, husbands spend about eleven hours. Children are reported to do about the same amount as husbands (Walker 1970). A 1975 study finds that, out of a sample of 340 couples, only 26 percent of the husbands spent some time cleaning, compared to 86 percent of the wives; 27 percent of the husbands contributed 2.5 hours per week cooking, whereas 93 percent of the wives contribute 8.5 hours. Only 7 of 340 husbands did laundry, compared to one half of the wives (Meissner 1975).

Recent time-budgeted studies also show that the husbands of wives who work for wages do not spend more time on housework than the husbands whose wives are full-time housewives (Hartmann 1981), although these men do report spending more time on housework (Pleck 1979). Women who work for wages spend fewer hours on housework (about 33 hours per week) than full-time housewives, but, of course, their total work week is then longer, contributing to the social speedup problems discussed in the previous section. In families with a child under one year of age, the full-time houseworker spends about 70 hours per week in housework, 30 hours of which are devoted to child care. Husbands in these families increase the amount of time they spend in child care to about 5 hours per week, but they spend less on other housework, leaving their total contribution to housework about the same (Hartmann 1981). Hartmann concludes from this data that "husbands may require more housework than they contribute" (1981:383). This conclusion is further supported by the finding that, *controlling for the size of families,* single women spend less time on housework than married women (Hartmann 1981; Morgan 1978).

Moreover, contrary to social myth, the advent of modern technology and household appliances has not significantly reduced the time women spend in housework (Hartmann 1976, 1981). The earliest information on time spent in housework was gathered in the 1920s under the guise of the new science of home economics and its emphasis on rational management (Vanek 1978). These studies show that then, as now, women spent approximately 52 hours per week doing housework. Although the amount of time spent on housework has not changed, the actual character of housework has.

In 1900, most American homes had no electricity and no running water; in 1920 one third of American families still lived on farms. By the 1930s, approximately 60 percent of American homes had electricity, opening the way for mechanical refrigerators and washing machines, and gas and electric ranges. Also in the 1920s, a variety of canned and processed foods had become available, reducing the time a housewife spent producing and preparing food. By 1940, 70 percent of American homes had indoor plumbing; in the 1950s, automatic washers replaced wringers; and in the 1960s, women's laundry work was changed by the introduction of dryers and wash-and-wear fabrics (Cowan 1976; Vanek

1978). In the 1970s, the fast-food industry offered to take the work of the housewife out of the home, although microwave ovens, food processors, and computerized home management systems increased the expectations of women's laboring within the home.

Although these technological and commercial developments create the potential for reducing women's work as housewives, ideological changes, as well as actual changes in the requirements of housework, contribute to the demands on a housewife's time. For instance, between 1920 and 1980, the amount of time spent on food preparation, cleaning, and sewing and mending decreased. However, the introduction of cheaper clothing and linens meant that there was more clothing and linen per household, and consequently, the time spent doing laundry increased. The invention of the automobile and the development of suburbs means that the housewife spends more time transporting family members and shopping. Housewives' managerial tasks in the household have increased as financial and medical records, grocery lists, deliveries, and repairs have become routine work (Vanek 1978). And finally, as child care has become more the work of individuals, not extended families, the amount of time spent in child care has increased.

The evolution of changes in household labor is part of the more general changes that have occurred in the relationship of the household to the economy, and is also related to changes in the economic structure of life. Also, the isolation of women's work as housewives is not inevitable; instead, it is a historically specific development that is tied to the modern structure of economic and household relations. Cross-cultural evidence demonstrates that women are not inevitably domestic. In many societies, even when women are engaged in childbearing and childrearing, their role in child care is accommodated to their role in the public economy—not the other way around (Friedl 1975; Malbin-Glazer 1976). In such societies, women's contributions to production are recognized and valued. Anthropological evidence indicates that women have more egalitarian roles in those societies where individuals are directly dependent on the well-being of the society as a whole, where there is no structural dichotomy between the public and domestic worlds, and where those who make decisions also carry them out (Leacock 1978). The modern role of the housewife, isolated and dependent in the private home, is a specific consequence of the historical transition to industrial capitalism. Because this transition affects women's role in the private household, as well as their role in the public economy, it is discussed at length in the concluding section.

HISTORICAL PERSPECTIVES ON WOMEN'S WORK

It is clear that gender stratification gives women different access to economic resources; it also results in the devaluation of women's labor both inside and outside the home. To understand why this occurs, we must examine the roots of this economic development to discover the societal processes upon which it is based. The theoretical perspectives developed by feminist scholars to interpret women's position will be discussed in more detail in Chapters 9 and 10. In this section, we will review the societal changes that affect the character of women's labor in industrialized capitalist societies. As we will see, the history of gender stratification in the Western world is intertwined with that of race stratification. Thus, although women's history is often recounted from the perspective of its effect on white women, a full analysis of the historical development of women's labor must account for the experiences of women of color as well.

A complete history of women's labor would also include their roles in preindustrial societies, for, as we have seen in previous sections, these earlier forms of social organization reveal much about the relationship of women's status to their roles in systems of production. But the character of women's labor in the contemporary economy is most significantly influenced by the transformation from domestically based production to industrialized production and a consumer-oriented market system. It is this transformation, and accompanying changes in the experiences of women of color, that this section will examine.

Historians describe this transformation in terms of three economic periods: the family-based economy, the family-wage economy, and the family-consumer economy (Tilly and Scott 1978). In the first period, the *family-based economy,* dating roughly from the seventeenth century to the early eighteenth century, the household was the basic unit of the economy because production occurred primarily in the home. As late as the seventeenth century, there was no sharp distinction between economic and domestic life because household members (including non-blood kin) were responsible for the production of goods. Work in this period would be defined as productive activity for household use, and all members of the household, including children, would contribute directly to household labor (Tilly and Scott 1978). The housewife in this setting would most likely supervise much of the household work, especially the labor of children; she would also be engaged in agriculture and the production of cloth and food. The typical household unit (in England and France) during this period was largely agricultural, although later, as cities developed, the wives of shopkeepers and artisans would also share in the household's work. In both rural and urban settings in the domestic economy, the work of women and children was interdependent with that of men. Although the tasks done by each might vary, "production and family life were inseparably intertwined and the household was the center around which resources, labor, and consumption were balanced" (Tilly and Scott 1978:12).

During the period of the domestic economy for white women, in Europe and the northern United States, black women and men were working as slaves on southern plantations, where they had no control over their labor and were legally the property of their masters. Black women and men were forcibly brought to the United States by the slave trade beginning in the early seventeenth century and persisting at least until 1807, when England and the United States agreed, at least in law, to prohibit the trade (Meier and Rudwick 1966). It is estimated that over 9.5 million Africans were transported to the United States, the Caribbean, and Brazil during this time, not counting the probably 20 million who died in passage (Genovese 1974; Meier and Rudwick 1966).

Black women in slavery worked in most of the same jobs as men; in addition, they worked in the master's home and took care of their own families at the day's end. As we will see in the following chapter, the double day for black women as slaves has special consequences for the development of black families. Black families never became a place for isolated and allegedly weak women, as they did in the dominant society.

The plantation economy functioned somewhat like the domestic economy because the plantation, like a household, functioned as the major unit of production. Under slavery, though, slaves provided most, if not all, of the productive labor, whereas white slave owners had total control and ownership of the system's resources. The plantation economy, in fact, represents a transition between an agriculturally based society and an industrialized one because the population of slaves worked as a cheap and fully controlled labor force. Not until after the abolition of slavery were black women and men able freely to enter the labor market and, even then, the dynamics of racism maintained blacks as an underclass who could never compete equally for the same jobs available to white women and men (Wilson 1978).

In the second period of the transformation to advanced capitalism, called the *family-wage economy,* the center of labor moved out of the household and into the factory system. This shift is the result of industrialization that began in England in the mid-eighteenth century, followed by France and the United States somewhat later. In the family-wage economy, workers earned their living outside the home and the household became dependent on wages that the workers brought home. The shift to wage labor and the production of commodities outside the home had several influences on the character of women's work. It led to the development of dual roles for women as paid laborers and as unpaid housewives (McBride 1976). With industrialization, the household was no longer the primary center of production, although women's work in the home was still socially and economically necessary. Yet, as the focus of work moved beyond the home, the worth of all persons became measured in terms of their earned wage; therefore, the work of women in the home was devalued. And with goods being produced largely outside the home for profit (not just exchange or subsistence), international mercantilism developed that further eroded the position of women (Dobash and Dobash 1979). In a wage system, producing, distributing, and purchasing goods require cash. Although women and children worked for wages in the factory system, they received less pay than men and, in fact, were chosen as workers because they were a cheap supply of labor. Male control of the wage labor system, along with the capitalist pursuit of greater profits, weakened women's earning power (Hartmann 1976). And because cash resources were needed to survive in the new economy, women became more financially dependent on men (Tilly and Scott 1978).

Black and immigrant women in the United States during this period worked primarily as domestics or in factory labor. Following slavery, the vast majority of black women were employed as private domestic workers; their wages were notoriously low and continue to be so today. At the same time, immigrant women in the Northeast for the most part filled factory jobs in the textiles and garment industries or, on the West Coast, worked in domestic, agricultural, and factory labor.

Throughout the period of the family-wage economy, at least until World War I, most single, working-class, and immigrant women worked as domestic servants. In 1870, one-half of all women wage earners in the United States were domestic workers. However, by 1920, the percentage of women wage earners working as domestics declined to 18.5 percent, reflecting the changes in women's employment as they entered new fields as clerical workers, teachers, and nurses.

The third period of economic change is called the *family-consumer economy*. This period, characteristic of the present state of affairs, is really an extension of the family-wage system. In this period, technological change, increased productivity, and the mass production of goods create households that specialize in consumption and reproduction (Tilly and Scott 1978). Although, in the family-consumer economy, economic production goes on outside the home, the labor of family members does contribute to their economic standing. As we have already seen, in this period, women's work as housewives is often coupled with their participation in paid labor. Thus, in the family-consumer economy, women's economic productivity is even higher than in the past (Tilly and Scott 1978). Public institutions (such as schools, welfare systems, and fast-food industry) take over activities that were once located in the household. Women, consequently, become defined primarily as consumers even though, in most cases, their wages are still necessary for household support.

In sum, middle and late nineteenth century in America brought about vast changes in the organization of labor, with enormous consequences for women's work even in the contemporary period. Rapid industrialization created not only a large working class but, as the century moved on, a large middle class as well. As production and commerce grew, management also became more complex, leading to vast increases in clerical and administrative occupations. For women workers, the invention of the typewriter created a new concentration of women in the clerical labor force.

The typewriter was introduced to the public in 1873 and, because there was a shortage of labor for the new jobs it created, women were recruited for typing jobs based on the ideological appeal that they were naturally more dextrous than men (Benet 1972). In other fields, too, women were recruited when labor shortages necessitated a new work force. As public education was expanded in the late nineteenth century, women were said to be naturally suited for a profession that required patience, nurturing, and the education of children. Similarly, when the middle class organized the public health movement of the early twentieth century to ward off the "contagions" of the poor, female nurses were recruited to serve doctors and to bring "feminine compassion" to the sick (Ehrenreich and English 1973).

The history of women in the labor force shows that women have served as a reserve army of labor. When there is a need for additional or cheaper workers, women are brought into the labor force and, as we will see, corresponding ideological definitions of women's place emerge to justify their social position.

The economic and technological changes that marked the transition from the domestic economy to the consumer economy were accompanied by changes in the ideological definition of womanhood. The "cult of true womanhood" (Kraditor 1968), popularized in the nineteenth century, glorified women's ideal place as the home, where women were seen to have a moral calling to serve their families. The aristocratic lady of leisure became a model to be emulated and set the ideal, although not the reality, for women of the bourgeois class. At the same time, the Protestant ethic, which stressed individualism, success, and competition in the workplace, also encouraged women to submerge their wills to piety, purity, and submissiveness (Kessler-Harris 1976). Thus, at least in bourgeois families, women's destiny became defined as a separate sphere in which home, duty to the family, and religion would prevail.

Women of the working class continued to work both in the factory and in the home. And the reality of their working lives in the early industrial period stands in contradiction to the myth of true womanhood. Only the most affluent families could maintain an idle woman; most women worked long hours in factories and then at home.

While the cult of true womanhood was at its peak, black women were working as slaves, and no ideal of femininity was bestowed upon them. In fact, the myth of the ideal woman could be created only at the expense of other women because black, immigrant, and poor women still performed the necessary household and factory tasks.

For example, around the turn of the twentieth century in the United States, the woman who stayed at home to do her own housework became a symbol of middle-class prosperity (Davis 1981). Consequently, black and immigrant women who had found employment as domestics were expelled from white middle-class homes and replaced by new technological devices that promised to make women's work easy. In fact, some of the advertising campaigns for new products in this period (such as irons) presented explicit images of these new products purging middle-class homes of the alleged germs and social diseases of black and Chinese women (Cowan 1976). The home, in fact, became depicted during this period as a bulwark of defense against the rapid social changes occurring in the industrial workplace. The new ideology of domesticity pictured women's place in the home as a moral alternative to the effects of the bustling, nervous organization of public labor. And because many of the industrial changes taking place involved the migration of blacks and immigrants to the cities, it can be said that the cult of domesticity was intertwined with the dynamics of racism. White, middle-class women were not only seen as pious and pure, they were also perceived as the moral antithesis of the allegedly inferior character of black, Oriental, and immigrant women.

At the same time, by the early twentieth century, middle-class women were expected to apply the skills and rational professional men to the maintenance of their homes. Inspired by modern models of rational management, housework, under the guise of the domestic science movement, was to be efficient, sanitary, and technologically streamlined. Order, system, and efficiency were the goals of domestic science, and the housewife was to become an engineer who would keep accurate records, color-code her appliances, maintain an efficient schedule, and, in the modern sense of the word, *manage* her home (Andrews and Andrews 1974). Once again, clean houses and efficient management were seen as the antithesis of immigrant lives. Racism in this period depicted blacks and immigrants as slovenly, diseased, and ridden with contagious germs (Higham 1965). Racist fears about the underclass propelled the middle classes to a new sense of themselves as both the moral agents of society and the social engineers of the future.

It is from this period that we have acquired many of our common household practices today. During the 1920s, many of the household designs that are now commonplace were introduced. Kitchens and bathrooms were to be pretty, as indicated in the following editorial:

Time was when kitchens were gloomy and dark, for keeping house was a gloomy business. . . . But now! gay colors are the order of the day. Red pots and pans! Blue gas stoves! . . . It is a rainbow, in which the cook sings at her work and never thinks of household tasks as drudgery. (*Ladies Home Journal,* March 1928; cited in Cowan 1976:150–151)

Old wooden furniture was painted pastel colors; new brides were advised to keep the gray out of their husbands' shirts; and protecting the family from germs became evidence of good maternal instincts (Cowan 1976). Thus, the ideology of domesticity added an emotional dimension to what had previously been the work of servants.

Women's roles in the home were further elaborated by the new importance placed on child care and the psychological life of infants and children. In the early twentieth century, the child became the leading figure in the family, and child psychology experts admonished mothers to turn their attention to their babies' emotional development and security (Ehrenreich and English 1978). In the end, both the concepts of housewife and motherhood emphasized new standards for women's services in the home. So, although technological change created the potential for a reduction in household labor, ideological shifts in the concept of women's roles increased the social requirements for women's work. Whereas housework before had been necessary labor, it now carried ideological significance as well. As contemporary ads imply, cleaning the rings from one's husband's collar is not only doing the laundry, it is an expression of love as well. These new standards of housework effectively raise the level of consumption by individual households, leading to the conclusion shared by many social scientists that consumption, not production, is one of the major functions of contemporary household units today.

The preceding discussion shows that an analysis of women's roles in economic production cannot be separated from their roles in family life. Although the family and the economy are usually perceived as separate institutions, they are, both in history and in the present, intertwined through the activities of production and reproduction. In the following chapter, we will examine the contemporary character of family life, as well as its evolution in industrial-capitalist societies.

CHAPTER 5

WOMEN AND THE FAMILY

INTRODUCTION

An 1889 housewife's guide proclaims:

Our boys are, in another score of years, to make the laws, heal the soul and bodies, formulate the science, and control the commerce of their generation. Fathers who, recognizing this great truth, do not prepare their sons to do their part toward accomplishing this work, are despised, and justly, by the community in which they live. Our girls are, in another score of years, to make the homes which are to make laws, heal souls and bodies, formulate science, and control the commerce of their generation. (Harland 1889:202)

The home is woman's place, so the historical legacy tells us. In the period when this guide was published, the glorification of the home and family was at its historical peak. The home was considered a moral sanctuary, and morality, which flourished in the home, was considered the work of women. It was women who would shape future generations. Thus, although their place was ideally limited to the domestic sphere, within that sphere they were charged with preserving and creating the moral fiber of society.

Today's families may seem quite different from this ideal because the family is one of our most rapidly changing social institutions. Today, for example, only about 13 percent of American families fit the supposed ideal of a two-parent family in which the man works and the woman stays home to care for the children (Ramey 1978). The vast majority of American families are now either two-earner families, female-headed or single-parent households, post-childbearing couples, or those who have no children. And if we consider families to include more alternative forms of household organization, cohabitors, gay and lesbian couples, singles, and various kinds of communal or cooperative living arrangements have to be included in our picture of the contemporary family.

Still, the social ideals of the family remain quite different from the realities of contemporary households. The family is still idealized as a private world—one in which family members are nurtured and prepared for their roles in the outside world. The family is also still perceived as the world of women—a place where, even if women are employed in the public sphere, they are expected to tend their children and manage the everyday affairs of the household. The realities of contemporary households and the persistence of the family ideal, then, create a series of contradictions—especially for women. On the one hand, the family is idealized as women's world. It is glorified, isolated, and assumed to be detached from public life, as well as being seen as an enclave for the development of family members' personalities and for the gratification of their physical and emotional needs. But at the same time, families have been undergoing rapid social changes, making it clear that families are situated within the larger context of political, economic, and social conditions—all of which are structured in accordance with the gender relations of society.

Thus, although we experience our family in terms of personal, intimate relationships, those relationships are conditioned by events that extend far beyond immediate family life. Yet, the family takes on great significance in the development of our individual lives. It is where we first encounter social expectations, where our physical needs are met, where our primary emotional bonds are first established, and where we first encounter systems of authority, power, and social conflict. Although family seems to be a personal experience, many of the strains associated with family life can be seen as stemming from the conflicts posed by the family's relationship to other social institutions. For example, unemployment, divorce, women's employment, and the welfare state are all experienced within the family, although they are also a part of broader social conditions.

This chapter will review sociological and feminist perspectives on the family and describe the contemporary structure of American households. It will discuss recent perspectives on the development of gender identities in the family and will review the historical emergence of modern family forms. The chapter includes a discussion of family violence, and the final section reviews issues regarding racism and the family.

SOCIOLOGICAL AND FEMINIST PERSPECTIVES ON THE FAMILY

All societies are organized around some form of kinship system, although the meaning of *family* changes in different cultural and historical contexts. Given the problems of attributing universality to the family, certain common characteristics of the family can be used as the basis for its definition. These include economic cooperation, common residence, socially approved sexual relations, reproduction, and childrearing (Gough 1975). Additionally, anthropologists note that, in most kinship systems, "marriage exists as a socially recognized, durable, although not necessarily life-long relationship, between individual men and women" (Gough 1975). It also appears that, in most societies, men have higher status and authority in the family than women (Gough 1975). Commonsense definitions of the family include blood ties, although as we will see in the following section, many contemporary families do not meet this criterion. In fact, in reality, many contemporary families also do not meet the standards of common residence, socially approved sexual relations, or reproduction and childrearing, nor do they all include marriage.

Thus, to discuss the family from the beginning poses a number of definitional problems, many of which stem from the concept of the traditional family as the ideal type, leaving all other family forms in some kind of deviant category. Feminist scholars have suggested a number of revisions in perspectives on the family, including the following: (1) the

family is a social, not a natural, unit; (2) primary emotional commitments occur outside, as well as inside, the family; (3) men and women
experience the family in different ways; (4) families are economic as
well as emotional and reproductive units of society; (5) the family ideal
is an ideological concept that does not necessarily reflect the realities of
family forms (Rapp, Ross, and Bridenthal 1979). We will discuss each
of these revisions in turn.

Feminist scholars insist that the family must be seen as a social, not
a natural, phenomenon and argue that the study of family life in the
past has been biased by assumptions that define it as a natural unit.
Feminist perceptives on the family lead in several directions, a major
one viewing the family as being in a state of constant transformation as
it interacts with the larger social world.

The assumption that families are natural or biological units prejudices our conceptions of the family by making it appear to be universal
and detached from the influence of other social institutions. In fact, the
meaning and character of family systems vary widely. Both historically
and in contemporary families, persons designated as kin may extend
beyond blood relations; adoption is a case in point. And as in the case
of illegitimate children, blood relations may sometimes be excluded
from the social network of the family. The traditional assumption that
family relations are natural stems from the ethnocentric attitude that
what is most common in our own culture is universally the most appropriate social form.

However, even a cursory look at cross-cultural studies of kinship systems reveals a great variety of family forms. For example, in poor rural
villages of the Dominican Republic, although single-mate patterns are
the dominant ideal, women usually have multiple partners, live on or
near the land of their own families, and have their children tended by
maternal kin (Brown 1975). And among the Chuckchee of Siberia,
adult women are allowed to marry boys two or three years of age. The
women care for the boys until they are adults, because the Chuckchee
believe that parental care will cement the marriage bond (Robertson
1977).

Moreover, within our own culture, the meaning and character of
family vary over time and among different groups in the society. Carol
Stack's (1974) work on the poor black family has shown, for instance,
how extended kin networks in the black community function as systems
for social and economic exchange. Participants who are recognized as
kin are those who share and meet socioeconomic obligations. Among

native American groups, in many tribes ancestry would traditionally be traced through maternal descent, young couples would reside with the woman's parents, and, wherever they lived, the woman assumed control of the household—including the distribution of game that her husband caught (Axtell 1981).

A second assumption that has biased traditional views of the family is the idea that the person's most significant emotional contacts take place primarily within the family. Although emotional life within the family is surely a powerful experience, we may have underestimated the emotional connections that exist between nonfamily members. Especially for women, we have assumed that their primary emotional tie is to their husband and children. Recent research on women's friendships reveals that this may not be true. New historical work shows that in the nineteenth century, female friendships included passionate and sensual relations (Cott 1977; Smith-Rosenberg 1975). It appears that the very ties that bind women to the home and to the emotional world of compassion and nurturance also bind them to each other. In contemporary life, because we have not asked the question, we are only now beginning to discover the powerful emotional bonds that women and men experience outside of their immediate family relations.

Third, scholars have incorrectly assumed that men and women (as well as children) experience the family in similar ways. Yet, as Bernard's (1972) research shows, marriage provides different experiential realities for wives and husbands and, we might assume, children. The assumption that families share and live in a harmony of interests is shattered when we consider the differences in family members' power (Blood and Wolfe 1960), the psychological conflict of parent-child relationships (Mitchell 1971; Weinstein and Platt 1969), and the vast extent of domestic violence (Dobash and Dobash 1979; Martin 1976). The assumption that all members of the family experience home life in similar ways is probably a reflection of our bias in studying the family primarily from the point of view of the dominant belief system.

Because we have tended to see families primarily as reproductive units, we have underestimated the economic functions of the family. Consequently, scholars now suggest that we think of the idea of the family as distinct from the household, since each has a distinct connotation. We tend to think of the family as involving blood ties; the household, on the other hand, implies the existence of a material, or economic, unit. Households are residential units that cannot be analyzed apart from their socioeconomic context. As Rapp, Ross, and Bridenthal describe them, "households are material units within which people pool resources and perform certain tasks. It is within households that people enter into relations of production, reproduction, and consumption with one another, and on one another's account" (1979:176).

This concept leads to the final point in feminist perspectives on the family. *Family* connotes a particular social ideal and, because of its singular form, the word implies that there is one dominant form of family life. Whereas *household* underscores the connection between residential units and the economic structure of society, *family* carries ideological significance as well (Rapp, Ross, and Bridenthal 1979). Distinguishing households from families allows us to recognize the diversity in people's lived experience and frees the discussion of household life from the traditional assumptions that have biased our study of families. Because most households no longer meet the family ideal, it seems appropriate to think of new language and concepts to describe this change. But old traditions die slowly, and it seems likely that the word *family* will remain in our consciousness and our analysis. Thus, this preceding discussion should point out the importance of recognizing that traditional concepts of the family are no longer adequate to describe the social facts of most people's family experience.

PORTRAITS OF CONTEMPORARY HOUSEHOLDS

What do American households look like? Statistically, among Western industrial nations, the United States still has the highest rate of marriage. In 1980, 61.1 percent of the American population was married. Single persons made up 25 percent of the population; 7.4 percent were widowed, and 5.8 percent were divorced. The marital status of the black and Hispanic populations is somewhat different. In 1980, 46.9 percent of the black population were married, 36.5 percent single, 8.9 percent widowed, and 7.7 percent divorced. Among the Hispanic population, 60.8 percent were married, 30.1 percent single, 5.2 percent divorced, and 3.9 percent widowed (U.S. Department of Commerce, Bureau of the Census 1981).

Men are more likely to be married than women (63.4 percent of men are married vs. 59 percent of women), although a greater proportion of men are also single—29.3 percent compared to 22.4 percent for women. The longer life expectancy of women also helps explain the fact that more women than men are widowed; 11.9 percent of the female popu-

Table 5.1   Marital Status of the Population Over Age 15, 1980 (as a percent age of the population)

	Total	Men	Women
All persons			
Single	25.7	29.3	22.4
Married, spouse present	58.0	60.8	55.4
Married, spouse absent	3.1	2.6	3.6
Widowed	7.4	2.5	11.9
Divorced	5.8	4.8	6.6
Whites			
Single	24.3	28.0	20.9
Married, spouse present	60.5	63.0	58.1
Married, spouse absent	2.4	2.1	2.7
Widowed	7.3	2.3	11.8
Divorced	5.6	4.7	6.4
Blacks			
Single	36.5	40.2	33.4
Married, spouse present	37.7	42.3	34.0
Married, spouse absent	9.2	7.2	10.9
Widowed	8.9	3.9	13.0
Divorced	7.7	6.4	8.7
Hispanics			
Single	30.1	32.6	27.6
Married, spouse present	55.1	58.2	52.1
Married, spouse absent	5.7	4.4	6.9
Widowed	3.9	1.4	6.4
Divorced	5.2	3.5	6.9

Source: U.S. Department of Commerce, Bureau of the Census. *Current Population Reports: Marital Status and Living Arrangements. March 1980,* Washington, D.C.: U.S. Government Printing Office, October 1981.

lation in 1980 were widowed, compared to 2.5 percent for men. Also, 6.6 percent of the female population were divorced, compared to 4.8 percent of men (U.S. Department of Commerce, Bureau of the Census 1981).

One of the most significant facts of household patterns is the large number of households headed by women, although changes in the definition of heads of household by the Bureau of the Census make this number difficult to assess and even more difficult to compare to the past. The bureau now distinguishes between families (defined as a group of two or more persons related by birth, marriage, or adoption and living together) and nonfamily households (households maintained by a person living alone or with nonrelatives only). It has also recently redefined the concept of a head of household.

Prior to 1980, the national census routinely classified the husband as the head of the family if he and his wife were living together. But as household responsibilities have become more equally shared, the Bureau of the Census has responded to social change by replacing the term *head of household* with *householder*. This term refers to the person in whose name the house is owned or rented. Although it is not an accurate measurement of who actually supports the household, it is intended to provide a better indication of the roles of women in the family.

The 1980 census shows that 10.8 percent of all households were families with female householders. Among blacks, families with female householders constitute 28.9 percent of all households; in Hispanic families, 15.9 percent of the total. Moreover, the number of nonfamily households with female householders is a significant percent of the total number of households (see Table 5.2). In total, the proportion of American households with women as householders is 24.1 percent of all white households, 43.4 percent of all black households, and 23.4 percent of Hispanic households. Again, given problems in the census definition of householder, these data should be interpreted with caution. But nevertheless, they do indicate the vast number of American households in which women take primary responsibility for household affairs.

Recent changes in the marital status of the population can also be seen among the young. Although people still marry at a rate similar to that of the past, they marry at a later age. In 1980, the median age for women at first marriage was 22.1 years; for men, 24.6 years. In 1959, women's age at first marriage was 20.2 years; men's 22.5 (Statistical Abstracts of the United States 1980; U.S. Department of Commerce, Bureau of the Census 1981). One result is that a larger proportion of the young population is single. In 1980, 50.2 percent of women and 68.6

Table 5.2 Households by Type and Race, 1980

	All Races	Whites	Blacks	Hispanics
All households	100.0%	100.0%	100.0%	100.0%
Family households	73.9	74.0	71.9	83.1
Married-couple families	60.9	63.4	39.9	63.6
Other family, male householder	2.2	2.0	3.1	3.6
Other family, female householder	10.8	8.6	28.9	15.9
Nonfamily households	26.1	26.0	28.1	16.9
Male householder	10.9	10.5	13.6	9.4
Female householder	15.3	15.5	14.5	7.5

Source: U.S. Department of Commerce, Bureau of the Census. *Current Publication Reports, Household and Family Characteristics, March 1980.* Washington, D.C.: U.S. Government Printing Office, September 1981.

percent of men between the ages of twenty and twenty-four were single; in 1960, only 28 percent of that age group were single (Richardson 1981; U.S. Department of Commerce, Bureau of the Census 1981).

It is also well known that marriages do not endure, as the ideal implies. The divorce rate in 1980 was 100 per 1,000 persons in the population, compared to 35 per 1,000 in 1960 (U.S. Department of Commerce, Bureau of the Census 1981). In the past, the remarriage rate has tended to equal the divorce rate, although since 1970 the remarriage rate has dropped, whereas the divorce rate continues to climb (Skolnick 1978). Men, however, still tend to remarry sooner and more often than women (Glick and Norton 1977).

Thus, although marriage is still an experience shared by a majority of the population, it is fraught with conflict and dissolution. Moreover, an ever-growing portion of the population finds itself living in family situations that deviate from the traditional family structure. Recent studies find that 16 percent of American homes are single-parent households; 23 percent are child-free or postchild-rearing marriages, 16 percent are dual-career families; and 4 percent are cohabitors (Ramey 1978). These and other alternative households patterns are now becoming more typical than the traditional family.

Recent increases in women's labor force participation have made dual-career couples a more common phenomenon. Fifty-three percent of all women in intact families are now in paid employment; 41 percent of them have children under 18 years of age and, in fact, nearly one third of all children under six years of age have working mothers (Moroney 1978; Nadelson and Nadelson 1980; Pifer 1978). Moreover, a 1981 survey finds that 12 percent of all white children, 20 percent of Hispanic children, and 50 percent of all black children are raised in homes maintained by women (Levitan and Belous 1981).

These changes are also reflected in the aspirations of the young. In 1967, 50 percent of women college students stated that a career was important to them in addition to being a wife and mother (Lozoff 1972). By 1971, 81 percent of college students held this view, including 91 percent of male students, who said that they wanted a wife with a career (Lozoff 1972). Also, 60 percent of male and female students thought that both parents should spend equal amounts of time with the children; 44 percent believed that household responsibility should be equally shared; and 70 percent of females and 40 percent of males thought that both persons should contribute equally to the family income.

In fact, these beliefs are usually not realized, even among dual-career

couples. Although wives who work for wages spend less time on housework than nonemployed wives, husbands of working wives spend no
more time on housework than husbands of wives who do not work
(Hartmann 1981). When wives are working in paid employment, it
appears that children contribute the additional labor for household
chores (Cherrin 1981; Poloma and Garland 1971). Moreover, wives
who work in full-time paid employment (based on 1977 data) contribute 36.7 percent of the family income (Bryson and Bryson 1980). The
median salary for husbands in these families is $14,286; for wives,
$8,696; the discrepancy can be explained as a function of wage discrim-
ination and sex-typed jobs that women face when they enter the labor
force. But as seen in the previous chapter, wives' paid work has become
an economic necessity, with two-earner families maintaining the highest
median income of all families.

The experience of dual-career couples often puts strains on their relationship because of the adaptations they must make in houschold
responsibilities and decision making. Especially when a traditional marriage evolves into a dual-career marriage, all members of the family
(including the children) may have difficulty adjusting to new roles. But
at the same time that couples face these new issues, there are also positive effects in changing traditional roles. Wives tend to experience
greater satisfaction with their jobs, and research indicates that children
develop more flexible and less stereotypic gender expectations in dual-
career families than in traditional ones (Cherrin 1981; Nadelson and
Nadelson 1980). Such findings are a direct contradiction to the idea,
widespread in popular thought, that the children of working mothers
experience maternal deprivation. The assumption that working mothers, but not working fathers, deprive their children of emotional bonding
is further evidence of the extent to which the family is idealized as the
responsibility of women.

Some dual-career couples, both married and unmarried, find it necessary, because of their job locations, to maintain separate residences.
These *commuter couples* also experience problems posed by their long-
distance arrangements, not the least of which are considerable trans-
portation and long-distance telephone expenses. However, researchers
find commuter marriages to be less stressful for older couples who have
been married longer, where at least one partner has an already established career, and where they are free from childrearing (Gross 1980).
Women also seem to be more comfortable with the commuter arrangement than men, probably because this relationship involves a recogni-

tion of their right to independence and a career of their own (Gerstel 1980; Gross 1980).

Regardless of the strains imposed on dual-career couples, research on marital strain shows no effect of wives' employment or degree of interest in their work on their marital adjustment or companionship (Locksley 1980). Wives' employment seems detrimental to marital adjustment mostly in families in which there are preschool children and the wife did not graduate from high school (Staines et al. 1978). But overall, researchers report that wives' employment in itself does not create marital dissatisfaction.

A current portrait of families and households must also include household relationships other than those of married couples. Single persons constitute a growing proportion of the population; in addition, the number of single-parent households has increased substantially. Single persons constituted 25.7 percent of the population in 1980; among black and Hispanic persons, the number of single persons is even higher (see Table 5.1). Single-parent households are now estimated to comprise 16 percent of all households (Ramey 1978), and this proportion is expected to increase further in the future (Ross and Sawhill 1975).

Recent trends among single persons include a profound increase in the numbers of persons who are cohabiting outside of marriage. Since 1970, the number of unmarried persons living together has more than doubled, with researchers now estimating that soon a majority of persons will experience this lifestyle at some point in their lives (Macklin 1978). Although the number is difficult to determine, there were approximately 1.1 million unmarried cohabiting couples in 1978, forming 2.3 percent of all couples living together. One-quarter of these cohabiting couples have children present; the others live with no other person present (Glick and Spanier 1980). Nearly half of the persons who comprise these couples have never been married, and among the never married, 85 percent are under thirty-five years of age. Among those who have once been married, 38 percent are under thirty-five; 30 percent are between thirty-five and fifty-four years of age; and 32 percent are fifty-five and over (Glick and Spanier 1980).

Compared to married couples, those who are living together are more likely to reside in metropolitan areas; 50 percent of cohabiting couples live in large metropolitan areas compared to 37 percent of married couples. One-quarter of these cohabiting couples are black and interracial; cohabitation is more common among black and interracial couples than among white couples (Glick and Spanier 1980). Although research on cohabiting couples is sparse, it appears that most of these relationships do not differ significantly from traditional marriages in terms of the household division of labor, gender roles, and egalitarian behavior (Macklin 1978; Stafford, Backman, and Dibona 1977).

In addition, households in which persons live alone have also increased in recent years, in part because of demographic changes in the proportion of aged persons in the population. In 1980, 58 percent of of all households included a husband and wife present, and 23 percent of persons lived alone. This pattern represents an increase of 40 percent merely since 1970, and the figure is expected to rise (Glick and Norton 1977). Moreover, two thirds of one-person households are maintained by women; half of one-person households are those of persons over sixty-five years of age. Like single-parent families, many of these persons also live in poverty; in 1980, 13.6 percent of all persons over sixty-five lived below the poverty line. Again, aging and poverty are complicated by race. Among black persons over sixty-five, 38.1 percent live below the poverty line. For Hispanics, 30.8 percent of this age group are poor. For whites, the proportion of poor elderly persons is 13.6 percent (U.S. Department of Commerce 1981).

Gay and lesbian households have seldom been investigated, and the research that has been done is often biased by the prejudice against homosexuality in this culture. Much of the traditional research on gay men and lesbian women assumes that homosexuality is pathological behavior, although new perspectives are beginning to show a more objective picture of gay and lesbian existence (Rich 1980; Swerdlow et al. 1980; Vida 1978).

Research on lesbian experiences finds that lesbian women tend to form extended networks of support that operate at local and national levels. In a sense, these support networks function like a large family except that, unlike patriarchal families, they tend to be nonauthoritarian and nonhierarchical (Lewis 1979). Within couples, lesbian relationships tend to be more companion-oriented and more flexible in social roles than are traditional couples (Tanner 1978). Moreover, lesbian households are less bound by traditional gender divisions of labor (Tanner 1978), and they tend to be more egalitarian (Taylor 1980).

There are no accurate statistics on the number of homosexual couples living together because public discrimination forces them into secrecy. Lesbian mothers may have to protect the custody of their children, although they have won the right to do so in some recent lawsuits by arguing that the quality of parenting, not sexuality, is the most important issue. Feminists argue that, when lesbian mothers have left unhappy marriages, the children may be more nurtured in lesbian households, where two women (or more) share the work of child care (Swerdlow et al. 1980). Fewer children live in male homosexual households, in part because women are still more likely to get custody of their children, but also because fewer male homosexuals live in long-term unions than do lesbian couples (Vida 1978).

These alternatives to traditional family life are indicative of the social changes influencing the contemporary character of the household. Demographic patterns and economic changes both contribute to the ever-changing portrait of the American family. Although some describe the family as the institution most reluctant to change (Lasch 1977), clearly the family is marked by both change and stability. In the next section, we will examine the historical changes that have led to the development of modern family forms.

HISTORICAL PERSPECTIVES ON MODERN FAMILIES

Twentieth-century families in the Western world are characterized by an emphasis on childrearing, the separation of home from work, and the idealization of the home as women's world. In addition, in the late twentieth century the family is also idealized as a private world—one where conflicts are supposed to be self-contained, without the intervention of the state. In reality, of course, the family is heavily entangled not only with economic institutions but also with the political state and its various social agencies. In fact, some have argued that the intervention of the state in family policies results in the "policing of families" (Donzelot 1979; Foucault 1967). Most feminists support the idea of public intervention in family policy, because they believe that new policies and agencies (such as battered wives' shelters and programs for displaced homemakers) are necessary to support women in transition.

The history of the western family reveals the events that have molded contemporary families. Discussion of this history shows how modern families emerge from more traditional forms; how the family is linked to the economy and the state; and how the family mediates between individual or personal life and the public, collective realm of society (Wermuth 1981). Moreover, in the absence of historical analysis, the family becomes an abstract form, void of its real context and social changes (Dobash and Dobash 1979; Weber 1947). Knowing the history of a contemporary institution is like knowing the biography of a good friend—it helps you understand the present.

It is impossible to pinpoint the exact time in history when the modern family first emerged. One could trace the patriarchal household to the early Roman family, one of the strongest patriarchal systems known. Or one could look to the medieval period as an era when courtly love and chivalry marked gender and class relations between men and women. *Patriarchal* households—defined as the rule of men over women—are found throughout Western history. But the modern household is generally depicted as having its origins (at least in the Western world) in the transformations of economic and political life found in the postmedieval period, roughly beginning in the fourteenth century.

Philip Aries (1962) locates the origins of the modern Western family in a series of gradual transformations that began in the fourteenth century and culminated in the seventeenth and eighteenth centuries. Starting in the fourteenth cenury, the wife's position in the household deteriorated as she lost the right ro replace her husband in the management of household affairs in the event of his death or insanity. By the sixteenth century, the wife was placed totally under the authority of her husband; any acts she performed without the authority of her husband or the law were considered null and void. At the end of the sixteenth century, the Church recognized the possibility of sanctification outside of the religious vocation. In other words, it became possible for institutions outside the church to be seen as sacred at this point, the family became an object of common piety. The marriage ceremony itself, in the seventeenth century, took on a religious form by becoming like a christening in which families gathered around the bride and groom.

Also in the sixteenth and seventeenth centuries, new importance was placed on the family as attitudes toward children changed. Greater intimacy between parents and children established a new moral climate and, although the extension of school education made education increasingly a matter for the school, the family began to center its emotional life on that of the child. By the eighteenth century, the family began to hold society at a distance, thereby initiating the idea of the family as an enclave of private life. Even the physical character of the household changed. Homes became less open; instead of being organized around large communal spaces, they became characterized by several rooms, each specialized by function (Aries 1962). This change is explained as the result of homes becoming more organized around domestic work as commerce and production became increasingly located in the public workplace.

It is important to note that this evolution of family life was specific to the noble class, middle class, and wealthy artisans and laborers. Even as late as the nineteenth century, the vast majority of the European population was still poor and lived like the medieval family, with children separated from their parents and the idea of the home and the family, as described above, nonexistent. But beginning in the nineteenth century and continuing through the present, the concept of the family, as it originated in the well-to-do classes, extended through other strata of society. Still, the concept of the family as we know it today—a privatized, emotional, and patriarchal sphere—has its origins in the aristocratic and bourgeois classes.

By the late eighteenth and early nineteenth centuries, these historical transformations led to what American historians have labeled the *cult of domesticity* (Cott 1977; Kraditor 1968). The ideology of domesticity gave women a limited and sex-specific role to play—namely, responsibility for the moral and everyday affairs of the home. This ideal, coupled with economic transformations in family life, limited women's idealized experience to the private world of the family. In actuality, of course, large numbers of women, especially from the working class, also performed wage labor. But the definition of womanhood as idealized femininity stemmed from the bourgeois origins of the cult of domesticity. The cult of domesticity also provided the conditions for women's involvement in moral reform movements and, ultimately, feminism because it encouraged women's nurturance to be turned toward social improvement (Cott 1977). But in the context of the family, the cult of true womanhood limited women's experience to affairs of the heart, not the mind. This ideal glorified women's role as homemaker at the same time that it fragmented the experience of women and men.

The idealized domestic role of women followed the transformations in women's labor that were described in the preceding chapter. To review briefly, prior to the seventeenth century, the work role of women was not marginal to the economy or the household. In fact, as late as the seventeenth century, the household and the economy were one, the household being the basic unit of production. Domestic life in the earlier period was not splintered from public life, and households, as the basic units of economic production, consisted not only of individuals related through marriage but also of individuals with economic relationships, particularly servants and apprentices. In such a setting, women's labor, as well as that of children, was publicly visible, equally valued, and known to be economically necessary.

The emergence of capitalism, with the related rise of mercantilism, industrialization, and a cash-based economy, eroded the position of women by shifting the center of production from the domestic unit to the public workplace. This separation not only devalued women's labor in the home, but it also made them more economically dependent on men (Tilly and Scott 1978). The emergence of a family-wage economy, as distinct from a family-based economy, transformed not only women's work but, equally important, the family and women's role within it.

When the workplace became separated from the home, the family, although still economically productive, became in the long run a site largely for the physical and social reproduction of workers and for the consumption of goods. As more goods were produced outside the home, the value of workers became perceived in terms of their earned wages. The social value of women, especially those left unpaid housewives, was diminished.

In addition, the status of women in the family was radically altered not only by changes in the economic organization of the household but also by political changes in the relationship of the family to the state. The displacement of large feudal households by the modern state enhanced the power of the husband over his wife. For example, in sixteenth-century England, the state assumed the powers of justice, punishment, military protection, and regulation of property originally assumed by feudal estates. At the same time, a massive propaganda campaign was initiated in support of the nuclear family. Family members were required to be loyal, subservient, and obedient to both the king and the husband (Stone 1975; cited in Dobash and Dobash 1979). Thus, the patriarchal family became the cornerstone—the basic social unit—for the emergence of the modern patriarchal state (Aires 1962; Foucault 1967). As capitalism has developed further, there has been a shift from private patriarchy within the family to public patriarchy centered in industry and government (Brown 1981). Although individual men may still hold power in families where they are present, the patriarchal state ensures that all women are subject to a patriarchal order. Thus, in contemporary society, social welfare systems, education, family courts, and reproductive policies are all controlled by men, even though their primary effect is upon women and children.

Historically, the patriarchal family and, ultimately, the state was hierarchically structured around the power of men and morally sanctioned by the patriarchal church. With the Protestant Reformation, an ever-increasing amount of religious socialization occurred within the home. Whereas Catholicism had sanctioned family life reluctantly (and thus forbade it to the clergy), the Puritans embraced the family as an exalted and natural (God-given) order. The Protestant ethic, as it emerged, blessed the family as a unit of material labor. The idea that one could do God's work in secular vocations encouraged a view of the family as sacred and as the place for spiritual life (Zaretsky 1976). In the end, the self-consciousness and individualism encouraged by the Protestant ethic helped ensure the subjective importance of the family. With the rise of capitalism, women's lower status in economic production was counterbalanced by their exalted status in the family as God's moral agents.

The historical development of the family shows the interrelationship of family life with the economic and political structure of society. The modern family is characterized by its dependence on the economic market, the isolation of women within the household, and the family's role in the economic consumption and acquisition of goods. The family is both a structure and an ideology and, at the ideological level, the glorification of personal life still remains.

Personal life emerged as a separate sphere of social life primarily with the development of capitalism (Zaretsky 1976). The split between work and home established by capitalism is related to a second schism—that between personal and public life. Modern capitalism depends on individual consumerism; thus, it encourages modern families to emphasize individualism, self-consciousness, and the search for personal identity. Yet, when personal identity is viewed as detached from objective material conditions, it becomes mystified. One can come to believe that personal liberation can occur without a change in the objective conditions of economic relations. The "plunge into subjectivity" (Zaretsky 1976:119) and its emphasis on life-style, consumerism, and personal awareness is a form of consciousness specific to and consistent with the ideological and economic needs of capitalist economies.

Modern families are also regulated by the patriarchal authority of the state and its various agencies. Especially in poor and working-class families, state agencies and reformers seeking to eliminate deviance regulate personal and family life through the work of professional experts. Even in the middle class, professional experts claim to know more about personal life, thereby defining individual and family needs and the character of contemporary social problems (Ehrenreich and English 1978; Illich 1977). In the end, the modern family is still nested within political and economic systems; yet, the ideology of personal life sees the family and the person as autonomous social forms. This structural and ideological character of the modern family, as influenced by capitalism and patriarchy, forms the basis for understanding gender roles in the contemporary family.

GENDER ROLES IN CONTEMPORARY FAMILIES

In its modern form, the family serves the functions of reproduction, emotional development, economic consumption, and caring for the young. Within the family, women's roles are organized around these functions, whereas men's roles (at least in the ideal) are defined as located in the public sphere. The man returns to the home for personal restoration, but it is largely women who are supposed to perform the work of the home.

The structural and ideological character of the family has several implications for the gender roles enacted within it. As we have already seen, the role of housewife has a specific economic and social function in the maintenance of family and economic life. In addition, the contemporary character of the family influences the practice of child care and the experience of motherhood and fatherhood.

Child care in American society is, by virtue of the character of the family, largely a system of private care. The parent-child unit is allegedly self-sufficient and, given the gender division of labor, the responsibility for child care falls almost exclusively on individual women. The experience of mothers (or other caretakers) and children is isolated within the home and is based on the assumption that children are best cared for by their biological mother. Exceptions to this design do exist, although even then the arrangements for child care are usually managed by the mother, and it is other women who do the work. So, although it is more and more impractical to do so, mothers usually have nearly exclusive responsibility for the everyday care of their children.

The privatized and exclusive character of child care seems especially inappropriate when we consider the labor force participation rate of mothers. As already noted, recent increases in the labor force participation rate are highest among women with children, especially women with children of preschool age. By 1977, 51 percent of all women with children worked; 41 percent of those with children under six years of age worked; and 35 percent of women with children under the age of three worked (Baxandall 1979). Yet, among children aged three to thirteen, 83 percent were cared for in their own home; 70 percent of these children were cared for by their parents or another relative. In fact, it is estimated that only 1.7 percent of American children are tended in group care (Baxandall 1979).

As Baxandall points out, depression and war have provided the major impetus for establishing public child care facilities in the United States. Although there was another expansion of day-care facilities in the early 1970s, since then the availability of such facilities has decreased. In fact, licensed and voluntary day-care centers in the United States now care for only one-sixth the number of children cared for at the end of World War II. This situation exists despite the fact that the labor force participation rate of women at that time was 38.1 percent compared to 52.3 percent today (Blau 1979; U.S. Department of Commerce, *Statistical Abstracts of the United States* 1980).

The historical origins of public day care in the United States are found in the Works Progress Administration (WPA) of the New Deal. In the 1930s, WPA day-care and nursery schools were designed to provide employment for needy teachers, child-care workers, cooks, janitors, nutritionists, and clerical workers during the Depression. By the end of the Depression and the beginning of World War I, when jobs were no longer in short supply, the WPA nurseries were eliminated. However, in 1941, the Lanham Act (also known as the Community Facilities Act) was passed by Congress to meet the day-care needs of mothers in wartime employment. The Lanham Act made matching federal funds available to states for the expansion of day-care centers and nursery schools. Following World War II, when women were no longer needed in the labor force, Congress withdrew funds for day care and most of the Lanham Act nurseries closed (Baxandall 1979).

Since World War II, federally funded day-care programs have been established for the poor. For example, Project Headstart, funded through the Office of Economic Opportunity, was designed primarily for children from families below the poverty line. More recently, cutbacks in federal funds for day care and other social science programs have nearly eliminated the option of federally supported day-care centers for most women.

In part, public attitudes toward day care are stigmatized by the association of day care with welfare services. But resistance to publicly supported day care also stems from the attitude that children cared for in the absence of mothers suffer from maternal deprivation. The fact that child care is defined as women's work is revealed by noting that, in spite of the relative absence of most fathers from the everyday life of the home, no one has suggested that children of working fathers suffer from paternal deprivation.

Thus, in child care, the myth persists that only the biological mother can best care for the child. Yet, the wear and tear that sole responsibility for child care imposes on the woman, limiting her ability to be a good mother, is only now being recognized. Few have considered that there may be beneficial effects on children who receive a wide variety of stimuli from different persons—no one of whom can maintain the same level of activity, enthusiasm, and curiosity as the child. Yet, in most situations, the structure of the contemporary family discourages shared child-care arrangements, leaving isolated mothers to draw on their own resources to make whatever arrangements are possible for the care of their children.

Moreover, child-centered families draw attention away from the experience of the mother by concentrating primarily on that of the child. For mothers, women's roles are idealized as all-loving, kind, gentle, and selfless. Yet, the objective conditions of motherhood in this society fill the role with contradictions, conflicts, and pleasures. Motherhood is, in fact, a social institution—one that is controlled by the systems of patriarchy and the economic relations in which it is embedded (Rich 1976). Like other institutions, motherhood involves a complex set of social relations organized around specific functions. Once established, institutions also involve a system of power relations, a division of labor, and the distribution of resources.

Viewing motherhood as an institution distinguishes motherhood as a social practice from the potential relationship between a woman and her children (Rich 1976). In this society, motherhood is specifically characterized by its isolation. Thus, although most young girls are socialized to become mothers, they are seldom prepared for the solitary activity of actually caring for children in the home. Jessie Bernard (1975) suggests, in fact, that when women marry, their early socialization for dependency is reversed, because as wives and mothers, they are expected to be responsible for both their husband and their children. The experience of motherhood then becomes a mixture of satisfaction and pleasure plus anger, frustration, and bitterness (Rich 1976). For children, the contradictions also appear, for as Rich says, "most of us first know both love and disappointment, power and tenderness, in the person of a woman" (1976:11). Because motherhood is a role exclusively reserved for women, women's identities develop in ways that reproduce mothering qualities.

Nancy Chodorow has explored this issue by asking how the psychological structures of gender emerge from the "asymmetrical organization of parenting" (1978:49). Chodorow begins by noting that the role of women as mothers is one of the few seemingly universal elements of the sexual division of labor. But instead of relying on explanations that see motherhood as a natural fact, she asks why the psychological characteristics of motherhood are reproduced so that women, and not men, want to be mothers and develop the capacity for nurturing others. According to Chodorow, "women, as mothers, produce daughters with mothering capacities and the desire to mother. These capacities and needs are built into and grow out of the mother-daughter relationship itself. By contrast, women as mothers (and men as not-mothers) produce sons whose nurturant capacities and needs have been curtailed and repressed" (1978:7).

Chodorow explains this process as the result of both the gender division of labor and the psychological processes it inspires. Both boys and girls, in order to become their own person, must separate—psychologically—from the parent. Because the parent most often present is a woman, the process of individuation is complicated by gender identity. Boys, who identify with the gender of the father, learn that their gender role is one of detachment and distance, because the father is seldom present in the home. Girls, on the other hand, identify with the gender of the mother; thus, their own psychological process of separation and individuation is less complete. Girls, then, "are more continuously embedded in and mediated by their ongoing relationship with their mother. They develop through and stress particularistic and affective relationships to others. A boy's identification processes are not likely to be so embedded in or mediated by a real affective relation to his father. At the same time, he tends to deny identification with and relationship to his mother and reject what he takes to be the feminine world; masculinity is defined as much negatively as possible. . . . Feminine identification processes are relational, whereas masculine identification processes tend to deny relationship" (1978:176). Thus, Chodorow explains how gendered personalities both reflect and re-create the gender division of labor in the household. Women become mothers because this role is consistent with their acquired psychological being; the fact that they are mothers, then, re-creates similar personality structures of nurturance in their daughters. Thus, the social organization of parenting creates psychic structures that orient the person to his or her social behavior. To reverse this process, so that men as fathers become more nurturant, will require that men be placed in the household on an equal basis with women. But because the organization of parenthood is tied to the organization of economic production, both the family and the economy must be transformed if we are to eliminate gender inequality.

Chodorow's analysis is psychoanalytic in its orientation; thus, the evidence for her argument is clinical evidence. As her critics point out, clinical evidence is weak because it rests on patients' accounts and psychoanalysts' interpretations of those accounts (Lorber et al. 1981). But, beyond the methodological criticisms, sociologists are concerned that Chodorow overemphasizes psychological processes in lieu of social structural conditions as the source of women's choice to become mothers. It is ideologically normal for women to become mothers; furthermore, given the inequality in men's and women's incomes, it is reasonable for fathers, not mothers, to be the primary wage earner in the family (Lorber et al. 1981:484). Other questions about the class, race, and culture bias of Chodorow's explanation can also be raised, for she assumes that the mother in the gender division of labor is a devalued woman. Although this is true in many cultures, including the dominant American culture, it is not universally true. An important test of her theory would involve the study of boys and girls who are raised by men or in cultures where women are not devalued and parenthood is more equally shared. We also need to consider the fact that the psychoanalytic perspective may not account for variations in the actual practices and relationships of mothers who are raising children. The mother's own personality, as well as the child-care arrangements she makes, may alter the degree to which her sons and daughters separate or do not separate themselves from her, and it certainly alters their relationship with her. But Chodorow's analysis gives us a provocative account of the formation of gender identity and its relationship to the social structure of the family.

Most importantly, Chodorow points out that the family is "a primary constituent of the male dominant social organization of gender and, as such, is as fundamental a constituent feature of society as a whole—of 'social structure'—as is the economy or the political organization" (Lorber et al. 1981:502). One is not dependent on or contained by the other;

people live in families, just as they live in societies. Chodorow's analysis has led us to see the importance of understanding "the gender politics of infancy" (Harding 1981) and the connection of masculine and feminine personalities not only to the social organization of families but also to self-other distinctions that constitute the basis for domination relations (Chodorow 1981; Harding 1981). In sum, although the cross-cultural evidence for Chodorow's work remains to be studied, she provides an insightful explanation of some of the effects of nuclear family relations, in which the woman's work as a mother is isolated from that of other persons and founded on the norm of exclusivity.

VIOLENCE IN THE FAMILY

Throughout this discussion of the family, isolation emerges as both an ideological and a structural characteristic of the modern family. We have already seen the contradictions and dilemmas that isolation poses for mothers. But the effects of isolation and the ethic of family privacy are no more vividly seen than in the high incidence of violence against women in the family. Wife battering, child abuse, and incest have only recently been brought to the public's attention, but all of them make the tensions of family life clear. And especially in the case of incest, they reveal the continuing dynamics of patriarchal relations.

Only in recent years has the sanctity of the private household been breeched so that these issues have come to our attention. What were once hidden problems now seem quite common and, although accurate measures of the extent of family violence are difficult to establish, researchers estimate that the problem is widespread across families in all classes and races (Dobash and Dobash 1979; Strauss, Gelles, and Steinmetz 1980). With regard to wife battering and child abuse, indirect evidence of their extent also comes from police records of domestic disturbances (Martin 1976), hospital emergency room files, family court records, homicide rates of women killed by husbands and lovers (Wolfgang 1958), and the great number of divorces that cite violence as the primary reason for ending the marriage (Chester and Streather 1972; Levinger 1966). Information on incest is even harder to obtain because social taboos against it make it one of the most hidden of social problems. But as victims of incest begin to speak out, it becomes apparent that the incest taboo is a taboo against discussing it, not doing it (Hamil 1981). It is important to point out that most official statistics on violence are also weighted against the poor because the middle and upper classes are better able to keep it secret.

Studies indicate that the overwhelming amount of domestic violence is directed against women (Dobash and Dobash 1979). Coupled with the idea that violence is purposeful behavior, this fact leads to the conclusion that violence against wives is a form of social control—one that emerges directly from the patriarchal structure and ideology of the family (Barry 1979). Because of the availability of research studies, this section will concentrate on the issue of wife beating, but as more information is revealed, many commonalities are likely to be found among wife beating, incest, and, as discussed in Chapter 7, rape. Child abuse, on the other hand, seems to be largely, but not exclusively, committed by women, probably reflecting the frustrations they experience in their isolated role in the family.

Historically, wife beating has been a legitimate way to express male authority. Scholars contend that the transformation from the feudal patriarchal household to the nuclear family had the effect of strengthening the husband's power over his wife by placing systems of authority directly in the hands of individual men, not in the indirect rule of the state. Thus, throughout the seventeenth, eighteenth, and nineteenth centuries, men could, within the law, beat their wives, and there was little community objection to their doing so as long as the method and extent of violence remained within certain tacit, and sometimes formally documented, limits. For example, eighteenth-century French law restricted violence against wives to "blows, thumps, kicks, or punches on the back if they leave no traces" and did not allow the use of "sharp edged or crushing instruments" (Castan 1976; cited in Dobash and Dobash 1979:56–57). One ancient code, from which we get the phrase *rule of thumb* allowed a man to beat his wife with a stick no thicker than his thumb (Dobash and Dobash 1977).

The historical context of wife beating provides a perspective with which to view the contemporary problem. Now, although wife beating is socially abhorred, it is at the same time widely legitimated through its humorous portrayal and in prevalent attitudes regarding privacy in marriage. Additionally, the attitude that victims bring violence on themselves (by not leaving) seems to discourage social intervention in violent relationships. As a result, the phenomenon of violence is widely misunderstood. Dobash and Dobash's (1979) study of Scottish wives gives us some understanding of how violence emerges in marriage and how it is tied to the social isolation of wives.

Dobash and Dobash traced the course of 109 relationships that resulted in battering, beginning with the initial courtship phase. During the period when couples first met, both maintained separate lives, including an independent social life with friends and individual commitments to their family, jobs, and education. As the couples' commitment to each other increased, the partners modified their social lives, although women did so more than men. One-quarter of the women studied went out with their own friends once a week or more, compared to nearly half of the men. The more serious the relationship became, the less time women spent with their own friends.

Prior to marriage, the women reported that sexual jealousy was the major conflict in the relationship, although arguments over jealousy seem to have had the purpose of confirming the couple's commitment to each other. The women became increasingly isolated from their friends prior to the marriage, and they reported believing that love would take care of any problems that existed in the relationship.

Both partners entered marriage with ideals about how the marriage would work, although after a time, it was clear that the husband's ideals would rule. Marriage, for the wife, involved an extreme constriction of her social world, and the husband began to believe that he could monopolize his wife, although she could not put similar demands upon him. He, as the representative to the outside world, was supposed to have authority, independence, and freedom; she could not question his movements.

In this study, 41 percent of the wives experienced their first attack within six months of the wedding; another 18 percent experienced an attack within the first year of marriage. The wives' response was one of surprise, shock, shame, and guilt, although both partners treated the incident as an exception and assumed, without discussion, that the issue had been resolved. Yet, as the marriage continued, conflicts repeatedly surfaced. Nearly two thirds of the couples reported sexual jealousy and expectations about domestic work as the source of conflict leading to violent episodes. The women reported that their social world moved more apart from their husband's as the marriage went on. The wives were mostly involved in the everyday matters of household management and child care, whereas the husbands were involved in their own work. However, the husbands still expected their wives to meet their immediate needs.

What is striking about these case studies is how common the patterns in these relationships are. Clearly, wife battering emerges from institutional arrangements that isolate women in the home and give men authority over them. Moreover, once a pattern of violence is established, wives believe they have no options. Most will, at some point, leave— even if temporarily (Dobash and Dobash 1979)—but their feeling that they have no place to go is usually a realistic assessment of their economic situation and their powerlessness to effect changes within the relationship (Martin 1976). In the courts, battered wives are faced with the problem of having to prosecute a man who is both their husband and, possibly, the father of their children. Moreover, even if the wife brings charges, when the husband is released, he returns to the home— perhaps more angry than when the violence began (Martin 1976). The movement to establish refuges for battered women has assisted many victims in responding to battering, and such centers have proliferated in communities throughout the country. But difficulties in funding such centers have caused many to close, and current cutbacks in social service funding seem likely to pose additional setbacks. Finally, the attitude that family problems are a private matter, to be resolved between two equal partners and within the confines of the home, creates resistance to social changes that could assist battered wives.

Feminists have pointed to violence as the logical result of both women's powerlessness in the family and a male culture that emphasizes aggression, domination, and violence. The modern form of the family leads women to be dependent on men economically and emotionally, and, as a result, the traditional family is a source of social conflict and a haven only for men (Hartmann 1981). The phenomenon of violence in the family shows clearly the problems that traditional family structures create for women. Feminist criticism of the family rests, in part, on the psychological, physical, and economic threats families pose for women. And it is for these reasons that feminists argue for a change in traditional family structures. These changes, intended to empower women, would not necessarily abolish the family, but they would create new values regarding women's work in the family and new rewards for women in the family, regardless of whether they are also working in the public labor force.

Before leaving our discussion of the family, it is important to discuss the experience of women of color in the family. Although these women share many of the problems of white women, their family relations also strengthen them in the face of oppression. Moreover, a review of the situation of women of color reveals the particular dynamics of racism in the organization of family life.

RACISM AND THE FAMILY

Many of the assumptions made in studies of minority families have been biased by the belief that these families are normal only when they conform to dominant groups norms (Staples and Mirandé 1980). In addition, minority families have also been targeted as the source of social disorganization in minority communities (Moynihan 1965) and as contributing to a lack of achievement among minority persons. These traditional interpretations of minority families stem from the confusion of ideology and objective social science research and demonstrate the extent to which racism has pervaded sociological research (Ladner 1971).

When minority families are studied on their own terms, a more objective picture of their character emerges—one that forces a reexamination of the assumptions we make about family life. The revisions in scholarship on minority families have come especially from studies of the black family in society and history, although recent work has also revised contemporary interpretations of Hispanic, Asian-American, and native American families.

Black families in America tend to be larger than white families, although the nonwhite birthrate is declining. Blacks also marry later than do whites, but the divorce rate of blacks is higher than that of whites. Also, a large and increasing proportion of black families and households are headed by women. When two spouses are present, black wives are more likely than white wives to work, and they contribute a larger share of the total family income.

Although these aggregate data give a partial portrait of the black family, they do not tell us about the actual content of these relationships and family systems. Also, discussions of the black family are often contaminated by value-laden terms such as *disorganization, maladjustment, and deterioration.* In fact, much of the discussion of black families has emerged from confusion over the use of the term *matriarchy* to refer to the fact of female-headed households. *Matriarchy* is defined as a social structure in which power is held by women. In black families, in which women are often the head of the household, they still have little power within the society; thus, the term *matriarchy* is misleading. It confounds the study of the family with racial and gender stereotypes of the black woman as dominating, castrating, and overbearing and, thus, distorts the reality of family life and turns the black woman's life into a myth (Staples 1971).

Because the dominant family ideal in this culture is the patriarchal family, much of the research on black families has attributed problems in the family to its woman-centered organization. The infamous Moynihan report, *The Negro Family: The Case for National Actions,* published as a federal study of the black community in 1965, cited the family as the cause of social disorganization in black America. In Moynihan's own words, "at the heart of the deterioration of the fabric of Negro society is the deterioration of the Negro family" (1965:5).

Moynihan's report attributed the origins of the family problem to the period of slavery and the social disorganization it created. Other studies of the black family have also cited slavery as creating female-headed families through the separation of family members by slave sales, the practice of slave breeding, and the disrespect paid to the black slave community (Frazier 1948). Others have traced the structure of black family life to its African origins, where polygamy and birth out of wedlock were more common (Herskovits 1958). Recent scholarship on the black family questions both of these conclusions, noting that locating the causes of contemporary family structure in the past downplays an analysis of family life within contemporary economic and social structures (Ryan 1971).

Herbert Gutman, a historian, argues that, if Moynihan was right in concluding that the structure of black families has its origins in the past, then we should expect the family to be less stable as we move backward in time. To test this assumption, Gutman traced five generations of kin as they adapted to the changes of postslavery American society. Part of his research is based on 1925 census data from New York City that show that 85 percent of kin-related black households at that time were double-headed; 32 of the 13,924 families had no father present; and five of six children under age six lived with both parents (Gutman 1976:xix). Based on this information, he concluded that female-headed households are a contemporary phenomenon, not just a historical remnant. His historical research is complemented by that of Genovese

(1974), who believes that slave owners used the family as a form of social control. Although Genovese does not deny that separation of families occurred, he suggests that it was often to the benefit of slave owners to maintain stable families as a way of preventing slave revolts. The slave family, according to Genovese, was subordinated to the economic interests of the owner. If it benefitted him, he would break up families for sale; in fact, most slave owners broke up families when they were under economic pressure (Genovese 1974:453).

Both Genovese's and Gutman's analyses indicate that slave families faced oppressive conditions that tested the adaptive capacities of men and women. Within slave communities, a subculture of resistance emerged in which family relations and women's role fostered resistance to dominant white institutions (Davis 1971, 1981). Because of the gender division of labor, black women in slavery provided domestic labor not only in the white household but also in their own. The labor they provided for their own family was the only labor not claimed by the ruling class; it was for the benefit of the slave community. As a result, black women's labor in the slave community "lay the foundation for some degree of autonomy" (Davis 1971:5), and the black woman became essential to the survival of the slave community. Moreover, because of her indispensable labor in the household of the oppressor, she developed a practical awareness of the oppressor's dependence on her. As Davis says, "the master needs the slave for more than the slave needs the master" (1971:6). Black women's consciousness of their oppression benefitted the slave community, as women were responsible for the socialization of future generations. Thus, the women in their roles in the family and community passed on a culture of resistance to oppressed kin (Caulfield 1974).

The picture of the black family emerging from these historical revisions is one of strength and resistance. In fact, Ladner (1971) suggests that traditional myths of the black matriarchy confuse black women's strength with domination. Because of racism, the black woman has not been subjected to the ideals of femininity, as have white women (Davis 1971). One result is found in the strong self-concept and higher educational and occupational aspirations that black women have for themselves compared to white women (Dill 1980; Epstein 1973; Myers 1975; Wilson 1980).

Rather than explaining the high incidence of female-headed households in black communities as the result of slavery or individual pathology, it makes sense to analyze the origins of black family life in terms of the patterns of urbanization, industrialization, and poverty in twentieth-century society (Billingsley 1966; Frazier 1948; Staples 1971).

In the early twentieth century, racial discrimination in the labor force denied black persons employment using the skills they had acquired in slavery. As a result, men could find only unskilled, often seasonal, and always underpaid employment; women were more likely to find steady, although also severely underpaid, employment in private domestic labor. In 1920, 41 percent of black women worked as servants and 20 percent as laundresses (Katzman 1978:74). Black women's labor thus made them steady providers for their family. As the twentieth century developed, continuing patterns of unemployment, the elimination of black men through war and imprisonment, and the conditions established for households by the social welfare system encouraged the formation of female-centered households.

The contemporary structure of black households must be understood in terms of both racism and sexism and the economic context in which they are embedded. As we look at black families without racist and sexist assumptions, we see that even in the poorest of families, systems of cooperation and social exchange characterize the organization of family life (McCray 1980; Stack 1974). The social and community ties that people generate in the face of poverty and oppression, in fact, appear stronger than some of the ties of nuclear families. This fact shows us that black families are not necessarily disorganized, but that they are not always organized according to dominant group ideals. If we understand this concept, then the role of women in the black family can be seen for the strength it creates, not the social destruction it allegedly causes. Black women continue to work to support their families (Rodgers-Rose 1980) and to hold high ideals for their children's future (Dill 1980). Sociological perspectives on black family life should recognize these ideals and begin their analysis there.

Similarly, research on other minority families needs to move away from pejorative assumptions about family organization. Studies on Mexican-American and Puerto Rican families, scant as they are, have often been founded on the assumption of the pathology of the family. For feminists, the study of these Hispanic families is especially important because of the value of machismo in the organization of family life. As a dominant force in patriarchal organization, machismo in the Hispanic family has been assumed to encourage aggressive, violent, and authoritarian behavior in men and saintly, virginal, submissive behavior in women (Staples and Mirandé 1980). But some researchers see machismo as a more benevolent feature of Hispanic families, encouraging honor, respect, and dignity among family members (Murillo 1971). Although these issues have yet to be examined by feminist scholars, some research shows that Hispanic families are more egalitarian than the ideal of machismo suggests (Baca Zinn 1976; Cromwell and Cromwell 1978; Mirandé 1979; Ybarra 1977), and that the Hispanic family is more woman-centered than prevailing stereotypes suggest (Baca Zinn 1976).

Research on Asian-American and native American families is similarly sparse and, in both cases, assimilation and acculturation are key concepts in understanding the transformations in family life. There are approximately 1.5 million individuals of Chinese, Japanese, Korean, Filipino, Vietnamese, Cambodian, Thai, and East Indian ancestries living in the United States (Yamauchi 1979; cited in Staples and Mirandé 1980). Although these persons conform more closely to middle-class American family norms than do other minorities, their family systems are marked by the tensions of generational changes in traditional cultures. American-born children may adapt American values, whereas their parents and grandparents may adhere to the more traditional and conservative family mores of their culture. Within Asian-American communities, ethnic cohesiveness and continuity through generations may be difficult to maintain, and families may experience conflict as a result (Staples and Mirandé 1980).

Among native Americans, family life-styles vary widely, as diversity among groups is a key element of culture. Also, the attempt to impose Western family forms on these people complicates the picture of native American family life. Interference in these cultures by social workers, the federal government, and other outsiders may have done more to promote family and cultural disorganization than to assist these groups. Among native American families, urbanization contributes to high rates of unemployment and dependence on public welfare (Miller 1975). Left to their own culture, native American families tend to rely on extended family networks to fulfill family functions (Redhorse 1979; Staples and Mirandé 1980). The imposition of Western standards on these traditional forms creates stress for the community and the family, because adapting to both traditional and dominant societal values poses difficulties for both individuals and families.

CONCLUSION

Consideration of the problems faced by minority families underscores the general point that families do not exist in a cultural and economic vacuum. Economic changes, racial and cultural conflicts, and gender relations interact to produce family systems. In sum, we can see that no single model of family life characterizes *the* American family, in spite of ideological beliefs to the contrary. Even the feminist perspective that family life is debilitating for women seems questionable when we consider the role of the family in the cultural resistance of minority groups. Sociological perspectives on family life should be sensitive to the interaction of the family with other social institutions and should keep in mind that the ideology of the family often, if not always, departs from the actual structure of both dominant- and subordinant-group family systems.

CHAPTER 6

WOMEN, HEALTH, AND REPRODUCTION

INTRODUCTION

Physical health is one of the most basic of life's privileges. Although we tend to think of our bodies as best cared for by personal hygiene and individual diet and health habits, in fact, physical health is heavily influenced by sociological factors. As one of those factors, gender plays a significant part in determining physical well-being and in influencing our bodily experience.

For instance, the likelihood that one will encounter stress, become overweight, experience hypertension, or become chronically ill is significantly affected by one's gender. National health statistics show that hypertension is more common among men than women until age fifty-five, when the pattern is reversed (Hess and Markson 1980). National data also show that, under age thirty-five, men are more likely to be overweight than women, although the reverse is true after this age (U.S. Department of Commerce, *Statistical Abstracts of the United States* 1980). Women are more vulnerable to chronic and acute diseases than are men, although men are more likely to become disabled by disease (Hess and Markson 1980). And in all cases, along with gender and age,

142

racial status is a complicating factor in each of these conditions. For example, blacks are far more likely to experience disability, to develop hypertension, and to suffer from poor nutrition (Hess and Markson 1980). And in the case of aging, only half of all nonwhite males and two thirds of nonwhite females born in 1974 can expect to live beyond age sixty-five. Comparable figures for whites are two thirds of white males born in that year living beyond age sixty-five and four fifths of white females (Hess and Markson 1980).

These data indicate that physical health is mediated by social and cultural organization. For this reason, gender roles influence not only what we will become but also how long our lives will be and how we are likely to die. The first section of this chapter reviews research on sex roles and health, showing how gender roles influence the distribution and experience of health and illness. This section is followed by a discussion of health and work, because where one works has many influences on physical well-being.

In addition to influencing the health of populations, gender relations in the society are reflected in institutional patterns of health care systems. As the feminist movement has shown (Ruzek 1978), health care institutions in this society are dominated by men, even though healing and caring for others have traditionally been defined as the work of women. Because of the sexist structure of health care in this society, women have had little control over their own reproductive lives. The third section of this chapter will discuss the politics of reproduction, especially surrounding the issues of abortion, pregnancy, and birth control. This section is followed by a review of the historical emergence of health care institutions and the process by which male domination in health care was established. Finally, the contemporary status of women in medicine and the feminist health care movement will be discussed. Throughout this chapter, we will see that gender relations are important in determining the character of health and reproduction in contemporary American society.

SEX ROLES AND HEALTH

Historically, patterns of male and female health change according to the social arrangements of the time. For instance, in the late nineteenth century, illness was quite fashionable for women--at least those of the upper middle and upper classes. Women in these classes were expected to be idle and faint; consequently, retiring to bed because of "nerves" was not only acceptable, but actually encouraged by medical practitioners (Ehrenreich and English 1973).

Differences in life expectancy for men and women did not emerge in American society until the beginning of the twentieth century. Even now, longer life expectancy for women occurs primarily in highly industrialized Western societies (Hess and Markson 1980). In America, death rates for both males and females have declined drastically since 1900, but there has been a trend toward a larger sex mortality differential (Ortmeyer 1979). Decreases in maternal mortality rates (death during pregnancy and childbirth) explain part of the increase in the sex mortality differential, but by far the greatest part of the difference is attributable to men's greater susceptibility to infectious diseases.

For both sexes, mortality caused by infectious disease has declined since 1900, but researchers cite differences in male and female roles and cultural practices as contributing to higher male death rates caused by infection. In particular, male occupational roles, more frequent travel and contact with strangers, and greater exposure to more people have been cited as contributing to the higher male death rate caused by infection (Graney 1977). In addition, health studies indicate that 75 percent of the increase in mortality differences by sex can be explained by increases in cigarette smoking, particularly among men in the twentieth century (Ortmeyer 1979). Cigarette smoking is known to contribute to greater cardiovascular and respiratory disease—a fact that, given changes in women's smoking patterns, may significantly alter the sex mortality differential in the future. Recent studies show a convergence in the number of men and women who are currently smoking and beginning to smoke; moreover, the evidence also shows that more men than women quit smoking (Dicken 1978). As a result, we might expect to see cardiovascular and respiratory diseases increase among women.

Particular health problems faced by men and women can be seen as consequences of their respective sex roles. The male role, for example, poses a number of hazards to physical health. Not only are men more likely than women to contract infectious disease and cardiovascular and respiratory illnesses, but they also have higher death rates caused by accidents, suicides, and homicides (Ortmeyer 1979). Men commit suicide three times as often as women, although women make four times as many attempts. The male-female suicide rate also increases with age.

Four times as many men as women commit suicide at age sixty-five, but at eighty-five years of age, twelve times as many men as women commit suicide (Miller 1978). Men are also four times more likely to be homicide victims than are women; black men are nearly six times as likely to die by homicide as white men (U.S. Department of Commerce, *Statistical Abstracts of the United States* 1980). Black women are four times as likely to die by homicide as white women and are slightly more likely than white men to die by homicide (U.S. Department of Commerce, *Statistical Abstracts of the United States* 1980). These patterns demonstrate the risks and stresses that are created by both racial and gender statuses in the society.

To summarize, it would appear that the work-oriented, ambitious, aggressive, and competitive life-style associated with the male role tends to produce heart diseases along with other health problems. Yet, the patterns of women's health reveal other problems, many of which are a function of women's status within both the society and the health care system. Women have higher rates of acute and chronic illness and a higher incidence of sick role behavior, as measured by the number of days of restricted activity and bed disability (Nathanson 1975). And although no sex differences are found in compliance with doctors' orders (Waldron and Johnston, 1976), women utilize the health care system more than men (even when controlling for pregnancy).

Women's health, like men's, varies according to the sociological features of their lives. In fact, much of the recent research on women and health reveals a direct link between women's roles and the likelihood of leading healthy lives. Several studies indicate that there are higher rates of reported illness among housewives than among women working outside the home (Nathanson 1980), indicating that employment generally has positive effects upon women's health. Moreover, housewives who have never worked outside the home are healthier than those who once worked but dropped out of the labor force to become full-time homemakers (Welch and Booth 1977). Employed women are also less likely than housewives to act out a sick role, and when employed women are sick, they tend to return to normal activities more quickly than do housewives (Nathanson 1980).

Some have interpreted these variations in health between housewives and employed women as indicating that feelings of self-esteem and accomplishment are the result of working in a society where paid work is the major basis of self-esteem (Nathanson 1980). However, most women's jobs certainly do not afford them the achievement and gratification traditionally associated with men's work; thus, this assumption must be cautiously considered. However, the housewife role in our society is devalued, which is likely to have serious repercussions for women in this position. We do know that, on the average, married women are less happy than single women or married men (Bernard 1971). The stress that they experience may be a contributing factor to their high rates of depression and physical illness.

Recent research also shows that mental health follows gender patterns in society. Most studies indicate higher rates of mental illness for women than for men, at least as indicated by hospital admissions, clinical treatment, and the duration of treatment (Gove and Tudor 1973). Some explain this finding as a result of women's secondary status in society, which, because it produces stress, makes women more mentally ill than men. Others argue that high rates of mental illness among women reflect the fact that women are more likely to report mental problems, seek help, and think of themselves as emotional and lacking self-control (Chesler 1972). This explanation interprets women's higher mental illness rate as the consequence of learned sex role behavior. Both explanations are probably correct, underscoring the point that mental as well as physical health is connected to the status of persons in society. These data suggest the need for change in women's traditional status—a point that is underscored by a recent study showing that women living in nontraditional relationships are less depressed than women living in traditional ones. Men living in nontraditional relationships are more depressed than comparable women (Rosenfeld 1980), which may indicate the personal needs and services that women in traditional relationships provide for men but not for themselves.

Racial oppression in this society further complicates patterns of health in men and women. Even accidents occur in different patterns among whites and blacks. Among black men, for example, death caused by accident is greater than for white men, except in the case of motor vehicle accidents (U.S. Department of Commerce, *Statistical Abstracts of the United States* 1980). Suicide rates among black men are lower than those for white men, although the former rate has risen in recent years; suicide rates for black women are half of those for white women (U.S. Department of Commerce, *Statistical Abstracts of the United States* 1980). It would appear that, although violent death is more common for black Americans, their cultural values prohibit suicidal behavior, which is found more commonly among whites.

Among women, race and social class significantly affect their chances for good health and for exercising some degree of control over their own bodies. For example, race is an important indicator of maternal mortality risk. Up to age forty, nonwhite women are twice as likely to die in childbirth as white women, and nonwhite women aged twenty-five to twenty-nine experience the same risks in childbirth as white women ten years older (Daniels and Weingarten 1979). Moreover, poor and black women do not have the same expectations as white women of being able to alter their birth experiences. As a result, they are less likely to question some of the obstetrical practices (such as separating the mother and newborn baby) that white, middle-class women have challenged (Hurst and Zambrana 1980).

Both historically and now, women of color and poor women have been denied control over their reproductive lives. Studies indicate that very high percentages of poor and minority women have been sterilized, often without their knowing consent. One study, conducted in the 1970s, found that 42.3 percent of the women living in East Harlem had had either a tubal ligation or a hysterectomy. In most cases, the doctor had recommended it to the patient but had given her incorrect information about the consequences (Hurst and Zambrana 1980). Other studies indicate that among samples of welfare mothers, approximately half have been sterilized (Corea 1977); welfare women have had approximately one third more sterilizations that other women (Gordon 1977; Lieberman 1975).

Sex differences in health indicate that our physical well-being is highly dependent on the conditions we face in our social environment and as part of our social roles. This fact is particularly evident when we look at occupational roles and the effect of work on our physical and mental health. And because, as we have seen in Chapter 4, work experience is a function of gender, women's health issues must be seen in the context of their place in the work force.

WOMEN, WORK, AND HEALTH

The mythology of work in this culture is that it provides an avenue for self-expression and the realization of personal goals. In fact, we are coming increasingly to see that work can be hazardous to both physical and mental health. Recent public attention to the toxic chemicals produced in industrial environments has heightened our awareness of the ways in which work environments pose hazards for workers. But until recently, most of the attention to this issue has focused on male workers, just as the male work role has often been cited as a source of anxiety and stress. Investigations by the Occupational Safety and Health Administration (OSHA) have resulted in increased information about the effects of toxic agents, carcinogens, and occupational accidents on the health of workers. Yet, when attention is given to women workers, the major focus is usually only on the dangers to their reproductive health. Studies of occupational health hazards have alerted us to many issues, but there is much to be learned, particularly about the effect of work on physical health.

One place to start is with the definition of work. As with other issues, gender-biased definitions have caused us to ignore the work environments of many women. One telling example comes from recent national surveys of cancer mortality in various occupational groups. These studies typically do not consider housework to be an occupation. Consequently, they have provided no data comparing cancer among housewives and other workers. A recent study shows, however, that housewives have a far greater death rate by cancer than any other occupational group of women (Morton and Ungs 1979). The work that women do in the home exposes them to a wide variety of toxic substances; moreover, none of these substances are subject to the control systems advocated for use in industrial settings, nor are the workers who use them instructed to wear protective equipment or to be periodically screened for toxic contamination. Additionally, although these substances are often used together during household cleaning, no one knows about their potentially hazardous combination. Because housework is seldom considered to be real work, little public attention has been given to the carcinogens and toxic substances used, nor has the high death rate by cancer among housewives been widely discussed.

When considering issues of work and health, it is easy to see that work and gender are closely bound together (Kelly 1979). Work hazards to women are almost exclusively focused on women's reproductive health, underscoring the point that women's roles in production and reproduction are closely intertwined (Petchesky 1979). Interestingly, however, few ever consider how reproductive hazards for men are related to their work (Wright 1979), leading to the erroneous conclusion, based on sexist premises, that only women reproduce. Clearly, occupational toxic agents and carcinogens can equally affect male sperm; yet, protective legislation against reproductive hazards is almost always aimed at female workers. Both the history of protective legislation and its contemporary status reveal this fact.

In the 1920s, the Women's League for Equal Opportunity staunchly opposed the protective legislation proposed by groups such as the Women's Trade Union League and the Consumer League of New York. They argued that consumer restrictions on the conditions of labor should be based upon the nature of the industry, not on the sex of the worker (Stellman 1977:36). Yet, history shows that protective laws apply specifically to women workers. The Supreme Court decision in *Muller* v. *Oregon,* for example, held in 1908 that it was constitutional to restrict the work day to ten hours for women only. Protecting workers from long work days and unhealthy environments is a reasonable action, but when applied only to women, these laws exclude women from jobs under the benign guise of protection (Chavkin 1979).

Contemporary protective legislation has also been used to exclude women from work in trades in which the hazards seem no greater than those in some traditionally sex-segregated female occupations. For instance, Title VII of the 1964 Civil Rights Act prohibited employment discrimination on the basis of sex, race, color, religion, and national origin. Yet, it also provided for bona fide occupational qualification (BFOQ), which made it lawful to hire on the basis of sex when sex is a reasonable qualification for performance on the job (Hill 1979). For instance, the BFOQ clause allowed women to be excluded from jobs exceeding weight-lifting limitations set only for women. That weight restrictions on women's work are based on gender stereotypes is clearly shown by the fact that such restrictions do not appear in occupations (such as waitressing) that are typically female and that involve strenuous physical effort. Subsequent court cases (*Weeks* v. *Southern Bell Telephone and Telegraph Company and Rosenfeld* v. *Southern Pacific Company*) ruled that individual women, like individual men, have to be given the opportunity to show that they are physically qualified for a job (Hill 1979).

The contradictions in protective labor legislation are especially clear in the case of policies alleged to protect women's reproductive health. An increasing number of working women are raising children at the same time. Moreover, more than 40 percent of women who have given birth in recent years also worked during their pregnancies (Hendershot 1977; Petchesky 1979). Arguments in favor of protective laws for women workers rest on the assumption that pregnant women and fetuses are especially susceptible to toxic chemicals, radiation, and other risks. Although there is little doubt that these hazards do affect pregnant women and fetuses (Hunt 1979), the issue is whether they affect the reproductive health of men as well. Legislation or company practices that apply to women only seem to rest on the faulty assumption that only women reproduce. Yet, we have evidence of the damaging effects of lead poisoning on male sperm, the excess of chromosomal aberrations among male vinyl chloride workers, and the causal relationship between the pesticide dibromochloropropane (DBCP) and male sterility (Wright 1979). Moreover, wives of male chloride workers have excessive rates of stillbirths and miscarriages (Infante 1975). Removing only women from jobs in which they may be exposed to these substances clearly does not protect the reproductive health of the population.

Gender-biased assumptions in protective regulations are intricately bound to the sex-segregated character of the labor force. Concern for women's health has not caused companies to remove workers from jobs traditionally considered women's work—in spite of known risks from mutagens, teratogens, and toxic substances that are found in occupations employing mostly women. For example, women who work in hospital operating rooms as nurse-anesthetists, anesthesiologists, and scrub personnel have higher rates of miscarriages and birth malformations than other groups of workers, but no one has argued that women should be excluded from these jobs (Hunt 1979; Wright 1979). Protective policies that restrict women from hazardous jobs seem to emerge only in higher-paying and traditionally male occupations in which women are now beginning to be employed (Chavkin 1979). Other occupations that pose equally serious hazards, but yet are poorly paid and filled by women, are usually excluded from protective legislation. Similarly, risks to the male reproductive system seldom are used to restrict their employment opportunities. In fact, one bizarre suggestion has been made that male workers exposed to sterility-causing DBCP might consider it a novel form of birth control (Wright 1979)!

Obviously, the health risks for both male and female workers are great. OSHA reports that 70,000 chemicals are being used in the workplace and that 2,000 new chemicals are introduced annually (Bell 1979). A 1978 government survey found that 20 percent of all cancer, heart, and lung diseases were attributable to chemicals and pollutants in the work environment and its products (Ortmeyer 1979). This estimate was probably a conservative one because it counted only those cases that could be directly attributed to this cause. Moreover, both men's and women's work involves stress and physical dangers other than toxic risks. Job-related stress leads to an increased risk of disease even without direct physical hazard on the job, and stress can be caused by a host of factors, including monotony, human relations, lack of control over one's work, time demands, insecurity, and relative powerlessness (Stellman 1977).

To limit occupational health hazards solely to women or solely to reproductive effects is to overlook the complexities of work and the various health hazards it creates. Job policies are needed that will protect all workers from health hazards posed by their jobs. Included would be policies that protect the reproductive health of men and women and provide a good system of reproductive leave for both sexes (Wright 1979). Moreover, toxic substances and radiation have a hazardous effect not only on workers in industrial plants but in surrounding communities as well. As Supreme Court Justice Felix Frankfurter said in 1916:

Once we cease to look upon the regulation of women in industry as exceptional, as the law's graciousness to a disabled class, and shift the emphasis from the fact that they are *women* to the fact that it is *industry* and the relation of industry to the community which is regulated, the whole problem is seen from a totally different aspect. (1916:367; cited in Hill 1979)

Discussion of women's health and work also cannot ignore the fact that, in spite of real risks to health posed by contemporary jobs, women who work, as far as we can tell, are healthier on the average than women who do not. Only the future will reveal the long-range effect of carcinogens, toxic substances, and radiation on human life, but current data indicate that employment has positive effects on women's health. There are higher rates of illness among housewives than among women who work for wages, although it is also true that the presence of children in the home makes women less likely to adopt a sick role (Nathanson 1975, 1980). Even with the additional burden of the double day, women who work for wages have better physical and mental health than women who do not.

This finding should not, however, lead us to conclude that women who work for wages are not subjected to stress and dissatisfaction. There is evidence that employed women drink more than unemployed ones, although no association has been found between drinking and the role conflicts experienced by women who are married and working for wages

(Parker 1980). In fact, in spite of the popular image of housewife alcoholics, marital status does not predict alcohol use for women. Among women, the frequency of drinking and the volume of consumption increase with education (Parker 1980).

Surveys of national drinking patterns show that housewives are less likely to be problem drinkers than are other groups of women. However, housewives are more likely to use mood-altering drugs than are working women and, thus, may be more likely to mix alcohol and other drugs (Sandmaier 1980). A 1975 National Opinion Research Center survey found the highest rate of drinking problems among women who were unsuccessfully looking for work, followed by working women who, because of their position in the labor force, face the stress of dead-end, low-income jobs (Sandmaier 1980). But the most marginal female alcoholics are skid row women, whose downward paths seem to begin with marital crises, compared to skid row men, who are more likely to begin their downward mobility following the loss of a job (Garrett and Bahr 1976). It is important to see, though, that in spite of these associations between employment and drinking, the greatest amount of female problem drinking occurs among women aged 18–20 years. Moreover, drinking among young women has dramatically increased in recent years, nearly closing the sex gap between male and female drinkers (Sandmaier 1980).

In sum, research on women's health and their work environments reveals a host of social problems. Although the specific hazards that workers face will vary depending on the type of work and the specific work conditions they face, there is a serious need for careful study of work-related health hazards. Policies that single out women as a restricted class cannot solve this problem, nor can ignoring the complexities of gender relations in the workplace. In the end, safe workplaces, both in industry and in the home, must be constructed for men and women alike. And as this discussion should show, the health issues faced by women at work are integrally tied to their status in the world of work.

THE POLITICS OF REPRODUCTION: ABORTION, BIRTH CONTROL, AND PREGNANCY

The issues of abortion, birth control, and pregnancy are at the heart of feminist politics and are core issues around which feminist analysis has been built. Contemporary feminists see women's right to control their own bodies as essential to the realization of other rights and opportunities in society. As the Boston Women's Health Collective has written, "one of our most fundamental rights as women is the right to choose whether and when to have children. Only when we are in control of that choice are we free to be all that we can be for ourselves, for children we already have or may have in the future, for our partners, for our communities" (1976:216).

Whether a woman experiences any one of these events as stressful or traumatic is at least partially due to the ways in which they are socially organized. Reproduction, although it is a physiological event, stands at the junction of nature and culture (Oakley 1979). Women do not simply get pregnant and give birth in the physical sense alone; they do so within a definite set of social relations (Petchesky 1980). These social arrangements vary not only historically but also cross-culturally. Feminist arguments about the social control of reproduction clearly take this fact into account. As Margaret Mead wrote following her early study of seven Pacific Island cultures:

> Whether childbirth is seen as a situation in which one risks death, or out of which one acquires a baby, or social status, or a right to Heaven, is not a matter of the actual statistics of maternal mortality, but of the view that a society takes of childbearing. Any argument about women's instinctively maternal behavior which insists that in this respect a biological substratum is stronger than every other learning experience that a female child faces, from birth on, must reckon with this great variety in the handling of childbirth. (Mead 1962:221)

Female control of reproduction is cross-culturally and historically the dominant social arrangement (Oakley 1979). Yet, in modern western societies, in the case of pregnancy and other reproductive issues, reproduction is controlled by men. Moreover, traditional social theories have largely ignored the question of reproduction, as if assuming that it is irrelevant in analyses of human experience and social organization.

Feminist perspectives on reproductive issues assert women's right to control their own bodies. Feminists see the medical profession as unresponsive to women's needs and as treating women's bodies as objects for medical manipulation. Not only are feminists distressed by the demeaning treatment women receive in medical institutions, but they are critical of the fact that it is men (either in medicine or in politics) who make decisions about reproductive issues (Ruzek 1978). The feminist position is that it is women's right to choose their reproductive status. Not only do feminists believe in individual rights on reproductive issues, but they also see that reproduction is embedded in systems of social power and social control (Petchesky 1980). The history of reproductive issues and their contemporary manifestations also shows that reproduction is directly entangled with class and race relations, in addition to relations of gender. Recent cutbacks in federal spending on abortion, a recurring history of sterilization abuse, and the manipulation of powerless women for medical experiments are all evidence of the powerlessness of women to control reproduction. This section will review the politics of reproduction focusing on three contemporary issues: birth control, abortion, and pregnancy.

Birth control, although a personal matter, is also controlled by decisions of the state, the social organization of scientific and medical institutions, and the normative system of public values and attitudes. Because birth control regulates sexual activity and population size, its significance extends beyond the individual relationships in which it is actually practiced. Moreover, the availability, form, and cultural significance of birth control bear directly on the role of women in society (Gordon 1977).

Many young women today probably take birth control for granted, although it was not long ago that the right to practice birth control was established in law, especially for the unmarried. A 1965 Supreme Court decision (*Griswold* v. *Connecticut*) established the first constitutional precedent that the use of birth control was a right, not a crime. However, this decision extended only to married persons; not until 1972 (in *Eisenstadt* v. *Baird*) were laws prohibiting the dispensing of contraceptives to any unmarried person, or by anyone other than a physician or pharmacist, held unconstitutional (Goldstein 1979). This decision was introduced following an incident in which Bill Baird, a long-time birth control activist, handed a package of vaginal foam to an unmarried young woman during a lecture on contraception at Boston University. Baird, in violation of a Massachusetts law that prohibited the distribution of nonprescribed contraceptives, was arrested and convicted of a felony before the case reached the Supreme Court.

Prior to the establishment of the constitutional right to birth control, laws varied from state to state and, even in those states where the distribution of birth control devices was legal, actual dispensing depended on the discretion of individual doctors. The effect was to shift the decision regarding birth control from women to men in the medical and judicial professions.

Since the early 1970s, birth control has become widely available, and evidence shows that an increasing number of women and men now engage in sexual intercourse prior to marriage. By age sixteen, one fifth of all American teenagers have had intercourse; by age nineteen, two thirds have had intercourse. Moreover, one in ten women has had at least one pregnancy by age seventeen, and one quarter of all women have had one pregnancy by age nineteen. Of these, eight in ten are premarital pregnancies (Zelnik, Kim, and Kantner 1979).

The high rate of teenage pregnancies has caused much concern over the issue of birth control and the sexual behavior of the young. Between 1971 and 1979, the teenage pregnancy rate doubled (Zelnick and Kantner 1980). In 1978, almost half of all births to women nineteen years old and under were to unmarried women (*New York Times,* October 26, 1981). One frequently asked question about teenage pregnancy is why, now that birth control is available, are these young women not using effective contraceptive methods? Studies show that teenager typically wait for several months after initiating sexual activity before using contraceptives (Zelnik and Kantner 1978). One recent study indicates that one third of teenage patients make their first visit to contraceptive clinics after they suspect that they are pregnant. Only 14 percent make the visit while they are still virgins; the remainder arrive after initiating sexual intercourse, and most of these girls do not seek contraceptive advice until after they have been sexually active for at least three months (Zabin and Clark 1981). This knowledge is particularly unsettling because it is known that one fifth of first premarital pregnancies among teenagers occur within the first month of sexual intercourse; another half occur within the first six months of intercourse (Zabin, Kantner, and Zelnik 1979).

Many have argued that a sociological reason for the nonuse of birth control among young women is that the regular use of contraceptives requires conscious recognition of oneself as sexually active (Luker 1975). Teenage sex tends to be episodic; for a young woman to make calculated plans for contraceptive protection requires her to see herself as a sexually active person. Cultural and legal proscriptions that encourage the denial of sexuality to young women seem likely only to exacerbate this situation.

The Adolescent Family Life law, passed by Congress in 1981, mandates that "caring services" be established to counsel teenage girls. Yet, only one third of the $30 million allocated for this program may be used for preventive services. Thus, "one of the major features of this bill is to promote adoption as a positive option for adolescent parents" (U.S.

Senate Committee on Labor and Human Resources 1981:9). Research does show that more young women are electing to keep their babies, although more are also having abortions (Westoff et al. 1980). But the Adolescent Family Life law prohibits the use of any funds for research on contraceptive development and bars recipients from the use of any funds to provide abortion counseling or services. In fact, the research funds under this act cannot be used for any research on abortion except to demonstrate its consequences—the strong implication being that research will be supported only when it shows the negative consequences of abortion. The law further restricts the options available to teenage women by requiring anyone using these services to inform her parents.

The issue of parental notification is rapidly changing in law and is of the utmost importance to feminists concerned about reproductive choice. In 1976 (*Planned Parenthood of Central Missouri* v. *Danforth*), the Supreme Court struck down a Missouri statute requiring every unmarried minor to have parental consent before having an abortion. The Court argued that minors, like adults, have a constitutional right to abortions; thus, blanket regulations of parental consent are unconstitutional. In 1979, this principle was reaffirmed in *Bellotte* v. *Baird* when a Massachusetts law requiring minors to have the consent of both parents or the authorization of a court, if they refused, was ruled unconstitutional. More recently, however, in a 1981 ruling (*H. L.* v. *Matheson*), the Supreme Court ruled that it is constitutional for a state to require physicians to notify parents of a minor seeking an abortion if the minor is living at home and dependent on them for support, if she does not claim to be mature enough to make the abortion decision on her own, and if she offers no special reasons why her parents should not be told (Donovan 1981). Although these conditions allow some flexibility in the event of such a situation, they obviously place young women in the situation of needing the approval of a court to proceed with an abortion. Court delays make the timeliness of such decisions critical, but, more fundamentally, such decisions clearly take the control of the woman's body out of her hands.

These directions in law are especially troubling when we consider the research on teenage sexuality, contraception, and parental relationships. A recent study shows that procrastination is the teenager's most frequent reason for delay in initiating contraceptive use. But the second most frequent reason is fear that parents will find out. One third of all teenagers delayed going to a clinic for this reason (Zabin and Clark 1981). Regulations that limit the options available to young girls (or anyone else) seem unlikely, then, to solve the problems associated with teenage pregnancy.

Restrictions on women's reproductive freedom are occurring in the context of an antiabortion movement that is attempting to limit further women's rights to choose abortion when necessary. Yet, the majority of American women and men support a woman's right to choose abortion. Recent surveys indicate that 67 percent of women believe that no legal obstacles should be put in the way of women who decide that an abortion is necessary. Thus, although a majority of women (56 percent) believe that abortion is morally wrong, they are in favor of leaving the choice to the individual concerned (*Life* November 1981). Other surveys show that support for abortion varies depending on the reason it is needed. In 1980, 80 percent of the population supported abortion in cases where the mother's health was seriously endangered; 83 percent where pregnancy resulted from rape; 83 percent where there was a serious chance for birth defect; 53 percent where the woman was from a low-income family and could not support any more children; 48 percent in cases where the woman was not married and did not want to marry the man; 47 percent if the woman was married but wanted no more children; and 41 percent for any reason. Moreover, this study shows that support for abortion has risen in the last fifteen years (Granberg and Granberg 1980).

Women's rights to choose abortions were established by the 1973 Supreme Court decision in *Roe v. Wade* and *Doe v. Bolton*. This decision held laws unconstitutional that prohibited abortion except where such laws are restricted to the last three months of pregnancy or to the stage of fetal viability (Goldstein 1979). The Court's decision acknowledged that on the issue of abortion, separately legitimate social concerns collided: (1) the constitutional right to privacy, (2) the right of the state to protect maternal health, and (3) the right of the state to protect developing life. Thus, the Court divided the gestation period into thirds and argued that in the first trimester the woman's right to decide her future privately, without interference from the state, took precedence over the other two rights. In the second trimester, the state cannot deny an abortion, but it can insist upon reasonable standards of medical procedure. In the third trimester, abortion may also be performed to preserve the life or health of the mother.

Although federal regulations on the availability of abortion are rapidly changing, feminists still insist that abortion should be an option for women who want them. Although many feminists may not choose abortions for themselves, they believe that it should be a woman's choice. Moreover, for those who believe that abortion is inherently immoral, feminists point to the historical and cross-cultural record, which indicates great variation in the social meaning and practice of abortion.

In some societies (such as those of Japan and some eastern European countries), abortion is a major method of population control (Luker 1975). And in America, abortion was not viewed as morally wrong (if performed prior to quickening at four or five months) until the second half of the nineteenth century. Prior to that time, abortion was a common practice and was often performed using drugs, potions, techniques, and remedies made popular in home medical guides. Abortion was viewed as relatively safe and was commonly assisted by midwives, "irregular" physicians, and physicians of the period. The earliest laws governing abortion were not enacted until 1821 and 1841, but these laws placed guilt only on those who used particular methods of inducing abortion that were feared unsafe. None of these laws punished women for having abortions; they were intended as regulations to ensure safe methods (Mohr 1978).

In the mid-nineteenth century, abortion became an increasingly widespread phenomenon, especially among white, married, Protestant women. During this period, abortion also became increasingly commercialized. One noted woman entrepreneur, Madame Restell, earned an enormous income from her abortion products and spent as much as $60,000 per year on advertising alone (Mohr 1978). As both the drug industry and the medical profession grew in the second half of the nineteenth century, more profits could be made by companies seizing control of the abortion market. Thus, in addition to eliminating midwives from the practice of abortion, the medical profession created laws and spread propaganda that altered the perception and practice of abortion.

These changes were additionally fueled by shifts in the class, racial, and ethnic structure of American life. The emerging new class of physicians were not only incensed by the flagrant commercialization of abortion, but they expressed the fear that the growing rate of abortion among the middle and upper classes would cause immigrants, blacks, and the poor to outbreed them. Spurred by the growth of Social Darwinism and an increasing nativist movement, the antiabortion crusade appealed to racist fears and portrayed abortion as the work of criminals, backward medical practitioners, and immoral social agents (Mohr 1978). Thus, beginning in the period between 1860 and 1880 and continuing through the first two thirds of the twentieth century, antiabortion policies included strict criminal laws about abortion and put absolute control of abortion in the hands of the medical profession. By these laws, women seeking abortions and their accomplices were defined as guilty of murder, abortion was defined as a criminal act, and the distribution of abortion and birth control information was deemed illegal. The public moralizing about abortion that we see in the late twentieth century has come historically from the emergence of new professional groups seeking to control abortion. Only very recently has abortion been seen as a moral issue stemming from religious beliefs.

The issue of abortion in feminist thought also requires a perspective on racism. The reproductive issues of abortion, birth control, and sterilization have particular significance for women of color. Although the majority of minority women support women's rights to abortion and birth control, history also shows that the birth control movement has been closely linked with racist movements for population control.

In the early twentieth century, when Margaret Sanger was organizing the birth control movement, white birth control reformers were campaigning to prevent so-called racial suicide by allowing the overpopulation of blacks, immigrants, the poor, and social misfits (Davis 1981; Gordon, 1977). The campaign for birth control was interwoven with genocidal movements to eliminate racial groups, and appeals for birth control were clearly intended to limit what was perceived as overbreeding among the poor. Sanger herself made this appeal part of her campaign and, thus, seemed to support the racist goals of the eugenics movement.

In the contemporary record, information on the sterilization of minority and poor women confirms that birth control and population control are often linked. As we have already seen, sterilization rates are highest among black and Puerto Rican women and female welfare recipients. In addition, a 1976 study reveals that 24 percent of all native American women of childbearing age have been sterilized (Davis 1981). These data raise the issue of the blurred distinction between forced and voluntary sterilization. Although forced sterilization is illegal, reports indicate that doctors and clinics do give misleading information to minority and poor clients. Although clients may technically agree to the procedure, they have frequently been misled or misinformed.

A noted example is found in the case of Minnie and Mary Alice Relf, twelve- and fourteen-year-old black girls. In 1973, their mother was told by the family planning clinic in Montgomery, Alabama, to sign a form authorizing shots for them. The girls had already been given the drug

Depo-Provera as a birth control measure, but the Montgomery clinic ordered that they be sterilized when this drug was found to cause cancer in animals (Davis 1981). The mother was led to believe that, in signing the authorization form, she was agreeing to more shots, but when it was learned that they had been permanently sterilized, a suit was filed against the clinic. The Southern Poverty Law Center, filing suit, contended that the agency had performed the operation because the girls were alledgedly "mentally retarded" and that, with "boys hanging around," sterilization was the most convenient method to prevent pregnancy (Corea 1977).

Subsequent federal investigations revealed a high incidence of sterilization of minors in other government-sponsored clinics. These incidents and a general history of the association among racism, sterilization, and birth control raise serious questions about contemporary findings that the hysterectomy rate among never-married black women is three to four times higher than that of never-married white women and that the hysterectomy rate for all women is highest in the South (Alan Gutmacher Institute, 1981). The politics of sterilization, coupled with the experimentation on Third World women for contraceptive development, indicates that racism is institutionalized in the health care system. Birth control, including abortion, is a necessary condition for the emancipation of women, but from a feminist and nonracist perspective, it must be a matter of choice. Reproductive issues are central to feminist analyses for change, and they are a clear case in which decisions made by men in the political, scientific, and medical communities take power away from women to direct their own lives. The next section will review the history of the medical profession and its control of female reproduction. The chapter will then conclude with a review of the contemporary institution of medicine and the role of women within it.

HISTORICAL PERSPECTIVES ON REPRODUCTION AND CHILDBIRTH

The emergence of modern medicine is usually seen as a conquest of ignorance and a triumph over superstition. Modern medical men are imbued with high status in our society and are perceived as learned, rational, and wise. Women also tend to view their doctors as explorers, pioneers, or therapists (Wolfson 1970), thus creating an image of the doctor as caring and adventurous at the same time that he is all-knowing and authoritative. Yet, there was a time when healing was almost solely the province of women. Particularly in matters of birth and child-rearing, women were perceived as the experts and birth was a female-centered, home affair (Dye 1980). Until the nineteenth century in this country, women presided over most births, in the presence of female friends and kin who provided comfort and aid to the childbearing woman (Wertz and Wertz 1977).

This section will review how men came to dominate the medical profession and to define and control the process of childbirth. Because childbirth was originally placed in the hands of women as midwives, developments in the history of childbirth provide a case study in which what was once a female-oriented process has come to be dominated and controlled by men. Although this section focuses primarily on childbirth, it also reveals more general patterns in the emergence of modern medicine. In the end, we will see how particular characteristics of medicine as an institution still take control of reproduction away from women.

Childbirth has a distinctive social history and one that is tied to the emergence of medicine as a profession, as well as to changes in the ideology and structure of women's roles in society. In colonial America, childbirth occurred in the home and in the presence of female family members and friends (Dye 1980; Scholten 1977). During this period, six to eight pregnancies were typical for women, as was a fear of pain and the possibility of death in childbirth. Female midwives who attended births generally practiced noninterventionist methods of delivery and, along with the other females present, provided comfort and emotional support for the laboring mother (Wertz and Wertz 1977). Records of the midwives' practices, successes, and failures are hard to find in this period, so it is difficult to know exactly how skilled or knowledgeable they were. Yet, information and experiences about childbirth were shared by women, and there is little indication in the historical record that midwives posed dangers for childbearing women. There are no recorded epidemics of puerperal fever, such as those that killed thousands of women when birth was moved to hospitals, and there are few recorded instances of midwives' incompetence in the colonial period (Wertz and Wertz 1977). Without romanticizing midwives and the process of birth, it appears that, unlike images of midwives that appeared later with the advent of scientific medicine, "the stereotype of the midwife as a curse upon women seems unfitting for colonial midwives" (Wertz and Wertz 1977:13).

Nevertheless, the pain associated with childbirth was a significant factor in women's desire for alternative practices. New interventionist techniques promised by the male founders of medical science appealed to women who sought relief from long and difficult labors. So, beginning in the mid-eighteenth century, a slow transition occurred in which birth was shifted from female to male control. American medical men took their lead from French and English physicians, who described the body as being like a machine and developed instruments or tools to intervene in natural bodily processes. Tools (such as forceps) promised to shorten labor and to make difficult labors more manageable, although such techniques were generally resisted by American and English women midwives, who believed that these techniques introduced new dangers and unsafe procedures to the natural process of birth.

In the mid-eighteenth and early nineteenth centuries, there was an open market for both female midwives and the medical men who were developing new birth techniques. Advances in knowledge about the physiology of labor, as well as various birth techniques, were taught in medical colleges—most of which were located in England and France. American men learned from these colleges but, because the government provided no financial support for medical education, women, with fewer financial resources than men, did not attend. However, medical education during this period was notoriously poor (Dye 1980), and many have argued that female midwives continued to have greater skills in birth, based on their practical experience, than did medically trained men (Ehrenreich and English 1978).

By the mid-nineteenth century, medical men had adopted an increasingly interventionist approach toward birth, whereas female midwives relied more upon the normal course of delivery. As an aside, Mary Wollstonecraft (1759–1797), an outspoken English feminist whom we will study in Chapter 9, deplored the takeover of childbirth by men and insisted that her daughter, Mary Shelley (author of *Frankenstein*), be born with a woman attendant. When the placenta was not delivered, a male midwife was called in, who, upon inserting his hand to withdraw it, caused Wollstonecraft to hemorrhage and later to die of puerperal fever. (Flexner 1972; Wertz and Wertz 1977). Studies indicate that, although physicians gained greater control of childbirth during this period, as late as the early twentieth century, midwives had high status

in their communities (Litoff 1978), maintained their own apprentice-
ship systems (Mongeau, Smith, and Maney 1961), and had better mortality records than medical men (Dye 1980).

Transformations in childbirth that ultimately resulted in the medical
model of contemporary birth were accelerated in the mid-nineteenth
century, when obstetrics was first developed as a medical specialty and
when Victorian cultural attitudes transformed bourgeois notions of
female sexuality. During the Victorian period, pregnancy was treated,
in the middle and upper classes, with shame and concealment. Because
the Victorian period severely restricted women's sexuality and because
pregnancy directly acknowledged their sexual activity, it became an
event to be hidden and concealed. For example, it is reported that Susan
B. Anthony's mother was embarrassed by her pregnancy (Wertz and
Wertz 1977). Like other bourgeois Victorian women, she disappeared
from public view when she was pregnant.

At the same time, the emergence of the medical profession provided
status to those classes that could afford new medical treatments. Families who could pay for it, especially in urban areas, began to go to medical specialists. Obstetrics was one of the first of these specialties,
although most women continued to employ women midwives because
they were more trusting of their noninterventionist techniques and more
comfortable in their modesty with other women (Bogdan 1978). Physicians themselves stated that medical midwifery was the key to a successful practice because, if they could eliminate midwives, it would be
a dependable market and its uncharted knowledge provided a chance
for the expansion of the physician's career (Barker-Benfield 1976;
Scholten 1977). In keeping with the Victorian sensibilities of the time,
the typical obstetrican (so renamed from male midwives to symbolize
their alleged professionalism) draped his client in cloth and avoided
looking at her body. Consequently, obstetrics with middle and upper-
class clients was commonly practiced by touch alone. Obstetricians thus
gained little knowledge of their female patients and relied upon experiments on poor and black women to advance their field. Following the
Civil War, maternity hospitals were established as charitable asylums
for poor and unmarried pregnant women. Stating that such places
would provide a more moral and sanitary environment than their own
homes, doctors provided free medical treatment for poor women (often
servants of the upper classes) in return for using these patients as
research subjects (Wertz and Wertz 1977). Because the physicians
would have violated the "ladylike" codes of the period by actually

examining an affluent woman's body, poor, black, and immigrant women in the charity hospital became research subjects for medical treatment and observation.

One of the most outrageous cases of experimentation is found in the practice of J. Marion Sims, originator of gynecology and early president of the American Medical Association. One of his early claims to fame was the discovery of ways to suture tears that occurred between the vagina and bladder and the vagina and anus. He developed these techniques by purchasing black female slaves, whom he kept in hospital quarters that he built in his own yard. Because he saw black slaves as enduring, passive, and helpless, he performed countless experimental operations on them without anesthesia. The pain he inflicted on them had to create unimaginable agony, yet this seemed not to faze him in his obsessive search for techniques to build his own career (Barker-Benfield 1976). Nor did it seem to bother upper-class women, who later erected a statue to him in Central Park because of their gratitude for his surgical method! (They, of course, experienced it only after the development of anesthesia.)

Sims, like other medical men of his day, believed that women's psychology stemmed from their sex organs, and he was anxious to perform clitoridectomies and oophorectomies (removal of the clitoris and ovaries). His drastic use of the knife seemed intended not for the betterment of women, but for the enhancement of his own career, because an aspiring specialist, then as now, made his name through the invention and publication of new techniques. Indeed, as one historian has noted, the operating rooms where female surgery was performed in the nineteenth century were essentially "an arena for an exchange between men" (Barker-Benfield 1976:101). Sims, in fact, developed gynecological procedures as if he were an explorer charting new frontiers; his own writings clearly show this to be his own metaphor about his work. He was the first to develop the speculum and says of it, "Introducing the bent handle of a spoon, I saw everything as no man had ever seen before. . . . I felt like an explorer in medicine who first views a new and important territory" (Barker-Benfield 1976:95). Other medical men, too, declared his "speculum to be to diseases of the womb . . . what the compass is to the mariner" (Barker-Benfield 1976:95).

The removal of childbirth from the home and the control of women contradicted the Victorian point of view that birth was a private matter, to be conducted in secrecy and within the domestic world. So, initially, delivery by men was seen as a breakdown of moral standards and an offense to female delicacy (Donegan 1978). But over time, as doctors promised safer and less painful births, women began to desire the new techniques they were offered. Most women wanted less painful childbirth, although in the late nineteenth century, the absence of pain in childbirth was associated with supposedly precivilized women—especially Indians and blacks. Racism in the middle and upper class defined more "primitive" peoples as closer to nature and, therefore, unlikely to experience childbirth pain. Thus, from the racist perspective of the bourgeois class, to experience pain and, therefore, to need relief from it became a sign of one's civilized nature. Needing relief from childbirth pain was also an indication of the social distance of the upper and middle classes from other strata of the society. Pain, then, became a mark of the "truly feminine"—a fact with its own paradoxical truth because childbirth pain and complications were greatly increased by the "civilized" practices of tight corsets, lack of exercise, fashionable illness, and airless rooms (Wertz and Wertz 1977).

Nonetheless, rather than change their cultural habits, middle- and upper-class women sought relief from childbirth pain and, thus, became more interested in the promises of modern medicine. But promises were all many of these techniques remained, for although they may have alleviated extreme pain, there is little evidence that childbirth was made any safer by medical men of the early twentieth century. Puerperal fever, later found to be caused by infections generated by unsanitary hospital procedures and interventionist techniques, became a major cause of maternal death (Wertz and Wertz 1977). Epidemics of puerperal fever killed thousands of women who sought painless deliveries through hospital births.

The number of births occurring in hospitals increased rapidly after the 1930s. Prior to this time, hospital birth had been primarily an urban phenomenon and, even there, had occurred on a large scale beginning only in the twentieth century. In 1930, only about 25 percent of all births took place in hospitals; by 1970, over 95 percent of all births occurred in hospitals (Wertz and Wertz 1977). Hospital births represent the ultimate transformation of birth from a female-centered, home activity to one that is male controlled and medically defined. The prevalence of hospital births followed a direct assault on women midwives in the second half of the nineteenth century, when propaganda to make women fear pregnancy and legislation to eliminate midwives combined to generate new definitions of women's place in childbirth and, more generally in medicine (Barker-Benfield 1976). Legislation between

1900 and 1930 made licensing for midwives a necessity. However, to obtain a license, midwives were required to get vouchers of their moral character from a member of the medical profession, to have their homes and outfits inspected by a physician's nurse, and to have attended births under the supervision of a physician. Because few physicians would provide these credentials, the number of practicing midwives radically declined. In New York City, for example, the number of practicing midwives declined from 3,000 in 1908 to 270 in 1939, 2 in 1957, and 1 in 1963 (Barker-Benfield 1976). Moreover, in most cases, women were excluded from medical schools and, if they wanted to enter the health care system, were relegated to secondary status as nurses (Ehrenreich and English 1978). Childbirth and, more generally, women's health had effectively been placed in the hands of male physicians.

The movement of childbirth to hospitals and medical men was further increased by popular racist fears of contagion and germs that were associated with poor, immigrant, and black people. The fads of genetic science and Social Darwinism of the 1920s and 1930s increased middle-class fears of associating with those from the lower strata of society. Coupled with the home economics movement of the 1920s that defined home environments as sources of germs and disease (see Chapter 5), popular opinions laced with racist and class ideologies further generated a social definition of childbirth as a scientific event to be placed under the authority of medical men.

Several features of modern medical practice emerged from these historical developments. They included the consolidation of medical authority, the subordination of woman-centered medical practices, a technological and mechanistic view of birth and women's bodies, hospital-centered childbirth, interventionist practices in childbirth and delivery, and the attitude that professional men know best how to respond to women's health.

These characteristics can each be seen in the way that childbirth is now routinely handled by the medical profession. It is, of course, located in hospitals, where doctors and the staff they control have final authority over delivery procedures. Recently, in the advent of the feminist health movement and the establishment of alternative birthing centers, some hospitals have established birthing rooms designed to provide more homelike atmospheres for delivering parents. But even in these rooms, ultimate authority lies with the physician, who may (and does) intervene in the birth process at any point.

Thus, the interventionist practices characterizing the rise of male

control over childbirth continue to dominate women's childbirth experiences. This fact is especially evident in the dramatic increase in the
number of cesarean sections being performed in hospitals throughout
the country. The National Center for Health Statistics states that since
1953, cesarean sections have increased from 3.7 percent of all births to
13.9 percent in 1978 (Corea 1980). Some hospitals report that as many
as one quarter of all births are performed by cesarean section (Corea
1980). In an age when childbirth is supposed to be safer and less threatening than in previous years, how do we explain the high proportion of
births using a process that clearly increases the risks to both mother
and child?

Researchers cite the routine practices of technological monitoring of
birth as contributing significantly to the increase in cesarean births.
Although some also mention physicians' greed for higher compensation
and their desire for predictable schedules as contributing to the incen-
tives to perform cesareans, it seems most likely that the social organization of childbirth around technological intervention is responsible for
the increase. Typically, the process of labor is now observed by an electronic fetal monitoring device that not only replaces the monitoring
originally performed by nurses but also keeps the laboring woman passively strapped to the device and immobile throughout the course of
labor. Even though changes in the baby's breathing and heartbeat are
routine features of the birth process, the close detection of these changes
by the electronic fetal monitor results in a high number of false indications of fetal distress (Corea 1980). Because of this situation, which
is complicated by doctors' fears of malpractice if an actually distressed
fetus is missed, doctors seem to react quickly to the slightest indication
of change in the fetal condition by performing a vast number of unnec-
essary cesarean sections.

Other practices in the obstetric management of birth have also been
criticized, including the separation of the mother and infant immediately following birth (Rossi 1977), the overuse of anesthetics that affect
the infant's nervous system, and the widespread use of birth positions
that immobilize the mother and increase the incidence of episiotomies
(Wertz and Wertz 1977). All of these practices contribute to better
hospital management, but they pose clear risks for mothers and their
children. Thus, it appears that in modern medical practice, the social
organization of hospital routines takes precedent over maternal and
infant well-being. Moreover, the expectation is that maternity clients
should maintain a passive attitude while trusting in the doctor's author-

ity and knowledge. This attitude is clearly conveyed by the following advice to pregnant women:

Because having a baby is such an important and unique event in life, possibly the greatest adventure in attaining complete womanhood, this time should be one of the most happy and exciting of your life, free of fear and worry and fully explained and understood.

We doctors who have worked together to make this experience and education available to you do so not only because we are spokesmen for other doctors, but, more important, because we are speaking for all mankind. . . . There is no substitute for "your" doctor's personal touch. (Record jacket, "Maternity and Motherhood," 1969).

Women have become increasingly critical of the conditions surrounding childbirth, and many groups have organized to create out-of-hospital birthing centers, more licensing and increased use of midwives, and greater consumer education to enhance women's control over childbirth. Although some reforms are being introduced, feminists argue that the process of childbirth still remains one of the fundamental ways in which women's reproductive abilities are subordinated to the definitions, practices, and controls of men. In the concluding section, we will look at the character of the modern medical profession and women's place within it.

WOMEN AND THE MEDICAL PROFESSION

When a woman seeks medical care from a physician, there are 93 chances out of 100 that the person she sees will be a man (U.S. Department of Commerce, *Statistical Abstracts of the United States* 1980). This fact is especially significant because women utilize the health care system more than do men, as measured by physician visits, hospital admissions, and the prescription of drugs (Nathanson 1975; U.S. Department of Commerce, *Statistical Abstracts of the United States* 1980; Wolcott 1979). Women's health care is intricately interwoven with the power of men in medicine and with profit structure of modern medicine. These factors influence the client-physician relationship, the quality of care received, and the status of women workers within the health care system. Feminist criticism of medical institutions is a response to both its political and its economic structure.

The most immediate context in which power relations can be seen in medicine is the doctor-patient relationship. Because two thirds of patient visits are by women (Walsh 1977) and 93 percent of doctors are men, this relationship is likely to reflect the gender roles in society as well as the roles of professionals and their clients. Both the doctor and the patient are likely to have expectations of the other that are conditioned by the status each occupies. We have already seen that women tend to see their doctors as explorers, pioneers, or therapists; doctors, on the other hand, are likely to see illness among their women patients as psychologically based (Wallen 1979). These definitions reflect gender role expectations because they indicate that male doctors are not taking women patients seriously, whereas women tend to view their doctors as all-knowing. In fact, an early study determined that clinicians (in this case, psychiatrists, psychologists, and social workers) held different standards of health for men and for women. Their concepts of healthy men were similar to their concepts of sex-unspecified healthy adults. But their concepts of healthy women were that they were submissive, not independent or adventurous, unaggressive, easily influenced, excitable, easily hurt, emotional, conceited about their appearance, and not objective (Broverman et al. 1970). If these definitions guide physicians' treatment of their clients, we would expect physicians to cure them according to gender role expectations that they think are appropriate.

Complicating this possibility is the fact that in medical schools, physicians are trained to view their patients as individual cases, not as representatives of their social structural milieu. Consequently, doctors sometime advise patients based on their conventional wisdom (Barrett and Roberts 1978). Particularly because the physician's background is likely to entail gendered assumptions about male and female patients, the advice he gives is influenced by sex-stereotypic roles and norms. Studies indicate that male doctors encourage male patients to see their problems as stemming from job stress, while locating women's problems in their family roles. Moreover, doctors are prone to view women's complaints as psychosomatic, leading them to prescribe psychotherapy instead of situational or structural changes that might alleviate their difficulties. Because of the physicians' tendencies to view cases as individual pathologies, neither male nor female patients are encouraged to consider the social structural origins of their difficulties (Barrett and Roberts 1978; Lorber 1975).

Other research reveals similar problems in doctor-patient consultations. Observations of consulting patterns reveal that women are given less complete and shorter explanations of their medical problems than are men, in spite of the fact that women ask more questions of their doctors. Because they are more inquisitive but receive less information, women experience frustration in their encounters with doctors. Because doctors see female illness as psychologically caused, they are also more pessimistic about the patients' recovery and, thus, give them less information about their condition (Wallen 1979).

The stereotypic attitudes of male doctors toward their women patients are consistent with the images of women encouraged in medical schools and in medical advertising. Medical texts, particularly in the area of gynecology, depict women as nurturing, passive, and powerless (Scully and Bart 1973). Medical advertisements typically show women as depressed, sullen, and afraid. There is also a strong association between the type of illness and the sex of the patient in medical ads. Women are shown as suffering from emotional illness, whereas men are seen as suffering from organic illness (Prather and Fidell 1975). These advertisements also play on cultural stereotypes, with men depicted in work settings and women shown in domestic roles or glamorous fashion poses (Mhant and Darroch 1975). Among other things, these images and sex role stereotypes, coupled with the profit structure of medical industries, have encouraged an extremely high rate of prescribed psychoactive drug use among women.

Testimony before the House Select Committee on Narcotics Abuse and Control in 1978 reveals that 42 percent of women, compared to 26 percent of men, have used prescribed tranquilizers; 21 percent of women and 17 percent of men have been prescribed sedatives; and, 17 percent of women as compared to 8 percent of men have used prescribed amphetamines (Wolcott 1979). Health professionals estimate that between 1 and 2 million women are addicted to legal drugs (Wolcott 1979). In part, the high rates of legal drug use are attributable to the belief that rising standards of living and technological advancement make relief available for every disease (Klass 1975). But the higher rates of legitimate drug use by women require a gender-specific explanation as well.

The example of Valium provides a case for examination. Valium (generically labeled diazepam) is the most frequently prescribed drug in the United States (Cant 1979). It is a minor tranquilizer that works as a central nervous system depressant. Valium is prescribed for a variety of reasons, including muscle relaxation, antianxiety, alcohol withdrawal, and the prevention of epileptic seizures (Pecis 1979). But for most users, Valium is taken in an attempt to overcome personal troubles.

The use of Valium is a societal issue as well, for it is tied to the gender relations between women and their physicians and, more broadly, to the political-economic structure of medicine. Research suggests that Valium is prescribed more often for women because they are more likely to seek help for their problems than are men (Nathanson 1975). Women are more free, because of their social roles, to report pain and seek help than are men, and physicians expect women to be emotional and men stoic (Cooperstock 1971). An alternative perspective is that, because of structured inequality, women's roles are more stressful and, consequently, women have more real complaints (Fidell 1973). A gender role perspective is helpful for putting medical issues in the context of how men and women define each other. But the roles alone do not explain the high rates of legitimate drug use by women or the broader issues of women's care in the medical system.

In the case of Valium, powerful economic and political interests capitalize on women as a market for a drug that brings massive profits to its producers. In 1975, it was estimated that the raw materials for Valium cost $87 per kilo; packaging and production cost an additional $487 per kilo. But the final retail price for this amount was $11,000—140 times the cost of materials and 20 times the total production cost (Pecis 1979; Pekkanen 1975). A large part of the cost of producing Valium is in advertising the drug to physicians; in 1973, 98 percent of Valium's wholesale price went to promotion and profit (Pekkanen 1975). Including other drugs, drug companies spend an average of $3,500 per physician per year promoting the sale of their products (McKinley 1978).

Because women constitute a majority of physician clients, they create a captive market for medical and drug establishments. Because women are reluctant to criticize their doctors, the medical profession is able to maintain its authority, while not challenging the societal basis of sex role stereotypes and the profit structure of medical practice. In sum, the problems of women's health care are manifested in the doctor-patient relationship but, ultimately, have their basis in the power of men in medical institutions and the profit structure of the medical profession.

The interaction of male power and profit systems is even more clear when we consider the status of women workers in the health care field. Women constitute 87 percent of health care workers (Walsh 1977); yet, they are systematically found in the least prestigious and most poorly paid positions in this field. Among doctors, women constitute a seven percent minority; among nurses, women are 98 percent of registered nurses, 10 percent of whom are black (Grimm 1978). Clearly, a sex-tracked system is at work wherein women become excluded from the upper echelons of medical care and are heavily concentrated in those positions that tend to be service-oriented.

Women who are nurses do not face the problem of existing in a male-dominated occupation, but their position relative to that of male professionals creates its own set of problems. Moreover, minority women and men in these fields also face the problems of racism and discrimination, which hamper their career development. Studies indicate that male physicians tend to think of themselves as leaders and of nurses and paramedics as their employees (Bates 1970). Consequently, nurses and other health care workers are put in a position in which male professionals hold authority over them, in addition to receiving greater material benefits. Moreover, men who do enter nursing tend to progress to higher echelons than women within the profession (compounding the problem of sexism that women in this field face (Grimm and Stern 1974). Research also shows that salaries in the nursing profession tend to be insensitive to the amount of experience one has had; for example, one survey finds that the difference between starting and maximum median wages for all status levels within nursing does not exceed 20 percent (Godfrey 1974).

Some have explained the poor salaries of nurses as a result of their lack of ambition. But this assumption is not supported by surveys that show that although more than half of male nurses believe that men have greater professional dedication than women, only 15 percent of female nurses hold this view (Lynn 1975). Moreover, although men are likely to believe that women nurses prefer male supervisors, 60 percent of female nurses disagree. More male nursing administrators (56 percent) than female administrators (39 percent) believe that the entry of men to nursing will upgrade the profession (Lynn 1975). Moreover, female nursing administrators are more likely aware that men are paid more than women for the same work. Women nursing administratiors are also more likely to believe that women are just as effective as men (Lynn 1975).

These data suggest that women nurses face sexist attitudes that define their work as less valuable than that of men. Moreover, on the job, nurses are subordinate to the doctor's authority; countless accounts have described the sexist putdowns, innuendoes, and insults that some doctors direct toward the nursing staff. More generally, physicians maintain a monopoly over medical knowledge and medical practice, even though nurses have more actual contact with hospitalized patients (Ehrenreich and English 1973).

The subordination of the nursing profession to the authority of doctors has resulted in a split between the activities of curing and caring. Stereotypically, nurses are alleged to provide nurturing, whereas doctors maintain the expertise in healing. Such a myth not only belittles the professional knowledge of nurses but also creates an atmosphere that may not work in the best interest of patients. As alternative medical practices have shown, a patient's health involves a complex configuration of physiological, emotional, and social systems. It would appear that a more useful system of medicine is one that integrates the process of healing with the complexities emerging from the interaction of these systems.

Among women who enter higher-status jobs (such as that of physician), most end up in the least prestigious specialties, such as pediatrics, obstetrics/gynecology, and general practice. There is, however, evidence of a recent change in this regard. By 1977, women comprised 24.7 percent of first-year medical students (Dubé 1977). In fact, between 1969 and 1976, the number of women in medical schools tripled; since 1959, the number of women in medical school has increased 700 percent (Walsh 1977). Because of the long period of training, internship, and residence, the impact of these changes on the composition of practicing physicians may not yet have been felt. Some data also show a growing tendency for women to enter traditionally male specialties (Kehrer 1976), although the percentage of women on medical faculties has remained unchanged since 1971 (Walsh 1977).

Some see these changes as signs of major breakthroughs for women in medicine, but this generation is not the first to witness such changes. At the turn of the twentieth century, women were a much larger proportion of all physicians, with some cities reporting almost 20 percent of all physicians to be women (Walsh 1977). The entry of women to medicine is historically closely aligned with feminism and the new opportunities it encouraged for women. Although the feminist movement at the turn of the century was quite different from contemporary feminism, it did encourage women, at least of the upper and middle classes, to use their skills, especially in areas perceived as helping professions. Since the turn of the century, women have been excluded from medicine through overt discrimination denying them entrance to medical schools and professional assignments and through informal practices whereby they received encouragement or support, were channeled into nursing schools, encountered hostility from peers, and were excluded from the old boy network that placed persons in their careers.

Women's lower status in the medical profession is often explained as the result of conflicts they experience in their family and work roles. For instance, some claim that women choose less prestigious specialties to accommodate their families, by working fewer hours and with less professional commitment. Yet, data on this point are contradictory (Lorber 1975), and recent surveys show an increase in full-time employment among female physicians (Mandelbaum 1978).

More pertinent to the status of women as physicians is a consideration of the structure of medical education and medical work as creating obstacles to women's advancement. Research cites the lack of sponsorship, sexual tracking systems, nonsupportive peer environments, and overt ridicule as contributing to the demise of women's medical careers (Lorber 1975). Yet, recently, there has been a reduction in women's attrition rates in medicine (Walsh 1977) as government policies prohibiting sex discrimination have disrupted the autonomy of male-dominated professional enterprises. Moreover, the current women's movement has helped create a climate of mutual support among women students and professionals, leading to the creation of an environment more conducive to women's success. Only the future will show us if these recent changes will continue to be effective in enhancing women's status. The historical record of women's decline in medical careers indicates that none of these gains can be taken for granted. Continual lobbying, network building among women, and federal support for women's medical education are all necessary for stabilizing the role of women in this profession.

CONCLUSION: THE WOMEN'S HEALTH MOVEMENT

The women's health movement has suggested various alternatives to traditional medical care, ranging from more consumer information to feminist self-help clinics (Ruzek 1978). As a social movement, the women's health movement is founded in reaction to the sexism of the medical profession and on criticism of traditional medical practices that deny women control of their own reproductive lives and physical health.

Although much of the women's health movement remains at the level of criticism, numerous groups are also organized to provide health care to women without the high-handed authority of traditional medical practitioners. Many of these organizations disseminate health care information, some offer direct services, and others work primarily as lobbying organizations, attempting to create changes in the health care system and its policies.

Altogether, the women's health movement has the goals of reducing differences in knowledge between patient and practitioner, challenging the mandate of physicians as the sole providers of health care, reducing the professional monopoly over goods and services, increasing the number of women practitioners, and organizing clients around health issues (Ruzek 1978). Whether the women's health movement can be successful in its goals remains to be seen. But its emergence is indicative of the dissatisfaction women have faced in health care institutions and over issues involving reproduction and health. As this chapter has shown, feminist perspectives on health and reproduction insist on women's right to control their own bodies. As long as the power to control women's bodies remains in the hands of men, feminists are likely to continue organizing on these issues.

WOMEN, CRIME, AND DEVIANCE

INTRODUCTION

On July 8, 1978, Bernadette Powell shot and killed her husband, Herman Smith. Powell's case became a feminist cause when it became known that Smith had frequently beaten her. Prior to her husband's death, Powell had obtained orders of protection from the family court and a divorce. One police officer testified in the later trial that he had suffered two cracked ribs when he once tried to arrest Smith for beating his wife. According to the trial evidence, on the night of the murder, after she picked him up from a card and drinking party, Smith allegedly pulled a gun on his wife and drove her around for hours, threatening to have her pumped full of heroin so that he could get custody of their children. She shot him several hours after he had kept her locked up in a motel room near the town where they both lived.

The prosecuting attorney in Powell's trial based much of his case on discrediting Powell's character. He asked if she didn't enjoy the beatings and if, in fact, she encouraged them. Her ex-husband was portrayed as a man who never got a break from a "castrating and manipulative" wife. Feminist supporters of Bernadette Powell were outraged when it was learned that the prosecuting attorney himself had just been divorced by his wife, following her numerous allegations (available in the files of the New York Supreme Court) that he had repeatedly hit, beat, and violently pushed her. Bernadette Powell, prosecuted by this man, was convicted of second-degree murder and sentenced to fifteen years in prison (Jones 1980).

Is Powell a victim of crime, or is she a violent murderer? Is her case indicative of the system of justice operating against the interests of women, or is it simply an example of rising rates of female crime? Whether her act was justified is also an important concern, although we will not discuss that issue here. But her case points to some of the complexities involved in a discussion of gender and crime.

Powell's case indicates that patterns in female crime are strongly connected to gender relations, and it is one of many situations in which women have killed their husbands after being repeatedly beaten and victimized. Moreover, Powell's case shows how sociological characteristics such as gender, as well as race and class, influence the judicial process and the treatment of women by the courts. Finally, Powell's case raises questions about recent increases in the female crime rate, causing us to wonder if women are becoming more criminally active or if they are simply more likely to be detected than in prior years.

This chapter begins with a review of sociological perspectives on crime and deviance, particularly as they have been developed to explain criminal and deviant behavior among women. Two sections follow that discuss women and social deviance and women and crime, respectively. As each of these sections will show, many of the assumptions made about female crime and deviance are based on gender expectations about women's roles in society. Furthermore, patterns of gender relations are also reflected in the actual crimes that women commit. The feminist movement has called attention to the fact that gender relations in this society generate a high degree of violence against women. The fourth section of this chapter reviews information on women as victims of crime and discusses the theoretical perspectives used to explain violence against women. Finally, women's position within the criminal justice system is discussed, particularly as the system treats women offenders. Throughout this chapter, we will see how crime is defined in relationship to gender, and is also complicated by race and social class.

SOCIOLOGICAL PERSPECTIVES ON WOMEN, CRIME, AND DEVIANCE

Female crime and deviance have only recently come to the attention of academic scholars. A few early studies (Lombroso 1920; Pollak 1950; Thomas 1923) of women's crime and deviance appear in the sociological literature, but most of them depict female deviance as rooted in their biological and psychological predispositions. Contemporary research has taken a critical examination of these assumptions as a starting point for analysis. Examining these early assumptions, thus, guides this review of contemporary issues surrounding crime and deviance among women.

Lombroso's work in the 1920s, although by now discredited, was one of the earliest studies of female crime. His highly racist and sexist ideas viewed crime as biologically based on differences between women and men, whites and blacks, the fit and the unfit. Lombroso believed that crime represented the survival of primitive traits; thus, his theory was explicitly linked to popular racist and sexist notions of the time (Higham 1965). Specifically, his explanation of female crime was based on the notion that women (and nonwhites) are less highly evolved than white men and, thus, are more susceptible to primitive urges. He also depicted women as less varied in their mental capacities and, generally, more passive and sedentary than men (Klein 1980). As he said, "Even the female criminal is monotonous and uniform compared with her male companion, just as in general woman is inferior to man" (1920:122, cited in Klein 1980:78).

In Lombroso's work, the cause of crime is located within individuals, not within their social circumstances. In the work of W. I. Thomas, a sociologist, more attention is paid to the role of social circumstances in producing crime. Thomas's work is central to contemporary perspectives on crime and deviance in that he establishes the theoretical and methodological foundation for the Chicago School of sociology and for what later became symbolic interactionism. This perspective sees deviance in terms of the social meaning it acquires and, therefore, is the basis for what is called *labeling theory*. Labeling theory suggests that deviance is in the eyes of the beholder. Those who are labeled as deviants may or may not have actually committed deviant acts, but if they are treated as deviant by the agents of the criminal justice system, then they may acquire deviant identities (Becker 1963). Although much of Thomas's work on the significance of meaning in attributing deviance to persons is of great importance to sociological thinking, his work on female deviance is seriously flawed because, like Lombroso, he traces female crime to biological differences between the sexes to deep-seated psychological "wishes" that are unique to young girls. In his early work, Thomas claims that females are biologically *anabolic*—motionless and conservative—whereas males are *katabolic*—destructive of energy, yet creative because of the outward flow of this drive. (As an aside, Thomas also sees monogamy as an accommodation to these basic urges because he believes that through monogamy women become domesticated and men become leaders!) Thomas's later work (*The Unadjusted Girl*, 1923) contains an important sociological insight—that female delinquency is a normal response to certain social conditions. But he still emphasizes that social behavior is a result of "primary wishes" that are derived from biological instincts. He identifies these wishes as the desire for new experience, security, response, and recognition; for women, there is the added wish for maternalism. In Thomas's view, middle-class people are less likely to commit crimes because they are more likely to control their natural desires. But delinquents are driven to crime because they long for new experiences. Girls, in particular, he says, engage in deviance to manipulate others, and their maternal instincts lead them to crimes, such as prostitution, in which he claims they are seeking love and tenderness (Klein 1980).

In sum, Thomas attributes motivational differences between males and females to internal, even biological, differences between the sexes. Although this biological explanation for sex differences is inadequate (see Chapter 2), Thomas did recognize differences in the attitudes of males and females and attempted to use these differences to explain patterns of delinquency and crime. His work, though seemingly crude to us now, has left an important message for more recent sociological work.

He attempts to find a behavioral basis for sex differences in male and female delinquency, and he tries, even if unsuccessfully, to relate those differences to attitudes that we now see as reflecting sex role socialization. Whether patterns of female crime can be properly attributed to sex role socialization is an important question that we will explore further in this chapter. But this suggestion opens the door for other sociological investigations. The major problem in Thomas's work, other than the sex role stereotyping of women as more manipulative, more emotional, and more desirous of love and tenderness than men, is that he portrayed sex differences as internal to individuals, not as a product of their social environment. But he contributes a second important insight on this point because he thinks that internal wishes and motivations can be directed by socialization and the manipulation of the social environment. Thus, his work establishes the liberal tradition in criminology that sees individual rehabilitation as the best solution to problems associated with deviant behavior. The liberal solution "requires that individual offenders be treated as undersocialized, as not fully adapted to the social values of society which represent their interests, and ultimately as being 'sick' rather than inherently evil or rationally opposed to the dominant values of society" (Smart 1977:37). Thus, liberal programs appeal to humanitarian values, but still ignore the social roots of social problems.

More recently, the work of Otto Pollak (1950) provides some of the early assumptions about female deviance. Like Lombroso and Thomas, Pollak traces women's deviance to their biological and psychological being; however, he reduces women's criminal behavior to sexuality and to what he assumes to be the natural character of sexual intercourse (Klein, 1980). Pollak claims that the basis for female crime is women's passive role in sexual intercourse. According to Pollak, women are able to conceal their sexual arousal from men and because of this physiological manipulation, women become socially deceitful. His major concern with female crime is the "masked" character of female criminality; he argues that the real extent of female crime is hidden from the public's view. Women, he contends, are deceitful and duplicitous; he sees them as the masterminds behind crime, manipulating men into committing offenses while they remain immune from prosecution. Pollak sees women as liars and interprets the hidden nature of their criminality as a reflection of their cunning behavior (Smart 1977). Moreover, in Pollak's view, men have been so duped by women that they protect women through chivalry and thus fear to charge and convict them for their crimes.

Although the views of Lombroso, Thomas, and Pollak appear quite outlandish now, the issues they raise continue to be addressed in current research, but in a quite different mode of explanation. Many still assume that delinquency can be traced to different emotional states in men and women, and they have looked to sexual character as the root of female criminality (Konopka 1966). Some who interpret female crime as a rebellion against sex roles want to restore women to their "proper" place in the social system (Klein 1973; Smart 1977). Current research and theory on female crime and deviance centers on the relationship of female deviance to gender roles. Following Lombroso, Thomas, and Pollak, criminologists ask whether and why women commit less crime and what the distinctive characteristics of female deviance are. Feminist perspectives on crime and deviance begin with a critical view of the sexist assumptions of criminological research. These assumptions include the fact that women's deviance is usually seen as sexual deviance and that women's crime is caused by physiological differences or internal motivations. From a feminist perspective, female crime and deviance must be seen within the context of societal gender relations; otherwise, any account of crime that is produced is liable to be misleading. Although feminists recognize that individual women may commit crimes or engage in deviant behavior, they see these acts as related to the status of women in society. Thus, any explanation of crime that views individual behavior as causally significant overlooks the more complex origins of deviant and criminal behavior.

Moreover, from a feminist perspective, the traditional questions that sociologists ask about women's crime and deviance are incomplete. For example, prior to the feminist movement, few criminologists asked about the experience of women as victims of crime and they did not inquire about how societal gender relations generate crimes committed specifically against women (such as rape, wife battering, and incest). In fact, studies of women as criminals and deviants have largely been limited to topics that feminists do not see as crime and deviance, such as prostitution, teenage promiscuity, and lesbianism. Crime and social deviance, thus, are inadequately defined when considering women's experience, and this recognition, along with the omission of a societal-level analysis of gender from earlier work, forms the basis for feminist studies of crime and deviant behavior. In the next section, we will discuss recent research on women and deviant behavior.

WOMEN AND SOCIAL DEVIANCE

This section describes sociological and feminist perspectives on deviance, beginning with the problems sociologists have faced in adequately defining the concept. After developing a sociological perspective on deviance and discussing some of the issues raised by studying deviance, we will note some of the specific problems feminists have identified in the study of deviant behavior and female deviance in particular.

Although deviance is a concept with many popular connotations, sociological definitions of deviance are based on three primary points: (1) deviance is social behavior that departs from conventional social norms; (2) deviance involves a process of social labeling; and (3) deviance becomes recognized within the context of social institutions that reflect the power structure and gender, race, and class relations of society. We will examine each of these ideas in turn, noting also some of the common assumptions that sociologists make about deviant behavior.

From a commonsense point of view, we might think of deviance as behavior that is bizarre, unconventional, and perhaps hard to understand. But from a sociological perspective, this definition is inadequate and misleading. First of all, what is unusual in one situation may be quite ordinary in another; second, even the most extraordinary behavior can often be understood if we know the context in which it occurs. Thus, sociologists define deviance as behavior that departs from conventional norms, noting that norms vary from one situation to another. Consequently, sociologists see deviance as located in a social context. Knowing and understanding this context is essential to understanding deviant behavior.

Although deviance is defined as behavior that departs from conventional norms, deviant behavior, like conventional behavior, is often guided by norms and rules, both formal and informal. In fact, deviance may be practiced in subcultures in which the social norms of the group encourage members to engage in deviant acts. One example comes from the research on gang rape, which shows that violence escalates when there is peer pressure to show off one's "masculinity" through increased aggression and abuse of the victim (Brownmiller 1975).

Another commonsense definition of deviance is that it is behavior that people disapprove of. But this idea too, is inaccurate because deviance is subject to social definition, and whether it is approved or disapproved depends upon who is doing the defining. Because deviance is situationally specific, it is sometimes difficult to distinguish deviant behavior from conventional behavior (Matza 1969). In fact, there is probably more overlap between deviant and conventional behavior than one might think. Most people engage in deviant behavior, sometimes on a regular basis. But whether they become identified as deviant may be a function of their social standing (including their sex, race, and class), the context of their deviant acts, and their ability to maintain a conventional identity.

For example, many would consider that the enjoyment of pornography is deviant behavior. It offends many people's moral sensibilities (including that of feminists, who see it as portraying women in a degrading and dehumanizing way). Yet, the easy availability of pornography, its widespread consumption, and its appearance even in the most respectable settings make it seem that pornography is a normal feature of everyday life. Moreover, whether one is perceived as deviant for reading or watching pornography depends upon one's social standing and the social context in which pornography is viewed. This fact is evident when we consider the deviant label attached to a frequenter of peep shows or pornography houses, in contrast to the socially legitimate label afforded to the young bachelor who keeps a copy of *Playboy* on his coffee table or bathroom reading rack. Moreover, when we analyze pornography as an economic industry, we see that its social organization is very similar (although perhaps more coercive) to that of other industries in which workers are exploited for profit and products are marketed by the use of women as sex objects.

This discussion brings us to the second major point that sociologists make about deviant behavior: Deviance involves a social labeling process (Becker 1963). One cannot be called deviant without being recognized as deviant, and sometimes persons become labeled as deviant regardless of whether they have actually engaged in deviant behavior. Becoming deviant involves societal reactions to one's behavior—or alleged behavior. In the absence of a deviant label, actual deviant behavior may have no consequences at all. But the process of being labeled as deviant may involve real changes in a person's self-image as well as his or her public identity. So, sociologists note that once one is labeled a deviant, it is likely that one becomes a deviant. But this new identity usually does not emerge suddenly or as the result of a single act. Instead, it involves a process of transformation wherein one adapts his or her self-image and behavior to the new identity being acquired (Lemert 1972). For example, in becoming a prostitute, a woman may slowly change her identity from a nondeviant status as a sexually active woman to a deviant status as a prostitute by exaggerating to herself that the exchange of sexuality for economic favors is typical of nondeviant women (Rosenblum 1975).

Finally, it is necessary to see that deviance occurs in the context of social institutions that have the power to label some persons as deviant and others as not. This fact is especially true to the degree that the official agents of these institutions carry sex, race, and class stereotypes or biases that make them more likely to discover deviance in some groups than in others. These agents include the police, judges, lawyers, prison guards, and others who may enter the official process of labeling deviant behavior (such as psychologists, psychiatrists, counselors, social workers, and teachers). Because these official agents of social institutions have the power to label some groups and persons as deviant and others as not, and because these institutions reflect the power structure and the systems of race, class, and gender relations in the society, deviance tends to be a label that falls most frequently on powerless persons in the society. Thus, the labeling of deviant behavior can be seen as involving a system of social control.

Sociologists who focus on deviance have suggested that it be studied from the point of view of the deviant actor (Becker 1963; Matza 1969). This method would allegedly prevent sociologists from seeing deviance only through official eyes and would create a more accurate portrayal of the deviant's social world. Many feminists studying deviance share this point of view, only adding that, traditionally, female deviance has been viewed through male eyes.

Prostitution, for example, has traditionally been described in terms of male demands for sexuality and females' supply of this service (McIntosh 1978). Although this is an apt description of the economic nature of prostitution, it also makes ideological assumptions about both male and female sexuality. Women are depicted as merely providing an outlet for male sexual needs and remaining sexually passive, while men are defined as having greater sexual urges than women. Prostitution is a sex-specific crime that punishes women, not men, for not subordinating their sexuality to monogamous marital relationships (McIntosh 1978). Were sociologists to study prostitution from the point of view of the prostitute, other questions would likely emerge.

For example, we might ask what the typical relationship between pimps and prostitutes is and how prostitutes view their pimps. One study finds that prostitutes laugh at the notion of having a pimp and say that only they use men to give them back-up protection. The men, on the other hand, thought they were pimps, even though the women did not think so (Pottieger 1981). Another issue that might be studied from the point of view of prostitutes is how they define their sexuality. Young delinquent girls, for example, have a more differentiated set of sexual mores than the simple virgin/whore dichotomy that is usually imposed upon them (Wilson 1978) This fact suggests that prostitutes, as well as delinquent and other girls, define their own sexual codes of conduct and negotiate them in social interaction.

A feminist perspective on prostitution also encourages interest in the female subculture among prostitutes. Typically, this subculture is assumed to be competitive and distrustful (Bryan 1965); yet, prostitutes work together and are dependent on each other for safety and support. Instead of assuming that they exploit each other, we might ask how their female group culture is established and maintained (Millman 1975). One study finds, for example, that clusters of four to five call girls maintain emotionally and financially reciprocal relations with each other. An exchange of clients is necessary to cover appointments if they are busy, to provide more than one woman if needed for their clients, or to aid financially troubled friends (Rosenblum 1975). Contrary to the idea that prostitutes have weak and exploitative relationships with each other, this research discovers an essential network existing among these women.

Feminist perspectives on deviant behavior are critical of traditional studies for their content, their omissions, their interpretations of female deviance, and even their assumptions about what counts as deviance. To a large extent, the study of female deviance has been ignored, making it easier for sexist interpretations of deviance to persist. When female deviance is studied, it is often relegated to a few categories of deviant behavior that evoke sexist stereotypes. Thus, studies of female deviance have typically been limited to behaviors that are linked with female sexuality (such as prostitution and promiscuity) or to behaviors seen as stemming from women's alleged inability to control their emotions (such as mental illness, alcoholism, and drug abuse). And interpretations of female deviance have been clearly tied to the sexual status attributed to women in this society. This tendency seems especially true when we compare the alleged deviance of women to that of men. A double standard of morality marks some behaviors as deviant in women that are not considered deviant when performed by men. A good example is the issue of teenage promiscuity—a value-laden concept, yet one that policymakers and official institutions take quite seriously. The double standard of morality marks promiscuity as a social problem only among young girls. Teenage boys are expected, if not encouraged, to be aggressive in their sexual encounters; girls who do the same thing are labeled as "loose" and are likely to be seen by officials as constituting a social problem.

The sexual status attributed to female deviants is also evident in the frequently made assumption (particularly among official agents of correctional and counseling institutions) that all female deviants are sexually deviant as well. For example, women junkies and alcoholics are frequently presumed to be sexually promiscuous as well and, in many jurisdictions, female delinquents charged with nonsexual deviant offenses may be routinely checked for virginity and/or venereal disease (Chesney-Lind 1977; Strouse 1972).

Another assumption that feminists criticized is the idea that females engage is less deviance and delinquency than do males (Cowie, Cowie, and Slater 1968). But if fewer females are detected, it may simply be because we assume that they are less deviant. Therefore, this assumption becomes a self-fulfilling prophecy. Moreover, if women are seen to be usually less deviant than men, then those women whose deviance is detected may be seen as more abnormal than their male counterparts (Smith 1978). This perspective would help explain the fact that when a woman is defined as deviant, more strict sanctions may be brought against her because she has greatly violated her gender role (Smith 1978).

Feminists have pointed out that those who study deviance usually choose topics that are exciting to them. Although they are not critical of this fact, they do point out that much of the research on deviance (because it is done largely by men) focuses on the most titillating aspects of deviant behavior (Millman 1975). Thus, much of the research on deviance (especially that of women) has a voyeuristic quality, particularly as it describes the intricacies of deviant behavior from the perspective of an outsider.

In their studies of deviant behavior, sociologists have often relied on ethnography. This is a descriptive method of investigation in which the recorder details all of the features of social organization of the people he or she is studying. Ethnographies have provided rich accounts of the everyday life of deviant actors because they are a good tool for observing the meanings and behaviors of deviant actors from their own perspective. But often, ethnographers overlook the fact the women occupy some of the same deviant scenes as men. So, only recently, as feminists have sensitized researchers to the existence of women, have we begun to get accounts of the everyday activities of female deviants (Prus and Vassilakopoulos 1979). Such studies are valuable for their details of the everyday activities of deviant persons, but they seldom provide any explanatory connection between the individual and the social institutions that perpetuate this behavior.

In studying deviance, sociologists have also tended to ignore issues that may appear mundane but are important in establishing complete accounts of the social world of the deviant. For instance, few have considered the effect that deviance might have on the lives of those in the deviant's social circle (Millman 1975). It is often these people—the family and friends of deviant actors—who must accommodate to the consequences of social deviance (including social stigma, embarrassment, ostracism, or imprisonment). Because sociologists focus on the public aspects of deviance, they ignore its emotional dimension and the accommodations that friends and families make to it.

With regard to female deviance, traditional sociological interpretations have often rested on sexist assumptions about male and female behavior. Many traditional studies of female deviance assume that female deviants have either lost control of their emotions or sexuality, or that they are exploitive, impulsive, or "doing it all for love" (Millman 1975). In addition, female deviance is often equated with female sexual pathology. Thus, the causes of female deviance are often attributed to individual maladjustment or a poor family background. It is true that some female deviance (including sexual deviance) does involve the individual's psycho-sexual adjustment. Often, in fact, child abuse, particularly sexual abuse by the father or other male kin, results in damage to female self-concepts and sexual identities (Jaget 1980). Consequently, such experiences may provoke a woman to engage in deviant behavior. But these events in her biography (which are by no means true for all female deviants) are not the sole or always the primary cause of deviant behavior.

Routine engagement in deviant behavior involves embarking on a deviant career and, like other careers, involves opportunity and socialization into new roles, as well as some reward (both material and psychological) for doing so. Moreover, individual maladjustment should also be seen as originating within institutional patterns of a patriarchal society. The incest victim is abused, not because of her own psychological derangement, but because of the institutional structure of patriarchal families, where men can demand sexual services, where they can exert power and authority, and where deviant sexual relations can be hidden through family privacy (Herman and Hirschman 1977). Furthermore, when individuals seek assistance for psychological problems, other institutional features of patriarchal society may interfere. The preponderance of male psychotherapists and the sexist assumptions of clinicians, social workers, and juvenile authorities not only prevent positive solutions but may even create further problems for individual deviants. When official agencies are contacted for help, the likelihood is high that the deviant will acquire a new label (criminal, juvenile delinquent, alcoholic or junkie), and this label will be seen as the problem to be dealt with. In consequence, the origins of the client's conflicts may be overlooked altogether, leading only to a further exacerbation of her problems.

In sum, explanations of female deviance have tended to be sex-specific, particularly because deviance in women, but seldom in men, is seen to emerge from problems in the woman's sexual identity or sexual behavior. This fact underscores the point that female deviance has traditionally been linked to female sexuality, as evident in explanations of female deviance as well as in the topics chosen for study. Nowhere is this tendency more clear than in traditional perspectives on female homosexuality—a subject that is almost always relegated to a deviant category.

The deviant label attached to lesbianism makes it appear that there is something perverted about loving persons of one's own sex. Much of the research on lesbianism and homosexuality assumes that this sexual preference is pathological. Consequently, the prevailing mode of explanation has been one of individual maladjustment. But lesbianism can just as well be seen as conscious resistance to conventional heterosexuality, by which women are defined as the adjuncts of men and female sexuality is seen as passive acquiescence to male demands. The volumes of research asserting that homosexuality needs correction are strong evidence of the compulsory nature of heterosexual institutions in the society (Rich 1980). Lesbianism and homosexuality are deviant, not because gay men and lesbian women are sick, but because they exist outside of the dominant expectations of a patriarchal and heterosexist society. It is the heterosexist structure of institutions that defines lesbians as deviant, invisible, and abhorrent. Inside lesbian-feminist communities, lesbian existence is viewed as a healthy response and conscious resistance to patriarchal domination.

In conclusion, sociological work on female deviance is only beginning to challenge the sex-stereotypic assumptions that have guided earlier work on the topic. As research emerges from a feminist perspective, we are beginning to see new issues and new perspectives for investigating the social problems that female deviants face. From these revisions, feminists hope to develop more complete and more analytically correct accounts of the experience of female deviants. In the next section, we will look at the specific questions encountered when studying the issue of women as criminals.

WOMEN AS CRIMINALS

Until recently, women's participation in crime has been ignored by criminologists. Criminologists are now asking new questions about women's involvement in criminal behavior and its relationship to female gender roles. An assertion runs throughout much of this research that the feminist movement and changes in women's status have created more opportunity for female crime (Adler 1975; Simon 1975). Thus, a central issue in the research on women and crime is the connection between crime rates and women's liberation.

The evidence shows that women commit much less crime than do men and, furthermore, that their crimes tend to be less serious than men's (Datesman and Scarpitti 1980; Simon 1975). However, women's participation in some crimes has increased in recent years, although not at the rapid rate implied by popular accounts. Three central questions asked in the research on women and crime are: Has women's crime increased and, if so, for what types of crime? Is the amount of female crime beginning to approximate the amount of male crime? How is female crime linked to gender roles, and have changes in traditional roles created more opportunities for women to commit crimes?

Available information on female crime comes primarily from official statistics (the FBI's *Uniform Crime Reports*), from self-report surveys, and from national victimization and crime surveys. Although each data source reveals different kinds of information, essentially they all create a consistent picture of female crime. Data on arrests show that the proportion of women arrested (as a percentage of all arrests) has increased over the last several decades (1932–1972) and that the increase in arrest rates for serious offenses is caused almost entirely by women's greater participation in property offenses, especially larceny (Simon 1975; Steffensmeier 1981). However, contrary to the sensationalized portrait of female crime drawn by the popular media, the proportion of arrests for women committing violent crimes has hardly changed since the 1940s (Simon 1976). The increase in the actual rate of violent crimes committed by women has been generally matched or exceeded by increases in violent crime by men (Steffensmeier 1981). Thus, the proportion of all violent crimes committed by women remains about the same.

In contrast, the gap in male-female property crime rates has narrowed substantially since 1960, as arrest rates for property crimes have increased much faster for adult females than for adult males. Specifically, women comprise one third of all those arrested for larceny, fraud, and embezzlement, although burglary and auto theft remain primarily male offenses (Steffensmeier 1981). Based on arrest rates, larceny is the most frequent female crime. In 1977, larceny constituted almost one quarter of all female arrests (Datesman and Scarpitti 1980). Criminologists point out that the vast majority of female larceny arrests are for shoplifting (Cameron 1964), although male shoplifters take more expensive merchandise (Cohen and Stark 1974).

Some have suggested that other property crimes, such as fraud and embezzlement, have increased for women because there are more opportunities for women to commit these crimes when their status in the labor market improves (Simon 1975). The evidence shows, however, that although women are approximating men in terms of total arrests for the category of fraud and embezzlement, fraud accounts for the largest percentage of these arrests (Datesman and Scarpitti 1980). Most women arrested for fraud are involved in small-profit offenses such as minor confidence games, welfare fraud, or being an accessory to fraudulent business practices (Hoffman-Bustamante 1973). Women do account for one quarter of all arrests for embezzlement (Steffensmeier 1981), but for them, it is also largely a petty crime. Eighty-one percent of the thefts in this category for women are for sums of money between $1 and $150; male embezzlers account for 70 percent of the thefts over $1,000 (Datesman and Scarpitti 1980). Although changes in women's position in the labor force may explain some of the increase in female embezzlement, large embezzlement schemes are still mostly attributed to men who remain in higher-level occupational positions and, therefore, have more opportunity to engage in white-collar crime. Moreover, a study of employee theft has found that, in the large retail organization studied, males account for 40 percent of the labor force but 56 percent of the thefts. Moreover, all of the persons in managerial positions committing thefts were males, whereas females accounted for a majority of the thefts in sales and clerical positions (Franklin 1979).

What, then, can we make of the relationship between female roles and their participation in crime? Many criminologists suggest that patterns of crime among women represent extensions of their traditional female roles. Activities such as shoplifting, credit card fraud, and the passing of bad checks result from the opportunities women have as consumers. Likewise, the crimes that are less frequent for women (such as armed robbery, aggravated assault, and major embezzlement) involve either physical strength or economic opportunity more typical of male sex roles. Several have argued that, as women's roles change, we can expect their involvement in criminal behavior to change as well. This argument deserves careful attention, however, because it is very easily misunderstood.

To begin with, even with increased economic opportunity for women in the labor force, the vast majority of women remain in low-paid, low-status jobs. Thus, it is an exaggeration to say that women's opportunities for crime are related to women's rapid advancement in the labor force. In fact, recent increases in poverty among women (Ehreneich and Stallard 1982) are probably more directly related to changes in women's criminal activity because sociologists have long pointed to the association between poverty and crime. Second, increases in female crime which show up in the arrest statistics do not necessarily reflect an increase in the actual extent of crime. Rather, these statistics may reflect an increase in the detection of female crime. This increased detection can occur in several ways.

First, it has been suggested that the feminist movement has created changes in public attitudes about female crime. So, although the amount of crime may remain the same, the police may be more likely to arrest women for offenses they commit (Datesman and Scarpitti 1980). A second argument is that changes in the rate of female crime do not result from changes in sex roles per se, but instead from broad structural changes in the economy, technology, legal systems, and law enforcement practices (Steffensmeier 1981b). Greater reliance in the last twenty years on self-service marketing and the use of credit cards has increased the opportunities for crime for all consumers. At the same time, detection systems (including national information systems, technological surveillance, and an expansion of private security forces) have increased the amount of social control and law enforcement. Thus, "the greater willingness of business officials to prosecute, the trend toward computerized records, and improvements in the detection of offenses such as shoplifting, bad checks, credit card fraud, and forged prescriptions would also tend to increase female, more than male, arrests for larceny, fraud, and forgery" (Steffensmeier 1981:63).

In sum, it is interesting that female crime is now being attributed to women's sex roles, whereas male crime is usually attributed to social structural characteristics. One pair of contemporary researchers even suggest that, although sociological interpretations explain part of the difference in male and female delinquency, the persistence of this difference should be explored as biologically based (Jensen and Eve 1976). A general theory of criminal behavior should be able to explain both male and female crime. Oddly enough, the sex roles perspective is seldom used to explain male crime, as if assuming that women have sex roles but men do not. Although the inclusion of a sex roles perspective (for both men and women) is an improvement on earlier thinking about crime, it does not, in itself, explain why men and women commit the crimes they do. Analyses of crime among women and men need to explain how sex differences in crime emerge not only from sex roles but also from institutional patterns in the society.

An alternative view of gender and crime can be found in radical perspectives on criminology. Instead of concentrating on the difference between the sexes in criminal behavior, radicals see that definitions of crime and arrests for crime serve as a system of social control. What counts as crime is established by powerful persons in the society, who define some acts as criminal in order to protect their own interests (Chambliss and Seidman 1971; Quinney 1970). Thus, what are considered criminal acts are primarily the crimes of the powerless, particularly crimes against property. Laws defining crime are made by the rich and politically powerful; at the same time, laws are created that allow for the legal acquisition of money by the wealthy.

From this perspective, we might ask why some behaviors are considered crimes and others are not. For feminists, this question is also important. For instance, as the example of abortion shows (see Chapter 6), historical changes in the law sometimes defined abortion as criminal behavior and other times did not. Moreover, these changes in abortion policy benefited medical doctors, who sought to gain control of the abortion market (Mohr 1978). Those who define crime do so for their own interests, and these interests have often worked against the interests of women. Consider, for instance, who would be considered criminal if our definition of crime included the control of another person's body. From this perspective, the normal practices of the medical profession might be considered criminal (see Chapter 6). The act of rape provides another case in point because, even now, in a majority of states rape within marriage is not legally defined as rape.

Feminist perspectives on crime and gender take a more broadly based view of criminal behavior than do traditional perspectives in criminology. Whereas traditional criminological research generally asks who committed the crime and why, feminists see crime within a holistic context of social power, gender relations, and economic stratification. Thus, from a feminist perspective, it is inadequate to ask simply why women commit fewer crimes than men. Feminists have directed attention not only to the crimes committed by women but even more to the crimes committed against women. A discussion of gender and crime is then incomplete without an inquiry about women as victims of crime.

WOMEN AS VICTIMS OF CRIME

Statistics indicate that, overall, women are less likely to be victimized by crime than men; however, there are important qualifications to make about this observation. To begin with, national data on victimization rates come primarily from the National Crime Panel Survey, a project sponsored by the Law Enforcement Assistance Administration. The National Crime Panel Survey is based on a national sample of households and businesses in which persons are asked to report crimes by which they were victimized in the preceding months. Because the surveys include crimes against businesses, they may distort the gap between male and female victimization because men are more likely to own businesses. The surveys are intended to give a more complete picture of crime than analyses based only on crimes reported to the police.

But problems remain, including sampling errors that have been found in the data, the likelihood of faulty recall among some research subjects, and the fact that many crimes might still have not been reported to the survey interviewers (Senna and Siegel 1981). Particularly in the case of rape, it is quite possible that, if a victim never reported it to the police, she might not report it to a researcher either.

Moreover, the National Crime Panel Surveys are restricted by asking only about FBI index crimes—homicide and nonnegligent manslaughter, forcible rape, aggravated assault, robbery, larceny, burglary, and auto theft. The surveys omit homicide, because it is believed that this crime is accurately documented in official records. Even more important, when considering the issue of violence against women, is that the National Crime Panel Surveys include no information about wife beating or incest—crimes against women that we know are largely hidden from public view.

Given these qualifications in the data, how can we characterize the victimization of women by crime? As noted earlier in this section, over-all, women are less likely to be victimized by crime than men. However, there are some groups of women and some crimes in which victimization rates are higher for women than they are for men. Also, some women are more likely to be victimized than others, and these categories reveal how victimization by crime is related to the political and economic powerlessness of women in society.

Specifically, black women and women between the ages of sixteen and nineteen are victimized by crime more than are men in general. Also, women between sixteen and twenty-four years of age are more likely to experience violent crime than are women of any other age. For crimes of theft, women between twelve and fifteen are the prime targets, and the victimization rates are inversely proportional to the age of the victim (Bowker 1981). Surprisingly, elderly women have the lowest rate of victimization by crime, suggesting that the amount of crime against the elderly of either sex has been grossly exaggerated in the media (Markson and Hess 1980).

Regardless of their actual victimization, at every age women have a greater fear of crime than do men. Women's fear of crime increases with age, the most fearful being elderly women who live alone (Burkhardt 1977; Markson and Hess 1980). Researchers find that women's fear of crime seems to restrict their freedom of action. Women take more precautions against crime than do men even though their fears of crime are not directly related to actual risk (as measured by crime rates in their neighborhoods). Women's perceived degree of risk probably encourages them to restrict their freedom and behavior, thus suggesting that women's fear of crime and their sense of personal vulnerability control their freedom of movement (Gordon et al. 1980).

Generally speaking, black men and women are more victimized by violent personal crimes such as rape, assault, and robbery. Whites are more victimized by property crimes, with blacks and those of Spanish origin experiencing 15 percent less property crime. However, in recent years, crimes against black, Spanish-American, and white women have increased, and there is little reason to expect that this trend will not continue (Bowker 1981).

Additional data on victimization rates underscore the idea that crimes against women reflect their powerlessness. Divorced and separated women are six times more likely to be raped or robbed than are married women; compared to married women, they are also five times more likely to be assaulted and 60 percent more likely to experience personal theft. Women who have never been married are also victimized more than are married women. One should not take these data to mean, however, that the married woman is safe from victimization. Research on violence against wives indicates a high degree of violence within the privacy of the household (Dobash and Dobash 1979). That these events do not show up in public records of crime should not lead us to the complacent conclusion that marriage protects women from crime and violence. Instead, empirical data on women and crime suggest that women's isolation (both inside and outside the home) is a common feature of crimes of violence against women.

The case of rape illustrates how isolation and powerlessness are features of crimes committed against women. Because it has been heavily researched by feminists and criminologists, it also provides a good example for explaining crimes of violence against women. In 1980, the Uniform Crime Statistics reported 82,088 cases of forcible rape in the United States. Because of underreporting, the FBI itself estimates that this figure represents only one fourth of the actual cases of forcible rape in that year. Moreover, the Uniform Crime Statistics on rape do not include those that result in death because these crimes are classified as homicides. Depending on the character of the incident, some rapes may be officially categorized as other forms of assault. Thus, most official statistics are likely to underestimate the actual extent of rape.

Specific data on which women are more likely to be raped also indicate the connection of rape to women's status in society; it is women of the lowest status who are most vulnerable to rape. Victimization surveys show that black women are slightly more likely to be raped than white women and that divorced or separated women are much more likely to be raped than women who have never been married. Married women are much less likely to be raped than are divorced, separated, or never-married women. For all women, the rape rate is three times higher for those with incomes under $3,000 per year (in 1975) than those with incomes of $15,000 or more. Also, unemployed women, and women living in households where they are not family members are seven times more likely to be raped than are wives. Finally, the probability of experiencing any form of personal victimization is directly related to the amount of time one spends in public places (Bowker 1981).

This information gives us a compelling picture of women's experience and its relationship to violence as a system of social control. Explanations of violence against women have usually suggested that its causes lie within the personalities and social backgrounds of individuals who commit violence. But the empirical data on women as victims indicate that the causes of violence lie, not in the characteristics of offenders, but in the social status of their victims. This is not to say that women are responsible for the violence committed against them. Quite the opposite; it locates the causes of violence within the political and economic status of women in society. This finding is revealed in a more detailed examination of explanations of rape, which can then be generally used to understand the causes of violence against women.

Theoretical explanations of rape can be broadly categorized in four groups: psychological theories, the subculture of violence theory, sex role learning theory and political-economic theory (Andersen and Renzetti 1980). We will look at each of these theories in turn and the criticisms of them. To begin with, psychological theories of rape look to individual characteristics of personality maladjustment and psychosexual development as the origins of men's motivation to rape. Explaining rape as a matter of individual psychopathology conforms to stereotypic notions of rapists as psychopathic and deviant, but it does not fit the evidence. That is, empirical studies have been unable to find consistent personality differences between men who rape and those who do not (Albin 1977). Moreover, because the vast majority of rapists go unidentified by official agencies, there is a tremendous bias in such studies. The men included in the studies are those who are most likely to be detained or incarcerated for rape, and because these men are more likely to be black, Hispanic, or poor, studies of rapists tend to be both class- and race-biased. The suggestion in the psychological studies that only abnormal men rape thus carries an implicit class and race bias that defines these men as deviant and psychologically deranged. At the same time, such studies underemphasize the causal contribution of the social environment to the occurrence of rape.

A second theory of the causes of rape comes from the subculture of violence perspective in criminology. This theory sees the social environment as the origin of violent behavior, but it is extremely biased by its differential emphasis on the behavior of black and working-class men. Susan Brownmiller popularized the use of the subculture of violence theory to explain rape in her best-seller, *Against Our Will* (1975). Adopted from Wolfgang and Feracuti (1967) and Amir (1971), the subculture of violence theory claims that violence is a cultural way of life in working-class and black communities; thus, its members come to take violence for granted, and it becomes a routine feature of everyday life. Male violence and aggression are explained in this perspective as adaptations to poverty, but the emphasis is placed upon the collective psychological maladjustment of minority and working-class populations. The problem with the subculture of violence thesis is not that violence in these communities is not a problem, but that this theory blames the presumedly pathological culture of these people for violent behavior.

Such a perspective begs the question of whether violence is more widespread in poor and working-class communities or whether it is just less hidden. Criminologists have frequently pointed out that the higher rape and violence rates found among minority and poor men largely reflect race and class discrimination in the criminal justice system. It is important to note that the most violent crimes (rape and homicide) show smaller race differences than the less violent crime of robbery (Hindelang 1978). This fact seemingly discredits the subculture of violence theory. Critics of this perspective also point out that violence is equally extensive in the dominant culture; it is just more easily hidden or legitimized as appropriately masculine behavior. In the end, the subculture of violence theory gives us an inadequate explanation of violence against women because, in its focus on society's underclasses, it does not explain why violence is also symptomatic of the dominant culture.

The third perspective used to explain rape comes from sex role learning theory. Feminists have suggested that the causes of rape can be traced to the dominant culture and its emphasis on masculinity as a learned pattern of aggression and domination (Griffin 1971). Unlike psychological and subcultural theories that emphasize deviations from the mainstream culture, feminist explanations see rape as an exaggeration of traditional sex roles (Clark and Lewis 1977). Sex role socialization theory provides a perspective on rape that is sensitive to the variety of contexts in which it occurs. For example, a large proportion of rapes are committed by persons who are known to the victim, especially among white and young female victims (Bowker 1981). Many of these violent events occur in the context of a date or some other relationship between the victim and the rapist. Researchers have noted that heterosexual relations typically involve some degree of seductive coercion on the part of the man, whereas women are expected to resist sexual relations (Clark and Lewis 1977). From the perspective of sex role learning theory, rape occurs because men learn to force women to have sexual relations against their will (Brownmiller 1975).

Understanding rape from this perspective helps us see how traditional sex role interaction encourages rape. But it is limited in that it focuses on the narrow context of interpersonal relations, socialization practices, and learned behavior. Although it is correct to see rape as connected to learned patterns in the culture, this perspective is inadequate without an understanding of how the cultural concepts of masculinity and femininity emerge from the actual status of women and men in the society.

Thus, feminists also suggest a fourth perspective on rape that explains violence against women as founded on the political and economic status of women in patriarchal and capitalist societies. This political-economic theory states that women have been historically defined as the property of men in these societies. For example, the rape of black women by white slave owners is evidence of the relationship between rape and the property status of women. Although women in contemporary society are no longer explicitly defined as the property of men, their use as sexual objects in advertising reduces their sexuality to a commodity. Moreover, images of violence against women in advertising and the popular media legitimate violent behavior against women and reiterate their status as sexual objects. To become an object is to become a piece of property, and this status, according to feminists, dehumanizes women and makes them an object for male violence.

Also, the fact that most rapists do not believe they have done anything wrong shows that violence against women carries some degree of legitimacy within the society (Clark and Lewis 1977). Those women who are perceived as the least valuable in the society are apparently most likely to be raped. This fact explains why black, poor, unemployed, and unmarried women are the most frequent victims of rape. Cross-cultural evidence also suggests that the level of violence against women is lowest in those societies where women have the most social, political, and economic autonomy (Friedl 1975; Parker 1978). In patriarchal societies, where men rule women, women lose their autonomy and are encouraged to be dependent on men. Research on rape victims shows that women who are not identified as belonging to a man (i.e., women who are alone in public, single, divorced, separated, or living with non-family members) are most victimized by rape. At the same time, as we have seen in Chapter 5, increasing social isolation seems to be a pattern in the phenomenon of wife beating (Dobash and Dobash 1979). And in the case of incest, the isolation of women in the privacy of family life keeps that act a closely guarded secret.

In conclusion, violence against women is based on the economic and political powerlessness of women living in patriarchal societies. Understanding violence against women requires an analysis that shows the relationship of violence to the structure of major social institutions. In this sense, stopping violence against women is intricately connected to the liberation of women from oppressive social and economic relations.

This discussion of women and crime has concentrated on the commission of crime, its victims, and its perpetrators. But the question remains of what happens to women when they enter the criminal justice system either as victims or as defendants. A review of this issue reveals once again how women's experience within particular social institutions is affected by gender relations and the overall status of women in society.

WOMEN IN THE CRIMINAL JUSTICE SYSTEM

The evidence on the position of women in the criminal justice system indicates that they are treated differently from men both as offenders and as victims. There is some question of whether paternalistic attitudes afford women offenders more lenient treatment than their male counterparts receive, and the research shows that, at least for some offenses, it does. However, an overall portrayal of women in the criminal justice system also indicates that, even though justice is symbolized by a blindfolded woman, equality of treatment by the law does not exist for women (Moulds 1980).

One factor in this inequality is the way women victims of crime are treated in the courts. Research, particularly in the area of rape, shows that women victims are not equally credible before the law. For example, in many rape trials, the victim's past sexual history is often introduced to discredit her testimony against her assailant. Only recently have some states reformed their legal statutes to make a woman's past sexual history inadmissible as evidence in a rape trial (Bienen 1977). Moreover, in spite of legal reforms, trial evidence indicates that lawyers' allegations about a woman's character may still be used to discredit her testimony or to make her appear to have an illegitimate claim (Randall and Rose 1981). Research also shows that certain characteristics of rape victims or a rape incident are likely to make the victim's testimony seem unsubstantiated. For this reason, police and prosecutors make judgments about the victim's credibility and the prosecutive merit of her case. If she had a prior relationship with her assailant, if she delayed reporting the crime, if she was under the influence of drugs or alcohol, or if she is a prostitute, a black woman, a welfare recipient, or a hitch-hiker—her case may be seen as unsubstantiated (Clark and Lewis 1977; Rose 1981; Wood 1981).

For women offenders who are brought before the criminal justice system, sexist stereotypes, prejudices against women, and a double standard of morality for men and women may influence the progress of their cases. Further, because women are often not taken as seriously as men in the society as a whole, it is not surprising that this bias reappears in police decisions and courtroom trials. For women offenders, the problem is equally serious. Even though paternalistic attitudes toward women in the courts sometimes provide them with protection, the fact remains that women offenders are treated according to gendered expectations about their behavior. Although paternalistic attitudes may appear to be benign, women offenders may actually be harmed by them because these attitudes may define women who break the law as needing more help than do male offenders.

This belief is particularly well illustrated in the juvenile justice system. In the name of protection or guidance, female delinquents are much more readily incarcerated for noncriminal offenses than are male delinquents. Young women are far more likely to be arrested for what are called status offenses than are boys. These offenses include behaviors that are at odds with conventional standards of morality (running away, incorrigibility, waywardness, and curfew violations), as opposed to actual criminal offenses. One study reports that 75 percent of girls compared to 25 percent of boys are brought to the juvenile justice system for status offenses, not criminal behavior. Boys are far more likely to go to court for criminal offenses: burglary, larceny, and car theft (Chesney-Lind 1977). Evidence from the juvenile system indicates that the court takes more severe sanctions against females than males for noncriminal status offenses, as girls are more likely to be held in jail or sent to juvenile detention facilities (Chesney-Lind 1981). Less severe dispositions are made, however, against girls than boys when criminal offenses are involved (Datesman and Scarpitti 1980). These differences hold for black juveniles as well, although there is somewhat less of a discrepancy in dispositions against black males and females when the charge is a criminal offense (Datesman and Scarpitti 1980).

The emphasis for juvenile treatment is on rehabilitation. In the case of girls, a frequent result is an attempt to bring them into line with traditional sex role expectations of passivity, submissiveness, conformity, and virginity (Haft 1980). In sum, sexual and moral misbehaviors are judged as more serious offenses for girls than for boys. This evidence indicates that the juvenile justice system operates *in loco parentis* and in accordance with traditional sex role stereotyping. For status offenders, the courts attempt to bring female youth into line with traditional moral standards for girls. For criminal offenders, it appears that women are still perceived as less serious, as not responsible for their behavior, and as less dangerous than men.

Considering all women offenders, women who become incarcerated constitute a small proportion of all prisoners. The proportion of women prisoners has always been approximately 4 percent of the total prison population, but since 1975, the number of women in prison has increased rapidly (Bowker 1981). A national survey of women prisoners finds that they are relatively young; two thirds are under thirty years old, and their median age is twenty-seven. Half of all imprisoned women are black. As with male prisoners, race and class biases in the criminal justice system operate to put more black and poor women in prison (Lewis 1981).

The family status of women prisoners shows that 20 percent are currently married, although almost two thirds have been married at some time. Three quarters of them have borne children and, of this group, three quarters had children living at home at the time of their arrest. Women prisoners tend to be less educated than women as a whole, and 40 percent were working at legitimate jobs just prior to their arrest; half have been on welfare at some time (Glick and Neto 1977).

Studies of women in prison find that 43 percent have been charged with violent crimes (Glick and Neto 1977); the remainder have been sentenced primarily for property crimes (29 percent) and drug offenses (22 percent). Other reports indicate that many women prisoners are charged as accessories to crimes committed by men, and they point out that many imprisoned women are charged with relatively minor offenses, such as prostitution, shoplifting, and drugs (Shakur and Chesimard 1978). Also, although it is popularly believed that women generally serve shorter sentences than men, women are sentenced to longer terms than men for the same crimes (Haft 1980).

The situation within prison for incarcerated women is quite different from that of men. As with men, the conditions faced by women in prison often include inadequate facilities, poor health care, separation from their families, and insufficient jobs and educational training. But women's prisons are typically smaller than men's prisons and somewhat more informal. There is a tendency for social control to be less rigid in women's prisons. For example, women in prison are often made childlike by pseudo-motherly attitudes on the part of prison guards (Shakur and Chesimard 1978). But although the outward appearance of the women's surroundings seems more benign, there is still strict control of their behavior and movements.

The activities made available for women prisoners often reflect sex role stereotypes, especially in the area of job training. Whereas male prisoners may learn skilled trades that are higher paid upon their release from prison, women are typically encouraged to learn housekeeping, hairdressing, sewing, and clerical skills (Haft 1980). When they leave prison, these skills prepare them only for poorly paid and sex-segregated occupations. Consequently, upon leaving prison, many find that illegal activities are more lucrative, and they may return to crime. It should be pointed out, however, that the recidivism rate for women offenders is less than that for men (Datesman and Scarpitti 1980).

Health facilities in women's prisons are mostly inadequate, particularly in meeting needs specific to women's medical and reproductive care. Many women enter prison with existing medical problems—the most frequent being drug addiction, psychiatric illness, hypertension, and respiratory disease (Novick et al. 1977). Although medical services for male prisoners are also notoriously poor (Goldsmith 1975), what services do exist are set up to deal with men; as a result, women's specific needs (especially for gynecological and obstetric care) may go unheeded. Women's privacy in health care may also be ignored, as in the case of institutions that provide sanitary napkins free of charge but require inmates to pay for tampons (Resnik and Shaw 1981). Even though some women may remain sexually active in prison (through occasional releases or relationships that develop within the prison), it is significant that women may also lose the right to use contraceptives in prison. Many prisons will not permit women prisoners to use particular birth control devices (such as diaphragms and intrauterine devices). For women who are pregnant or become so in prison, long waits for medical evaluations may make abortion a high risk, and some facilities do not allow abortions at all. Should a woman prisoner carry through her pregnancy, she may not receive an adequate diet and prenatal care, and when she gives birth, she may be separated from her child. Nursing is then impossible and, at worst, the child may be placed in a foster home

(Resnik and Shaw 1981). There is evidence that, in spite of these problems, women prisoners do attempt to meet their own health needs. They are critical of prison health facilities and, in some cases, attempt to implement home techniques of health care, including herbal remedies and self-examination (Resnik and Shaw 1981).

In sum, the conditions in women's prisons often lead them to fend for themselves. In the face of these conditions, research indicates that women's own social networks in prison are more supportive and affectionate than those formed in male prisons. Giallombardo's early study (1966) found that women in prison form pseudo-families, with prisoners taking different roles in relation each other (such as mother, daughter, and sister). Her observation has since been replicated by others, although it may be more common among juveniles (Proper 1976). Many have interpreted this phenomenon as a reflection of the external values and cultural expectations that society has for all women. According to this argument, women in prison bring external norms, values, and beliefs that define women in stereotypic family roles; these norms and roles are then reflected in prison subcultures.

An alternative explanation emphasizes women's active construction of a supportive subculture, rather than their passive acquiescence to external sex roles. Thus, women prisoners form a conscious culture of resistance like those of other oppressed groups who, in the context of domination, create and maintain networks of mutual support (Caulfield 1974). Cultures of resistance often take the form of conscious affirmation of cultural differences in the face of external domination. Although women in prison do not all come from similar cultural backgrounds, the subcultures they form in prison exhibit resourcefulness, flexibility, and creativity in the social relations they develop. The perspective of a culture of resistance emphasizes that they are not merely passive victims of their situation; instead, they develop adaptive strategies to cope with the conditions they face.

Part of this subculture is reflected in the homosexual relationships that emerge between some women prisoners. Compared to homosexuality among male prisoners, which tends to be founded on coercion or prostitution, women prisoners put more emphasis on love than physical sex in homosexual relations. Because lesbianism in women's prisons occurs in the context of love, sexual coercion is a rare event (Bowker 1981). Moreover, many loving relationships between women emerge in prison subcultures without an overt sexual relationship, whereas such relationships are less evident in men's prisons (Bowker 1981).

CONCLUSION

This chapter shows how gender differences and the status of women in society shape the experience of women both as victims and offenders in crime and deviance. Although reforms in the criminal justice system are needed for both men and women, this chapter demonstrates that changes specific to women must be addressed. Feminist perspectives on crime and deviance argue that crime occurs in the context of gender relations, along with those of class and race. Understanding crime and deviance merely in terms of sex differences does not explain the feminist idea that institutionalized patterns of gender relations influence the behavior of women as well as the behavior of men. Thus, a thorough analysis of gender and crime must include the full context of women's criminal behavior and the victimization of women by male violence. Therefore, the simple addition of sex differences in sociological work on crime will not explain the full process by which gender organizes patterns of crime and deviance in society.

PART THREE

FEMINIST THEORY AND SOCIAL CHANGE

C H A P T E R

SEXISM AND THE SOCIAL CONSTRUCTION OF KNOWLEDGE

INTRODUCTION

Standing with one leg propped on an oversized box and with her cleavage pouring out of a sequined skintight halter top, a young woman declares, "I'm more satisfied!" Is this a peep show or a suggestive photograph in a girlie magazine? No, it is an advertisement for cigarettes that can be found in any one of a variety of mass-circulated magazines (*Essence* January 1982). Another advertisement states, "Part of the art of being a woman is knowing when not to be too much of a lady" (*Cosmopolitan* December 1981). Although ads such as these evoke an image of women as beguiling and seductive, others seem designed to make women fearful—fearful of aging, fearful of being overweight, or fearful of being without men. Some intimidate women by their implied threats of danger, as in the sales campaign for shoes that warns, "When you go out for the evening, leave your lights on"—the "lights" referring to spike-heeled, open-toed, strapped sandals!

Advertisements are only one source for the ideas about women that are generated in the mass media and popular culture. Popular music, advice columns, television shows, and other cultural materials all carry explicit and implicit suggestions regarding the appropriate social roles for women and men. Although the sexism found in these cultural artifacts may not be as overt as that of prior generations, sexist images and ideas about women persist that associate women primarily with sexuality or homemaking. Men, on the other hand, are most frequently depicted in work roles or postures in which, unlike women, they are dominant, aggressive, and self-assured.

The ideas about women and men that these cultural objects portray greatly influence our thinking about gender roles in society. As images, they convey an impression about the proper role of women, their sexual identity, and their self-consciousness. The ideas we hold about women and men, whether overtly sexist or more subtle in their expression, create social definitions that we use to understand ourselves and the society we live in.

Previous chapters have studied the status of women within the institutional structure of American society. They show the actual conditions of social life that influence gender relations in the society, and they demonstrate that transformations in gender relations must involve changes in the material conditions of women's experiences. In the discussion of sex role socialization, for example, the argument was made that changes in consciousness alone cannot liberate women from their oppression in a sexist society. Yet, we are likely to agree that changes in consciousness must be part of broader attempts to transform gender relations. The ideas that people have of one another do guide their behavior, even though there is no direct fit between what people believe and say and what they actually do (Deutscher 1973). But certainly, what is known or believed about women and gender relations, even when it is based on distortions of social realities, influences our mental experiences. These experiences, in turn, become part of the basis for sexist social arrangements.

A sociological perspective on ideas recognizes that social reality is composed of both ideas and actual material conditions. Each has a tremendous influence on our lives. Ideas, although based in the interpretive realm of thought and subjectivity, direct our behavior and constrain the ways in which we see each other and others see us. Ideas also have a political reality because they affect how society works, who gets rewarded, and what things should and should not be. For example, if we believe that women's proper place is in the home, we are not likely to object to the sexist practices of employer discrimination. However, if we believe that women are as capable as men, we are likely to support policies and changes that would make more opportunities available to them.

This chapter studies sexism as an idea, especially as it is reproduced in the media and academic institutions. Although these systems are not the exclusive sources of sexist ideas, they exert a powerful influence on the way we define reality and women's role within it. Although it is easy to oversimplify the influence of these systems, there is little doubt that both of them have a tremendous impact on the ways in which we define our society and ourselves within it. In fact, it can be argued that in a highly complex technological-industrial society, these systems of communication play an increasingly important part in the generation and transmission of ideas.

Moreover, as the feminist movement has shown, images of women conveyed by the media and in educational materials have been based on distortions and stereotypes that legitimate the status quo at the same time that they falsely represent the actual experience of women in the society. Thus, the ideas we acquire regarding gender relations poorly prepare us for the realities we will face. As we will see in the concluding section, these contradictions in social myths and realities have created much of the impetus for feminism as a social movement. But presently, our focus is on the content of these images, their origins in institutional systems of gender and power, and the ways in which they establish a definition, however misleading, of social reality.

This chapter begins by explaining the perspective of the sociology of knowledge—a subfield in sociology that examines the social origins of ideas. This section is followed by a discussion of images of women in the media. The final material presented in this chapter deals with women in academic knowledge and the reformulations of that knowledge that the feminist movement has generated.

THE SOCIOLOGY OF KNOWLEDGE

The sociology of knowledge begins with the premise that ideas emerge from particular social and historical settings and that this social structural context shapes, although it does not determine, human consciousness and interpretations of reality. Studies in the sociology of knowledge thus relate ideas and consciousness to social structure and human culture. Intellectually, this perspective originates primarily in the works of Karl Marx and Karl Mannheim, both of whom, in distinct ways, grappled with the relationship between human knowledge and human existence. It was Mannheim who, in the early twentieth century, labeled the study of the sociology of knowledge and delineated its specific program; but Marx's study of ideology and consciousness is the intellectual precursor of this endeavor. We will first consider Marx's ideas about the social construction of knowledge, following it with a discussion of Mannheim.

Marx begins his study of human ideas with the premise that the existence of living human beings, that is, their actual activities and material conditions, form the basis for human history and the ideas generated in this history. Although Marx recognizes that human beings live within particular physical settings (including climatic, geographical, and geological conditions), it is the social relationships formed in these settings that comprise human society. In other words, human beings transform their environmental conditions through the activities in which they engage. Marx argues that human beings are distinguished from animals by the fact of their consciousness; and although we now know that other animal species have linguistic abilities and rudimentary systems of social organization, nevertheless no other species has the capacity of humans for the elaboration of culture. Human society and history emerge as people use their labor to create their social environment.

Marx's theory of ideas originates with his argument that ideas follow from human behavior. In other words, thinking and the products of thinking are derived from the actual activity in which human beings engage. Marx discards the philosophical view that what humans think, imagine, or conceive precedes their actual life experiences. Thus, within Marx's framework, it is not the consciousness of persons that forms the bonds (and chains) of human society. Rather, specific relationships among people shape human society and, therefore, the ideas of its people.

Marx is not denying that social relations involve an interpretive dimension. He is arguing, however, that ideas emerge from our material reality. This theory has important consequences for social change, for it implies that changes in consciousness alone do not constitute the social changes necessary for the liberation of people. Instead, it is the material conditions of society that must be changed if we are to liberate people from oppression.

Marx goes one step further by arguing that within society, the dominant ideas of any period are the ideas of the ruling class. It is they who have the power to influence the intellectual production and distribution of ideas. Consequently, although persons ordinarily form their ideas within the context of their practical experience, ideas produced within powerful institutions take on an objective form that extends beyond us and acts as a system of social control. In fact, Marx goes on to say that in societies with a complex division of labor, a split develops between mental and material labor. Those who work with their hands are not those who produce the society's dominant ideas. Thus, especially for persons who are not in the ruling class, the dominant ideas of a society stand in contradiction to their experience.

An excellent example comes from the feminist scholar Dorothy Smith. She argues that the social organization of complex societies establishes a bifurcation of consciousness wherein the mind and body are considered to be different modes of experience. Coupled with a gender-based division of labor, the structure of work (especially in intellectual careers) engages in mental work men who are seemingly detached from physical needs. But this bifurcation is possible only because the labor of women provides for men's physical needs and mediates their social relations (Smith 1975).

A Marxist perspective relates ideas directly to the material conditions in which they are produced. This view is summed up by Marx's statement that "it is not the consciousness of men that determines their being, but, on the contrary, their social being that determines their consciousness" (Tucker 1972:4). In capitalist societies, those who own the means of production also determine the ruling ideas of the period. As Marx wrote, "The ideas of the ruling class are in every epoch the ruling ideas: i.e., the class which is the ruling material force of society, is at the same time its ruling intellectual force. The class which has the means of material production at its disposal, has control at the same time over the means of mental production, so that thereby, generally speaking, the ideas of those who lack the means of mental production are subject to it" (*The German Ideology;* in Tucker 1972:136).

Under capitalism, consciousness is determined by class relations, for even though persons will normally try to identify what is in their best interest, under capitalism the ruling class controls the production of ideas. Also, even though humans create practical ideas from experience, most of our experience is determined by capitalist relations of production. Thus, the ideas that are disseminated through communications systems, including language, serve to authorize a reality that the ruling class would like us to believe. Marx's theory is fundamental to understanding sexism as an idea that preserves the interests of dominant groups. Sexism justifies the power of men over women and, therefore, sanctions male domination. Furthermore, according to Marx, when subordinate groups accept the world view of dominant groups, they are engaged in "false consciousness." The fact that some women believe sexist ideas only reflects their false consciousness and shows how dominant groups have the power to control the production of ideas.

Marx's theory of consciousness is complemented by that of Karl Mannheim (1893–1947), who further developed the sociology of knowledge. Mannheim's sociology of knowledge seeks to discover the historical circumstances of knowledge by relating ideas to the conditions under which they are produced. His work also provides the foundation for feminist scholarship because he develops the thought that ideas grow out of the relationship of knowledge to social structure. Feminists (as we discussed in Chapter 1 and will further elaborate in this chapter) suggest that what has been taken as knowledge reflects the system of male domination in which it is produced. This insight stems from the work of Mannheim, who relates what is known to the social existence of the knower. By doing so, Mannheim and feminist scholars who have followed him challenge the idea that objectivity is based on the detachment of the knower from the surrounding environment. Mannheim suggests that the individual does not think alone. Not only do persons participate in what others have thought prior to the individual's existence, but even more fundamentally, all social thought involves a "community of knowing" (1936:31). Ideas expressed by a person are, therefore, functions of the person's experience as well as his or her social and historical milieu. The task of the sociology of knowledge is to discover the relational character of thought, meaning that it studies how ideas are embedded in the social experience of their producers and the social-historical milieu within which ideas are formed. Intellectual change must likewise be seen in the context of social change, and all ideas must be evaluated within the context of their social making. This view is true not only for the grand ideas of intellectual history but also for the consciousness of human beings in their ordinary experience (Berger and Luckmann 1966). Mannheim suggests that new ideas are most likely generated during periods of rapid social change. He explains this belief by suggesting that as long as group traditions remain stable, then traditional world views remain intact. New ideas appear when old traditions are breaking up, although the persistence of customary ways of thinking is also likely to make new ideas appear to be "curiosities, errors, ambiguities, or heresies" (1936:7).

Mannheim is best known for his study of ideology. *Ideology* refers to a system of beliefs about the world that involve distortions of reality at the same time that they provide justification for the status quo. Following from Marx, Mannheim sees ideology as serving the interests of groups in the society who justify their position by distorting social definitions of reality. Ideologies serve the powerful by presenting us with a definition of reality that is false and yet orders our comprehension of the surrounding world. When ideas emerge from ideology, they operate as a form of social control by defining the status quo to be the proper state of affairs.

In terms of Mannheim's work, sexism can be understood as an ideology that defends the traditional status of women in society. Although, as Mannheim says, no single idea constitutes an ideological belief system, the collective totality of an ideology (such as sexism) permeates our consciousness and our comprehension of the world in which we live. It is here that the sociology of knowledge merges with the political goals of feminism because in debunking sexist ideology, the social-historical origins of sexist thought are found and new definitions of reality can be forged. Although Mannheim is careful to distinguish political argument from academic thought, he recognizes that the unmasking of ideological systems is a function of sociological theory. Thus, politics and theory are interconnected (although not identical) because both recognize the relatedness of ideas to social structure.

For feminists, the sociology of knowledge creates the theoretical framework in which sexism and the generation of ideas about women can be understood. The theoretical perspectives of Marx and Mannheim underlie the analysis of sexism and knowledge that feminists have offered. Understanding the perspective of the sociology of knowledge helps us make sense of the images of women in the media, the gender bias of academic studies, and the patriarchal structure of popular culture. The fundamental issues of the sociology of knowledge perspective are to understand how ideas reproduce our definitions of social reality, who produces ideas, under what conditions ideas are made, and the consequences of ideas and beliefs that, in the case of sexism, systematically define women in stereotypical and distorted terms. We will first review the images of women in the media and see how these images reproduce sexist ideology.

IMAGES OF WOMEN IN THE MEDIA

Even a cursory review of the image of gender roles in the mass media shows that women and men are portrayed in stereotypical ways. Not only are they cast in traditional roles, but both men and women are omitted from roles that portray them in a variety of social contexts. Women tend to be portrayed in roles in which they are trivialized, condemned, or narrowly defined, resulting in the "symbolic annihilation" of women by the media (Tuchman, Daniels, and Benét 1978). Men, on the other hand, are usually depicted in high-status roles in which they dominate women (Lemon 1978).

The research method most often used to study media images is called *content analysis*. This method is a descriptive one whereby researchers analyze the actual content of documents or programs. By counting particular items within a defined category, researchers are able to systematize their observations of the content of the media (Wiseman and Aron 1970).

Content analyses of television show that, during prime-time hours, men make up a large majority of all the characters shown. Moreover, women prime-time characters are found primarily in comedies and men in dramas, giving the impression that men are to be taken seriously and women are not (Tuchman, Daniels, and Benét 1978). Content analysis also shows that men on television are more likely depicted in high status occupations than are women (Lemon 1978), and women are more likely depicted in family roles than work roles (Busby 1975). In fact, 75 percent of all television ads using women are for products found in the kitchen or the bathroom (Tuchman, Daniels, and Benét 1978).

Images of men and women on television reinforce not only gender stereotypes but those of class and race as well. Studies of dominance in television shows find that both men and women of high occupational status are more likely found in dramas than in comedies. Working-class characters are more frequently depicted in comedies, where they are presented in class stereotypical roles (such as Schneider on "One Day at a Time"). The impression is then given that working-class lives are funny, whereas serious drama occurs elsewhere. Defining dominance as behavior that influences, controls, persuades, prohibits, dictates, leads, directs, restrains, or organizes the behavior of others, studies find that white men are most dominant on television except in situation comedies, where low-status women tend to be more dominant than low-status men (Lemon 1978).

These patterns are further complicated by race. White men and women are far more numerous on television than minority men and women. This trend is particularly noticeable in the "disappearing" roles that blacks, Hispanics, and Asian-Americans often play in television dramas. On popular shows such as "Dallas" and daytime soap operas, minority women and men silently appear in backgrounds to cater to the needs of dominant households or individuals. Also, in popular shows such as "Quincy" and "Hawaii Five-O," minority persons frequently portray assistants to leading white male actors. In their interactions, the minority character is deferential, respectful, and dutiful to his dominant partner.

In a slightly different vein, black women in situation comedies dominate more than any other characters. In crime dramas, although black and white men are more dominant than either black or white women, black women are shown as more dominant than white women. On all shows, black women are usually portrayed as dominant in all black interactions. Such depictions of black women reproduce racist stereotypes of the mythical black matriarch by casting black women in the role of humorous but dominating characters. In this example, as well as others, television acts as a system of social control, narrowing our understanding of people's experience, discrediting and ridiculing serious subjects such as racism and sexism, and undercutting any resistance that the public might generate against dominant social institutions (Gerbner 1978).

In children's television programming, sexist stereotypes are probably at their worst—a particularly disturbing fact considering the number of hours children spend watching television. Television acts as a powerful agent of socialization for young children. Ninety-six percent of American homes are equipped with at least one television, and these sets are turned on an average of six hours per day. By the time an American child is fifteen years old, he or she will have spent more hours watching television than attending school (Sprafkin and Liebert 1978). A study of sixth through ninth graders finds that 40 percent of the children watch television for five hours or more per day; 25 percent watch for six or more hours per day; and only 10 percent report watching for less than two hours per day (Gross and Jeffries-Fox 1978).

What do children see when they watch television? Children's cartoons include even fewer women than do adult shows and, as in adult shows, female characters are likely to be seen as comical, as located only in family roles, or as victims of male violence (Gerbner 1978; Liebert, Neale, and Davidson 1973). The influence of gender stereotyping on television can be seen in the fact that children who watch the most television are those with the most stereotypic sex role values (Frueh and McGhee 1975). And a large proportion of elementary school children report that they learn about how blacks look and dress by watching television (Greenburg 1972).

As we increasingly rely on television and other media for information about our society, these restrictive images of women and minorities become especially troublesome. Segregation by race and by sex in the real world keeps us distant from each other and gives us little access to the experiences of others. Thus, it is likely that, for many, the media present the only information they know about people with whom they have had no direct experience and the only information about places where they have never been.

The nature of printed and electronic media is such that once an image is represented, it loses the fluid character it would have in reality. Thus, ideas and characters appear fixed, giving a singular impression of reality. Moreover, the mass media carry a certain authority, particularly because they provide a common basis for public interaction. Even the news, where we hope to get factual, objective reporting of world events, is packaged with authoritative commentaries, moral admonitions, comic relief, and sensationalized presentations. Because of the televised or recorded format of the news, all items appear equally serious, resulting in the trivialization and ultimate distortion of world events. Moreover, the gender biases common in fictional media also appear in the news, where women are underrepresented as reporters and commentators, where female reporters are more likely to report on "soft" news or human interest stories, where news about women is seldom found, and where, when it does appear, it is likely to celebrate traditional sex role values.

The mass media have slightly improved their images of women in the past few years, but these changes should be seen in the context of social control. Some suggest that television acts as a national religion in the contemporary world because it establishes a common culture and is resistant to cultural change. Television

is used by practically all the people and is used practically all the time. It col
lects the most heterogeneous public of groups, classes, races, and sexes, and
nationalities in history into a national audience that has nothing in common
except television or shared messages. Television thereby becomes the common
basis for social interaction among a very widely dispersed and diverse national
community. As such, it can only be compared, in terms of its functions, not to
any other medium but to the preindustrial notion of religion. (Gerbner
1978:47)

If television provides for the maintenance of culture, then it must
resist social movements that challenge the culture and seek to transform
social institutions. The media do not fully resist such changes; rather,
they defend the traditional system by coopting new images that social
movements generate. Consequently, we now see "liberated" images of
women in the media, but ones that still carry stereotypic gender
assumptions. For example, women may now be shown as working, but
these women are all beautiful, young, rich, and thin. At the same time,
because the media cannot ignore the feminist movement, it is portrayed
as trivial (as represented in the media phrase *women's lib*), and feminists are shown as extremists or as acceptable only when they are
moderate.

Women's magazines have been more responsive to social change than
other media, in part because of changes in the experiences of their audience (Tuchman, Daniels, and Benét 1978). Yet, these magazines still
portray women in sex role sterotypes in which youth and good looks are
emphasized and women are still defined by the men in their lives or by
their absence (Flora 1971; Tuchman, Daniels, and Benét 1978). Some
class differences in images of women also appear in women's magazines;
those with middle-class audiences have been more responsive to changes
in women's roles. One study comparing magazines with working-class
and middle-class readers finds that by 1975 working-class fiction was
more likely to portray women in dependent and passive roles than was
fiction in midde-class magazines. In 1970 the reverse had been true,
indicating that the media have responded more to changes in the lives
of middle-class women than to others (Flora 1979).

Content analyses of the media tell us a great deal about the image of
women in modern society. But these descriptions alone provide no direct
evidence of the character of communication systems, their audiences
and producers, and their actual effects. To understand these issues, we
require other material to provide theoretical direction to empirical
observations about the media, their content, organization, and effects.

Perspectives that have been used to explain women's depiction by the media are presented in the following section.

EXPLAINING WOMEN'S DEPICTION BY THE MEDIA

Understanding women's depiction by the media would not be so important if we did not assume that there is some relationship between media images and social reality. This is not to say that the images are real because we have already seen how they involve distortions and misrepresentations. But feminists assume that there is some relationship between images and reality, either because images reflect social values about women's roles or because images create social ideals upon which people model their behavior and attitudes. Moreover, these images are produced by actual working people, so that even if we see them as social myths, they remain connected to the social systems in which they emerge. Creating a theory of women's depiction by the mass media involves explaining the relationship between media images and the social worlds in which they are produced and consumed.

Several approaches have been taken by sociologists and communications specialists to explain the depiction of women by the media. These include the reflection hypothesis, sex role learning theory, gender inequality approaches to media organization, and socioeconomic approaches to media organization (Tuchman 1979). Each of these approaches has its own strengths and weaknesses, which are discussed here.

The first and theoretically the most simple explanation is called the *reflection hypothesis* (Tuchman 1979; Tuchman, Daniels, and Benét 1978). This hypothesis assumes that the mass media reflect the values of the general population. Thus, the images are seen to represent dominant ideals within the population, particularly because the capitalistic structure of the media is dependent upon appealing to the largest consumer audience. According to Gerbner (1978), the ideals of the population are incorporated into symbolic representations. The reflection hypothesis asserts that, although media images exist as make-believe, they do encapsulate dominant social beliefs and images.

The volumes of data produced by marketing researchers and ratings scales indicate that popular appeal is definitely significant in decisions about programming content. Observations of shows such as soap operas also show that television attempts to incorporate social issues into its programming that reflect, even if in an overblown way, the experiences (or, at least, the wishes) of its viewers. Although viewers may escape into soap operas as a relief from daily life, the fact that they can do so rests upon some form of identification (even if fanciful) with the characters and the situations they are in (Modleski 1980).

But the reflection hypothesis leaves several questions unanswered. To begin with, as content analysis studies have shown, much if not most of what the media depicts is not synchronized with real conditions in people's lives. In part, this phenomenon is explainable by a time lag between cultural changes and changes in the media (Tuchman, Daniels, and Benét 1978). It is also explainable by the fact that the media portray ideals, not truths. Nevertheless, people may not actually believe what they see in the media and, if they do, it may be because the media create their beliefs as much as it emerges from them. Thus, a causal question is asked in theoretical explanations of media images: Do the media reflect or create popular values? The reflection hypothesis makes the first assumption. Other explanations begin with the second one.

Feminists believe that the values reflected in the media represent the most conservative and sexist views of women and men. Moreover, they assume that sexist images in the media encourage role modeling. That is to say, "the media's deleterious role models, when internalized, prevent and impede female accomplishments. They also encourage both women and men to define women in terms of men (as sex objects) or in the context of the family" (Tuchman 1979). The assumption that the media encourage role modeling has been the basis for organized challenges by feminist groups that are opposed to sex role stereotyping in the media. Children's programs especially have been examined for their effect upon children's development (Gross and Jeffries-Fox 1978; Sprafkin and Liebert 1978), and even the more liberated shows such as "Sesame Street," have been criticized for their portrayals of female characters (Cathey-Calvert n.d.).

Feminist opposition to sex role stereotypes in the media often assumes that these stereotypes encourage people to model their behavior in stereotypic ways. But the role modeling argument involves naive theoretical assumptions that the media should truthfully reproduce social life and that there is some causal connection between the content of the media and its social effects (Tuchman 1979). In other words, the role modeling argument assumes that media images produce stimuli that, when mediated by social variables (such as age, gender, race, and class), have predictable responses from the public. This portrayal of social reality and human responses to the environment entails a pessimistic view of human beings as totally passive receptacles for whatever media inputs are poured into them. People may, in fact, view media images much more critically or even with cynicism, making it unlikely that they would modify their behavior in accordance with them. However, this possibility does not deny the fact that people, especially children, do learn from the media. This criticism of role modeling theory suggests that it is an oversimplified perspective.

Although both the reflection hypothesis and the role modeling argument alert us to the fit between images and reality, neither adequately explains the reasons for sexism in the media. Thus, scholars have attempted to explain sexism in media content by studying gender inequality within media organizations. This perspective assumes that women's subordinate position in the media influences the ideas produced therein. If women are absent from the power positions where ideas and images are produced, then their world view and experience will not be reflected in the ideas that organizations produce (Smith 1975). Moreover, those who occupy power positions come to share a common world view, so that the ideas they produce reflect the values of the ruling elite.

There is little doubt that women remain in subordinate positions in media organizations. They work in sex-segregated media jobs and are in a tiny proportion of reporters, writers, announcers, and managers in television and radio stations and on the major networks (Deckard 1975). And despite a spurt of hiring around 1970, the number of women holding administrative positions in the media has declined (Tuchman 1979). These data are convincing evidence that more women need to be hired if they are to have equality in media organizations, but do they explain the images of women produced by the media? The argument that increasing the presence of women in the media will transform images of women assumes that men and women hold different sex role values; this belief has simply not been demonstrated in research. Women and men in the fields of journalism and television production seem to share the same stereotypes of women, and most female journalism students believe that the majority of women prefer traditional content in women's magazines (Orwant and Cantor 1977). Female editors of women's pages also share the preferences of their male counterparts (Merritt and Gross 1978), and women make the same judgments as men regarding the general news (Phillips 1975).

These comparisons make sense if we recognize that persons who work in organizations become socialized to accept the organization's values. Those who do not conform are less likely to build successful careers. Hence, organizational workers more often than not adopt the values of the organizations in which they are employed. Within the media, professional attitudes discourage workers from offending the networks; thus, professionalism encourages workers to conform to the bureaucratic and capitalist values of their organization (Tuchman 1979). This influence affects the way men and women workers portray gender issues in the media because the organizational culture would encourage them not to appear too controversial. Values promoting the idea of individualism and upward mobility are so much a part of this culture that even feminism becomes portrayed in the media in terms of individual achievement, consumerism, personal style, and individual rewards (Ehrenreich 1978; Tuchman 1979). That men and women working in the media adopt similar values tells us, not so much that men and women think alike, but that all workers' behaviors and attitudes are shaped by the organizations in which they are employed (Kanter 1977).

Thus, a fourth perspective used to explain sexism in the media is a socioeconomic approach that attributes sexism to the capitalist structure of media organizations. According to this approach, it is in the interests of sponsors to foster images that are consistent with the products they sell. Many of these products encourage particular values, such as obsessive cleanliness, which is necessary to sell the myriad household cleaning products placed on the market. The depiction in the media of housewives who are pathologically concerned with cleanliness (Kilbourne 1979) reflects the manufacturers' attempts to sell their products.

This perspective also claims that it is in the interests of a capitalist power elite to discourage images of reality that would foster discontent. Thus, not only will sponsors promote any values that will sell, but they will also encourage traditional views that uphold the status quo while discouraging those that challenge it. When they do respond to social criticism, they do so within the limits of existing institutions. For example, following the civil rights movement, when pressure was generated to increase the number of blacks in the media, more blacks appeared in advertisements and on television programs, but they were mostly depicted in middle-class settings with dominant value systems and without radical criticism of the social system. Similarly, as noted previously, the feminist movement was, in its early days, depicted by the media as trivial and extremist. As the movement gained public support, the media selected its more moderate programs and leaders for public display.

This perspective does remind us that the media are owned and controlled by the major corporations of American society. One example comes from the popular magazine *Cosmopolitan,* which is owned by the Hearst Corporation—the same organization that controls several major newspapers, has representatives on the board of regents of the University of California, and owns vast amounts of property and other business organizations. Similar examples are found in other corporate conglomerates that own networks, newspapers, and recording companies. From this perspective, Marx's idea is true that those who control economic production also control the manufacture and dissemination of ideas.

The economic structure of the media explains much about how women are exploited through commercialism. Thus, this perspective has frequently been cited by feminists as the reason that women are portrayed either as sex objects or as household caretakers. These values, they point out, are consistent with capitalist needs to maintain women's services in the home and to make commercial objects out of everything, including sexuality (Mitchell 1974).

But in itself, this explanation encourages a conspiratorial view of media owners and management who, although they are motivated by economic profit, may not have the specific intent of exploiting women. But this perspective, along with the gender inequality approach, gives us a more complete understanding of sexism in the media. Observing the economic and social organization of the media causes us to ask who produces media images and how these images define legitimate forms of social reality. Thus, images of women become specifically tied to their economic and social origins.

The feminist sociologist Dorothy Smith suggests that "social forms of thought originate in a practice of ruling—or management, or administration, or other forms of social control. They are located in and originate from definite positions of dominance in the society. They are not merely that floating thing, the 'culture'" (1975:355). Because of this logic, it is suggested that the concept of images be discarded by feminists because it connotes a somewhat vacuous and abstract idea and underplays the social production and reproduction of thought (Tuchman 1979).

Alternatively, women's depictions in the media can be seen as social myths by which the meaning of society and women's place within it is established. Anthropologists study social myths to gain an insight into the culture and social organization of a people. Myths provide an interpretation of social truths, beliefs, and relationships that guide a society in its vision of the past, present, and future. Myths establish a "universe of discourse" that integrates and controls its members, gives them a common reality, and creates structures for what is said, done, and believed (Tuchman 1979). By creating a universe of discourse among their audience, the media act as powerful agents of social control. They engage people in passive fantasies, encourage dreams and visions that are consistent with the social structure, and establish a common basis for social interaction. Therefore, in a fundamental way, the depiction of women in the media infiltrates our social consciousness and embeds itself in our imagination. In sum, the media establish popular culture, which, in turn, establishes our definitions of social reality.

The media are powerful sources for communicating sexist ideas about men and women and their roles in society. What we absorb from the media is learned subtly and informally and in the context of everyday life. But in addition to the influence of the media and the popular culture they represent, sexism is also learned through the formal process of education. In the next section, we will look at the social construction of knowledge as it occurs in academic settings. This section will show especially how feminism has encouraged transformations in academic knowledge so as to better understand the position of men and women in society.

WOMEN AS OUTSIDERS IN THE SOCIAL CONSTRUCTION OF KNOWLEDGE

The pursuit of knowledge has always been considered the work of men (Sherman and Beck 1979). In the history of education, women have been outsiders. Either they were excluded by formal admissions policies or they were tracked into sex-typed fields and specialties. Although women have now been present in the university system for more than a century, they still have the status of outsiders because they are not yet as numerous as men in the academic professions and, when they are present, they are not as highly placed in the educational system. As this section will show, women's status as outsiders also has important ramifications for the way in which academic knowledge is constructed and the way women are defined within it. Academic knowledge is created within specific institutional structures. Because the production of research and scholarship is tied to the setting in which it develops, the noticeable absence or invisibility of women in these settings has contributed to "the symbolic annihilation of women" (Tuchman, Daniels, and Benét 1978).

Commonsense attitudes about scholarship may make it seem odd to think of it as institutionalized. Popular images of university scholarship tend to see it as produced in "ivory towers"—places with little connection either to common sense or to the events of everyday life. Thus, scholarship is perceived as if it were somehow detached from the events of the world at large. But the popular connotations of the word *scholarship* overlook the fact that the institutions in which scholarship is produced share the same characteristics that are found in other institutions.

Institutions are *established* patterns of behavior with a particular and recognized *purpose,* and they include specific *participants* who *share expectations* and act in *specific roles* with *rights and duties* attached to them (Payer 1977). Institutions define reality for us insofar as they exist as objective entities in our experience. They are "experienced as existing over and beyond the individuals who 'happen' to embody them at the moment. In other words, the institutions are experienced as a reality of their own, a reality that confronts the individual as an external and coercive fact" (Berger and Luckmann 1966:58).

A closer look at institutions where scholarship is created reveals that there are unequal distributions of resources within them, power relationships between dominant and subordinate groups, beliefs and attitudes that define the work of some as more legitimate than that of others, and socialization processes by which newcomers are taught the ways of the system. And just as in other institutions, for those who do not conform, a variety of sanctions can be applied, ranging from ridicule to exclusion.

Moreover, persons who participate in the life of an institution intersubjectively share in its definitions of reality and its definitions of themselves. Thus, what becomes known is tacitly known among the participants in given systems of meaning. And as the collective cognitions of the institution's members become taken for granted, the institution becomes reified. That is to say, it is assumed to have an objective (i.e., real) existence even though its objective existence is subjectively based. The process of reification is complete when the relationship between the institution and its origins (in other words, its social development) is forgotten. Institutions

are not only here-and-now, given, and self-evident, but also arise within particular and historic environments, and in response to certain felt interests and needs; and as these interests are served, and needs are met and continue to be met in certain typical ways, actions are repeated, grow into patterns, and become firmly entrenched in practice and consciousness. It is just at this stage, when practice and habits pass over into highly organized forms, that we begin to speak of "institutions" as opposed to mere custom or habitual activity. (Payer 1977:30).

From this perspective on institutions, it is possible to see that those who are not fully integrated into the institutional structure are least likely to share the conventional wisdom of the institution as a whole. Women have stood as outsiders to these institutions, and their status as outsiders is critical in explaining the origins of feminist scholarship.

Most women who enter academic life will find themselves alone, or nearly so, in a group of men. Statistically, they constitute a small minority of the persons in all but the most traditionally female disciplines in American universities (Hornig 1980). Women are not only under-represented as faculty in higher education, they are also less likely to be tenured (see Table 8.1). This situation is partly explained by the fact that women are more concentrated at the lower ranks than men (see

Table 8.1 Percent of Faculty with Tenure, 1980–1981

	Number of Faculty Members (All Ranks Combined)		Percent with Tenure (All Ranks Combined)	
	Male	**Female**	**Male**	**Female**
Public universities	73,754	16,807	6.5%	0.6%
Private universities	26,480	6,516	66.3%	36.5%
Other public four-year institutions	81,928	28,945	70.9%	50.2%
Other private four-year institutions	44,114	16,685	59.8%	37.4%
Public two-year institutions	40,711	22,224	79.3%	67.5%
Private two-year institutions	967	749	57.3%	39.5%
All institutions (public and private)	267,954	91,926	70.0%	49.7%

Source: "Fact File: Faculty Tenure Rates, 1980–81," *Chronicle of Higher Education,* September 30, 1981:10.

Table 8.2). Although women have made slight gains in academic rank in recent years, they still remain predominantly at lower levels and in less prestigious institutions.

Women's token status in academia has several consequences both for the personal experiences of women academics and for the state of knowledge in general. At the personal level, women may find that their personalities (formed as they are through cultural expectations of femininity) are at odds with the values and behaviors surrounding them. This dilemma is best described by Alice Rossi, who wrote in 1970:

women who are intellectually or politically brilliant are more readily accepted by men if they are also properly feminine in their style and deportment with men. This helps to assure that there will be few women of achievement for men to 'exempt' from the general category of women, since the traits associated with traditional femininity—softness, compliance, sweetness—are rarely found together with the contradictory qualities of a vigorous and questioning intellect, and a willingness to persist on a problem against conventional assumptions. (1970:36)

The isolation women encounter in academic life (as well as other work organizations) creates a feeling of standing out—if only by reason of their differences (Epstein 1970; Kanter 1977). Moreover, women will probably find that, in their professions, their experience is translated into the concepts and categories that have been used to describe male experience. And as women begin to rethink the character of scholarship in their disciplines, they are frequently charged with being trivial, insignificant, or simply "into that women's stuff"!

Table 8.2   Faculty by Rank and Sex, 1980–1981 (All Institutions)

Rank	Number of Male Faculty	Percent of Male Faculty at This Rank	Number of Female Faculty	Percent of Female Faculty at This Rank	Women as % of All Faculty at This Rank
Full professor	91,888	34.3%	10,295	11.2%	10.1%
Associate professor	75,000	28.0	19,046	20.7	20.3
Assistant professor	60,628	22.6	32,252	35.1	34.7
Instructor	13,649	5.1	14,833	16.1	52.1
Lecturer	3,272	1.2	2,827	3.1	46.4
No rank	23,517	8.8	12,673	13.8	35.0
Total	267,954		91,926		

Source: "Fact File: Faculty Tenure Rates, 1980–81," *Chronicle of Higher Education,* September 30, 1981:10.

The personal consequences of women's status in academia are troubling and, no doubt, result in the demise of many women's careers. But women's status in the academic disciplines has also influenced what is known about them. Male domination of academic institutions influences the social production of knowledge because the existing schemes of understanding have been created within a particular setting, one in which men have authority over women. In sociology, for example, "how sociology is thought—its methods, conceptual schemes and theories have been based on and built up within the male social universe—even when women have participated in its doing" (Smith 1974:7). Because the male-constituted world stands in authority over women (both inside and outside the academy), sociologists "impose the concepts and terms in which the world of men is thought as the concepts and terms in which women must think about their world" (Smith 1974:7). Women then become outsiders, not only because their status in universities is less than that of men, but also because they are estranged from the dominant world view surrounding them in academic life.

Sociological theory provides insight in understanding how the status of outsiders influences their perspectives. Georg Simmel (1858–1918) describes a stranger as one who is "fixed within a particular spatial group whose boundaries are similar to spatial boundaries. But his [sic] position in this group is determined, essentially, by the fact that he has not belonged to it from the beginning, that he imports qualities into it which do not and cannot stem from the group itself" (1950:402). Thus, the stranger (or the outsider) is both close to and distant from the group and its beliefs. The outsider is both involved with and indifferent to the shared perspectives of the group as a whole. This detachment creates critical distance, so that what is taken for granted by group members may be held in doubt by outsiders. As feminists have put it, "the outsider is denied the filtered vision that allows men to live without too troubling an insight" (Gornick 1971:126).

Feminist criticism of the social sciences also describes the vision that women as outsiders bring to intellectual life. The feminist sociologist Marcia Westkott writes:

When women realize that we are simultaneously immersed in and estranged from both our own particular discipline and the Western intellectual tradition generally, a personal tension develops that informs the critical dialogue. This tension, rooted in the contradiction of women's belonging and not belonging, provides the basis for knowing deeply and personally that which we criticize.

A personally experienced, culturally-based contradiction means that in some fundamental way we as critics also oppose ourselves, or, at least, that part of us continues to sustain the very basis of our own estrangement. Hence, the personal struggle of being both an insider and outsider is not only a source of knowledge and insight, but also a source of self-criticism. (1979:422)

In the history of sociological thought, marginality and alienation, especially during periods of rapid social change, have produced many valuable insights (Collins and Makowsky 1978; Nisbet 1970). That scientific thinking, including sociological thinking, emerges in periods of uncertainty testifies to the idea that doubt and transformation foster the development of personal and collective creative thought. As suggested by C. Wright Mills, personal and societal troubles that destroy the façades of conventional wisdom also form the scientific basis of the sociological and feminist imaginations.

For outsiders, their paradoxical closeness to and remoteness from social groups may result in new perspectives on knowledge. It is the outsider who suspends belief in the taken-for-granted attitudes of institutions. Feminists have concluded that in this way the status of women in intellectual life results in new methodologies and new perspectives of thought.

Because of the influence of the feminist movement, women who entered the academic world in the 1970s did so while they were self-conscious of their status as women. As these women saw that gender influenced all aspects of their lives, they also began to recognize the gender bias inherent within the traditional scholarship of the academic fields. Consequently, the work done by feminist scholars has entailed an ongoing critique of the distortions that gender bias has created within traditional academic knowledge.

FEMINISM AND THE SOCIAL CONSTRUCTION OF KNOWLEDGE

Feminists argue that what we come to know as a result of being educated is thoroughly infused with gendered assumptions about the character of the social world, its problems, its inhabitants, and its meaning. This critique of traditional scholarship forms the basis for the emergence of feminist scholarship and the introduction of new modes of analysis in most of the academic fields. Revisions in the traditional canons of knowledge by feminist scholars have been closely tied to the women's movement and have, in many disciplines, transformed some of the basic assumptions about the relationship of women and men—both to each other and to the world in which they live.

As already discussed in Chapter 1, feminist scholarship began by noting the omission of women from scholarly research and sought to remedy this bias by adding women and their experience to scholarly projects. In this way, women's contributions to society and history were recognized, although there were no fundamental shifts in the basic concepts and ideas of academic thinking. This approach was soon followed by the recognition that, just as gender patterns our social being and consciousness, so does it organize the process of thinking by which ideas are formed. Therefore, feminist scholarship has moved to challenge some of the fundamental concepts, theories, and substantive facts of the academic disciplines.

In sociology, this movement is best represented by Dorothy Smith, whose work in the sociology of knowledge challenges some fundamental conceptions of objectivity, social research, and the construction of sociological theory. Smith (1979) begins with a fundamental sociological point—that social experience and consciousness are conditioned by the social location of our existence. As Smith shows, men and women have quite different life situations. To the extent that their situations differ, their consciousness, culture, conceptions, and ideas are also different. Smith's work begins with the premise that the real activity of women— their roles in production and reproduction—form the basis for their ideas. Because sex/gender systems organize our social relations and because intellectual thought is shaped by social relations, then the sex/ gender system also shapes our perspectives as social thinkers and social researchers.

In sociology, the problems that feminist scholars find contradict the established image of sociology as objective and value-free. Introductory students, for instance, are taught that sociological inquiry relies on the procedures of the scientific method, particularly because scientific inquiry is seen as contributing to the objectivity of social research. For instance, in two introductory textbooks we read:

Sociology is a science. It is a system of knowledge in which all statements about reality must be based on objectivity and carefully collected observations. . . . Sociology is not just a series of exercises in casual observation or "educated guessing," but a meticulous and objective science. (Goodman and Marx 1982:8)

The sociological perspective relies on the scientific method for answers to its inquiries about social life. . . . Social science uses the scientific method . . . to observe, to establish consistent regularities, to predict future behavior, and eventually to control events. (Baldridge 1980:8–9)

Although feminists do not reject the use of the scientific method in sociological study, this picture of sociology raises two distinct but related issues. The first involves the connection between theory and politics; the second involves discussion of the concept of objectivity and its relationship to the social production of knowledge.

If one assumes, as most would, that social and scientific theory must be free of political commitments, then the very phrase *feminist theory* seems to be a contradiction in terms. Theory is allegedly void of social purpose, and its legitimacy, in the scientific framework, depends on its ability to explain events in the empirical world. What, then, does feminist theory mean, and how do we account for the connection it makes between theoretical construction and political commitment?

The history of modern science demonstrates that science has often been tied to the cause of social reform (Mendelsohn 1977). In the seventeenth century, as modern science began, scientific inquiry was justified for its specific social value. Moreover, the legitimacy of scientific inquiry rested on the same principles of reform that today sound like feminist social practices—antiauthoritarianism, progressiveness, antielitism, educational reform, humanitarianism, and the unity of experience and knowing (Van Den Daele 1977). Contemporary debates about the social and political application of scientific knowledge (such as the examples of nuclear energy and the atomic bomb) also indicate that even in scientific circles the question of scientific purpose is not separate from the practice of scientific inquiry.

Historically, the scientific movement also emerged in specific opposition to the canons of traditional belief, especially as a challenge to the state and the political authority of the church. As one historian of science writes, "the breakdown of older patterns of authority and traditionally-held dogmas or consensus positions allows much broader boundaries for exploration and the staking out of positions previously proscribed—either tacitly or implicitly" (Mendelsohn 1977:10). By removing the blinders of earlier commitments, scientists have argued that more objective inquiry would provide the new facts and new perspectives needed to meet the needs of emerging social institutions. Similarly, feminists argue that the neutral claims of traditional scholarship mask nonobjective interpretations of women's lives that have been produced. According to feminist inquiry, new perspectives on women's lives, and specifically, ones that challenge sexist assumptions, will result in more accurate explanations of women's experiences. Feminists still use scientific methods in their studies, but they claim that their work is more objective because it is more inclusive of all persons' experiences.

Thus, a central question in feminist scholarship is the issue of objectivity and its relationship to the process of knowing (Harding 1982). According to standard arguments about sociological research, rigorous observation and the use of the scientific method eliminate observer bias. But in the feminist critique, the observer is not a neutral party. Because knowledge is socially produced, feminists argue that the particular experiences and attitudes that observers bring to their work influence what they study, how they study it, and what they conclude about it (Keller 1978). Untangling the relationship between the knower and the known is a primary issue in feminist thought.

In sociology, these ideas have been most fully developed by Dorothy Smith (1979). She makes several important points in considering the issue of objectivity. First, she notes that all research is done from a particular standpoint or location in the social system. The world is known from the perspective of the researcher. In any given research project, we must know both the subjects's and the researcher's point of entry. Most often, sociologists enter research projects through official institutions (such as the schools, the police, or social welfare agencies). Consequently, the work they do may support the system as it is. Instead, Smith suggests that most objective inquiries can be produced only by those with the least interest in maintaining the status quo.

She explains this idea by using an example from the German philosopher Hegel. Suppose we consider a master and a slave and want to comprehend the world in which they live. Both of them live in the same world, but their experience within that world is quite different. The master takes the slave's labor (in fact, his or her existence) for granted; thus, the master's needs are immediately satisfied. The slave, on the other hand, conforms to the master's will; his or her labor is an object of the master's consciousness. The organization of this relationship is invisible to the master. If the master were describing the world they both inhabit, his account would be less objective because the structures of that world are invisible to him. But the slave's description of the world would include the master, plus the fact of his or her labor and its transformation to the status of an object. Consequently, the slave is more objective because his or her account is both more complete and more directly related to the empirical events within the relationship.

Similarly, in the case of women, when we begin describing the world by examining women's experience, the knowledge we create does not merely add to the already established constructs of sociological thought. The experience of women, like that of the slave, has been invisible. Women inhabit the same world as men; in fact, women's labor shapes men's experience in the world (through housework and the maintenance of social and bodily relations). Women's labor makes the male mode of operation—detached and rational—possible; yet, it remains invisible to men as the dominant class. An objective sociological account of reality must make sense of both women's and men's experiences and, therefore, must be constructed from the vantage point of both.

Smith (1981) also argues that sociological research and theory must situate social actors within their everyday worlds. In other words, unless research begins with the ordinary facts of lives, then the knowledge that sociologists construct will be both alienating and apart from the actual experiences of human actors. Sociological analysis begins with what social actors immediately experience but goes beyond it by discovering the social-institutional context of their lives. Although the institutional context of everyday experience is not immediately visible to those who experience it, the sociological perspective makes this context available and, thus, is a powerful agent of social change. Like the perspective of C. Wright Mills, Smith is working to establish the relationship between social structure and everyday life. This relationship is especially important in comprehending women's experience, because the affairs of everyday life are the specific area of women's expertise. Given the gender division of labor, women are charged with maintaining everyday life. To overlook it or to treat it as insignificant is to deny women's reality as an important part of social existence.

In sum, feminists have both introduced women's experience into sociological knowledge and have shown how traditional knowledge has been generated from specific gender relations. Informed by the empirical facts of women's experience and recognizing the influence of gender relations in the development of knowledge, the feminist perspective has created new analyses of the social order and established new goals for social change. Although feminist scholarship does not discard all the insights and understandings from past sociological thought, it does revise the assumptions, content, and purpose of sociological inquiry (Westkott 1979). Feminist scholarship emerges specifically from the feminist consciousness and has followed a clear path of development. The origins of feminist scholarship are found within women's cultural experience—first, as the simple recognition that a collective wrong has been suffered. The feminist movement emerged when women organized to correct these wrongs; the social movement itself then generated new forms of women's culture. Finally, feminist consciousness is producing autonomously defined modes of thinking and theory, and thinking has been shifted from male-centered to female-centered perspectives. With that change, new modes of analysis are emerging (DuBois et al., 1980).

The following two chapters review the development of feminist theory as it emerges from liberal and radical perspectives. These chapters will show that different theoretical perspectives in feminist analysis provide different insights into the status of women in society. Each perspective has its own strengths and weaknesses, although the dialogue emerging from them provides a rich account by which to understand gender relations. As we will see, too, each theoretical perspective presents a different interpretation of the social world. Therefore, the assumptions, observations, and conclusions that we make regarding women's status will vary depending on the theoretical position that we take. But understanding women's status requires the broadly based perspective that theoretical discussion provides. Hopefully, this review of feminist theory will guide interpretations of the issues and research studies that the first two parts of this book provide.

C H A P T E R 9

FEMINISM AND SOCIAL REFORM: THE LIBERAL PERSPECTIVE

INTRODUCTION

The theoretical and political frameworks of feminist thought emerge from some of the classical traditions of social and political theory. However, as we will see, in considering issues about women's lives, feminists have revised some of these classical perspectives to explain better the position of women in society. But, like the intellectual traditions from which feminist thought stems, feminist theory is organized around varying assumptions about social organization and social change. As a result, many of the empirical conclusions of social research that have been reviewed in preceding chapters lend themselves to different interpretations and implications for change, depending on the theoretical position that is used to understand them.

Because theoretical perspectives inform interpretations of observed events in the social world, it is necessary to understand the theoretical underpinnings of positions we adopt in scholarly and political analysis.

Particularly since feminism has moved into the mainstream of American life, many people identify themselves as feminists with little understanding of the liberal framework they assume (Eisenstein 1981). Whether one assumes a liberal or a radical feminist stance, examining the intellectual roots of different feminist perspectives provides a more complete understanding of the assumptions of a given perspective, as well as the different programs for social change which given perspectives imply. Consequently, careful study of particular feminist frameworks enables us to answer questions about women's status in society more accurately and, therefore, allows for a better assessment of possible directions for social change.

To date, three major theoretical perspectives have been developed in feminist theory. They include liberal feminism, Marxist or socialist feminism, and radical feminism. Liberal feminism emphasizes social and legal reform through policies designed to create equal opportunities for women. In addition, liberal feminism emphasizes the sex role socialization process as the origin of sex differences, thereby assuming that changes in socialization practices and the reeducation of the public will result in more liberated and egalitarian gender relations.

Marxist or socialist feminism is a more radical perspective that sees the origins of women's oppression in the systems of capitalism and patriarchy. Classical Marxists, in fact, see the oppression of women as stemming primarily from capitalism, in which women are defined as the property of men and the accumulation of profit necessitates the exploitation of women's labor. Socialist feminists have criticized traditional Marxism for reducing women's status to capitalism alone, noting that women are also oppressed in precapitalist- and noncapitalist-based social systems. Although maintaining the importance of class systems and the economic relations of capitalism in their analyses, socialist feminists see capitalism as interacting with patriarchy to create women's oppression.

Radical feminists, on the other hand, see patriarchy per se as the primary cause of women's oppression. They look to the devaluation of women in all patriarchal societies as evidence of the centrality of patriarchy in determining women's status. Within American culture, they trace women's oppression to the patriarchal control of female sexuality and male domination in social institutions.

Each of these perspectives will be detailed more thoroughly. Liberal feminism is the subject of this chapter, and socialist feminism and radical feminism are discussed in Chapter 10. As we will see, no single perspective provides the singularly most correct analysis of women's place in society. As our review will show, each perspective has its own conceptual strengths and weaknesses and, thus, is able to answer some questions better than others. Together, these feminist theoretical perspectives provide a rich and engaging analysis of women in society.

The adequacy of each perspective should be assessed, in part, in terms of its ability to address several fundamental issues in feminist thought. Most importantly, because feminism purports to liberate *all* women, a sound feminist analysis must be able to address the relationship of race, class, and gender. The adequancy of a given theoretical and political framework must be judged according to the perspective on race and class (as well as gender) that it provides.

In addition to explaining how race, class, and gender intersect in women's experience, feminist perspectives must address some of the central issues that are encountered in thinking about women. These issues follow from the topics that have organized the preceding chapters of this book. They include understanding the issue of nature versus nurture (including the process of sex role socialization); interpreting women's status in work and the family; explaining the social control of female reproduction, health, and sexuality; comprehending female crime and deviance and their connection to gender relations; and relating the ideology of sexism to the social institutions in which it is produced.

The review of feminist theory begins with liberal feminism—the most mainstream feminist perspective. This chapter begins by discussing the general perspective of liberalism and the origins of liberal feminism in the liberal tradition. Following this introduction of liberalism, the chapter reviews the work of early (eighteenth- and nineteenth-century) liberal feminists, particularly the writings of Mary Wollstonecraft and the first woman sociologist, Harriet Martineau. An extended discussion of John Stuart Mill and Harriet Taylor Mill is given because their collected works form a major part of the intellectual origins of contemporary feminism. Finally, the chapter reviews the contemporary liberal feminist perspective as it is found in feminist politics and theory.

THE ORIGINS OF LIBERALISM

The origins of contemporary liberal feminism reach back to the seventeenth- and eighteenth-century Age of Enlightenment in Western

Europe (also known as the Age of Reason). This period fostered an array of political, social, and intellectual movements, most of them characterized by an explicit faith in the capacity of human reason to generate social reform. As the setting for the early philosophies of feminism, the Age of Enlightenment is noted for its libertarian ideals, its pleas for humanitarian reform, and its conviction that "reason shall set us free" (Rossi 1973).

The philosophy of the period provided the theme for major changes in Western social organization (including the French and American Revolutions), and it set the stage for the eventual development of social-scientific thought and the emergence of sociology as an academic field. The historical context of early feminist thought is found in conditions that inspired more general appeals to social reform through the application of human reason. It is worthwhile to examine some of the transformations that mark the period and that provide the historical arena for the emergence of contemporary liberal feminism.

The two most notable developments that influenced broad-scale change in the West were the consolidation and expansion of a world system of capital (Wallerstein 1976) and a decline in the traditional sacred authority of religion (Nisbet 1970). The development of Western capitalism created new systems of inequality marked by the displacement of the poor from rural land and the concentration of wealth in the hands of the new capitalist class. The related developments of urbanization and industrialization also planted the seeds of the social problems that continue to confront us in the late twentieth century—urban crowding and the development of slums, pollution and waste, poverty, crime, and new tensions in family life. But in the Age of Enlightenment, political thinkers who observed these changes also delighted in the decline of the influence of the sacred authority of the church and the secular feudal state. The Enlightenment thinkers fostered the hope that the human ability to reason would provide societies with reasonable solutions to the new problems they encountered.

Thus, one of the central tenets of Enlightenment philosophy and the political-social thought it inspired was that free, critical inquiry was to be the cornerstone for the future. At heart, the Enlightenment thinkers were optimists, and they seemed undaunted by the vast problems surrounding them. Although, in retrospect, they can be criticized for their naive faith in human rationality, their work is also praised for its emphasis on nondogmatic discussion and open inquiry (Hughes 1958).

Their libertarian ideals challenged the power of feudal elites and assumed that the future was in the hands of the masses. And as they considered the development of history, they envisioned a decline in the brutal and "uncivilized" physical abuses of the past (deTocqueville 1945). They believed that the church, identified by most Enlightenment thinkers as the villain of past repression, would continue to decline in its authoritarian influence; modern society would instead be regulated by the rational construction of democratic government.

The influence of the Enlightenment extends beyond the eighteenth century, laying the foundation for the development of social science in the nineteenth and twentieth centuries and influencing later thinkers, such as John Stuart Mill, in the nineteenth century. Sociology, in particular, is indebted to the Enlightenment for its emphasis on the application of reason and the scientific method to the solution of social problems. Early sociological thinkers, such as Auguste Comte (1798–1857) and Henry Saint-Simon (1760–1825), believed that social knowledge would take the form of social laws, telling us how the social world operated and, therefore, how we could engineer positive changes. The simplicity of their faith in sociology as the ultimate science is now apparent, but their influence on the positivist methods of sociology is immeasurable. The positivism they inspired and that others have developed assumes that the techniques of scientific observation in the physical sciences can be used in the discovery of social behavior. Their insistence on the application of sociological knowledge for engineering social change continues to influence the activities of modern social planners.

The philosophy of liberalism emerging in this period rests on two central principles—one, the concept of individual liberty, and the other, an emphasis upon human reason as the basis for humanitarian social change. In liberal feminism, these philosophical ideals are the basis for the principle of equal opportunity and social reform. Consequently, much of the focus of social change among liberal feminists groups lies in the construction of legislation and in the regulation of employment practices. According to the liberal perspective, the obstacles to equal rights for women (and other groups, as well) lie in traditional laws and practices that deny the same individul rights to women that men already have.

The liberal perspective assumes that persons can create humanitarian change through the use of human rationality. Injustice is viewed as due to irrationality and ignorance; reason and the pursuit of knowledge are believed to be the source of social change. Consequently, liberal policies for change rely upon a faith in the process of social reform. Liberal feminists' practical solutions to inequality include programs that prohibit discrimination (such as affirmative action and equal opportunity policies). Liberal feminism also seeks the reform of individuals through, for example, the resocialization of children and the relearning of appropriate social roles for adults. A central emphasis of the liberal perspective is that all persons' abilities are culturally learned; therefore, egalitarian gender relations will follow from relearning traditional sex role attitudes and behaviors.

The popularity of the liberal perspective makes it difficult to identify as a specific social and political philosophy. It is the philosophical backdrop to many contemporary programs for change, and it has been widely adopted by diverse groups, such as those advocating assertiveness training and self-awareness workshops for women and political action groups such as the National Organization for Women. Commonly, liberalism also encourages the acceptance of diverse life-styles, because it sees life-style as a matter of individual choice. Within the liberal perspective, persons and the societies they create should be tolerant and respectful of the choices persons make. Because the person has the civil right to exercise his or her freedom, societies should not erect barriers to individual liberties. The liberal perspective, like other feminist perspectives, rejects the conservative view that persons assume their status in life because of ascribed (biological) characteristics. The different statuses that people acquire can be attributed to social learning and the denial of opportunity. Thus, liberal feminists (along with other feminists) reject the conservative belief that women arc bound to particular roles and statuses because of their biological capacity to bear children.

In sum, the liberal perspective of feminism assumes that the inequality of women stems both from their deprivation of equal rights and from their learned reluctance to exercise them. The goal of liberal feminism is equality—the construction of a social world where all persons can exercise individual freedon. At its heart, the liberal perspective is a philosophy based on the principle of individual liberty. In the liberal framework, every person should be allowed to exercise freedom of choice, unfettered by either public opinion or law. In effect, all persons should be given equal opportunities, and civil rights should be extended to all. The liberal feminist platform , then, supports reforms such as the Equal Rights Amendment, which, if it were enacted, would amend the Constitution to state: "Equality of rights under the law shall not be denied or abridged by the United States or by any state on the basis of sex."

Several criticisms of the liberal perspective can be made, and these issues will be discussed in the concluding section. But the criticisms can be summarized by saying that liberal feminism asks mainly for changes in the way individuals, because of their group characteristics, are treated in the existing social system. For example, the major change advocated by liberal feminists is that more women should be admitted to the existing political and economic systems. Because of the centrality of individual liberty to the liberal perspective,

liberals do not criticize *as such* inequalities in wealth, position, and power. What they do criticize is their distribution on the grounds of some inherited and not obviously relevant characteristic such as family, race, or sex. Liberals believe that each individual should be able to rise in society as her or his talents permit, unhindered by restraints of law or custom. (Jaggar and Struhl 1978:82)

The liberal perspective emphasizes gradual reform and is distinguished from more radical perspectives by the fact that liberals believe that progress and social change can be made within the structure of existing political and economic institutions.

The birth of liberalism during the Enlightenment provides the context for its emphasis on human liberty and social reform. It is in this period that the stage was set for the emergence of feminism and its pleas for the emancipation of women.

THE EARLY FEMINISTS

The legacy of the Enlightenment, as it is recorded in the historical record, was a period characterized by the ascendency of reason over tradition, the outreach of humanitarianism to dispossessed groups, and general improvement in the condition of humanity. Therefore, the Enlightenment period is often interpreted as the origin of contemporary social throught.

We are not sure what the Enlightenment was like for women, because its recorded history has been largely that of men's accomplishments. We do know that women's historical experience differs significantly from men's (Kelly-Gadol 1976), (Lerner 1976) and feminist historians have suggested that the Enlightenment is no exception. They would argue that the Age of Reason is a reference only to the reason of certain men; during this same era, women's work was idealized as belonging in the emotional world of the home. Nevertheless, women's labor (both in the home and outside of it) constituted a major part of the society's economic productivity. Most women still produced marketable goods in the home and, as factories became the site for production, women and children were employed for long hours at low wages.

But both women and the working class seem to have been left out of the Age of Reason. The intellectual movement of the Enlightenment was largely based on the thought of bourgeois white men; during this same period in the United States, black women and men were still in the bonds of slavery. The legacy of the Enlightenment as the triumph of reason is a celebration of the preeminence of men's rational power. Women, on the other hand, were identified with the irrational and emotional side of life. The ascent of rationality about which historical legends of the Enlightenment inform us can be seen the ascent of male rational power over the presumed emotionality and inferiority of women.

This revision casts a different light on long-standing interpretations of the intellectual history of the period. Feminist historians who have studied the philosophies of the major Enlightenment thinkers (Rousseau, Diderot, and Condorcet) conclude that, although the Enlightenment philosophy had the potential to decry the sexist ideas of sacred tradition, most of the Enlightenment thinkers ignored the revolutionary potential of their ideas of change in women's lives (Kleinbaum 1977). Among women thinkers of the period, there are some notable exceptions. Most of them, however, never escaped the class-biased boundaries of their own experience. But women thinkers of the time such as Mary Wollstonecraft, Abigail Adams, Margaret Fuller, and Judith Sargent Murray, produced some of the earliest feminist work (Rossi 1973). Later (in the nineteenth century), John Stuart Mill was to become an exception among male philosophers, as he adopted a strikingly feminist position on the emancipation of women. Together with his collaborator, Harriet Taylor Mill, John Stuart Mill produced a series of essays that have now become the cornerstone of modern liberal feminism. The Mills' work is studied later in this chapter. The roots of liberal feminism are first traced to the work of Mary Wollstonecraft.

Mary Wollstonecraft (1759–1797) provides the first philosophical foundation for modern feminism. Her essay, *A Vindication of the Rights of Women,* first published in London in 1792, was so provocative that editions of it quickly appeared in Dublin, Paris, and New York (Poston 1975). So astutely did she outline the position of women that her essay was equally provocative to women who discussed it in consciousness-raising groups in the 1960s and 1970s. Her words continue to inspire women almost 200 years after the original edition was published—a testimony to the influence Mary Wollstonecraft has had.

Mary Wollstonecraft left her home as a teenager in 1778. Distressed by her father's excessive demands for obedience and her family's continued poverty, she wandered from town to town in the countryside of Wales and England (Rossi 1973). Her independence and self-sufficiency established a lifetime pattern of refusing to submit to authority—both in her life and in her writings. She later wrote:

I will venture to affirm, that a girl, whose spirits have not been damped by inactivity, or innocence tainted by false name, will always be a romp, and the doll will never excite attention unless confinement allows her no alternative. Girls and boys, in short, would play harmlessly together, if the distinction of sex was not inculcated long before nature makes any difference. I will go further and affirm, as an indisputable fact, that most of the women, in the circle of my observation, who have acted like rational creatures, or shown any vigour of intellect, have accidentally been allowed to run wild. (1975:43)

Her concern with subservience to authority recurs as a central theme in her work, and it is tied to her argument that learning and socialization are responsible for the formation of mind. Foretelling generations of feminists to come, Wollstonecraft argued that sex role characteristics were the result of education (used broadly in her work to mean all social learning). What appeared to be the natural weakness of women was the result of their lack of liberty and their dependence on men. She writes, "All the differences that I can discern, arises from the superior advantage of liberty, which enables the former to see more of life" (Wollstonecraft 1975:23). She goes on to say:

it is vain to expect virtue from women till they are in some degree independent of men; nay, it is vain to expect that strength of natural affection which would make them good wives and mothers. Whilst they are absolutely dependent on their husbands they will be cunning, mean and selfish, and the men who can be gratified by the fawning fondness of spaniel-like affection have not much delicacy, for love is not to be bought; its silken wings are instantly shriveled up when anything besides a return in kind is sought (1975:144)

Throughout her essay, Wollstonecraft emphasizes that blind submission to authority not only limits social and political freedom but also inhibits the development of mental reasoning. Like others in the Enlightenment, she imagines that the downfall of tyranny will occur as society becomes organized around the principle of rational thought. She writes, "Tyrants would have cause to tremble if reason were to become the rule of duty in any of the relations of life, for the light might spread till perfect day appeared" (1975:150).

Wollstonecraft equates the life of a dutiful soldier to that of a well-socialized woman:

they both acquire manners before morals, and a knowledge of life before they have, from reflection, any acquaintance with the grand ideal outline of human nature. The consequence is natural; satisfied with common nature, they become a prey to prejudices, and taking all their opinions on credit, they submit blindly to authority. So that, if they have any sense, it is a kind of instinctive glance, that catches propositions, and decides with respect to manners but fails when arguments are to be pursued below the surface, or opinions analyzed. (1975:24).

More than other early feminists, Wollstonecraft was sensitive to the issue of social class and the artifical distinctions among persons that she believed social class created. She directed her arguments especially to leisure-class women, for, she said, it is in that class that women are most dependent on men. She held in contempt the idleness of mind and attention to gentility that she believed wealth produced: "The education of the rich tends to render them vain and helpless, and the unfolding mind is not strengthened by the practice of those duties which dignify the human character" (1975:9). "The preposterous distinctions of rank, which render civilization a curse by dividing the world between voluptuous tyrants and cunning envious dependents, corrupt, almost equally, every class of people, because respectability is not attached to the discharge of the relative duties of life, but to the station" (1975:144). Although she recognizes that her observations are of a particular social class, she gives little, if any, attention to women of other classes and cultures. Thus, although her analysis is sensitive to the issue of class, she develops little perspective on the experience of women in the lower classes.

Wollstonecraft's outspoken portrayals of femininity, authority, and property relations earned her a lifetime of insults and insinuations about her bad character. Her contemporaries indexed articles written about her under the topic "prostitution" (Rossi 1973; Wardle 1951); more recently, her feminist beliefs have raised charges that she was "pitifully weak," "consumed with penis envy," and an "extreme neurotic" (Lundberg and Farnham 1947). These same critics write, "Out of her illness arose the ideology of feminism, which was to express the feelings of so many women in years to come" (Lundberg and Farnham 1947:145–159).

Wollstonecraft's work is a powerful criticism of the feminine role and its connection to power and social control. Her writing typifies the passion with which the Enlightenment thinkers pursued their condemnations of traditional authority, and it stands as one of the most persuasive accounts of the effects of women's subservience on their powers of thought, behavior, and self-concept. Her statement that more egalitarian education was needed to liberate women sounds as if it could have been written yesterday. It is a tribute to Wollstonecraft's own capacities for reason and her unchecked passion for justice that her words continue to inspire two centuries after they were written.

Not long after Wollstonecraft's death in 1797, another woman was born who could appropriately be called the mother of sociology. Little recognized in contemporary histories of sociological thought, the Englishwoman Harriet Martineau (1802–1876) was one of the first to use field observation as a method for the development of social knowledge. She was the translator of Auguste Comte's (the father of sociology) *Positive Philosophy;* and, like her counterpart, Alexis deTocqueville, she traveled widely in America, producing a descriptive and analytic account of her observations in her book *Society in America* (1837). Her other book, *How to Observe Manners and Morals* (1838), is the first methodology book in sociology, for in it she details the method of participant observation as she developed it in her own work (Lipset 1962; Rossi 1973).

Like many of the early feminists, Martineau matched her concern for women's emancipation with her support for the American abolition movement. Her outspokenness on the slavery issue, coupled with her daring to travel as a single woman in nineteenth-century America, generated threats against her life. She was eventually forced to restrict her travels to the northern section of the country, but her analysis insists upon the right of women to speak their conscience. She writes:

The whole apparatus of opinion is brought to bear offensively upon individuals among women who exercise freedom of mind in deciding upon what duty is, and the methods by which it is to be pursued. . . . The reproach in all the many similar cases I know is, not that the ladies hold anti-slavery opinions, but that they act upon them. The incessant outcry about the retiring modesty of the sex proves the opinion of the censors to be that fidelity to conscience is inconsistent with retiring modesty. If it be so, let the modesty succumb. (1837:158–159)

And, as Marx and Engels were also later to proclaim, she writes: "If a test of civilization be sought, none can be so sure as the condition of that half of society over which the other half has power" (1837:156).

The connection Martineau makes between the abolition and feminist movements is indicative of the association that early feminists had with the anitslavery movement in America. Historians have argued that American women learned of their own oppression through their participation in the abolition struggle. But more recent work argues that women did not discover their oppression through abolition; instead, their dissatisfaction with their own position led to women's involvement in and apprecation for the abolitionist cause (DuBois 1978). Their involvement in the antislavery movement taught early early feminists not that they were oppressed, but how to understand their situation and act to change it. White women who worked in the abolition movement gained an understanding of the concept of institutional power and adopted the political conviction of natural rights for all individuals, regardless of race or sex. But their analysis of racial and sexual oppression remained at the level of analogy. Early feminists did not develop an understanding that took account of the historical specificity of the black experience in America, nor did they ever make the kind of analysis that could adequately account for class and other cultural differences among women (DuBois 1978). As a result, the liberal tradition of feminism that was established by leaders such as Elizabeth Cady Stanton (1815–1902) and Susan B. Anthony (1820–1906) began and continued with an inadequate comprehension of race and class issues in women's experience.

Martineau's own analysis of race and class is filled with contradictions. She appeals to justice and freedom, yet maintains the ethnic stereotypes typical of her period. She writes:

the English, soon find it impossible to get American domestic help at all, and they are consigned to the tender mercies of the low Irish; and everyone knows what kind of servants they commonly are. Some few of them are the best domestics in America; those who know how to value a respectable home, a steady sufficient income, the honour of being trusted, and the security of valuable friends for life; but too many of them are unsettled, reckless, solvenly; some dishonest, and some intemporate. (1837:171–172)

Martineau's work stands as an example of early feminist thought, complete with its class and race contradictions. More generally, in spite of appeals to reason, free will, humanitarianism, and liberty, liberal feminism has never adequately addressed the issues of race and class inequality. In stating that racism and sexism are analogous forms of oppression, liberal feminism suggests an analysis that would take race, class, and gender into account. But as the concluding section of this chapter will show, this analysis is never provided by liberal feminists, leaving the theoretical and political task of comprehending race, class, and gender oppression to other thinkers.

JOHN STUART MILL AND HARRIET TAYLOR MILL

No thinkers have been more significant in the development of liberal feminism than John Stuart Mill (1806–1873) and Harriet Taylor Mill (1807–1858). *The Subjection of Women,* first published in 1851, was the philosophical inspiration for the British suffrage movement and, like Wollstonecraft's *A Vindication of the Rights of Women,* continues to be studied. The analysis that the Mills develop is the philosophical backbone of liberal feminist politics. Their essays go farther than Wollstonecraft or Martineau in that they relate women's oppression to a systemic critique of liberty and the relations between the sexes. A review of the Mills' work provides an analysis of the particular assumptions and modes of thinking that are characteristic of liberal feminism.

From an early age, John Stuart Mill was steeped in the rigors of intellectual thought and disciplined study. Under his father's stern supervision, he began a course of study at age three that created his intellectual genius at the same time that it apparently robbed him of emotional gratification (Rossi 1970). His life was one of continuous intellectual production mixed with political activism and long struggles with emotional depression. His father's intense emphasis on rational thought left Mill with a long struggle to "cultivate the feelings," an accomplishment perhaps best made though his strong relationship with Harriet Taylor (later to become Harriet Taylor Mill).

The relationship between John Stuart Mill and Harriet Taylor is one that matches romantic commitment and intellectual collaboration with a fervor for individual liberty; so passionate and unusual was their life together that it is still the subject of discussion (Rossi 1970). Through their correspondence and conversation with each other, their published ideas were formed. Mill himself wrote that the ideas in *The Subjection of Women* (published after Harriet's death) belonged to his wife and had emerged from their vast discussions on a topic dear to them both (Rossi 1970). Yet, over the years, scholars have seldom given Harriet Mill the recognition she deserves for her contribution to these works or, for that matter, to her own writing. The fact that Harriet Taylor Mill has so seldom been cited in the many detailed reviews of the Mills' work underscores the sexist character of philosophical criticism and points out how little credit has been given to women thinkers of the past. Alice Rossi makes a convincing case that the Mills' work was a joint effort, even though it was published under his name. She also argues that *Enfranchisement of Women* (published in 1851) was actually written by Harriet Mill (Rossi 1970). Through this review, their works will be interpreted as a collaborative effort.

Taken together, the Mills' eassys provide the most comprehensive statement of the liberal perspective of feminist thought. The issues they raise can be grouped into several key areas—the logic of inquiry, the issue of sex differences, work and the family, and the process of modernization and social change.

The Logic of Inquiry

The logic of the Mills' arguments is typical of that inspired by the rational perspective of the Enlightenment thinkers. In fact, the introduction to *The Subjection of Women* speaks of the difficulty of arguing against opinions that are steadfastly located in the emotions. Convictions, the Mills claim, fare poorly in argumentative debate, for the resistance of conviction to reason makes rational argument impossible. Strong feelings, they maintain, are impenetrable by rational debate. Consequently, those who argue against almost universally held opinions will, most certainly, have a hard time being heard. In discussing the subordination of women, the Mills clearly argue that open inquiry—especially listening to women's voices—is a prerequisite to establishing knowledge of women's lives. They write:

We may safely assert that the knowledge which men can acquire of women, even as they have been and are, without reference to what they might be, is wretchedly imperfect and superficial and always will be so, until women themselves have told all they have to tell. . . . Let us remember in what manner, up to a recent time, the expression, even by a male author, of uncustomary opinions, or what are deemed eccentric feelings, usually was, and in some degree still is, received; and we may form some faint conception under what impediments a women, who is brought up to think custom and opinion her sovereign rule, attempts to express in books anything drawn from the depths of her own nature. (Rossi 1970:152–153)

Knowing that their ideas in *The Subjection of Women* would be controversial, the Mills began their argument with a premise that both makes their own assumptions clear and places the burden of proof to the contrary on those who would oppose human liberty. Their premise is this:

The burden of proof is supposed to be with those who are against liberty, who contend for any restriction or prohibition, either any limitation of the general freedom of human action, or any disqualification or disparity of privlege affecting one person or kind of persons, as compared with others. The *a priori* presumption is in favor of freedom and impartiality (Mill 1970:3)

Thus, the Mills present the starting point of their argument, as well as the central concept in the liberal perspective—that all persons have equal liberty and, therefore, that human institutions should treat all alike. Their words, in fact, provide the philosophy behind the modern practice of equal employment opportunity and equality before the law. They write, "The law should be no respector of persons, but should treat all alike, save where dissimilarity of treatment is required by positive reasons, either justice or of policy" (1970:4).

In sum, the logic of their analysis is one of rational argument, but argument that assumes that human liberty is a natural right and one that should not be denied on the basis of any individual or group characteristics. But as the style of their writing shows, their rationality is coupled with a passionate emphasis on the necessity for liberating social changes.

Sex Differences and Social Learning

Throughout their essays, the Mills imagine alternatives to existing relationships between the sexes, and they show how social conditions create sex-specific attitudes and arrangements that their opponents use to discredit the claim of women's equality. By imagining new alternatives, the Mills show how a change in the relationship of the sexes would likely alter the characteristics usually throught to be natural differences between the sexes. They make their argument by showing that there is no reasonable defense for the current state of affairs and by arguing that the creation of liberty for women would benefit not just women but society as a whole. The social benefits of liberation would include "doubling the mass of mental faculties available for the higher service of humanity" (1970:153), overcoming the selfish attitudes and self-worshiping characteristics of humanity (1970:148), and enhancing the "softening influence" (1970:156) of women's moral tendencies.

What is considered to be natural is only what is taken for granted, they argue. And foretelling the thoughts of contemporary feminists, they write:

Was there ever any domination which did not appear natural to those who possessed it? There was a time when the division of mankind into two classes, a small one of masters and a numerous one of slaves, appeared, even to the most cultivated minds, to be a natural, and the only natural, condition of the human race. . . . Did not the slave owners of the Southern United States maintain the same doctrine, with all the fanaticism with which men cling to the theories that justify their passions and legitimate their personal interests? (1970:20–21)

They go on to say:

The smallest acquaintance with human life in the Middle Ages, shows how supremely natural the dominion of feudal nobility over men of low condition appeared to the nobility themselves, and how unnatural the conception seemed, of a person of the inferior class claiming equality with them, or exercising authority over them. It hardly seemed less so to the class held in subjection. The emancipated serfs and burgesses, even in their most vigorous struggles, never made any pretension to a share of authority; they only demanded more or less of a limitation to the power of tyrannizing over them. So is it that unnatural generally means only uncustomary, and that everything which is usual appears natural? The subjection of women to men being a universal custom, any departure from it quite naturally appears unnatural. (Mill 22–23)

Like contemporary social scientists, the Mills clearly see that what appears natural is primarily the result of social learning. They continue by saying that one can know what persons actually are only by comprehending their social experience. In their words, "We cannot isolate a human being from the circumstances of his condition, so as to ascertain experimentally what he would have been by nature; but we can consider what he is, and what his circumstances have been, and whether the one would have been capable of producing the other" (1970:126).

The Mills obviously believe that women had been held in such an unnatural state of submission and domination that it was impossible to make claims about natural sex differences. All that we see as masculinity or feminity, they contend, is the result of learned, not actual, differences. So, they write, "women have always hiterto been kept, as far as regards spontaneous development, in so unnatural a state, that their nature cannot but have been greatly distorted and disguised" (1970:104–105). They go on, "I deny that any one knows, or can know, the nature of the sexes, as long as they have only been seen in their present relation to one another" (1970:38), and say, "one thing we may be certain of—that what is contrary to women's nature to do, they will never be made to do by simply giving their nature free play" (1970:48).

The Mills make the case for liberty by seeing the detrimental effects of social learning or, in their words, education and custom, under a state of subjection. They assume that persons construct their social arrangements and social identities, although some may have more power than others to do so. Human beings, they argue, are rational and creative. Only by removing constraints and obstacles to liberty can the free expression of rational choice and humane social development be encouraged. According to the Mills, human beings have a natural right to self-expression that unnatural systems of authority and rule take away.

Thus, the Mills' concept of liberty rests on the idea of voluntary contracts among human actors. Accordingly, they argue that marriage ties should be based on free and voluntary choice and that law, in marriage and other areas, should treat all alike—giving no unnatural advantage to one group or another. The purpose of *The Subjection of Women* is, in fact, to show the following:

the principle which regulates the existing social relations between the two sexes—and legal subordination of one sex to the other—is wrong in itself, and now one of the chief hindrances to human improvements; and that it ought to be replaced by a principle of perfect equality, admitting no power or privilege on the one side, nor disability on the other. (1970:1)

Harriet Taylor Mill, in her own essay, *Enfranchisement of Women,* argues, in addition, that "we deny the right of any portion of the species to decide for another portion, or any individual for another individual, what is and what is not their proper sphere" (Rossi 1970:100). Although the Mills differ on their opinions about women's place in marriage, their attitude toward the self-determination of the sexes is clearly one that denies the right of one to restrain the other. As they write, "The law which is to be observed by both should surely be made by both; yet, as hitherto, by the stronger only" (Rossi 1970:68). This premise in their work is also the foundation for their ideas on women's place in the workplace and the family.

Work and the Family

The Mills' belief in individual liberty is also seen in their arguments on women's occupations. They believe in the *laissez-faire* operation of the economic market, meaning that they favor a nonintervention approach to economic processes. Their assumption is that, if persons are free to choose their occupation, then the best qualified will fill the positions most appropriate to their talent. Then the occupational system will work in the best interests of all.

These assumptions are grounded in the earlier work of the British economist Adam Smith. Smith maintains that the economic market should be based on open competition and a lack of regulation or interference. According to Smith, this *laissez-faire* policy best suits what he thinks are the laws of the market. He identifies the laws of the market as stemming from the self-interest of individuals. Open competition between individuals will establish a harmony of interests as individuals mutually compete to establish reasonable prices for the sale of goods. Because Smith believes this process to be the natural law of the market, he concludes that the most effective policy is a hands-off or laissez- faire approach.

Although the Mills do not speak so directly about the laws of the economy, they similarly assume that free competition is the key to economic equity—at least in terms of occupational choice. So, in *The Subjection of Women,* they write:

It is not that all processes are supposed to be equally good, or all persons to be equally qualified for everything; but that freedom of individual choice is now known to be the only thing which procures the adoption of the best processes, and draws each operation into the hands of those who are best qualified for it. . . . In consonance with this doctrine, it is felt to be an overstepping of the proper bounds of authority to fix beforehand on some general presumption, that certain persons are not fit to do certain things. (1970:32)

But the Mills' arguments about an open choice of occupation have one important qualifier. In spite of their general position on the emancipation of women, John Stuart Mill and Harriet Taylor Mill disagree about women's preferred occupation. John Stuart Mill believes that the occupation women should (and would) choose is marriage. He argues that in marriage, women's work is to be the moral educators of children and to be themselves objects of beauty and adornment. Thus, regardless of his advocacy of an open marketplace, in his correspondence with Harriet Taylor, he writes:

it does not follow that a woman should actually support herself because she should be *capable* of doing so: in the natural course of events she will *not*. It is not desirable to burden the labour market with a double number of competitors. In a healthy state of things, the husband would be able by his single exertions to earn all that is necessary for both: and there would be no need that the wife should take part in the mere providing of what is required to *support* life: it will be for the happiness of both that her occupation should rather be to adorn and beautify it. (John Stuart Mill and Harriet Taylor Mill, *Early Essays on Marriage and Divorce;* in Rossi 1970:74–75) (Emphasis by John Stuart Mill.)

Later in *The Subjection of Women,* Mill writes:

in an otherwise just state of things, it is not, therefore, I think, a desirable custom that the wife should contribute by her labour to the income of the family. . . . Like a man when he chooses a profession, so, when a woman marries, it may in general be understood that she makes choice of the management of a household, and the bringing up of a family, as the first call upon her exertions, during as many years of her life as may be required for the purpose; and that she renounces, not all other objects and occupations, but all which are not consistent with the requirement of this. (1970:88–89)

In other words, in spite of his general arguments to the contrary, John Stuart Mill thinks that women are more self-sacrificing than men and that they will by *nature* want marriage. Only a free market, however, will sort out which individuals have this nature and which do not. Still, he would prefer not to change the traditional activities of women in the family. He writes, "The education which it *does* belong to mothers to give . . . is the training of the affections. . . . The great occupation of women should be to beautify life" (Rossi 1970:76).

Harriet Taylor Mill seriously disagrees with Mill on this subject, and her arguments show her to be the more radical of the two. In *The Enfranchisement of Women,* she argues, "To say that women must be excluded from active life because maternity disqualifies them for it, is in fact to say, that every other career should be forbidden them in order that maternity may be their only resource" (Rossi 1970:105). And in the same essay, she says, "Let every occupation be open to all, without favour or discouragement to any, and employments will fall into the hands of those men or women who are found by experience to be most capable of worthily exercising them" (Rossi 1970: 100–101).

The disagreement between John Stuart Mill and Harriet Taylor Mill indicates one of the shortcomings in this philosophy of emancipation. He stops short of advocating full equality for women, because he does not support major changes in family relations (Goldstein 1980). Harriet Taylor Mill's analysis is more far-reaching because she argues for the unqualified equality of women with men. Both of them, however, fail to make a radical analysis of women's status because their assumptions ignore the limits to individual free choice that are created by the system of stratification.

The Mills' analysis of occupation is characterized by meritocratic assumptions. *Meritocracies* are systems in which persons hold their positions allegedly based on their individual talents and personal choices. Although meritocracies do supposedly resist ascriptive hierarchies (i.e., those based on characteristics such as sex or race), they still maintain hierarchical organization (Harding 1979). Because the Mills' analysis ignores questions such as how talent is distributed, how talent is created or recognized, and how merit is defined, they do not analyze how social systems are marked by unequal powers, privileges, and rewards. In short, their analysis does not overcome inequality; it simply replaces educational, occupational, and legal inequality by gender with other forms of distinction.

Because the Mills do not develop a theory of social class or a perspective on racism, their view of the emancipation of women is based primarily on the optimistic belief that social progress is marked by the increased liberty of the individual. As a central tenet in liberal philosophy, this concept of individual liberty leaves unanswered the question of how institutions are structured around collective inequality. At the same time, the liberal perspective implies that individual liberty will result in the social transformation of the whole society. This belief is made especially clear in the Mills' writing on modernization and social change.

Modernization and Social Change

The picture of the future that liberalism portrays tends to be an optimistic one. Likewise, its view of history assumes that modern Western civilization is more progressive than in the past because, in the Mills' language, the modern, advanced state leaves behind the tyrannies and repressions of the past. Thus, they conceptualize history in terms of progressive improvement, and they imagine the future as lacking the subjugation and repression of the past.

In keeping with the Enlightenment perspective, the Mills assume that the historical rule of force is ending with the development of modern rationalized institutions. History, they argue, replaces the use of force with the use of reason. Accordingly, social organization is no longer based on ascriptive roles, but rather upon the achieved merit of individuals. The Mills write:

For what is the peculiar character of the modern world—the difference which chiefly distinguishes modern institutions, modern social ideas, modern life itself, from those of times long past? It is, that human beings are no longer born to their place in life, and chained down by an inexorable bond to the place they are born to, but are free to employ their faculties, and such favourable chances as offer, to achieve the lot which may appear to them most desirable. (1970:29–30)

The Mills' attitude toward this alleged change is consistent with their desire for equality of choice. Their plea for the enfranchisement of women is based on the argument that women are the only exception to an otherwise emancipated world. So, they write:

At present, in the more *improved* countries, the disabilities of women are the only case, save one, in which laws and institutions take persons at their birth, and ordain that they shall never in their lives be allowed to compete for certain things. The one exception is that of royalty. . . . The disabilities, therefore, to which women are subject from the mere fact of their birth, are the solitary examples of the kind in modern legislation. (1970:35; emphasis added)

Although this essay was published following the emancipation of the slaves in the United States, the Mills' arguments reveal naive optimism about the actual disenfranchisement of many social groups. Although it may be true that broad-scale legislation had struck down many ascriptive barriers in the law, in practice the law, the economy, and social custom continue to oppress a large majority of the society. In the United States, for example, the enfranchisement of women—white and black—did not occur until 1920. The Mills' naiveté in considering that inequality of rights was a "relic of the past" (1869:30) rests solely on their belief that rationality will provide a new moral base for society. The Mills envision the Western world as the most advanced of all forms of civilization. Yet, this view is both *ethnocentric* (meaning that it regards one's own group as superior to all others) and is founded on class-based and race-based assumptions about the desirability of present social arrangements. The Mills' commitment to rationality as a moral basis for society blinds them to the facts of continuing inequality and oppression of underprivileged peoples in the contemporary Western world.

The Mills' optimism about social change also leads them to assume that women's status has necessarily improved over time. They write:

Experience does say, that every step in improvement has been so invariably accompanied by a step in raising the social position of women, that historians and philosophers have been led to adopt their elevation or disbasement as on the whole the surest test and most correct measure of the civilization of a people or an age. Through all the progressive period of human history, the condition of women has been approaching nearer to equality with men. (1970:37)

But feminist studies have shown that women's status has not necessarily improved with time (Kelly-Gadol 1975). In Western culture, women's status has fluctuated depending upon developments in industrialization, capitalism, the advent of technology, and transformations in patriarchal relations. The Mills' assumption that the position of women is necessarily improving is a reflection of their sincere commitment to bringing about that change. But because they do not study specific historical developments in women's roles created by capitalism and patriarchy, their analysis of social change has a hollow ring.

However, these criticisms aside, the Mills' arguments for the emancipation of women still stand as provocative, replete with insightful ideas on the relationship of gender inequality to other systems of unjust authroity and the repression of individual freedom. Their failures result from what they did not explain, not from the errors of their inquiry. However, criticism notwithstanding, it is uncanny how truthful the Mills' ideas seem today. Apart from the particular eloquence of their style, their words could be those of a contemporary feminist. This discovery is, in fact, rather disheartening for it indicates how little the status of women has changed since the Mills' time.

LIBERALISM AND THE FEMINIST MOVEMENT

The contemporary feminist movement has two major branches—women's rights and women's liberation (Hole and Levine 1971). The women's rights branch is reform-oriented and is based on liberal feminism, whereas the women's liberation branch is the more radical of the two. Both emerge under specific social and historical conditions, particularly in the experience of white, middle-class women. Understanding the reform and radical perspectives requires a brief analysis of the origins of the contemporary feminist movement.

Transformations in women's roles occurring during the 1950s and 1960s that influence the development of feminism include changes in women's labor force participation, a change in women's fertility patterns, increases in women's educational level, and ideological patterns that glamorize women's domestic life. In the 1950s, women were idealized as happy housewives whose primary purpose was to care for their husbands and children. In this decade, women were marrying younger, but also having fewer children because wide-spread use of contraception gave women control over their fertility. At the same time, white middle-class women were better educated and, although their education was intended to make them better wives and mothers, they were acquiring many of the same skills as men. For women in the home, technological changes in housework simplified physical tasks, but they increased consumption and new patterns of family life in automobile-based suburbs complicated the role of housewives. Although there was less physical labor associated with housework, housewives had to be constantly available to their children. Whatever time was saved by labor-saving appliances was more than replaced by increased shopping, transporting of children, and nurturing of family members. The dominant ideology of housework and motherhood told women that their work in the home would bring them fulfillment and gratification but, in fact, many found the experience to be depressing, isolating, and boring. This situation created a crisis for middle-class women in the family that was brought to the widespread attention of the public by the appearance of Betty Friedan's best-seller, *The Feminine Mystique,* in 1963. Friedan identified "the problem that has no name" for white, middle-class housewives—namely, that their isolation in the family was the source of their discontent. Friedan's book critically assailed the establishment (including mass advertising, women's magazines, and Freudian psychology) as contributing to women's problems. The chord she struck was soon repeated by a number of critical assessments of women's roles that appeared in academic and popular literature (Evans 1979).

In addition to experiencing a crisis in domestic life, women were, at the same time, appearing in the labor force in greater numbers. Throughout the 1950s, women from middle-income families entered the labor force at a faster rate than any other group. And they were working not just in the years prior to marriage but in addition to their marriage and family roles. Although married women's work experience was defined in terms of helping their families, it broadened their horizons at the same time that it made them conscious of discrimination in the workplace. Thus, the decade of the 1950s and the early 1960s created a self-conscious cohort of women who lived in the contradictions of a society that idealized their role and promised them opportunity and gratification while it devalued their labor and denied them self-expression.

Professional women working within established institutions began pressuring politicans to recognize the problems facing American women. Thus, in 1961, although it was likely done for political reasons, President John F. Kennedy appointed a Presidential Commission on the Status of Women, chaired by Eleanor Roosevelt. The commission was charged with documenting "prejudices and outmoded customs that act as barriers to the full realization of women's basic rights" (Hole and Levine 1971:18) and with making recommendations designed to alleviate the problem. The commission report, *American Women,* was released in 1963, the same year that Friedan's *The Feminine Mystique* appeared.

The commission's report made a number of recommendations involving employment and labor discrimination. It was the basis for the Equal

Pay Act of 1963 requiring that men and women receive equal pay for equal work performed under equal conditions (Hole and Levine 1971:28ff). Problems in enforcing this law and exemptions that were later attached to it prohibited the act from making the radical changes it implied. Thus, the commission's work had only a moderate affect. Moreover, the commission held steadfastly to the idea that the nuclear family was the foundation of American history and that women's role in the family was an invaluable and necessary resource. Although recognizing the contribution that women made to the home, the commission ignored the effects of home life on women that Friedan's book so strikingly portrayed.

These developments within both the government and the society provide the context for women to begin to question their traditional roles, but it remained for major social movements of the period to crystallize the vague discontent that women felt. Consequently, the birth of contemporary feminism must be seen as stemming from the civil rights movement and, later, the anti-Vietnam War and student movements.

The civil rights movement was initiated within black communities of the South during the 1950s as a challenge to public racial segregation and white racial prejudice. But like the nineteenth-century American feminists who developed their feminist politics through participation in the abolitionist movement (DuBois 1978), white women working in the civil rights movement soom saw their own oppression as similar to the racial injustices against which they were organizing. White women worked in the civil rights movement out of their felt need to remedy the inequities of racial injustice, which they saw as a moral issue calling for their humanitarian participation. For white women and men, joining the civil rights movement required a radical departure from the dominant beliefs and practices of white society. Their challenge to the status quo on racial issues was soon to influence the way they also interpreted other social issues (Evans 1979).

Between 1963 and 1965, white liberals from the North (especially male and female college students) went to the South in great numbers to assist in the civil rights struggle. The nonviolent direct-action projects in which they engaged (voter registration drives, protest marches, and sit-ins) forced them to encounter institutional racism and generated a new consciousness not only of racial issues but of the institutional structure of American society (Rothschild 1979). Most importantly, the civil rights movement's emphasis on examining the roots of oppression caused many white poeple to look into their own experience so as to comprehend their relationship to dominant institutions. In so doing, white women in the movement began to see the origins of their own oppression—both as they had learned sexism in their own lives and as it was reflected in the public institutions of society.

In spite of a growing feminist consciousness, sexual politics within the civil rights movement divided black and white women for two reasons. First, white women in the movement often proved their social liberalism by having sexual relations with black men. Although this action was encouraged by the permissive atmosphere in the movement, it discouraged solidarity between black and white women (Rothschild 1979). Second, both white and black women believed that the movement had failed to address the issue of sexual inequality. Black women in SNCC (the Student Non-Violent Coordinating Committee) wrote position papers protesting the fact that women in the movement were relegated to clerical work, were not given leadership and decision-making positions, and were belittlingly referred to as girls. But white women, supporting the idea that the movement should be led by blacks, were reluctant to present their own analysis of sexism and distrust between black and white women prevented their alliance against male sexism (Evans 1979).

Throughout the summers of 1964 and 1965, the position of whites in the civil rights movement became increasingly precarious. Black disillusionment with white liberals and the ideology of black power eventually resulted in the exclusion of whites from SNCC in 1965. Thus, at the very time that women were becoming more conscious of their ties to each other, both white and black women ended up working in movements that were even more male-dominated and less open to an examination of sex inequality. For black women, the black power movement explicitly appealed to the power of black men and the role of black women as supporters of men. White women, after their exclusion from the black power movement, were now found in male-dominated white activist groups, organizing around antiwar and student issues. These movements once again relegated them to traditionally women's work and treated them as sexual objects for the pleasure of radical men. By applying the analysis of racial injustice they had learned in the civil rights movement to their own oppression as women, white feminists emerged from the ranks of other activist groups (Evans 1979).

By the late 1960s, the feminists had developed their own social movement, including a variety of organizations, local conscious-raising groups, and political demonstrations. In theory and in practice, women within the feminist movement have developed different perspectives on women's issues and different strategies for social change. Liberal organizations, such as the National Organization for Women, founded in 1966, work primarily within the established economic and political system. Liberal feminists, using the civil rights perspective, see feminism essentially as extending equal rights to women. More radical feminists, as we will see in the following chapter, see the need for a more fundamental restructuring of American institutions. However, contemporary feminist perspectives are not perfectly separated from each other. Although different orientations emphasize different assumptions and programs, there is, in fact, much overlap in the theoretical and political analyses that feminists use.

Contemporary liberal feminism is, however, characterized fundamentally by its emphasis on individual rights and equal opportunity. It does not, as more radical feminism does, challenge the systems of capitalism and patriarchy, but it attempts to reform these systems so as to give women an equal place within them. Liberal feminist organizations (such as the National Organization for Women, the National Women's Political Caucus, and the National Abortion Rights Action League) work primarily within the existing political system through extensive lobbying, legislative reform, and the pursuit of fair employment practice.

The gains inspired by liberal feminism in recent years have made significant changes in women's lives. On issues ranging from equity in employment to reproductive rights, liberal reforms have resulted in increased opportunities for women and increased public consciousness of women's rights. The fact that liberal feminism works largely within exisitng institutions has, most likely, contributed to its broad-based support.

The strengths of the liberal feminist position are its insistence on individual freedom, its toleration for diverse life-styles, and its support of economic, social, and political reform. These strengths reflect the bourgeois origins of liberal throught, which emphasizes the importance and autonomy of the individual. One reason liberalism is accepted as the norm for feminists is that its philosophy reflects Western cultural values of individualism and personal achievement (Eisenstein 1981). But its strengths are also its weaknessess, for each of these positions has serious limitations that the liberal framework does not address. Consider, for example, the issues of individual liberty and tolerance liberals accord to diverse life-styles. Many probably agree that it is important to tolerate the individual's rights to choose his or her life-style. Thus, the liberal perspective encourage us to say, for example, that lesbians are entitled to live as they please. What liberalism does not do is to recognize that heterosexuality is institutionalized in this society and, thus, is made compulsory for all except those who are deviant. From a liberal perspective, lesbianism is tolerated as a deviant choice, but it is not seen as a positive alternative to the patriarchal control of female sexuality.

Similarly, on race and class issues, the liberal perspective fails to explain the institutionalized basis for race and class oppression. By claiming that all persons, regardless of race, class, or sex, should have equal opportunities, liberals accept the existing system as valid without analyzing the racism, sexism, and class system upon which it is based. From a liberal feminist perspective, black women's experience is one among many. But explaining how white women's and white men's experience is also conditioned by racism is not part of the liberal program. Liberal feminism sees race as a barrier to the individual freedom of blacks, but it does not see that the position of white women is tied to that of women of color.

Liberal feminism's perspective on individual rights does remind us that social change must provide the basis for individual well-being. Therefore, it is premised on humanistic ethics for social change. Some feminists also argue that liberal feminism recognizes that women form a sexual class (Eisenstein 1981). Because liberal feminism is based on the premise that individuals are autonomous beings, it does recognize that women are independent of men. Early feminists (such as Wollstonecraft and the Mills) viewed women as having an independent and collective existence apart from men. They are not merely different as individuals. But liberal feminist programs for change leave this point underdeveloped by offering solutions that would simply grant individual rights. Therefore, liberal feminism to some extent denies the connections between individuals and leaves its political goal as one of equality. But in saying that women should be equal to men, liberal feminism does not specify which men women want to be equal to; thus, it glosses over the class and race structure of societal relations (Eisenstein 1981).

As a result, liberal feminism leaves much unanswered. It does not explain the emergence of gender inequality, nor can it account, other than by analogy, for effects of race and class stratification on the conditions of women's lives. Its analysis for change is limited to issues of equal opportunity and individual choice. As a political ethic, it insists upon individual liberty and challenges any social, political, and economic practice that discriminates against persons on the basis of group or individual characteristics. It remains for more radical perspectives to explain the casual conditions of women's oppression and its relationship to race and class oppression.

C H A P T E R 10

RADICAL ALTERNATIVES: SOCIALIST AND RADICAL FEMINISM

INTRODUCTION

Radical perspectives in feminist theory arise from the critique of liberalism and also from a dialogue with Marxist perspectives on women's position in society. Two radical alternatives to liberal feminism are socialist feminism, which sees women's oppression as primarily based in capitalism and its interrelationship with patriarchal gender relations, and radical feminism, which sees patriarchal social relations as the primary cause of women's oppression.

Whereas the liberal framework emphasizes learned sex roles and the denial of opportunities as the primary causes of women's oppression, radical perspectives attempt to explain how gender develops and persists as a social, economic, and political category. The radical analysis goes beyond the goal of including women in existing societal institutions by arguing that dominant institutions are characterized by gender, race, and class oppression. The specific process by which this oppression occurs forms points of divergence between socialist and radical feminist perspectives.

Radical feminists criticize liberal feminists for assuming that sexism is largely a remnant of traditional beliefs and practices. Because of their indignation over the continuation of past practices, liberal feminists have widely documented the effects of discrimination and have tried to locate the institutional practices and policies that foster continuing discrimination. As shown in the previous chapter, the liberal feminist perspective takes women's equality with men as its major political goal. In distinct contrast to this perspective, socialist and radical feminism challenge the social, political, and economic analysis of the liberal perspective. Equality, these alternatives suggest, would only put some women on a par with men, without transforming the conditions of oppression that produce gender as well as class and race relations. This chapter reviews socialist and radical feminism and shows how each emerges from an ongoing debate with Marxist theory and its analysis of gender, class, and race relations.

The focus of this presentation is on the contemporary issues posed by these perspectives, although their intellectual origins are rooted in the nineteenth century and in an ongoing dialogue with Marx since that time. As feminist analysis has shifted from liberal concerns with equality and sex roles, new questions have arisen regarding gender as a social, political, and economic category. In relation to Marxist theory, these questions ask how gender is socially produced and reproduced and how it is related to class analysis. Further, they ask whether women's oppression is a consequence of class oppression and how patriarchy—simply defined as rule by men—is linked to class relations. Each of these analytical questions is developed in this chapter, but first, some additional historical background to the emergence of feminism and a review of classical Marxist analysis are presented.

THE POLITICAL CONTEXT OF RADICAL FEMINIST PERSPECTIVES

The intellectual origins of radical feminist analyses date back to the nineteenth century and the same intellectual and political climate that stimulated liberal thinking. The political and economic changes of this period fostered a mix of social thought and social protest, most notably found in the work of Karl Marx (1818–1883) and his collaborator, Friedrich Engels (1820–1895). Marx and Engels's major essay, *The Communist Manifesto,* was published in Paris in 1848, the same year and city as John Stuart Mill's primary work, *On Liberty.* The differences between the radical perspective of Marx and Engels and the liberal perspective of Mill point to the profound controversies over the analysis of social structure and social change that historical changes in the structure of Western society were generating.

The middle and second half of the nineteenth century in Western Europe and America was marked by the vast growth of capitalism and the rapid expansion of industrialization, along with widespread social and political changes inspired by the French Revolution and, in the United States, by the elimination of slavery, the expansion of western territories, and urbanization. The climate of social reform that began in this period set the stage for the British suffrage movement and the American feminist movement of the late nineteenth and early twentieth centuries. The political discourse that this period fostered created a diversity of political and social thought that, in the case of sociological theory, continues to this day (Bramson 1961; Zeitlin 1968).

Nineteenth-century feminism is typically characterized as a reform movement whose ideas are rooted in the liberal thought of persons such as John Stuart Mill and Harriet Taylor Mill. But the politics of this movement also emerged through debate and action between radical and reform leaders. Some groups in the nineteenth- and early-twentieth-century feminist movement were as much influenced by class and union politics as they were by the spirit of moral reform characterizing the women's rights approach of nineteenth-century feminism. Case studies of both the suffrage movement (DuBois 1978) and the women's trade union movement (Dye 1975) reveal the complexities of the movements' attempt to grapple with the complexities of class, race, and gender politics. In the end, however, most of the nineteenth-century feminists were unable to transcend the class biases of their middle-class majority leadership. Some feminist leaders, such as Susan B. Anthony, also used prevailing racist and anti-immigrant sentiments to attract members and to articulate movement ideologies (DuBois 1978; Dye 1975). These failures to unite women across classes and races limited the effectiveness of nineteenth-century feminism, but a radical tradition for alliances with working-class women and the beginnings of an analysis linking gender, race, and class oppression can be found in some of the feminists of this period.

Many of the feminists of this period were also socialists and worked for radical causes in addition to their feminist politics. Charlotte Perkins Gilman's (1860–1935) socialist analysis is suggested in *Women and Economics* (published in 1898), where she proposed that housework should be communally organized, particularly for working mothers, who were appearing in the labor force at this time. She suggested that apartment houses have one common kitchen where all families could be served and that cleaning, child care, nursing, and teaching should be paid professional work. The responsibility for this work should not fall on individual families, but instead on apartment house managers (Rossi 1973). Other radical thinkers of the time, such as Emma Goldman (1869–1940) and Agnes Smedley (1892–1950), did not define feminism as their primary cause, but they clearly linked the oppression of women to other forms of economic and political oppression.

The more recent emergence of feminism in the 1960s and 1970s shows a similar diversity of feminist politics and thought and, as discussed in the previous chapter, is linked with other radical social movements. Both liberal and radical feminism emerged in the 1960s and early 1970s as part of the critical social movement developing at the time. The liberal and radical wings of the movement, however, inspired different constituencies and developed different strategies for change. The liberal wing attracted older working women, especially in the professions, and its organizations tended to reflect the more traditional style of their politics. Liberal organizations are typically more formal, with leadership and authority hierarchically ordered, and with formal procedures and membership rules (Freeman 1973).

The more radical feminist groups emerging from the New Left drew their participants from women who were critical of the often sexist and patronizing behavior of radical men (Evans 1979). Their early political analysis was forged from the appeals to justice that the leftist movements had articulated and that women felt were being denied to them. The style and organization of more radical feminist groups also reflect their more radical ideological base. In the beginning, participants in the radical branches of the feminist movement tended to be younger than their liberal counterparts, and the organization of their groups was nonhierarchical, mass-based, and with informal procedures and networks (Freeman 1973). The looser, more flexible style of discussion in radical groups encouraged analyses that were not only more critical of establishment systems but also more person-oriented and more likely to engage individuals in examining their own experience and its relationship to institutionalized sexism. Thus, the radical branches of feminism recognized that personal life was tied to the structure of public institutions and would be altered as these institutions changed. From the beginning, the more radical forms of feminism were more likely to engage in analysis including the dynamics of gender, class, and race.

As the radical analysis has developed, two different perspectives have emerged: socialist feminism and radical feminism. Although each has developed as a criticism of liberal feminism, both are also a response to the analysis of women developed in classical Marxism. To understand radical feminist perspectives, then, requires some familiarity with the analysis of Marx and Engels. A summary of their major ideas follows.

THE MARXIST PERSPECTIVE

Among scholars, Marxist thought is one of the most influential and insightful analyses of modern intellectual history. And in the case of sociology, some argue that most sociological theory developed as a dialogue with the ideas that Marx inspired (Zeitlin 1968). Certainly, for modern feminism, Marxist ideas are pivotal. Marx himself began writing as a student, first at the University of Bonn (1835–1836) and then at the University of Berlin (1836–1841), where he was involved in some of the most politically and intellectually controversial movements of his time. He was active in a group known as the Young Hegelians, who based their studies and activities on the work of the German philosopher Hegel (1770–1832). Hegel's philosophy is based on the idea that persons create their world by perceiving it; thus, ideas are the objective facts through which human beings construct their world. Hegel's philosophy, furthermore, sees the "real" as emanating from the "divine" (Giddens 1971:3), and Christian theology is an important foundation for his work. The Young Hegelians followed Hegel's concern with theology and adopted his philosophical perspective, until their outlook was radically transformed by the appearance of Ludwig Feuerbach's work, *The Essence of Christianity,* in 1841. Feuerbach (1804–1872) reversed the philosophy of ideas in Hegel's work by arguing that ideas follow the existence of human action. Feuerbach writes, "Thought proceeds from being, not being from thought" (Giddens 1971:3). From Feuerbach's thesis, the divine was a construction of human thought; human activity, not ideas, provides the basis for social reality.

This philosophy led Marx's teacher and sponsor, Bruno Bauer (1809–

1882), to assert that the Bible was a historical document and that Christian theology was a social and historical myth. Bauer was consequently dismissed from the university, as he was declared to be dangerous to the state. For Marx, in a university system where one's future was dependent on academic sponsorship, Bauer's dismissal meant the end of his academic career. Although Marx received his doctorate of philosophy from the University of Jena in 1841, he, who had once been predicted to be the most outstanding professor of his time, was never to hold a university post. The remainder of his life was spent in political exile and in poverty. He continued to write, working occasionally as a journalist, but he was forced to move from Germany to Paris and later to London as he was expelled by various governments. In 1849 he moved to London, where he was to spend the last thirty-four years of his life. His family was extremely poor; several of his children died of malnutrition and disease. Loans from his friend and collaborator, Friedrich Engels, supported the family, along with Marx's occasional journalism jobs. Throughout this difficult time, Marx continued writing and studying, and produced several works that would change the course of world history and the history of social thought.

The ideas Marx developed always reflected the early influence of Hegel and Feuerbach and resulted in a theoretical perspective called *historical materialism* (also referred to as *dialectical materialism*). The central thesis of historical materialism is that persons live in interaction with their social and physical environments. Thus, human consciousness is formed by the interplay between persons as subjects and as objects in the world in which they live. The movement of human history, from a historical materialist perspective, involves the continuous creation and re-creation of human life. Thus, persons' relationship to their environment is mediated by the particular historical and societal milieu of which they are a part. Specifically, for Marx, the materialist thesis sees human production—what men and women actually do—as the basis for social structure. Thus, the cause of social change, for Marx, lies not in ideas and values that are abstracted from human experience. Instead, he sees societal change as emerging from the social relations and activities that themselves emerge through human labor and systems of production (Giddens 1971).

Because Marx assumes that by nature human beings are working animals, he concludes that if human work is oppressive, then all social life is distorted. Human beings do more than merely exist; they reach their full human potential for creative living through social consciousness and their struggle against oppression. According to Marx, systems of production that distort human potential and, consequently, deny the realization of the species must be transformed through political revolt.

Marx explicitly rejects a biologically determinist view of human nature, because he sees human production and reproduction as adapting to social and physical environments. Different forms of social organization produce different social relations, because, in Marxist theory, the systems of human production and reproduction create the conditions for everyday life. Marx and Engels define *production* as the labor humans perform and *reproduction* as the physical re-creation of both the species and the social systems in which human beings reproduce. In Engels's words, production and reproduction are the central features of human society:

According to the materialistic conception, the determining factor in history is, in the final instance, the production and reproduction of immediate life. This, again, is of a two-fold character: on the one side, the production of the means of existence, of food, clothing and shelter and the tools necessary for that production; on the other side, the production of human beings themselves, the propagation of the species. The social organization under which the people of a particular historical epoch and a particular country live is determined by both kinds of production; by the stage of development of labor on the one hand and of the family on the other. (Engels 1972:71–72).

Feminists have argued that Marx and Engels never fulfilled their promise of developing a materialist perspective to account for productive *and* reproductive activity (Eisenstein 1979; Flax 1976). Marx and Engels also clearly place reproduction solely within the family. But they devote most of their analysis to class relations and systems of production, the alienation of human labor, and the struggle of the working classes against capitalism. So, in spite of their recognition of the dual importance of production and reproduction, their analysis subordinates reproduction and the family to economic systems of production. As we will see, classical Marxism sees women's oppression as a reflection of the more fundamental form of oppression by class. Thus, sexism is a secondary phenomenon and, assumedly, will disappear with a revolution in class relations. It is on this point that socialist and radical feminists depart from classical Marxist feminists, because they would argue that the oppression of women itself is fundamental (Jaggar and Struhl 1978).

The materialist perspective of Marx and Engels sees human activity (as it is engaged in productive relations) as the mainspring of social change and as the determining feature of social organization. In Marx's analysis, the economic mode of production forms the *infrastructure* of social organization; other institutions form the *superstructure,* meaning that they reflect the essential character of the economic system.

In the Western capitalist societies that Marx observed, the economic infrastructure was marked primarily by class struggle—the division of society into groups characterized by their relationship to the means of production. Under capitalism, two new major classes emerge: capitalists, who own the means of production, and the proletariat (or working class), who sell their labor for wages to capitalist owners. Two minor classes also exist—the petty bourgeoisie (merchants, managers, and artisans, for example), who become functionally dependent on capitalism, although they do not own the means of production; and the lumpenproletariat, who have no place in capitalist economics because they have no direct role in producing profit and who form, in Marx and Engels's words, "the 'dangerous class,' the social scum, that passively rotting mass thrown off by the lowest layers of old society" (Tucker 1972:25).

The Marxist concept of class differs significantly from that of non-Marxist social scientists, who use it to refer to stratified status or income hierarchies (see Chapter 4). *Class,* in the Marxist sense, refers specifically to the relationship of a group to the societal means of production; thus, it indicates a system of relationships, not a unit of like persons. Similarly, the concept of *ownership* refers not to the accumulation of goods (which in Marxist theory may occur in any class) but to the actual ownership of a society's productive enterprises.

Society emerges, according to Marxist thought, through class struggle; according to Marx and Engels, "the history of all hitherto society is the history of class struggles" (1970:16). Classes emerge as a society produces a surplus; as a division of labor emerges, thereby allowing for surplus production, the accumulation of a surplus can be appropriated by one group. As a result, this group stands in an exploitative relationship to the mass of producers, and class conflict is established (Giddens 1971). Marx and Engels point out that the first division of labor is the division of labor by sex for the purpose of propagating children; gender thus provides the first class antagonism. However, they (and subsequent Marxist thinkers) leave this point without further development.

As capitalism develops, the capitalist class appropriates the wealth produced by the subordinate classes because the capitalists have the power to control the conditions under which other classes work. The working class owns only its labor, which it must sell for wages; the capitalists, in turn, have the power to determine what wages they will pay and the conditions under which people work. As capitalists try to increase their profit, they do so at the increasing expense of laborers. Profit comes from the fact that workers produce more value than the wages they receive. The craft of distinctive workers becomes less important than the value of mass-produced commodities. Material objects, then, take on greater value than the workers who produce them. In effect, in Marxist analysis, the value of individual human activity decreases as the material value of the products created increases.

Therefore, human beings become alienated in the sense that they do not control or own the products of their labor; they choose neither the form nor the use of the products they make. Additionally, workers are alienated from each other, and they become alienated from themselves because they do not exercise the human ability to transform nature to their own design.

Politically, according to Marx, workers must seize the means of production (and, feminists would add, reproduction); the accumulation of profit in the hands of a few must be eliminated. Marxists see that social changes that do not strike at the material basis of social life—capital accumulation by the owning class—will be insufficient because they will not change the underlying causes of social organization.

The materialist thesis is also central to the perspective on consciousness and ideas that is developed throughout Marxist theory. Systems of knowledge take their historical form in response to the economic mode of production. Marx argues that the ideas of a period are a reflection of the interests of the ruling class (see Chapter 8).

Marx writes:

The production of ideas, of conceptions, of consciousness, is at first directly interwoven with the material activity and the material intercourse of men, the language of real life. . . . We do not set out from what men say, imagine, conceive nor from men as narrated, thought of, imagined, conceived, in order to arrive at men in the flesh. We set out from real, active men, and on the basis of their real life-processes we demonstrate the development of the ideological reflexes and echoes of this life process. (Marx, *The German Ideology;* in Tucker 1972:118–119)

Basic to this perspective on the sociology of knowledge is the proposition that "it is not the consciousness of men that determines their being, but, on the contrary, their social being that determines their consciousness" (Marx, preface to *A Contribution to the Critique of Political Economy;* in Tucker 1972:4). Those who own the means of production also determine the ruling ideas of the period.

Consciousness is determined by class relations, for even though persons will normally try to identify what is their best interest, under capitalism the ruling class controls the production of ideas. Also, even though humans create practical ideas from experience, most of our experience is determined by capitalist relations of production. Thus, the ideas that are disseminated through communications systems, including language, serve to authorize a reality that the ruling class would like us to believe. In this sense, ideas become *ideology*—understood to mean a system of beliefs that legitimate and maintain the status quo.

For feminists, Marx's work on ideology is fundamental to their understanding of sexism. Sexism, as an ideology that justifies the power of men over women, emerges not in the best interest of women but as a defense of male domination. Like other ideologies, sexist ideology is a means by which one class rules a society and sanctions the society's social relations. The extent to which women believe in the precepts of sexist ideology is only a reflection of the powers of coercion (whether subtle or overt) and social control.

False consciousness emerges as the subordinate group accepts the world view of the dominant class. Because, as history moves, consciousness also changes, then at the time that workers see the nature of their exploitation, false consciousness would be transformed into class consciousness and workers would take the revolutionary struggle into their own hands. Marx's theory goes beyond academic analysis because central to his work is the idea that theory must be connected to social and political practice (*praxis,* in his words). Social criticism has no value unless coupled with material change; in *The German Ideology,* he writes:

all forms and products of consciousness cannot be dissolved by mental criticism, by resolution into "self-consciousness" or transformation into "apparitions," "spectres," "fancies," etc., but only by the practical overthrow of the actual social relations which gave rise to this idealistic humbug; that not criticism, but revolution is the driving force of history. (Tucker 1972:128)

Thus, Marx sees human beings as potentially revolutionary because their capabilities for creative work and social consciousness far exceed those allowed them under capitalist organization (Eisenstein 1979). This fact provides the basis for optimism in Marx's work, for it lays the foundation for radical change and the transformation from human oppression to human liberation.

Marx and Engels's analysis of women's oppression is drawn mostly from their writing on the family, especially Engels's essay, *The Origins of the Family, State and Property,* published in 1884 after Marx's death. Feminists who, in the beginning of the contemporary women's movement, were looking for alternative analyses to the liberal perspective began with this classical Marxist perspective. Their later criticisms of Marx and Engels are based primarily on the discussion of the family proposed by Marx and Engels.

Although Engels states in the preface to *The Origins of the Family, State and Property* that production and reproduction together are the determining factors of history, family relations are discussed as derived from the economic mode of production. From a Marxist perspective, in capitalist societies, forms of the family change as class relations change, thus making family relations secondary to economic and class relations. In keeping with their perspective on the social origins of ideas, Marx and Engels would say, however, that the social image of the family is an idealized one that disguises the real economic structure of family relations.

They describe the family under capitalism as a microcosm of the society's larger class relations; so, particularly in bourgeois families, the wife is the proletariat. Engels writes:

In the great majority of cases today, at least in the possessing classes, the husband is obliged to earn a living and support his family and that in itself gives him a position of supremacy, without any need for special legal ties and privileges. Within the family he is the bourgeois and the wife represents the proletariat. (Engels 1972:137)

Monogamous marriage, Marx and Engels argue, develops as part of the formation of private property. Particularly in the bourgeois family, the development of private property creates the need to determine lineage for the purpose of inheritance. Engels writes:

Monogamy arose from the concentration of considerable wealth in the hands of a single individual—a man—and from the need to bequeath this wealth to the children of that man and of no other. For this purpose, the monogamy of the woman was required, not that of the man, so this monogamy of the woman did not in any way interfere with open or concealed polygamy on the part of the man. (Engels 1972:138)

Engels does not explain how men and not women came to control property. Therefore, feminists have criticized the Marxist perspective for not explaining the origins of patriarchy.

Marx and Engels discuss marriage as being, for women, a form of prostitution. Engels writes:

marriage is conditioned by the class position of the parties and is to that extent always a marriage of convenience.... This marriage of convenience turns often enough into crassest prostitution—sometimes of both partners, but far more commonly of the woman, who only differs from the ordinary courtesan in that she does not let out her body on piece-work as a wage-worker, but sells it once and for all into slavery. (1972:134)

Marx and Engels define marriage as based on economic relations, although they make it clear that they would prefer to see it based on individual sex-love. In marriage and the family, Marx and Engels recognize the woman's role is to be responsible for household management and child care. They argue that household work becomes a private service under advanced capitalism, because it loses the public character it has in earlier forms of economic life. In advanced capitalism, the work of the housewife is both a private service to the male head of the household and an unpaid economic service to the society as a whole. Marx and Engels conclude that "the modern individual family is founded on the open or concealed domestic slavery of the wife, and modern society is a mass composed of these individual families as its molecules" (Engels 1972:137).

Based on their analysis of the family, Marx and Engels see emancipatory social change in family relations as occurring only with the abolition of private property. Although they maintain a wish for monogamous relationships, they want monogamy to be the expression of a sexual commitment based on love, not property. Furthermore, although they do not use the modern language of double standards, what they hope for is monogamy for *both* men and women, not masked polygamy for men and monogamy for women.

Because Marx and Engels see male supremacy in the family as originating with the accumulation of property and the development of class relations, they suggest that the liberation of women will occur as the result of class struggle. Women's status is derived from the economic organization of society; therefore, the liberation of women will follow automatically from the revolution of the workers and the abolition of private property. Thus, although Marx and Engels note that the gender division of labor is the first class oppression, their analysis assumes that women's oppression is secondary to oppression by class and that because it is entirely caused by class oppression, women will be liberated as soon as class oppression is ended.

It is on this point that socialist and radical feminists begin their critique of Marx. These feminists agree with much of Marx and Engels's analysis, but they disagree that the oppression of women is secondary to class oppression. Socialist feminists essentially agree with Marx's theory of class relations, although they believe that gender relations are equally important in the determination of historical social relations.

Radical feminists, on the other hand, identify patriarchy as an autonomous historical fact and consider gender relations to be the fundamental form of oppression. Class and race oppression, radical feminists argue, are extensions of patriarchal inequality. Accordingly, radical feminists see the abolition of male supremacy as their primary political goal. Although radical feminists differ in the extent to which they use Marxist theory, both socialist and radical feminists would agree that Marx and Engels ignored their own observations on gender oppression. The Marxist assumption that gender oppression would disappear with the abolition of private property too easily assumes that gender is of secondary importance in the determination of social, political, and economic relations.

SOCIALIST FEMINISM

The emergence of socialist feminism in the 1970s stems largely from feminists' dissatisfaction with classical Marxist perspectives on women and the family. Marx and Engels, socialist feminists would argue, do not seriously consider their own point that sexual division of labor is the first form of class antagonism. Consequently, they too easily assume that economic class relations are the most critical relations defining women's place in society. Too many questions—cross-cultural, historical, and contemporary—stand in the way of such a theoretical assumption. Are women subordinated to men in preclass societies? Why does women's oppression continue even in socialist societies? Where, in advanced capitalist societies, do women fit in the Marxist definition of class?

Questions such as these lead socialist feminists to conclude that women's oppression cannot be reduced to capitalism alone, although capitalism remains as a highly significant source of women's oppression. The socialist feminist perspective begins with the point that, although economic class relations are important in determining women's status, gender relations may be equally important. Socialist feminists would then argue that class and gender relations intersect in advanced capitalist societies (Hartmann 1976) and that class relations alone do not account for the location of women and men in social life (Jaggar and Struhl 1978). Moreover, according to this perspective, eradicating social class inequality alone will not necessarily eliminate sexism as well.

As feminists ask these new questions, they have begun a dialogue with Marxist theory and an independent theoretical tradition in feminist studies. They question how biological and social reproduction are tied to the mode of production, how patriarchal relations are tied to the development and maintenance of class relations, whether women's oppression is primarily a question of gender or class, and how systems of race, class, and gender oppression interact with each other.

On the first point, feminists argue that Marx and Engels ignore their statement that forms of production and reproduction constitute the basis for social organization. Marxist theory defines *reproduction* as the social (as well as physical) production of workers. The family is the place, in advanced capitalism, where workers are restored (through food and shelter) so as to be able to reenter the labor force on a daily basis. Also, reproduction in the family includes the socialization of workers to capitalist values and personalities. Implicit in the classical Marxist argument is the idea that the family is a separate force in history, although one subordinate to the forces of production. Although Marx and Engels note historical changes in the family as a productive unit, they do not develop an analysis of women's place in the family, nor do they explain the sexual politics of male-female relations in the family in any terms other than property relations.

One of the first feminist theories attempting to fill this void was Shulamith Firestone's *The Dialectic of Sex* (1970). In it, she uses the method of dialectical materialism to analyze the status of women. She compliments Marx and Engels for their dialectical perspective—one that sees history as an emerging process of social action and reaction—and she accepts their materialist proposition as the correct analysis of economic development. But she argues that Marx and Engels are mistaken in giving a strictly economic interpretation to the oppression of women. In her own analysis, she argues that just as the underclasses must seize the means of production as a way to eliminate economic classes, so must women control the means of reproduction if they are to eliminate the inequality of sexual classes. Firestone's controversial conclusion includes the advocacy of technological innovation through artificial reproduction and the consequent elimination of sexist institutions of childbirth and childrearing. She writes:

The reproduction of the species by one sex for the benefit of both would be replaced by (at least the option of) artificial reproduction: children would be born to both sexes equally, or independently of either, however one chooses to look at it; the dependence of the child on the mother (and vice versa) would give way to a greatly shortened dependence on a small group of others in general, and any remaining inferiority to adults in physical strength would be compensated for culturally. The division of labor would be ended by the elimination of labor altogether (cybernation). The tyranny of the biological family would be broken. (1971:11).

Although her biological determinism is neither consistent with Marxist solutions nor agreeable to all feminists, her argument underscores the importance of considering reproduction, along with production, as necessary in explaining the status of women.

Firestone's analysis was followed by Juliet Mitchell's classical work, *Woman's Estate* (1971), which at the time it was published provided the most comprehensive theory of women's position in advanced capitalist societies. Mitchell also distinguishes socialist and radical feminist perspectives by defining socialist feminism as a Marxist framework and radical feminism as a perspective on women's oppression as rooted in male ego psychology. She argues that radical feminism explains the ideological and psychological oppression of women, whereas socialist feminism explains the complexity of class relations both among women *and* between women and men. Mitchell argues that both theories are wrong when each is considered independently of the other, and she offers an analysis that ties women's economic role explicitly to their roles within the family. Although both socialist and radical feminism have developed further since Mitchell discussed them, her work provides the foundation for understanding current feminist theory.

Mitchell begins with the classical Marxist premise that the economic mode of production is the defining factor of social organization, but she argues that, in Marx and Engels's theory, the liberation of women remains an abstract ideal, not a problem to be explained. Marx and Engels assume that the liberation of women will occur with the transition from capitalism to socialism. Mitchell contends that a specific theory of women's oppression is needed if the liberation of women is to occur with the transition from capitalism to socialism. Although women's role in production is central to their oppression, Mitchell includes an analysis of women's role in reproduction, sexuality, and the socialization of children. She argues that the subordination of women involves the interplay of these key structures with the economic mode of production. The structure of production embraces the structure of the family, which, in turn, includes the structures of sexuality, reproduction, and socialization. Mitchell writes:

> The contemporary family can be seen as a triptych of sexual, reproductive, and socializatory functions (the women's world) embraced by production (the man's world)—precisely a structure which in the final instance is determined by the economy. The exclusion of women from production—social human activity—and their confinement to a monolithic condensation of functions within a unity—the family . . . is the root cause of the contemporary social definition of women as *natural* beings. (1971:148).

To some extent, Mitchell agrees with Firestone that technological development must be a precondition for the liberation of women. This conclusion is also consistent with Marx's perception that technological advances, if under the political and economic control of *all* humans, can liberate persons allowing them to fulfill their creative potential. Mitchell argues that women were excluded from production in the past because of their presumed physical weakness and the involuntary character of childbearing. Technological developments and automation have now lessened the necessity for physical strength in labor, and the development of contraception makes childbearing a voluntary act. Because contraception makes it possible to separate sexual and reproductive activity, Mitchell argues that the ideological basis of the family life as the unit of sexual and reproductive activity is destroyed. And because biological and social parentage need not be performed by the same person, she concludes that the development of technology and industrialization now makes the liberation of women a possibility. She concludes that "probably it is only in the highly developed societies of the West that an authentic liberation of women can be envisaged today" (1971:121).

Based on her theory, Mitchell assumes that "the entry of women fully into public industry and the right to earn a living wage" (171:148–149) must be a fundamental goal of women's emancipation movements. The exclusion of women from public industry, their restriction to the private world of the family (where socialization, reproduction, and sexuality are located), and their lack of control over women's work form the basis for their subordination. The ideological assumption of women's dominance in the family obscures their inferior role in production, she argues. Women's full entry into the system of production, coupled with policies to transform the character of family relations, form the practical implications of the argument she develops.

Mitchell raises a number of issues that remain central to feminist theory. For one, she opens the feminist discussion of the relationship of the family to the economy. In Mitchell's analysis, the family has both an economic and an ideological role in capitalist systems. As industrial capitalism of the nineteenth and twentieth centuries developed, the family changed from a unit of production to a unit of consumption. Because of the way the family contains women's work in reproduction, sexuality, and socialization, several specific consequences of the family's economic-ideological functions occur for women. The process of consumption obviously supports economic life, but in more subtle ways, it affects the status of women. Sexuality, for example, becomes intermixed with a consumption ethic; under modern capitalism, sexuality becomes marketable. Although this fact supposedly means more sexual freedom for women, it clearly increases their use as sexual objects (1971:142). The economic function of the modern family is also reflected in socialization and reproductive practices because it is in the family that workers are created and sustained for their labor force participation. A capitalist work force supports capitalist enterprises by leaving women with the responsibility for creating the personalities that are appropriate to a capitalist labor force.

In addition, Mitchell argues that the family's ideological role supports the rationale and the inherent contradictions of advanced capitalist societies. The ideology of the family supports values of individualism and personal freedom at the same time that it favors individual accumulation of property. The family becomes typified as a "haven in a heartless world" (Lasch 1977) where persons are free to be themselves and to consume goods at their pleasure. An essential contradiction of capitalism lies in the fact that, as capitalism develops, private property as well as the real choices necessary for personal freedom are taken away from the masses. So, the individualism and freedom that the ideology of the family promise stand in opposition to the fact that capitalism makes these social and economic ideals impossible to realize.

For Mitchell, the result is a self-contradictory system in which, ideologically, women are asked to hold together a system that cannot operate as it is supposed to. Although many feminists would disagree with Mitchell's analysis, this task constitutes women's oppression. She writes, "The family is a stronghold of what capitalism needs to preserve but actually destroys: private property and individualism. The housewife-mother is the guardian and representative of these. She is a backward, conservative force—and this is what her oppression means. . . . The 'freedom' of the housewife is her isolation" (1971:161). According to Mitchell, the one area of women's power—the socialization of children—becomes a mystique for their own oppression. In Mitchell's second book, *Psychoanalysis and Feminism* (1974), she points out that the process of socialization only projects the mother's anxieties and frustrations onto her children. Mitchell concludes that the overemphasis in the contemporary family on emotional development and individual growth is a rationale for denying women full social and economic participation.

Mitchell's book lays the cause of women's oppression directly on the development of capitalism and the exclusion of women from equal participation in the labor force. Her solution to women's oppression is to eliminate the division of labor by gender and, ultimately, to support the transition from capitalism to socialism. Although she is critical of classical Marxist theory, she still relies on economic production as the primary cause of women's position. Since the publication of her book, socialist feminist theory has developed around several of the issues that Mitchell first suggested.

In particular, Mitchell's work calls attention to the division between public and private spheres of social and economic life. Rosaldo and Lamphere (1974), for instance pick up Mitchell's point and argue that women's relegation to the private, domestic sphere excludes them from public life and, thus, from equal access to social and economic resources. Recent feminist theory is more critical of this argument, although the question of the division in public and private spheres is still central to feminist analyses (Elshtain 1974). Recently, the increasing entry of middle-aged, married women and mothers into the labor force, makes it less true that women are confined to the home. Still, women's work in public labor is often said to mirror and extend the private services they provide in the home. Others have argued, more fundamentally, with Rosaldo and Lamphere and Mitchell by demonstrating that women's confinement to the private sphere is largely a white, middle-class phenomenon (Lewis 1977) and, thus, is a race- and class-bound analysis. But without arguing that women's exclusion from the public sphere is the primary basis for their subordination, feminists continue to point out that a theory of women's position must account for the relationship of the private, domestic realm to the public realm of social and economic life (Sacks 1975).

Zaretsky (1976), for example, argues that the supposed split in the public and private spheres obscures the economic role of the family. The production of food, shelter, and emotional nurturance, along with sexuality and reproduction, is a basic material necessity; consequently, even if it is unpaid, housework constitutes socially necessary labor. The idea that the private labor of women is separate from publicly productive labor is, in his analysis, specific to the historical development of capitalism. He argues that the idea of the family as separate from the productive world *and* as the sphere of women originated in the nineteenth century with the rise of industrial capitalism. At this time, women's work was ideologically defined as taking place in the home (Cott 1977) even though most working-class, poor, and minority women continued to work in factories, domestic service, agriculture, and other forms of public labor. Whereas others trace the division of the public and private spheres to earlier historical periods (Elshtain 1974), Zaretsky's work points to the specific dynamics of this split under advanced capitalism.

What is innovative in his work is his equation of the public-private split with a second division—that between the newly emerging concept of personal life and the collective life as found in the social division of labor. Zaretsky writes, "This 'split' between the socialized labour of the capitalist enterprise and the private labour of women in the home is closely related to a second 'split'—between our 'personal' lives and our place within the social division of labour" (1976:29). Personal life, emerging under capitalism, appears to be an autonomous process—as if persons' private lives were governed by their own internal laws. Accordingly, Zaretsky argues that human relations become seen as an end in themselves, detached from the material world of economic fact. Individuals appear unique, and the subjective sphere of self and life-style takes preeminence over the economic relations that, for Zaretsky, define social organization.

Zaretsky's analysis shows how, in the advanced capitalist family, women's primary responsibility is for an emotional world that is ideological in character. Like Mitchell, he sees that advanced capitalism eliminates the production of goods as the basis of the family. But he adds to her analysis that the seeming independence of personal life is a falsehood. Consequently, socialist feminist theory and practice must include the elimination of capitalism *and* the transformation of the family and personal life.

Although Mitchell and Zaretsky point to the dynamics of family life as it is related to economic life, they still maintain the material perspective of Marxism by arguing that the economic mode of production provides the essential basis for social organization. Their socialist feminist position makes the important point that change in women's status will come only through the transformation of capitalist relations, along with independent efforts to transform family relations as well. Socialist feminism shares with classical Marxism the idea that the oppression of women is primarily an economic fact, although it is buttressed by ideological delusions about the family. Socialist feminism makes the additional point that women's oppression must be related to their position in the private world of reproduction and the family. In sum, socialist feminism makes the first suggestion that women's oppression extends beyond the area of economic production. As we will see, socialist feminists have recently incorporated an analysis of patriarchy into their theoretical analysis. But the inclusion of patriarchy follows from the analysis developed by radical feminists, so it is to their ideas that we will now turn.

RADICAL FEMINISM

At the same time that socialist feminism was developing, other feminists were arguing that male domination per se was the basis for women's oppression. Radical feminists define *patriarchy* as a "sexual system of power in which the male possesses superior power and economic privilege" (Eisenstein 1979:17), and they view patriarchy as an autonomous social, historical, and political force. Whereas socialist feminism emphasizes the economic basis of gender relations, radical feminism emphasizes male power, privilege, and psychological development as the bases of social relations. Radical feminism sees patriarchal relations as more fundamental than class relations in determining women's lives.

Since its inception, the radical feminist position has taken several different directions, some of them more explicitly tied to Marxism than others. Some current radical feminist thought is totally apart from the materialist thesis in Marxist work, locating the causes of oppression solely within patriarchal culture and its control of women (Daly 1978). But much of radical feminism has developed specifically because of Marxist perspectives to explain adequately the emergence and persistence of patriarchy. Thus, some early radical feminists attempted to explain the origins of patriarchy by claiming that women controlled many of the early hunting and gathering societies, but men organized themselves to conquer women by force, thereby also gaining control of originally woman-centered forms of social organization. This position is spelled out by Charlotte Bunch:

The first division of labor, in pre-history, was based on sex: men hunted, women built the villages, took care of children, and farmed. Women collectively controlled the land, language, culture, and the communities. Men were able to conquer women with the weapons that they developed for hunting when it became clear that women were leading a more stable, peaceful, and desirable existence. We do not know exactly how this conquest took place, but it is clear that the original imperialism was male over female: the male claiming the female body and her service as his territory (or property). (1978:37).

The radical feminist claim that matriarchal society predates the emergence of patriarchy is a debatable point. Popular feminist accounts claim a universal matriarchal history in human social organization (Davis 1971), but anthropological evidence gives a more cautious interpretation. Research on the transition from primate to human society indicates a high level of cooperation between males and females in early human societies (Zihlman 1978), but studies of early hunting and gathering societies show that, although many groups were matrilineal, they tended to be egalitarian, not matriarchal (Leacock 1978). Anthropologists conclude that more careful conceptual definitions of power, authority, influence, and status are needed before we can accurately describe women's role in the evolution of human society (Webster 1975) and before we can make claims about the existence of matriarchal societies. It is the case that women's social position has not always been, in every society or in every way, subordinate to that of men (Sacks 1975). But the radical feminist account of a universal preexisting matriarchy is also a skeptical claim. The arrangements between women and men vary widely from society to society and across history, and it has taken a great amount of new anthropological research to untangle the early history of male-female relations (Reiter 1975). Moreover, in traditional anthropological accounts, scholars have often projected contemporary assumptions of male supremacy and female social roles into the pasts they have studied (Hubbard 1979). Only now are scholars beginning to find answers to the questions that arise from considering the origins of women's oppression.

So, the question posed is: how did men gain control of the systems of production and reproduction, and how is women's oppression tied to the development of class systems? Radical feminists concentrate on the first half of the question. They argue that male control of women cannot be simply explained as based on class oppression and, as the feminist anthropologist Gayle Rubin has written, "no analysis of the reproduction of labor can explain foot-binding, chastity belts, or any of the incredible array of Byzantine, fetishized indignities, let alone the more ordinary ones, which have been inflicted upon women in various times and places" (1975:163). In part, the strength of the radical feminist position is that it is better able to explain male violence against women and the many cultural practices designed to control female sexuality and reproduction.

Rubin's own work on the genesis of women's oppression centers on the concept of *sex/gender system* as the "set of arrangements by which a society transforms biological sexuality into products of human activity, and in which these transformed sexual needs are satisfied" (1975:159). For Rubin, the oppression of women lies in social systems that create male solidarity, not simply in systems of economic production. Kinship systems, as the observable form of sex/gender systems, relate persons through social categories that may or may not have their basis in biological relations. Beginning with Levi-Strauss's theory in which the essence of kinship systems is the exchange of women (usually through marriage), Rubin goes on to say that "the subordination of women can be seen as a product of the relationships by which sex and gender are organized and produced" (1975:177). The solidarity expressed through the exchange of women represents solidarity between men. According to Rubin, "the 'exchange' of women is a seductive and powerful concept. It is attractive in that it places the oppression of women within social systems, rather than in biology. Moreover, it suggests that we look for the ultimate locus of women's oppression within the traffic in women, rather than within the traffic in merchandise" (1975:175).

Rubin also develops the idea that gender is a socially imposed division of the sexes that is reproduced through the production of gender identities. As socialization theory has argued, persons are not created in a gender-neutral process. Their personalities represent the gendered categories around which kinship systems are organized. Thus, in the radical feminist analysis, the production of gender sets the preconditions for other forms of domination (Harding 1981). Men first learn to dominate women, setting a pattern for the domination of others. Economic systems may determine who these others are, but sex and gender systems establish the preconditions for domination to emerge. In the end, radical feminism sees systems of domination based on class, race, or tribe as extensions of the underlying politics of male supremacy (Bunch 1975).

In radical feminist politics, patriarchal institutions create myths and forms of social organization that constrain women to exist in male-centered worlds (Daly 1978). The radical feminist solution to women's subordination is the establishment of women-centered beliefs and systems. For some, this movement has produced the separatist philosophy of radical lesbian feminism (Bunch 1975; Daly 1978), whereby a woman-identified world would be re-created through the attachments women have to each other, not to men.

In sum, the radical feminist position has called attention to the concept of patriarchy by challenging the economic framework of socialist-feminist theory. But in emphasizing the importance of patriarchy, the radical feminist position itself tends to downplay the effects of class systems on women's oppression. Thus, the dialogue between socialist and radical feminists has resulted in a synthesis of the two perspectives in which capitalism and patriarchy taken together are seen as the origins of women's oppression. In this synthesis, the psychological production of gender, the organization of sex/gender systems (including male control of female reproduction and sexuality), and capitalism are seen as the underlying determinants of women's subordination to men.

CONNECTING SOCIALIST AND RADICAL FEMINISM

The assumption in radical feminist analyses that gender relations are more fundamental than class relations has posed important causal questions for feminist theory. The dialogue between radical feminists and socialist feminists has formulated new insights that reject the ahistorical and universalist claims in some radical feminist accounts, but that reckon with the empirical observation that patriarchal relations do precede and exist independently of class relations. Although women in general are not equal to men in class societies, recent anthropological works show that male property ownership is not the sole basis for male supremacy (Sacks 1975). Within this new synthesis, socialist feminists who might earlier have rejected the radical feminist perspective as a causal theory are now taking radical feminist perspectives on patriarchy seriously. Although socialist feminists still reject the universalist and ahistorical assumptions frequently found in radical feminist accounts (Rosaldo 1980), they are grappling with the fact that the oppression of women predates the development of class society and, therefore, are trying to relate gender domination more carefully to patriarchal relations and other forms of oppression.

Hartmann's (1976) analysis of the interaction of patriarchal structures and the development of capitalism is one of the earliest works to make this synthesis. She argues that in precapitalist societies men controlled the labor of women and children in the family and "that in so doing men learned the techniques of hierarchical organization and control" (1976:138). As larger systems of exchange formed beyond local communities, men were faced with the problem of maintaining their control over women. Through the long-standing institution of patriarchy, men learned techniques of social control that, when capitalism emerged in Western societies, were transformed from direct and personal systems of control to indirect and impersonal systems of social control. Hartmann's analysis sees capitalism as emerging in interaction with and reinforcing patriarchy, but patriarchy is not the sole cause of gender inequality. Many have pointed out, in fact, that the categories of capitalist systems are potentially sex-blind. Gender stratification developed as a particular hierarchy under capitalism because the precondition of the sexual division of labor was extended to newly emerging systems of wage labor.

Hartmann's argument continues by arguing that "job segregation by sex ... is the primary mechanism in capitalist society that maintains the superiority of men over women" (1976:139). She documents her argument through historical review of the change from cottage and farm production to industrial factory systems and the transformation of household industry, pointing out that the development of capitalism had a more severe impact on women than it did men. Not only was women's productive role in the family altered, but they became more economically dependent on men. Thus, the gender division of labor is transformed from one of interdependence to one of the dependence of women on men. The crux of Hartmann's research lies in her analysis of men's control of the wage-labor market, where she says the reason men excluded, rather than organized, women workers "is explained, not by capitalism, but by patriarchal relations between men and women: men wanted to assure that women would continue to perform the appropriate tasks at home" (1976:155). Men benefit both from the higher wages they receive *and* from the household division of labor in which they receive women's services.

Although Hartmann's analysis explains much about job segregation by sex and about the interplay of capitalism and patriarchy, it still does not explain the origins of gender stratification. In fact, her work concludes, as earlier suggested by radical feminists, that we will not be able to eliminate the sexual division of labor until we have understood and transformed the process of the social production of gender.

The synthesis of radical and socialist feminism shows how women's role in the *division of labor* (simply defined as the work that different groups of people do) explains much about their position in the society as a whole. Current research in anthropology demonstrates that the gender division of labor in preclass hunting and gathering societies is not as rigidly divided along "man the hunter" and "female the gatherer" lines as has been assumed in traditional anthropological research (Lamphere 1977; Slocum 1975). Where a gender division of labor exists, women's roles are often seen as "complementary and equal" to those of men (Lamphere 1977; Matthiasson 1974), leading many to conclude that women's power in society is directly related to their contribution to production and the extent to which they control the resources they produce (Friedl 1975; Leacock 1978; Sanday 1973). These revisions of earlier assumptions show that our visions of societal development and gender stratification have been clouded by the cultural bias entailed in Western male-defined social research; also they show that women's contributions to social organization and development have been highly underrated (Zihlman 1978). But more profoundly, they indicate that the emergence of gender inequality is more complex than Marxist accounts of the preeminence of capitalism can explain (Flax 1976).

For feminist theory, the question emerges as to whether, especially in complex societies, groups can maintain a sex division of labor and still have economic, political, and social freedom for women and men. Can women remain different but equal, or must differences between the sexes be eliminated altogether? Moreover, can changes in the gender division of labor eliminate women's subordination, or must we also consider transformations in the social production of gender? How, in effect, is the social production of gender tied to the modes of economic life that have emerged in modern Western societies?

Anthropological work on women's roles in more egalitarian societies begins to shed light on the necessary conditions for egalitarianism between women and women. In studying the social organization of hunting and gathering societies with relatively egalitarian gender relations, Leacock identifies three social structural conditions that seem necessary to produce egalitarianism: (1) the ties of collective economic dependency link *all* individuals directly to the well-being of the group as a whole; (2) the public and private spheres are not dichotomized; and (3) decisions are made by those who will also carry them out (1978:247).

On the first point, Leacock emphasizes that all members of an egalitarian society would be necessary to the system of production. They need not, it would seem, all contribute in the same way, but they would all be seen as equally valuable—quite a contrast to the socially and economically devalued labor of women under capitalism. Second, Leacock shows how the separation of the public and the private invites the restriction of women to the family. Other anthropologists, too, argue that the restriction of women to domestic work is an important precondition for the subordination of women. Domestic labor is production for the use of society's members, whereas public production creates goods for exchange. Because production for exchange takes on greater value than production for use, any group that is restricted to production for use is likely to be devalued (Sacks 1975). Moreover, in modern societies, the separation of the public and the private also invites ideological oppression of women that claims they are more fit for domestic life and, therefore, more likely to be restricted to it.

Finally, Leacock's analysis suggests that no group should have authority over the experience of others. Were women to be involved in the decision-making processes that affect them, they would exercise control over their own lives. Again, this arrangement would be the reverse of the contemporary situation, in which men rule even on matters, such as female reproduction, that greatly influence the course of women's experience. The development of modern patriarchy puts men in positions of authority in public and private institutions. The historical shift placing more authority in industry and government has meant that men control (through public patriarchy) areas that deeply affect womens lives—family law, welfare practices, reproductive issues, work policies, and the prosecution of male violence (Brown 1981). Leacock's analysis raises the question of how different gender relations might be in a society where women and men controlled decisions pertinent to their lives; where persons engaged in equally valuable labor, and where all members of the society were equally responsible for household work. Chodorow's (1978) work on the production of gender (see Chapter 5) suggests that such a society would produce men and women with less stereotypical personalities and, consequently, more flexibility in creating new social arrangements.

In sum, a synthesis between radical and socialist feminism gives us a new direction for social theory. It suggests that we ground a discussion of women's position in the dynamics of the gender division of labor, the emergence of class systems, the formation of patriarchal relations, and the social organization of the family. In all, a complete theory of women's oppression must explain not only women's role in production but also the patriarchal control of female reproduction and sexuality (too often demonstrated through male violence against women). Feminist theory, from a radical perspective, thus directs us to look at the material conditions of women's lives and in so doing, to explain the basis for their oppression not only by gender but also by race and by class. At this point in time, this issue is perhaps the most important one in the development of feminist theory.

CONCLUSION: EXPLAINING RACE, CLASS, AND GENDER

A comprehensive analysis of women's position must include insights and issues from all three feminist perspectives: liberal feminism, socialist feminism, and radical feminism. Each contributes important information on women's situation, although no one of them adequately explains the intersection of race oppression with oppression by gender and class. To date, feminist theory has not provided a complete analysis of race.

Early feminist work suggests that sex oppression is analogous to race oppression, by arguing that sexism has effects on its victims similar to those of racism (Hacker 1951) and that discriminatory policies based on sex are comparable to those based on race (Stimpson 1971). This reasoning by analogy, however, was more often an attempt to prove the existence of sexism than to analyze the conditions of minority women's experience. The first attempts to describe minority women's conditions were usually described as "double jeopardy," suggesting the cumulative effect of race and gender exploitation. Although these arguments are descriptively valuable, they are analytically limited. The analogy between sex and race, for instance, falls apart when we consider the particular experience of black, Hispanic, Asian-American, and native American women. And the idea that race and gender oppression are cumulative, although suggestive of the burdens these women face, does not explain the complex dynamics of race, gender, and class inequality.

Within the feminist movement, white feminists have often asked why black women are reluctant to identify with the women's movement. At the same time, minority women perceive the women's movement as a white, middle-class cause that misunderstands or ignores their experience. Although research shows that even more black women than white women support feminist issues (Hemmons 1980), black women are reluctant to affiliate with a movement that divides them against black men or that generalizes its politics and analysis from the experience of the dominant group (Eichelberger 1977). Third World feminists themselves insist on an analysis that synthesizes the major systems of oppression (Combahee River Collective 1979; Smith 1979) and that speaks to the particular conditions that Third World women face in their lives (Hemmons 1980; Lewis 1977; Moraga and Anzaldúa 1981). Each of the feminist perspectives reviewed here implies a different understanding of race.

The liberal feminist analysis shares many assumptions with an assimilationist perspective on race relations (Glazer 1971; Gordon 1964). Assimilation theory assumes that as barriers of race discrimination are removed, minorities will move into the system and become assimilated with the dominant culture. Like liberal feminism, assimilation theory strives for liberal political goals that will establish sex- and color-blind categories to place people in economic and social statuses. Although this vision may depict an ideal world and although its emphasis on civil rights is shared by all feminists, it offers little analysis of the persistence of race in equality, and it assumes that to become liberated, one must deny the particular conditions of one's experience (Rich 1979).

Socialist feminism provides the best starting point for an analysis of race, but only when its concern with the political economy of class and gender is extended to include race issues. The experience of all women is inextricably tied to the development of class relations; moreover, the development of productive and reproductive relations under capitalism provides much of the basis for the exploitation of racial groups in this country. The economic perspective of socialist feminism should also remind us that the liberation of white women from domestic labor has rested upon the availability of black and other minority domestic workers (Dill 1980), although this fact is frequently forgotten in feminist analyses. Moreover, the history of contraceptive technologies that helped liberate women followed experimentation on Third World women (Barker-Benfield 1976; Reid 1975). The socialist feminist perspective used in developing an economic framework for women's oppression tells us much about the interplay of gender and class, but it "does not entail a corresponding awareness of cultural differences" (Simons 1979:389). Without such a full-blown analysis, the assumptions of socialist feminism remain blind to the experience of women most oppressed by class, race, and gender domination.

Finally, the radical feminist perspective assumes that gender is the primary form of oppression and that class and race are extensions of patriarchal domination (Daly 1978). This perspective is perhaps the most problematic in providing a theory of race oppression. In assuming that patriarchy is the cause of women's oppression, it divides minority women and men and takes the experience of white American women as the universal social experience. In locating the causes of oppression in the domination of men, radical feminism provides no explanation of the powerlessness that minority men and women experience together. Its insistence that eliminating sexism is the key to eliminating racism has a hollow ring to Third World women who face oppression on both counts and who have likely experienced racism as a more fundamental (or at least equally fundamental) fact of their lives. Radical women of color clearly recognize that sexism exists in their communities. But attributing the primary cause of their experience to patriarchy belies the racism they encounter not only from men but from white feminists as well (Moraga and Anzaldúa 1981).

In sum, a perspective on race demands more careful analysis using each of the feminist theories reviewed here. Assumptions throughout feminist research about such matters as the dependency of women on men, the learned helplessness of women, and the debilitating effects of the family on women are all called into question from a Third World feminist perspective. Developing an analysis of race is the most important task of feminist theory because without it, theory and research that describe and explain the experience of *all* women cannot be established. As a result, without an analysis of race, feminists cannot hope to find solutions to liberation for all women.

C O N C L U S I O N

The theoretical perspectives reviewed here make the point that social change is informed by different premises about the social organization of society. The different feminist perspectives examined here each suggest different kinds of social change. Therefore, for feminists to realize their goals for an egalitarian society requires careful examination of the underlying assumptions of given theoretical and political perspectives. As Karl Mannheim suggests, "A theory is wrong if in a given practical situation, it uses concepts and categories which, if taken seriously, would prevent man from adjusting himself at that historical stage" (1936:95).

Liberal feminism emphasizes that social change should establish individual civil rights so that no one is denied access to the existing social-economic system based on sex, race, or class. Liberal feminism also tells us that sexism is the result of past traditions and learned psychology; consequently, it suggests reform in sex role socialization practices and puts much of its faith in the raised consciousness of future generations. The political tactics of liberal feminism are primarily those of interest group politics in which liberal feminists attempt to increase the political influence and power of women. Their political strategy involves building coalitions that align the issues of feminism with other political causes, thereby increasing the strength of the women's movement. This strategy also has its costs, however, because political compromises mean that only the most moderate feminist demands can gain the support necessary for a solid coalition.

Socialist and radical feminism, on the other hand, locate the cause of sexism in the fundamental character of political and economic institutions. These perspectives pose a challenge to the very basis of our social existence by suggesting that revolutionary changes need to be made in the systems of capitalism and patriarchy.

Socialist feminists make the issue of social class central to their theoretical analysis and argue that classical Marxist theory has obscured the economic and social role of women. In their dialogue with Marx and Engels, socialist feminists go beyond seeing women as just another victim of capitalism by making women's liberation central to all struggles for revolutionary change. They suggest that the issue of class alone cannot account for the complex relationship between the family, reproduction, and productive relations in the society. Nonetheless, the class analysis that socialist feminists include does necessitate understanding the experience of women of all classes and races. Both socialist and radical feminists take a material perspective on social life—that is, they see things (including those with subjective value, such as ideas, personalities, and social values) as taking on objective value through the relations of human production and reproduction. In the materialist perspective, the actual work and activity of men and women constitutes the social world; therefore, to change that world requires a change in the actual labor and reproductive relations among human beings.

Because of their Marxist perspective, socialist feminists often align themselves with other oppressed groups in their programs for social change. Their politics remain Marxist in tone, but with the added issue of ending women's oppression in ways that traditional Marxists overlook. Their strategies, then, are analytical and practical—seeking to find the common grounds of oppression and trying to establish collective ways to solve the problems that communities and individuals experience.

Distinct from socialist feminism, radical feminism locates the development of sexism in the independent existence of patriarchy and the social relations that it generates. Thus, the radical feminist perspective asks us to look at the structure of consciousness—not just as it is reproduced through sex roles but specifically as it reflects the patriarchal organization of society. Radical feminism suggests that only the elimination of patriarchy will result in the liberation of women in society. Much of the strategy of radical feminist programs for change has been to redefine social relations by creating a woman-centered culture. Radical feminists emphasize the positive capacities of women by focusing on the creative dimensions of women's experience. Radical feminists celebrate the creative dimension of women's lives, specifically because women's culture and experience are seen as resisting patriarchal social relations.

The distinctions drawn here among these three feminist perspectives are in no way a perfect description of any. In theory and in practice, there are as many shared ideas and politics among feminists as there are differences. But discussion of the different feminist perspectives demonstrates that the questions that feminists raise have different answers and that they are as complex as the systems that they seek to change. Also, the substantive observations of empirical research on gender and women's lives that have been made by social research can be understood in the context of the larger theoretical issues that surround them. This research literature documents the experience of women in society, whereas the theoretical issues describe the possibilities for creating change in women's position. Thus, in sociology, at least, the thrust of the feminist movement has been to observe and interpret women's experience with the larger purpose of creating a nonsexist society.

If we take direction from all three feminist perspectives, it seems that a nonsexist society would be a society with no race, gender, and class distinctions in the production and distribution of economic resources. It would also be a society where power is not distributed by virtue of one's class, race, or gender and where individual civil rights are respected and maintained. And finally, such a society would have to respect and encourage traditional female values, but not restrict them to only one-half of the population, who, by virtue of their gender, are categorized as subordinate to the other. Although that society seems a long way off, feminist research and theory provide the guidelines for creating it.

BIBLIOGRAPHY

ACKER, J. "Women and Stratification: A Review of Recent Literature." *Contemporary Sociology,* **9**(1980):25–35.

ADLER, F. *Sisters in Crime.* New York: McGraw-Hill, 1975.

ALBIN, R. "Review Essay: Psychological Studies of Rape." *Signs,* **3**(Winter 1977):423–435.

ALDRICH, M. L. "Women in Science." *Signs,* **4**(Autumn 1978):126–135.

ALMQUIST, E. "Women in the Labor Force." *Signs,* **2**(Summer 1977):843–855.

——— *Minorities, Gender, and Work.* Lexington, Mass.: D. C. Heath, 1979.

ALMQUIST, E., and WEHRLE-EINHORN, J. L. "The Double Disadvantaged: Minority Women in the Labor Force." In A. Stromberg and S. Harkess (eds.), *Women Working.* Palo Alto, Calif.: Mayfield, 1978, 63–88.

AMIR, M. *Patterns of Forcible Rape.* Chicago: University of Chicago Press, 1971.

ANDERSEN, M. "Corporate Wives: Longing for Liberation or Satisfied with the Status Quo?" *Urban Life,* **10**(1981):311–327.

ANDERSEN, M., RENZETTI, C. "Rape Crisis Counseling and the Culture of Individualism." *Contemporary Crises,* **4**(1980):323–339.

ANDREWS, W. and ANDREWS, D. C. "Technology and the Housewife in Nineteenth Century America." *Women's Studies,* **2**(1974):309–328.

ARIES, P. *Centuries of Childhood.* New York: Vintage, 1962.

AXELSON, L. "The Working Wife: Differences in Perception Among Negro and White Males." *Journal of Marriage and the Family,* **32**(1970):457–464.

AXTELL, J. *The Indian Peoples of Eastern America: A Documentary History of the Sexes.* New York: Oxford University Press, 1981.

BABCO, E. *Salaries of Scientists, Engineers, and Technicians: A Summary of Salary Surveys.* Washington, D.C.: Scientific Manpower Commission, 1981.

BACA-ZINN, M. "Chicanas: Power and Control in the Domestic Sphere." *De Colores,* **2**(Fall 1976):19–31.

BAKER, S. H. "Women in Blue-Collar and Service Occupations." In A. Stromberg and S. Harkess (eds.), *Women Working.* Palo Alto, Calif.: Mayfield, 1978, 339–376.

BALDRIDGE, J. V. *Sociology.* New York: Wiley, 1980.

BANDURA, A., and WALTERS, R. H. *Social Learning and Personality Development.* New York: Holt, Rinehart & Winston, 1963.

BARKER-BENFIELD, G. J. *Horrors of the Half-Known Life.* New York: Harper & Row, 1976.

BARRETT, M. and ROBERTS, H. "Doctors and Their Patients." In C. Smart and B. Smart (eds.), *Women, Sexuality, and Social Control.* London: Routledge & Kegan Paul, 1978, 41–52.

BARRY, K. *Female Sexual Slavery.* Englewood Cliffs, N.J.: Prentice-Hall, 1979.

BART, P. "The Loneliness of the Long-Distance Mother." In J. Freeman (ed.), *Women: A Feminist Perspective.* Palo Alto, Calif.: Mayfield, 1979, 245–261.

BATES, B. "Doctor and Nurse: Changing Roles and Relations." *New England Journal of Medicine,* **283**(1970):129–134.

BAXANDALL, R. F. "Who Shall Care for Our Children? The History and Development of Day Care in the United States." In J. Freemen (ed.), *Women: A Feminist Perspective.* Palo Alto, Calif.: Mayfield, 1979, 134–149.

BECK, E. M., HORAN, P. M., and TOLBERT, C. M. II. "Stratification in a Dual Economy: A Sectoral Model of Earnings Determination." *American Sociological Review,* 43(1978):704–20.

BECKER, H. *The Outsiders.* New York: Free Press, 1963.

BELL, C. "Women and Work: An Economic Appraisal." In A. Stromberg and S. Harkess (eds.), *Women Working.* Palo Alto, Calif.: Mayfield, 1978, 10–28.

——— "Implementing Safety and Health Regulations for Women in the Workplace." *Feminist Studies,* **5**(Summer 1979):286–301.

BELL, I. P. "The Double Standard: Age." In J. Freeman (ed.), *Women: A Feminist Perspective.* Palo Alto, Calif.: Mayfield, 1979, 233–244.

BEM, S. "Psychology Looks at Sex Roles: Where Have All the Androgynous People Gone?" Paper presented at the UCLA Symposium on Women, May 1972.

BEM, S., and BEM, D. J. "Training the Woman to Know Her Place: The Power of a Non-conscious Ideology." In M. Garskof (ed.), *Roles Women Play: Readings Toward Women's Liberation.* Belmont, Calif.: Brooks/Cole, 1971.

BENET, M. K. *The Secretarial Ghetto.* New York: McGraw-Hill, 1972.

BENSTON, M. "The Political Economy of Women's Liberation." *Monthly Review,* **21**(1969):13–27.

BERGER, P. *Invitation to Sociology.* Garden City, N.Y.: Doubleday-Anchor, 1963.

BERGER, D., and LUCKMANN, T. *The Social Construction of Reality.* Garden City, N.Y.: Doubleday-Anchor, 1966.

BERNARD, J. "The Paradox of the Happy Marriage." In V. Gornick and B. Moran (eds.), *Woman in Sexist Society*. New York: New American Library, 1971, 145–162.

———— "Marriage: His and Hers." *Ms.,* 1(1972):46ff.

———— *The Future of Marriage*. New York: Bantam Books, 1973.

———— *Women, Wives, Mothers: Values and Options*. Chicago: Aldine, 1975.

———— *The Female World*. New York: Free Press, 1981.

BERQUIST, V. A. "Women's Participation in Labor Organizations." *Monthly Labor Review,* 97–10(1974):3–9.

BERRY, J. W. "Ecological and Cultural Factors in Spatial Perceptual Development." *Canadian Journal of Behavioral Science,* 3(1971):324–336.

BIENEN, L. "Rape II." *Women's Rights Law Reporter* 3(Spring/Summer 1977):90–137.

BILLINGSLEY, A. *Black Families in White America*. Englewood Cliffs, N.J.: Prentice-Hall, 1966.

BLAU, F. "Women in the Labor Force: An Overview." In J. Freeman (ed.), *Women: A Feminist Perspective*. Palo Alto, Calif.: Mayfield, 1979, 265–289.

BLAU, F., and JUSENIUS, C. L. "Economists' Approaches to Sex Segregation in the Labor Market: An Appraisal." *Signs,* 1(Spring 1976):181–199.

BLAU, P., and DUNCAN, O. D. *The American Occupational Structure*. New York: Wiley, 1967.

BLOOD, R. D., and WOLFE, D. M. *Husbands and Wives*. New York: Free Press, 1960.

BLUMBERG, R. L. *Stratification: Socioeconomic and Sex Equality*. Dubuque, Iowa: William C. Brown, 1978.

BOALS, K. "Political Science." *Signs,* 1(Autumn 1975):161–174.

BOCK, E. W., and WEBBER, I. "Suicide Among the Elderly: Isolating Widowhood and Mitigating Alternatives." *Journal of Marriage and the Family,* 34(1972):24–31.

BOGDAN, J. "Care or Cure? Childbirth Practices in Nineteenth-Century America." *Feminist Studies,* 4(1978):92–99.

Boston Women's Health Collective. *Our Bodies, Ourselves*. New York: Simon & Schuster, 1976.

BOWKER, L. H. "Gender Differences in Prisoner Subcultures." In L. Bowker (ed.), *Women and Crime in America*. New York: 1981, 409–419.

———— "Women As Victims: An Examination of the Results of L.E.A.A.'s National Crime Survey Program." In L. Bowker (ed.), *Women and Crime in America*. New York: Macmillan, 1981, 158–179.

BRAMSON, L. *The Political Context of Sociology*. Princeton, N.J.: Princeton University Press, 1961.

BRISCOE, A. M. "Hormones and Gender." In E. Tobach and B. Rosoff (eds.), *Genes and Gender*. New York: Gordian Press, 1978, 31–50.

BROVERMAN, I. K., BROVERMAN, D. M., CLARKSON, F., ROSENKRANTZ, P., and VOGEL, S. "Sex Role Stereotypes and Clinical Judgement of Mental Health." *Journal of Consulting and Clinical Psychology,* **34**(1970):1–7.

BROWN, C. "Mothers, Fathers, and Children: From Private to Public Patriarchy." In L. Sargent (ed.), *Women and Revolution.* New York: South End Press, 1981, 239–267.

BROWN, S. E. "Love Unites Them and Hunger Separates Them." In R. Reiter (ed.), *Toward an Anthropology of Women.* New York: Monthly Review Press, 1975, 322–332.

BROWNMILLER, S. *Against Our Will.* New York: Simon & Schuster, 1975.

BRUGH, A. E., and BEEDE, B. "American Librarianship." *Signs,* **1**(Summer 1976):943–956.

BRYAN, J. H. "Apprenticeships in Prostitution." *Social Problems,* **12**(Winter 1965):287–297.

BRYSON, J., and BRYSON, R. "Salary and Job Performance Differences in Dual-Career Couples." In Pepitone-Rockwell (ed.), *Dual-Career Couples.* Beverly Hills, Calif.: Sage, 1980, 241–259.

BUNCH, C. "Lesbians in Revolt." In N. Myron and C. Bunch (eds.), *Lesbianism and the Women's Movement.* Oakland, Calif.: Diana Press, 1975, 29–38.

BURKHARDT, J. E. *Crime and the Elderly—Their Perceptions and Their Reactions.* Rockville, Md.: National Criminal Justice Reference Service, Microfiche Program, 1977.

BUSBY, L. J. "Sex-role Research on the Mass Media." *Journal of Communication,* **25**(1975):107–131.

CAMERON, M. O. *The Booster and the Snitch.* Glencoe, Ill.: Free Press, 1964.

CANT, G. "Valiumania." *New York Times Magazine,* **6**(February 1, 1976), 34ff.

CARRINGTON, C. H. "Depression in Black Women: A Theoretical Appraisal." In L. F. Rodgers-Rose (ed.), *The Black Woman.* Beverly Hills, Calif.: Sage, 1980, 265–272.

CARROLL, B. *Liberating Women's History.* Urbana, Ill.: University of Illinois Press, 1976.

CATHEY-CALVERT, C. "Sexism on Sesame Street." Know, P.O. Box 86031, Pittsburgh, PA 15221.

CAULFIELD, M. D. "Imperialism, the Family, and Cultures of Resistance." *Socialist Revolution,* **20**(1974):67–85.

CHAMBLISS, W. and SEIDMAN, R. *Law, Order and Power.* Reading, Mass.: Addison-Wesley, 1971.

CHAVKIN, W. "Occupational Hazards to Reproduction: A Review Essay and Annotated Bibliography." *Feminist Studies,* **5**(Summer 1979):310–325.

CHERRIN, S. "The Dual Occupational Family and Children's Gender Expectations." Unpublished M.A. thesis, University of Delaware, Newark, 1981.

CHESLER, P. *Women and Madness.* Garden City, N.Y.: Doubleday, 1972.

CHESNEY-LIND, M. "Judicial Paternalism and the Female Status Offender." In L. Bowker (ed.), *Women and Crime in America.* New York: Macmillan, 1981, 354–366.

CHESTER, R., and STREATHER J., "Cruelty in English Divorce: Some Empirical Findings." *Journal of Marriage and the Family,* **34**(1972):706–710.

CHILD, I., POTTER, E., and LEVINE, E. "Children's Textbooks and Personality Development: An Exploration in the Social Psychology of Education." In M. L. Haimonitz and N. R. Haimonitz (eds.), *Human Development: Selected Readings.* New York: Crowell, 1960, 292–305.

CHISWICK, B., FACKLER, J., O'NEILL, J., and POLACHEK, S. "The Effect of Occupation on Race and Sex Differences in Hourly Earnings." *Public Use Data,* **3**(1975):2–9.

CHODOROW, N. *The Reproduction of Mothering.* Berkeley: University of California Press, 1978.

CICONE, M. V., and RUBLE, D. N. "Beliefs About Males." *The Journal of Social Issues,* **34**(Winter 1978):5–16.

CLARK, L., and LEWIS, D. *Rape: The Price of Coercive Sexuality.* Toronto: Women's Press, 1977.

CLAY, V. S. *Women: Menopause and Middle Age.* Know, Inc., Pittsburgh, 1977.

COATES, B., ANDERSON, E. P., and HARTUP W. W., "Interrelations in the Attachment Behavior of Human Infants." *Development Psychology,* **6**(1972):218–230.

COHEN, L., and STARK, R. "Discriminatory Labeling and the Five-Finger Discount—An Empirical Analysis of Differential Shoplifting Dispositions." *Journal of Research in Crime and Delinquency,* **11**(1974):25–39.

COLLINS, M. "Ageism in the Medical Profession." Paper presented at the Women's Caucus, Annual Meeting of the American Public Health Association, Miami, 1976.

COLLINS, R., and MAKOWSKY, M. *The Discovery of Society.* New York: Random House, 1978.

Combahee River Collective. "A Black Feminist Statement." In Z. R. Eisenstein (ed.), *Capitalist Patriarchy and the Case for Socialist Feminism.* New York: Monthly Review Press, 1979.

COMFORT, A. "Likelihood of Human Pheromones." *Nature,* **230**(1971):432–433.

COOPERSTOCK, R. "Sex Differences in the Use of Mood-Modifying Drugs: An Explanatory Model." *Journal of Health and Social Behavior,* **12**(1971):238–244.

COREA, G. *The Hidden Malpractice.* New York: William Morrow, 1977.

——— "The Caesarian Epidemic." *Mother Jones,* **5**(1980):28ff.

COTT, N. *The Bonds of Womanhood.* New Haven, Conn.: Yale University Press, 1977.

COWAN, R. S. "Two Washes in the Morning and a Bridge Party at Night: The American Housewife Between the Wars." *Women's Studies,* 3(1976):147–171.

COWIE, J., COWIE, V., and SLATER, E. *Delinquency in Girls.* London: Heinemann, 1968.

CROMWELL, V., and CROMWELL, R. "Perceived Dominance in Decision-Making and Conflict Resolution Among Black and Chicano Couples." *Journal of Marriage and the Family,* 40(1978):748–759.

CURRIE, E., DUNN, R., and FOGARTY, D. "The New Immiseration: Stagflation, Inequality and the Working Class." *Socialist Review,* 10(1980):7–31.

DALY, M. *Gyn/Ecology.* Boston: Beacon Press, 1978.

DANIELS, P., and WEINGARTEN, K. "A New Look at the Medical Risks in Late Childbearing." *Women and Health,* 4(Spring 1979):5–36.

DATESMAN, S., and SCARPITTI, F. (eds.), *Women, Crime, and Justice.* New York: Oxford University Press, 1980.

DAVIS, A., "Reflections on Black Women's Role in the Community of Slaves." *The Black Scholar,* 3(1971):2–15.

———— *Women, Race and Class.* New York: Random House, 1981.

DEAUX, K., WHITE, L., and FARRIS, E. "Skill Versus Luck: Field and Laboratory Studies of Male and Female Preferences." *Journal of Personality and Social Psychology,* 32(1975):629–636.

DEBEAUVOIR, S. *The Second Sex.* New York: Knopf, 1952.

DECKARD, B. *The Women's Movement.* New York: Harper & Row, 1975.

DEFLEUR, M. L., D'ANTONIO, W. V., and DEFLEUR, L. N. *Sociology: Human Society.* Glenview, Ill.: Scott, Foresman, 1977.

DELANEY, J., LUPTON, M. J., and TOTH, E. *The Curse: A Cultural History of Menstruation.* New York: New American Library, 1976.

DETOCQUEVILLE, A. *Democracy in America.* New York: Knopf, 1945.

DEUTSCHER, I. *What We Say/What We Do.* Glenview, Ill.: Scott, Foresman, 1973.

DICKEN, C. "Sex Roles, Smoking, and Smoking Cessation." *Journal of Health and Social Behavior,* 19(1978):324–334.

DILL, B. T. "The Dialectics of Black Womanhood." *Signs,* 4(Spring 1979):543–555.

———— "'The Means to Put My Children Through': Childrearing Goals and Strategies Among Black Female Domestic Servants." In L. F. Rodgers Rose (ed.), *The Black Woman.* Beverly Hills, Calif.: Sage, 1980, 107–123.

DINNERSTEIN, D. *The Mermaid and the Minotaur.* New York: Harper-Colophon, 1976.

DOBASH, R. E., and DOBASH, R. "Love, Honor, and Obey: Institutional Ideologies and the Struggle for Battered Women." *Contemporary Crises,* 1(1977):403–415.

———— *Violence Against Wives.* New York: Free Press, 1979.

DOERINGER, P. B., and PIORE, M. J. *Internal Labor Markets and Manpower Analysis.* Lexington, Mass.: D. C. Heath, 1971.

DOMINICK, J., and RAUCH, G. "The Image of Women in Network TV Commercials." *Journal of Broadcasting,* **16**(1972):259–265.

DONEGAN, J. *Women and Men Midwives: Medicine, Morality and Misogyny in Early America.* Westport, Conn.: Greenwood Press, 1978.

DONOVAN, P. "Parental Notification: Is It Settled?" *Family Planning Perspectives,* **13**(1981):243–246.

DONZELOT, J. *The Policing of Families.* New York: Pantheon, 1979.

DUBÉ, W. R. "Datagram: Medical Student Enrollment." *Journal of Medical Education,* **52**(1977):164–166.

DUBOIS, E. C. *Feminism and Suffrage.* Ithaca, N.Y.: Cornell University Press, 1978.

DUBOIS, E. C., BUHLE, M. J., KAPLAN, T., LERNER, G., and SMITH-ROSENBERG, C. "Politics and Culture in Women's History: A Symposium." *Feminist Studies,* **6**(Summer 1980):26–64.

DURKHEIM, E. *The Division of Labor in Society.* Glencoe, Ill.: Free Press, 1947.

DYE, N. S. "Creating a Feminist Alliance: Sisterhood and Class Conflict in the New York Women's Trade Union League, 1903–1914." *Feminist Studies,* **2**(1975):24–38.

———— "History of Childbirth in America." *Signs,* **6**(1980):97–108.

EAGLY, A., and CARLI, L. "Sex of Researchers and Sex-Typed Communications as Determinants of Sex Differences in Influenceability: A Meta-analysis of Social Influence Studies." *Psychological Bulletin,* **90**(1981):1–20.

EHRENREICH, B. "Combat in the Media Zone." *Seven Days,* **2**(1978):13–14.

EHRENREICH, B., and ENGLISH, D. *Complaints and Disorders.* Old Westbury, Conn.: Feminist Press, 1973.

———— *For Her Own Good.* Garden City, N.Y.: Anchor-Doubleday, 1978.

———— *Witches, Midwives, and Nurses: A History of Women Healers.* Old Westbury, Conn.: Feminist Press, 1973.

EHRENREICH, B. and STALLARD, K. "The Nouveau Poor." *Ms.* **11**(1982):217–224.

EICHELBERGER, B. *"Voices on Black Feminism."* Quest, **3**(Spring 1977):16–27.

EISENSTEIN, Z. (ed.). *Socialist Feminism and the Case for Capitalist Patriarchy.* New York: Monthly Review Press, 1979.

———— *The Radical Future of Liberal Feminism.* New York: Longmans, 1981.

ELSHSTAIN, J. B. "Moral Woman and Immoral Man." *Politics and Society,* **4**(1974):453–473.

ENGELS, F. *The Origin of the Family, Private Property, and the State.* Ed. with an introduction by E. Leacock. New York: International 1972.

ENGLISH, D. "The Politics of Porn." *Mother Jones,* **5**(1980):20ff.

EPSTEIN, C. *Woman's Place: Options and Limits in Professional Careers.* Berkeley: University of California Press, 1970.

———— "Positive Effects of the Multiple Negative: Explaining the Success of Black Professional Women." *American Journal of Sociology,* **78**(1973):912–935.

ERNEST, J. "Mathematics and Sex." *American Mathematical Monthly,* **83**(1976):595–614.

EVANS, S. *Personal Politics: The Roots of Women's Liberation in the Civil Rights Movement and the New Left.* New York: Knopf, 1979.

FAULS, L. B., and SMITH, W. D. "Sex-Role Learning of Five-Year Olds." *Journal of Genetic Psychology,* **89**(1956):105–117.

FEATHERMAN, D. L., and HAUSER, R. M. "Sexual Inequalities and Socioeconomic Achievement in the U.S., 1962–1973." *American Sociological Review,* **41**(1976):462–483.

FENNEMA, E., and SHERMAN, J. A. "Sex-related Differences in Mathematics Achievement, Spatial Visualization, and Affective Factors." *American Educational Research Journal,* **14**(Winter 1977):51–71.

FIDELL, L. S. "Put Her Down on Drugs: Prescribed Drug Usage in Women." Paper presented at the Western Psychological Association Meeting, Anaheim, Calif., 1973.

FIGES, E. *Patriarchal Attitudes.* New York: Stein and Day, 1970.

FIRESTONE, S. *The Dialectic of Sex: The Case for Feminist Revolution.* New York: William Morrow, 1970.

FLACKS, R., and TURKEL, G. "Radical Sociology: The Emergence of Neo-Marxian Perspectives in U.S. Sociology." *Annual Review of Sociology,* **4**(1978):193–238.

FLAX, J. "Do Feminists Need Marxism?" *Quest,* **3**(Summer 1976):46–58.

FLEMING, W. *Arts and Ideas.* New York: Holt, Rinehart & Winston, 1974.

FLEXNER, E. *Mary Wollstonecraft: A Biography.* New York: Coward, McCann, and Geoghegan, 1972.

FLING, S., and MANOSEVITZ, M. "Sex Typing in Nursery School Children's Play Interests." *Developmental Psychology,* **7**(1972): 146–152.

FLORA, C. B. "The Passive Female: Her Comparative Image by Class and Culture in Women's Magazine Fiction." *Journal of Marriage and the Family,* **33**(1971):435–444.

———— "Changes in Women's Status in Women's Magazine Fiction: Differences by Social Class." *Social Problems,* **26**(1979):558–569.

FOUCAULT, M. *Madness and Civilization: A History of Insanity in the Age of Reason.* London: Social Science, 1967.

FOX, L. H., FENNEMA, E., and SHERMAN, J. (eds.). *Women and Mathematics: Research Perspectives for Change.* Washington, D.C.: National Institute of Education, November 1977.

FRANKFURTER, F. "Hours of Labor and Realism in Constitutional Law." *Harvard Law Review,* **29**(1916):353–373.

FRANKLIN, A. "Criminology in the Workplace: A Comparison of Male and Female Offenders." In F. Adler and R. J. Simon (eds.), *The Criminology of Deviant Women.* Boston: Houghton-Mifflin, 1979, 167–179.

FRAZIER, E. F. *The Negro Family in the United States.* New York: Citadel Press, 1948.

FREEMAN, J. "The Origins of the Women's Liberation Movement." *American Journal of Sociology,* **78**(1973):792–811.

FRIEDAN, B. *The Feminine Mystique.* New York: Norton, 1963.

FRIEDL, E. *Women and Men.* New York: Holt, Rinehart & Winston, 1975.

FRIEDMAN, M., and ROSENMAN, R. H. *Type A Behavior and Your Heart.* New York: Knopf, 1974.

FRIEZE, I., PARSONS, J., JOHNSON, P., RUBLE, D. N., and ZELLMAN G. (eds.). *Women and Sex Roles.* New York: Norton, 1978.

FRIEZE, I., and RAMSEY, S. J. "Nonverbal Maintenance of Traditional Sex Roles." *Journal of Social Issues,* **32**(1976):133–141.

FRUEH, T., and McGHEE, P. E. "Traditional Sex Role Development and Amount of Time Spent Watching Television." *Development Psychology,* **11**(1975):109.

FULLERTON, H. N. "The 1995 Labor Force: A First Look." *Monthly Labor Review,* **103**(1980):11–21.

GARRETT, G. R., and BAHR, H. M. "The Family Backgrounds of Skid Row Women." *Signs,* **2**(Winter 1976):369–381.

GENOVESE, E. *Roll, Jordan, Roll.* New York: Pantheon, 1974.

GERBNER, G. "The Dynamics of Cultural Resistance." In G. Tuchman, A. K. Daniels, and J. Benét (eds.), *Hearth and Home: Images of Women in the Media.* New York: Oxford University Press, 1978, 46–50.

GERSTEL, N. R. "Commuter Marriage: Constraints on Spouses." Paper presented at the Annual Meeting of the American Sociological Association, San Francisco, 1978.

GHENT, W. *Our Benevolent Feudalism.* New York: Macmillan, 1902.

GIALLOMBARDO, R. *Society of Women: A Study of a Women's Prison.* New York: Wiley, 1966.

GIDDENS, A. *Capitalism and Modern Social Theory: An Analysis of the Writings of Marx, Durkheim, and Max Weber.* Cambridge: Cambridge University Press, 1971.

GILLIGAN, C. "Woman's Place in Man's Life Cycle." *Harvard Educational Review,* **49**(1979):431–446.

GLAZER, N. "America's Race Paradox." In P. Rose (ed.), *Nation of Nations.* New York: Random House, 1971, 165–180.

GLICK, P. C., and NORTON, A. J. "Marrying, Divorcing, and Living Together in the U.S. Today." *Population Bulletin,* **32**(1977):2–38.

GLICK, P. C., and SPANIER, G. B. "Married and Unmarried Cohabitation in the U.S." *Journal of Marriage and the Family,* **42**(1980):19–30.

GLICK, R. M., and NETO, V. V. *National Study of Women's Correctional Programs.* Washington, D.C.: U.S. Government Printing Office, 1977.

GODFREY, M. A. "Nurses' Salaries Around the Country." *Nursing '74* **4**(1974):54–55.

GOLDBERG, S., and LEWIS, M. "Play Behavior in the Year-old Infant: Early Sex Differences." *Child Development,* **40**(1969):21–31.

GOLDBERG, S. *The Inevitability of Patriarchy.* New York: William Morrow, 1974.

GOLDSMITH, S. *Prison Health: Travesty of Justice.* New York: Prodist, 1975.

GOLDSTEIN, L. *The Constitutional Rights of Women.* New York: Longmans, 1979.

—— "Mill, Marx, and Women's Liberation." *Journal of the History of Philosophy,* **18**(1980):319–334.

GOODE, W. J. "Community Within a Community: The Professions." *American Sociological Review,* **22**(1957):195–200.

GOODMAN, N., and MARX, G. T. *Society Today.* New York: CRM/Random House, 1982.

GORDON, L. *Woman's Body/Woman's Right.* New York: Penguin Books, 1977.

GORDON, M. T., RIGER, S., LEBAILLY, R. K., and HEATH, L. "Crime, Women, and the Quality of Urban Life." *Signs.* **5**:3 supplement(Spring 1980):5144–5160.

GORDON, M. *Assimilation in American Life: The Role of Race, Religion, and National Origin.* New York: Oxford University Press, 1964.

GORNICK, V. "Woman As Outsider." In V. Gornick and B. Moran (eds.), *Woman in Sexist Society.* New York: Basic Books, 1971, 126–144.

GOUGH, K. "The Origin of the Family." In R. Reiter (ed.), *Toward an Anthropology of Women.* New York: Monthly Review Press, 1975.

GOULD, C. C., and WARTOSKY, M. W. *Women and Philosophy.* New York: Putnam, 1976.

GOVE, W., and TUDOR, J. "Adult Sex Roles and Mental Illness." *American Journal of Sociology,* **78**(1973):812–835.

GRANBERG, D. G., and GRANBERG, B. W. "Abortion Attitudes, 1965–1980: Trends and Determinants." *Family Planning Perspectives,* **12**(1980):250–261.

GRANEY, M. J. "An Exploration of the Social Factors Influencing the Sex Differential in Mortality." Paper presented at the Thirtieth Annual Meeting of the Gerontological Society, San Francisco, 1977.

GREENBURG, B. "Children's Reactions to TV Blacks." *Journalism Quarterly,* **49**(1972):5–14.

GRIFFIN, S. "Rape: The All-American Crime." *Ramparts,* **10**(1971):26–35.

GRIMM, J. W. "Women in Female-Dominated Professions." In A. Stromberg and S. Harkess (eds.), *Women Working*. Palo Alto, Calif.: Mayfield, 1978, 293–315.

GRIMM, J. W., and STERN, R. N. "Sex Roles and Internal Labor Market Structures: the 'Female' Semi-professions." *Social Problems,* **21**(1974):690–705.

GROSS, E. "Plus ça Change . . . ? The Sexual Structure of Occupations Over Time." *Social Problems,* **16**(Fall 1968):198–208.

GROSS, H. "Couples Who Live Apart: Two Types." *Journal of Marriage and the Family,* **42**(1980):567–576.

GROSS, L., and JEFFRIES-FOX, S. N. "What Do You Want To Be When You Grow Up, Little Girl?" In G. Tuchman, A. K. Daniels, and J. Benét (eds.), *Hearth and Home: Images of Women in the Mass Media.* New York: Oxford University Press, 1978, 240–265.

GROSSMAN, A. S. "Women in Domestic Work: Yesterday and Today." *Monthly Labor Review,* **103**(1980):17–21.

Alan Gutmacher Institute. "Sterilization Rates Rose Most for Women 15–24 Before 1976 and 1978." *Family Planning Perspectives,* **13**(1981):236–237.

GUTMAN, H. *The Black Family in Slavery and Freedom.* New York: Vintage, 1976.

HACKER, H. "Women as a Minority Group." *Social Forces* **30**(1951):60–69.

HACKER, S. L. "Sex Stratification, Technology, and Organizational Change: A Longitudinal Case Study of AT&T." *Social Problems,* **26**(1979):539–569.

———— "Farming Out the Home: Women and Agribusiness." In J. R. Kaplan (ed.), *A Woman's Conflict: The Special Relationship Between Women and Food.* Englewood Cliffs, N.J.: Prentice-Hall, 1980, 233–263.

HAFT, M. "Women in Prison: Discriminatory Practices and Some Legal Solutions." In S. Datesman and F. Scarpitti (eds.), *Women, Crime and Society.* New York: Oxford University Press, 1980, 320–338.

HAMIL, C. "Incest." Paper presented at the Research on Women Series, University of Delaware, Newark, September 1981.

HARDING, S. "Is the Equality of Opportunity Principle Democratic?" *Philosophical Forum* **10**(1978–79):206–223.

———— "Gender Politics of Infancy." *Quest,* **5**(1981):53–70.

———— "What Is the Real Material Base of Patriarchy and Capital?" In L. Sargent (ed.), *Women and Revolution.* Boston: South End Press, 1981, 135–163.

———— "Surpassing the Thought of Men: Towards a Feminist Epistemology." In S. Harding and M. B. Hintikka (eds.), *Discovering Reality: Feminist Perspectives on Epistemology, Metaphysics, Methodology, and the Philosophy of Science.* Dordrecht: Rieder, 1983.

HARLAND, M. *House and Home: The Complete Housewives' Guide.* Philadelphia: Clawson, 1889.

HARRISON, J. "Men's Roles and Men's Lives." *Signs,* 4(Winter 1978):324–336.

HARTLEY, R. E. "Sex Role Pressures and the Socialization of the Male Child." *Psychological Reports,* 5(1959):457–468.

HARTMANN, H. "Capitalism, Patriarchy, and Job Segregation by Sex." *Signs,* 1:3, Part 2(Spring 1976):137–169.

———— "The Family As the Locus of Gender, Class, and Political Struggle: The Example of Housework." *Signs,* 6(Spring 1981):366–394.

HAWKES G., and TAYLOR, M. "Power Structure in Mexican and Mexican-American Farm Labor Families." *Journal of Marriage and the Family,* 37(1975):807–811.

HAWKINS, R. A., and OAKEY, R. E. "Estimation of Oestrone Sulphate, Oestradiol-17B and Oestrone in Peripheral Plasma: Concentrations During the Menstrual Cycle and in Men." *Journal of Endocrinology,* 60(1974):3–17.

HEMMONS, W. M. "The Women's Liberation Movement: Understanding Black Women's Attitudes." In L. F. Rodgers-Rose (ed.), *The Black Woman.* Beverly Hills, Calif., Sage, 1980, 285–299.

HENDERSHOT, G. E. "Pregnant Workers in the U.S." *Advancedata.* National Center for Health Statistics, U. S. Department of Health, Education, and Welfare, No. 11, September 15, 1977.

HENLEY, N., and FREEMAN, J. "The Sexual Politics of Interpersonal Behavior." In J. Freeman (ed.), *Women: A Feminist Perspective.* Palo Alto, Calif.: Mayfield, 1979, 474–486.

HERMAN, J., and HIRSCHMAN, L. "Father-Daughter Incest." *Signs,* 2(Summer 1977):735–756.

HERSKOVITS, M. *The Myth of the Negro Past.* Boston: Beacon Press, 1958.

HESS, B. B. "Sex Roles, Life Course, and Friendship." Paper presented at Miami University, Ohio, 1977.

HESS, B. B., and MARKSON, E. W. *Aging and Old Age.* New York: Macmillan, 1980.

HIGHAM, J. *Strangers in the Land.* New York: Atheneum, 1965.

HILL, A. C. "Protection of Women Workers and the Courts: A Legal Case History." *Feminist Studies,* 5(Summer 1979):247-273.

HILTON, T. L., and BERGLUND, G. W. "Sex Differences in Mathematical Achievement: A Longitudinal Study." *Journal of Educational Research,* 67(1974):231–237.

HINDELANG, M. "Race and Involvement in Crime." *American Sociological Review,* 43(1978):93–109.

HOCHSCHILD, A. R. "A Review of Sex Role Research." *American Journal of Sociology,* 78(1973):1011–1029.

———— "The Sociology of Feeling and Emotion." In M. Millman and R. M. Kanter (eds.), *Another Voice.* Garden City, N.Y.: Doubleday-Anchor, 1975, 280–307.

HOFFMAN-BUSTAMANTE, D. "The Nature of Female Delinquency." *Issues in Criminology,* **8**(Fall 1973):117–36.

HOFSTADTER, R. *Social Darwinism in American Thought.* New York: Braziller, 1959.

HOLE, J., and LEVINE, E. (eds.). *Rebirth of Feminism.* New York: Quadrangle Books, 1971.

HORAN, P. M. "Is Status Attainment Research Atheoretical?" *American Sociological Review,* **4**(1978):534–540.

HORNER, M. "Toward an Understanding of Achievement-Related Conflicts in Women." *Journal of Social Issues,* **28**(1972):157–175.

HORNIG, L. S. "Untenured and Tenuous: The Status of Women Faculty." *Annals of the American Academy of Political and Social Science,* **448**(1980):115–125.

HOSKEN, F. P. *The Hosken Report: Genital and Sexual Mutilation of Females.* Lexington, Mass.: Women's International Network News, 1979.

HOWE, L. K. *Pink Collar Workers.* New York: Putnam, 1977.

HOYENGA, K. B., and HOYENGA K. *The Question of Sex Differences: Psychological, Cultural, and Biological Issues.* Boston, Little, Brown, 1979.

HUBBARD, R. "Have Only Men Evolved?" In R. Hubbard, M. S. Henifin, and B. Fried (eds.), *Women Look at Biology Looking at Women.* Cambridge, Mass.: Schenckman, 1979, 7–36.

HUGHES, H. S. *Consciousness and Society.* New York: Knopf, 1958.

HUNT, V. R. "A Brief History of Women Workers and Hazards in the Workplace." *Feminist Studies,* **5**(Summer 1979):274–285.

HURST, M., and ZAMBRANA, R. E. "The Health Careers of Urban Women: A Study in East Harlem." *Signs,* **5**:3 Supplement(Spring 1980):S112–S126.

ILLICH, I. *Disabling Professions.* Salem, N.H.: Boyars, 1977.

INFANTE, P. "Genetic Risks of Vinyl Chloride." *Lancet,* **3**(1975):734–735.

JACKLIN, C. N., MacCOBY, E. E., and DICK, A. E. "Barrier Behavior and Toy Preference: Sex Differences (and Their Absence) in the Year-Old Child." *Child Development,* **44**(1973):196–200.

JACOBS, R. *Life After Youth: Female, Forty, What Next?* Boston: Beacon Press, 1979.

JACOBSON, D. "The Women of North and Central India: Goddesses and Wives." In C. Matthiasson (ed.), *Many Sisters.* New York: Free Press, 1974, 99–175.

JAGET, C. (ed.). *Prostitutes: Our Life.* Bristol: Falling Wall Press, 1980.

JAGGAR, A., and STRUHL, P. R. *Feminist Frameworks: Alternative Theoretical Accounts of the Relations Between Women and Men.* New York: McGraw-Hill, 1978.

JAQUETTE, J. S. "Political Science." *Signs,* **2**(Autumn 1976):147–164.

JENSEN, G. J., and EVE, R. "Sex Differences in Delinquency." *Criminology,* **13**(1976):427–448.

Joffe, C. "Sex Role Socialization and the Nursery School: As the Twig Is Bent." *Journal of Marriage and the Family,* **33**(1971):467–475.

Jones, A. *Women Who Kill.* New York: Holt, Rinehart & Winston, 1980.

Journard, S. M. "Some Lethal Aspects of the Male Role." In J. Pleck and J. Sawyer (eds.), *Men and Masculinity.* Englewood Cliffs, N.J.: Spectrum Books, 1974, 21–29.

Jusenius, C. L. "Review Essay: Economics." *Signs,* **2**(Autumn 1976):177–189.

Kagan, J., and Lewis, M. "Studies of Attention in the Human Infant." *Merrill-Palmer Quarterly,* **11**(1965):95–137.

Kalleberg, A. L., and Griffin L. "Class, Occupation, and Inequality in Job Rewards." *American Journal of Sociology,* **85**(1980):731–768.

Kanter, R. M. *Men and Women of the Corporation.* New York: Basic Books, 1977.

Katzman, D. "Domestic Service: Women's Work." In A. Stromberg and S. Harkess (eds.), *Women Working.* Palo Alto, Calif.: Mayfield, 1978, 377–391.

Kehrer, B. H. "Factors Affecting the Incomes of Men and Women Physicians: An Exploratory Analysis." *Journal of Human Resources,* **11**(Fall 1976):526–545.

Keller, E. F. "Gender and Science." *Psychoanalysis and Contemporary Thought,* **1**(1978):409–433.

Kelly, J. "The Double Vision of Feminist Theory: A Postscript to the 'Women and Power' Conference." *Feminist Studies,* **5**(Spring 1979):216–227.

Kelly-Gadol, J. "The Social Relations of the Sexes: Methodological Implications of Women's History." *Signs,* **1**(Summer 1976):809–824.

Kessler-Harris, A. "Women, Work, and the Social Order." In B. A. Carroll (ed.), *Liberating Women's History.* Urbana, Ill. University of Illinois Press, 1976, 330–343.

Kilbourne, J. "Killing Us Softly." Film. Cambridge, Mass.: Cambridge Documentary Films, 1979.

Klass, A. *There's Gold in Them Thar Pills.* London: Penguin Books, 1975.

Klein, D. "The Etiology of Female Crime: A Review of the Literature." In S. K. Datesman and F. R. Scarpitti (eds.), *Women, Crime, and Justice.* New York: Oxford University Press, 1980, 70–105.

Kleinbaum, A. R. "Women in the Age of Light." In R. Bridenthal and C. Koonz (eds.). *Becoming Visible: Women in European History.* Boston: Houghton-Mifflin, 1977, 217–235.

Kluckhohn, C. *Culture and Behavior.* New York: Free Press, 1962.

Kohlberg, L. "A Cognitive-Developmental Analysis of Children's Sex Role Concepts and Attitudes." In E. Maccoby (ed.), *The Development of Sex Differences.* Stanford, Calif.: Stanford University Press, 1966, 82–166.

Kolodny, A. "Literary Criticism." *Signs,* **2**(Winter 1976):404–421.

KOMAROVSKY, M. *Women in the Modern World.* Boston: Little, Brown, 1953.

KONOPKA, G. *The Adolescent Girl in Conflict.* Englewood Cliffs, N.J.: Prentice-Hall, 1966.

KRADITOR, E. *Up from the Pedestal: Selected Writings in the History of American Feminism.* Chicago: Quadrangle Books, 1968.

LAMBERT, H. H. "Biology and Equality: A Perspective on Sex Differences." *Signs,* **4**(Autumn 1978):97–117.

LADNER, J. *Tomorrow's Tomorrow.* Garden City, N.Y.: Doubleday-Anchor, 1971.

LAMPHERE, L. "Anthropology." *Signs,* **2**(Spring 1977):612-627.

LASCH, C. *Haven in a Heartless World: The Family Besieged.* New York: Basic Books, 1977.

LEACOCK, E. "Women's Status in Egalitarian Society." *Contemporary Anthropology,* **19**(1978):247–275.

LEGHORN, L., and PARKER, K. *Woman's Worth: Sexual Economics and the World of Women.* Boston: Routledge & Kegan Paul, 1981.

LEMERT, E. *Human Deviance, Social Problems, and Social Control.* Englewood Cliffs, N.J.: Prentice-Hall, 1972.

LEMON, J. "Dominant or Dominated? Women on Prime-Time Television." In G. Tuchman, A. K. Daniels, and J. Benét (eds.), *Hearth and Home: Images of Women in the Mass Media.* New York: Oxford University Press, 1978, 51–68.

LERNER, G. "Placing Women in History: A 1975 Perspective." In B. Carroll (ed.), *Liberating Women's History.* Urbana, Ill.: University of Illinois Press, 1976, 357–367.

LEVER, J. "Sex Differences in the Complexity of Children's Play and Games." *American Sociological Review,* **43**(1978):471–83.

LEVINE, A., and CRUMRINE, J. "Women and the Fear of Success: A Problem in Replication." *American Journal of Sociology,* **80**(1975):964–974.

LEVINGER, G. "Sources of Marital Dissatisfaction Among Applicants for Divorce." *American Journal of Orthopsychiatry,* **36**(1966):803–807.

LEVITAN, S. A., and BELOUS, R. "Working Wives and Mothers: What Happens to Family Life?" *Monthly Labor Review,* **104**(1981):26–30.

LEWIS, D. K. "A Response to Inequality: Black Women, Racism, and Sexism." *Signs,* **3**(Winter 1977):339–361.

——— "Black Women Offenders and Criminal Justice." In M. Q. Warren (ed.), *Comparing Female and Male Offenders.* Beverly Hills, Calif.: Sage, 1981, 89–105.

LEWIS, R. A. "Emotional Intimacy Among Men." *The Journal of Social Issues,* **34**(Winter 1978):108–121.

LEWIS, S. G. *Sunday's Women: A Report on Lesbian Life Today.* Boston: Beacon Press, 1979.

LIEBERMAN, S. "The Politics of Population Control." *Majority Report,* **14**(1975).

LIEBERT, R. M., NEALE, J. N., and DAVIDSON, E. S. *The Early Window: Effects of Television on Children and Youth.* New York: Pergamon, 1973.

Life, "Abortion: Women Speak Out; 4(1981):45–50.

LIPSET, S. M. (eds.). *Harriet Martineau: Society in America.* New York: Doubleday, 1962.

LITOFF, J. B. *American Midwives, 1860 to the Present.* Westport, Conn.: Greenwood Press, 1978.

LIVSON, F. B. "Cultural Faces of Eve." Paper presented at the Annual Meeting of the American Psychological Association, San Francisco, 1977.

LLOYD, C. (ed.), *Sex, Discrimination and the Division of Labor.* New York: Columbia University Press, 1975.

LOCKSLEY, A. "On the Effects of Wives' Employment on Marital Adjustment and Companionship." *Journal of Marriage and the Family,* **42**(1980):337–346.

LOMBROSO, N. *The Female Offender.* New York: Appleton, 1920.

LOPATA, H. Z. *Occupation: Housewife.* New York: Oxford University Press, 1971.

———— *Widowhood in an American City.* Cambridge, Mass.: Schenckman, 1973.

LOPATA, H. Z., and THORNE, B. "On the Term 'Sex Roles'." *Signs,* **3**(Spring 1978):718–721.

LOPATE, C. *Women in Medicine.* Baltimore: Johns Hopkins University Press, 1968.

LORBER, J. "Women and Medical Sociology: Invisible Professionals and Ubiquitous Patients." In M. Millman and R. M. Kanter (eds.), *Another Voice.* Garden City, N.Y.: Doubleday-Anchor, 1975, 75–105.

LORBER, J., COSER, R. L., ROSSI, A. S., and CHODOROW, N. "On 'The Reproduction of Mothering': A Methodological Debate." *Signs,* **6**(1981):482–514.

LOZOFF, M. "Changing Life Style and Role Perceptions of Men and Women Students." Paper presented at Radcliffe College, Cambridge, Mass., 1972.

LUKER, K. *Taking Chances.* Berkeley: University of California Press, 1975.

LUNDBERG, F., and FARNHAM, M. *Modern Woman: The Lost Sex.* New York: Harper, 1947.

LYNN, N. B., VADEN, A. G., and VADEN, R.E. "The Challenge of Men in a Woman's World." *Public Personnel Management,* **4**(1975):4–17.

MACCOBY, E. E. *The Development of Sex Differences.* Stanford, Calif.: Stanford University Press, 1966.

MACCOBY, E. E., and JACKLIN, C. N. *The Psychology of Sex Differences.* Stanford, Calif.: Stanford University Press, 1974.

MACKLIN, E. D. "Nonmarital Heterosexual Cohabitation." *Marriage and Family Review,* **1**(1978):1–12.

MALBIN-GLAZER, N. "Housework." *Signs,* **1**(Summer 1976):905–922.

MANDELBAUM, D. R. "Women in Medicine." *Signs,* **4**(Autumn 1978):136–145.

MANNHEIM, K. *Ideology and Utopia.* New York: Harcourt, Brace, and World, 1936.

MANT, A., and DARROCH, D. "Media Images and Medical Images." *Social Science and Medicine,* **9**(1975):613–618.

MARKSON, E. W., and HESS, B. B. "Older Women in the City." *Signs,* **5**(Spring 1980):S127–S141.

MARTIN, D. *Battered Wives.* San Francisco: Glide, 1976.

MARTINEAU, H. *Society in America.* Paris: Baudry's European Library, 1837.

———— *How to Observe Manners and Morals.* London: C. Knight, 1838.

MARX, K. and ENGELS, F. *The Communist Manifesto.* New York: Pathfinder Press, 1970.

MASTERS, W. H., and JOHNSON, V. E. *Human Sexual Response.* Boston: Little, Brown, 1966.

MATTHIASSON, C. *Many Sisters.* New York: Free Press, 1974.

MATZA, D. *Becoming Deviant.* Englewood Cliffs, N.J.: Prentice-Hall, 1969.

MAXWELL, B. D. *Employment of Minority Ph.D.'s: Changes Over Time.* Washington, D.C.: National Academy Press, 1981.

MCBRIDE, T. *The Domestic Revolution.* London: Croom Helms, 1976.

MCCLINTOCK, M. "Menstrual Synchrony and Suppression." *Nature,* **229**(1971):244–245.

MCCONNELL-GINET, S. "Intonation in a Man's World." *Signs,* **3**(Spring 1978):541–559.

MCCRAY, C. A. "The Black Woman and Family Roles." In L. F. Rodgers-Rose (ed.), *The Black Woman.* Beverly Hills, Calif.: Sage, 1980, 67–78.

MCINTOSH, M. "Who Needs Prostitutes?" In C. Smart and B. Smart (eds.), *Women, Sexuality, and Social Control.* London: Routledge & Kegan Paul, 1978, 53–64.

MCKINLEY, J. "The Drug Pusher in the Grey Flannel Suit." *Playboy,* **25**(1978):165ff.

MCNULTY, D. J. "Differences in Pay Between Men and Women Workers." *Monthly Labor Review,* **90**(1967):40–43.

MEAD, M. *Sex and Temperament in Three Primitive Societies.* New York: Dell, 1949.

———— *Male and Female.* Harmondsworth: Penguin Books, 1962.

Mead Johnson and Company. "Names for Boys and Girls." Evansville, Ind., 1978.

MEHRABIAN, A. "Verbal and Nonverbal Interaction of Strangers in a Waiting Situation." *Journal of Experimental Research in Personality,* **5**(1971):127–38.

MEIER, A., and RUDWICK, E. *From Plantation to Ghetto.* New York: Hill & Wang, 1966.

MEISSNER, M. et al. "No Exit for Wives: Sexual Division of Labour and the Cumulation of Household Demands." *Canadian Review of Sociology and Anthropology,* **12**(1975):424–439.

MENDELSOHN, E. "The Social Construction of Scientific Knowledge." In E. Mendelsohn, P. Weingart, and R. Whitley (eds.), *The Social Production of Scientific Knowledge.* Dordrecht: Riedel, 1977, 3–26.

MERRITT, S., and GROSS, H. "Women's Page/Life Style Editors: Does Sex Make a Difference?" *Journalism Quarterly,* **55**(1978):508–519.

MEYER, W. J., and THOMPSON, G. G. "Sex Differences in the Distribution of Teacher Approval and Disapproval Among Sixth-grade Children." *Journal of Educational Psychology,* **47**(1956):385–397.

MILL, J. S. *The Subjection of Women.* New York: Source Book Press, 1970.

MILLER, D. *American Indian Socialization to Urban Life.* San Francisco: Institute for Scientific Analysis, 1975.

MILLER, M. "Geriatric Suicide: The Arizona Study." *The Gerontologist,* **18**(1978):488–495.

MILLMAN, M. "She Did It All for Love." In M. Millman and R. M. Kanter (eds.), *Another Voice.* Garden City, N.Y.: Doubleday-Anchor, 1975, 251–279.

MILLMAN, M., and KANTER, R. M. (eds.). *Another Voice.* Garden City, N.Y.: Doubleday-Anchor, 1975.

MILLS, C. W. *The Sociological Imagination.* New York: Oxford University Press, 1959.

MILTON, G. A. "Five Studies of the Relation Between Sex Role Identification and Achievement in Problem Solving." Department of Industrial Administration, Department of Psychology, Yale University, December 1958.

MINCER, J., and POLACHECK, S. "Family Investments in Human Capital: Earnings of Women." *Journal of Political Economy,* **82**(1974):76–111.

MIRANDÉ, A. "Machismo: A Reinterpretation of Male Dominance in the Chicano Family." *The Family Coordinator,* **28**(1979):473–479.

MISCHEL, W. "Sex-typing and Socialization." In P. H. Mussen (ed.), *Carmichael's Manual of Child Psychology,* 3rd ed., Vol. 2. New York: Wiley, 1970.

MITCHELL, J. *Woman's Estate.* New York: Pantheon Books, 1971.

——— *Psychoanalysis and Feminism.* New York: Pantheon Books, 1974.

MODLESKI, T. "The Disappearing Act: A Study of Harlequin Romances." *Signs,* **5**(Spring 1980):435–448.

MOHR, J. *Abortion in America.* New York: Oxford University Press, 1978.

MONEY, J., and EHRHARDT, A. A. *Man, Woman, Boy and Girl: The Differentiation and Dimorphism of Gender Identity from Conception to Maturity.* Baltimore: Johns Hopkins University Press, 1972.

MONGEAU, B., SMITH, H. L., and MANEY, A. C. "The 'Granny' Midwife: Changing Roles and Functions of a Folk Practitioner." *American Journal of Sociology,* **66**(1961):497–505.

MORAGA, C., and ANZALDÚA, G. *This Bridge Called My Back: Radical Writings by Women of Color.* Watertown, Mass.: Persephone Press, 1981.

MORGAN, J. N. "A Potpourri of New Data Gathered from Interviews with

Husbands and Wives." In G. J. Duncan and J. N. Morgan (eds.), *Five Thousand American Families: Patterns of Economic Progress.* Ann Arbor, Mich.: University of Michigan Press, 1978, 367–401.

MORIN, S. F., and GARFINKLE, E. M. "Male Homophobia." *The Journal of Social Issues,* **34**(Winter 1978):29–47.

MORONEY, R. "Note from the Editor." *Urban and Social Change Review,* **11**(1978):2.

MORTON, W., and UNGS, T. "Cancer Mortality in the Major Cottage Industry." *Women and Health,* **4**(Winter 1979):305–354.

MOULDS, E. F. "Chivalry and Paternalism: Disparities of Treatment in the Criminal Justice System." In S. Datesman and F. Scarpitti (eds.), *Women, Crime, and Justice.* New York: Oxford University Press, 1980, 277–299.

MOYNIHAN, D. P. *The Negro Family: The Case for National Action.* Washington, D.C.: U.S. Government Printing Office, 1965.

MURILLO, N. "The Mexican American Family." In N. Wagner and M. Hang (eds.), *Chicanos: Social and Psychological Perspectives.* St. Louis: Mosby, 1971, 97–108.

MYERS, L. W. "Black Women and Self Esteem." In M. Millman and R. M. Kanter (eds.), *Another Voice.* Garden City, N.Y.: Doubleday-Anchor, 1975, 240–250.

NADELSON, C., and NADELSON, T. "Dual-Career Marriages: Benefits and Costs." In F. Pepitone-Rockwell (ed.), *Dual-Career Couples.* Beverly Hills, Calif.: Sage, 1980, 91–109.

NATHANSON, C. "Illness and the Feminine Role: A Theoretical Review." *Social Science and Medicine,* **9**(1975):57–62.

——— "Social Roles and Health Status Among Women: The Significance of Employment," *Social Science and Medicine,* **14A**(1980):463–471.

National Research Council Committee on the Education and Employment of Women in Science and Engineering. *Career Outcomes in a Matched Sample of Men and Women Ph.Ds.* Washington, D.C.: National Academy Press, 1981.

NEUGARTEN, B. L. (ed.). *Middle Age and Aging.* Chicago: University of Chicago Press, 1975.

NISBET, R. A. *The Social Bond: An Introduction to the Study of Society.* New York: Knopf, 1970.

NOCHLIN, L. "Why Are There No Great Women Artists?" In V. Gornick and B. Moran (eds.), *Women in Sexist Society.* New York: Basic Books, 1971, 480–510.

NOVICK, L., DELLA PENNA, R., SCHWERTZ, M., REMMLINGERT, E., and LOEWENSTEIN, R. "Health Status of the New York City Prison Population." *Medical Care,* **205**(1977):205–216.

OAKLEY, A. *The Sociology of Housework.* London: Mertin Robertson, 1974.

——— *Woman's Work: The Housewife, Past and Present.* New York: Pantheon Books, 1975.

——— "A Case of Maternity: Paradigms of Women as Maternity Cases." *Signs,* **4**(Summer 1979):607–631.

OLESEN, V. L., and KATSURANIS, F. "Urban Nomads: Women in Temporary Clerical Services." In A. Stromberg and S. Harkess (eds.), *Women Working.* Palo Alto, Calif.: Mayfield, 1978, 316–338.

OPPENHEIMER, V. K. "The Sex-Labeling of Jobs." *Industrial Relations,* **220**(1968):219–234.

ORTMEYER, L. E. "Female's Natural Advantage? Or, the Unhealthy Environment of Males?" *Women and Health,* **4**(Summer 1979):121–133.

ORWANT, J. E., and CANTOR, M. "How Sex Stereotyping Affects Perceptions of News Preferences." *Journalism Quarterly,* **54**(Spring 1977):99ff.

PARKER, D., PARKER, E., WOLZ, M., and HARFORD, T. "Sex Differences and Alcohol Consumption: A Research Note." *Journal of Health and Social Behavior,* **21**(1980):43–48.

PARKER, S. "Women in Foraging Societies." Paper presented at the Research on Women Series, University of Delaware, 1978.

PARLEE, M. B. "Psychology: Review Essay." *Signs,* **1**(Autumn 1975):119–138.

PATTERSON, M. and ENGELBERG, L. "Women in Male-dominated Professions." In A. Stromberg and S. Harkess (eds.), *Women Working.* Palo Alto, Calif.: Mayfield, 1978, 266–292.

PAYER, M. "Is Traditional Scholarship Value Free? Toward a Critical Theory." Paper presented at the Scholar and the Feminist IV, Barnard College, New York, 1977.

PECIS, K. "Val-i-um/val-e-em/n. Latin. To Be Well and Strong." Paper presented at the Research on Women Series, University of Delaware, 1979.

PEDERSON, D. M., SHINEDLING, M. M., and JOHNSON, D. L. "Effects of Sex of Examiner and Subject on Children's Quantitative Test Performance." *Journal of Personality and Social Psychology,* **10**(1968):251–254.

PEKKANEN, N. "Controlling Librium and Valium: The Tranquilizer War." *New Republic,* **173**(1975):17–19.

PETCHESKY, R. "Women, Reproductive Hazards and the Politics of Protection." *Feminist Studies,* **5**(Summer 1979):233–246.

——— "Reproductive Freedom: Beyond a Woman's Right to Choose." *Signs,* **5**(Summer 1980):661–685.

PHILLIPS, E. B. "The Artists of Everyday Life: Journalists, Their Craft, and Their Consciousness." Ph.D. dissertation, Syracuse University, 1975.

PIAGET, J. *The Moral Judgement of the Child.* New York: Free Press, 1965.

PIERCE, C. "Philosophy: Review Essay." *Signs,* **1**(Winter 1975):487–503.

PIFER, A. "Women and Working: Toward a New Society." *Urban and Social Change Review,* **11**(1978):3–11.

PLECK, J. H. "Men's Family Work: Three Perspectives and Some New Data."

Unpublished paper, Wellesley College Center for Research on Women, Wellesley, Mass., 1979.

PLECK, J. H., and BRANNON, R. (eds.). "Male Roles and the Male Experience." *Journal of Social Issues,* **34**(1978):1-195.

PLECK, J. H., and SAWYER, J. (eds.) *Men and Masculinity.* Englewood Cliffs, N.J.: Prentice-Hall, 1974.

POLACHEK, S. W. "Discontinuous Labor Force Participation and Its Effect on Women's Market Earnings." In C. Lloyd (ed.), *Sex, Discrimination, and the Division of Labor.* New York: Columbia University Press, 1975, 90–122.

POLLAK, O. *The Criminology of Women.* Philadelphia: University of Pennsylvania Press, 1950.

POLOMA, M. M., and GARLAND, T. N. "The Married Professional Woman: A Study in the Tolerance of Domestication." *Journal of Marriage and the Family,* **33**(1971):531–540.

POSTON, C. (ed.). *A Vindication on the Rights of Woman.* New York: Norton, 1975, 2–10.

POTTIEGER, A. Personal correspondence, March 1981.

POTTKER, J., and FISHEL, A. *Sex Bias in the Schools.* Cranbury, N.J.: Associated University Presses, Inc., 1977.

POWERS, E., and BULTENA, G. "Sex Differences in Intimate Friendships of Old Age." *Journal of Marriage and the Family,* **38**(1976):739–747.

POWERS, M. "Menstruation and Reproduction: An Oglala Case." *Signs,* **6**(Autumn 1980):54–65.

PRATHER, J., and FIDELL, L. S. "Sex Differences in the Content and Style of Medical Advertisements." *Social Science and Medicine,* **9**(1975):23–26.

President's Commission on the Status of Women. *American Women.* Washington, D.C.: U.S. Government Printing Office, 1963.

PROPPER, A. "Importation and Deprivation Perspectives on Homosexuality in Correctional Institutions: An Empirical Test of Their Relative Efficacy." Ph.D. dissertation, University of Michigan, 1976.

PRUS, R. C., and VASSILAKOPOULOS, S. "Desk Clerks and Hookers: Hustling in a Shady Hotel." *Urban Life,* **8**(1979):52–72.

QUINNEY, R. *The Social Reality of Crime.* Boston: Little, Brown, 1970.

RAMEY, J. "Experimental Family Forms—The Family of the Future." *Marriage and Family Review,* **1**(1978):1–9.

RANDALL, S. C., and ROSE, V. M. "Barriers to Becoming a 'Successful' Rape Victim." In L. Bowker (ed.), *Women and Crime in America.* New York: Macmillan, 1981, 336–353.

RAPP, R., ROSS, E., and BRIDENTHAL, R. "Examining Family History." *Feminist Studies,* **5**(Spring 1979):174–200.

REDHORSE, J. G., LEWIS, R., FEIT, M., and DECKER, J. "American Indian Elders: Needs and Aspirations in Institutional and Home Health Care." Manuscript, Arizona State University, 1979.

REES, A., and SCHULTZ, G. P. *Workers and Wages in an Urban Labor Market.* Chicago: Univeristy of Chicago Press, 1970.

REID, I. S. "Science, Politics, and Race." *Signs,* 1(Winter 1975):397–422.

REITER, R. R. (ed.). *Toward an Anthropology of Women.* New York: Monthly Review Press, 1975.

REITZ, R. *Menopause: A Positive Approach.* Radnor, Pa.: Chilton, 1977.

RESNIK, J., and SHAW, N. "Prisoners of Their Sex: Health Problems of Incarcerated Women." *Prison Law Monitor.* 3(1981):55ff.

RHEINGOLD, H. L., and COOK, K. V. "The Contents of Boys' and Girls' Rooms as an Index of Parent's Behavior." *Child Development,* 46(1975):459–463.

RICH, A. *Of Woman Born: Motherhood As Experience and Institution.* New York: Norton, 1976.

———— "Disloyal to Civilization: Feminism, Racism, and Gynephobia." *Chrysalis,* No. 7(Summer-Fall 1979):9–28.

———— "Compulsory Heterosexuality and Lesbian Existence." *Signs,* 5(Summer 1980):631–660.

RICHARDSON, L. W. *The Dynamics of Sex and Gender.* Boston: Houghton, Mifflin, 1981.

ROBERTSON, I. *Sociology,* New York: Worth, 1977.

RODGERS-ROSE, L. F. (ed.). *The Black Woman.* Beverly Hills, Calif.: Sage, 1980.

ROOKS, E., and KING, R. "A Study of the Marriage Role Expectations of Black Adolescents." *Adolescence,* 8(1973):317–324.

Roper Organization, Inc. *The 1980 Virginia Slims American Women's Opinion Poll.* Storrs, Conn.: The Roper Center, 1980.

RORVIK, D. M. *Brave New Baby: Promise and Peril of the Biological Revolution.* Garden City, N.Y.: Doubleday, 1971.

ROSALDO, M. Z. "Use and Abuse of Anthropology: Reflections on Feminism and Cross-cultural Understanding." *Signs,* 5(Spring 1980):389–417.

ROSALDO, M. Z., and LAMPHERE, L. (eds.). *Women, Culture, and Society.* Stanford, Calif.: Stanford University Press, 1974.

ROSENBLUM, K. E. "Female Deviance and the Female Sex Role: A Preliminary Investigation." *British Journal of Sociology,* 26(1975):169–185.

ROSENFELD, S. "Sex Differences in Depression: Do Women Always Have Higher Rates?" *Journal of Health and Social Behavior,* 21(1980):33–42.

ROSOW, I. "And Then We Were Old." *Trans-Action/Society,* 2(1965):20–26.

ROSS, D. M., and ROSS, S. A. "Resistance by Preschool Boys to Sex-Inappropriate Behavior." *Journal of Educational Psychology,* 63(1972):342–346.

ROSS, H. L., and SAWHILL, V. *Time of Transition: the Growth of Families Headed by Women.* Washington, D.C.: Urban Institute, 1975.

ROSSI, A. "A Biosocial Perspective on Parenting." *Daedulus,* 106(Spring 1977):1–31.

Rossi, A. (ed.). *Essays on Sex Equality*. Chicago: University of Chicago Press, 1970.
———— *The Feminist Papers*. New York: Columbia University Press, 1973.
Rossi, A. S., and Rossi, P. E. "Body Time and Social Time: Mood Patterns by Menstrual Cycle Phase and Day of the Week: *Social Science Research,* **6**(1977):273–308.
Rothschild, M. A. "White Women Volunteers in the Freedom Summers." *Feminist Studies,* **5**(Fall 1979):466–495.
Rubin, G. "The Traffic in Women." In R. Reiter (ed.), *Toward an Anthropology of Women*. New York: Monthly Review Press, 1975, 157–211.
Rubin, J. Z., Provenzano, F. J., and Luria, Z. "The Eye of the Beholder: Parents' Views on Sex of Newborns." *American Journal of Orthopsychiatry,* **44**(1974):512–519.
Ruzek, S. *The Women's Health Movement: Feminist Alternatives to Medical Control*. New York: Praeger, 1978.
Ryan, W. *Blaming the Victim*. New York: Random House, 1971.
Sacks, K. "Engels Revisited: Women, the Organization of Production, and Private Property." In R. Reiter (ed.), *Toward an Anthropology of Women*. New York: Monthly Review Press, 1975, 211–234.
Sahlins, M. *The Use and Abuse of Biology: An Anthropological Critique of Sociobiology*. London: Tavistock, 1977.
Sanday, P. "Toward a Theory of the Status of Women." *American Anthropology,* **75**(1973):1682–1700.
Sandmaier, M. *The Invisible Alcoholic: Women and Alcohol Abuse in America*. New York: McGraw-Hill, 1980.
Sario, T., Jacklin, C. N., and Tittle, C. K. "Sex Role Stereotyping in the Public Schools." *Harvard Educational Review,* **43**(1973):386–404.
Schlozman, K. L. "Women and Unemployment." In J. Freeman (ed.), *Women: A Feminist Perspective*. Palo Alto, Calif.: Mayfield, 1979, 290–312.
Scholten, C. M. "On the Importance of the Obstetric Art: Changing Customs of Childbirth in America." *The William and Mary Quarterly,* **34**(1977):426–445.
Schwendinger, H., and Schwendinger, J. R. *Sociologists of the Chair: A Radical Analysis of the Formative Years of North American Sociology*. New York: Basic Books, 1974.
Scully, D., and Bart, P. "A Funny Thing Happened on the Way to the Orifice: Women in Gynecology Textbooks." *American Journal of Sociology,* **78**(1973):1045–50.
Sears, R. R., Maccoby, E., and Levin, H. *Patterns of Child Rearing*. Evanston, Ill.: Row, Peterson, 1959.
Senna, J., and Siegel, L. *Introduction to Criminal Justice*. St. Paul, Minn.: West, 1981.
Serbin, L. A., and O'Leary, K. D. "How Nursery Schools Teach Girls to Shut Up." *Psychology Today,* **9**(1975):56ff.

SERBIN, L. A., O'LEARY, K. D., KENT, R., and TOLNICK, I. J. "A Comparison of Teacher Response to the Preacademic and Problem Behavior of Boys and Girls." *Child Development,* **44**(1973):776–804.

SHAKUR, A., and CHESIMARD, J. "Women in Prison: How We Are." *The Black Scholar,* **9**(1978):8–15.

SHERMAN, J. "Problems of Sex Differences in Space Perception and Aspects of Intellectual Functioning." *Psychological Review,* **74**(1967):290–299.

SHERMAN, J., and BECK, E. T., (eds.). *The Prism of Sex: Essays in the Sociology of Knowledge.* Madison, Wisc.: University of Wisconsin Press, 1979.

SIMMEL, G. "The Stranger." In K. Wolff (ed.), *The Sociology of Georg Simmel.* New York: Free Press, 1950, 402–408.

SIMON, R. *Women and Crime.* Lexington, Mass.: Lexington Books, 1975.

———— "American Women and Crime." In L. Bowker (ed.), *Women and Crime in America.* New York: Macmillan, 1981, 18–39.

SIMONS, M. "Racism and Feminism: A Schism in the Sisterhood." *Feminist Studies,* **5**(Summer 1979):384–401.

SKOLNICK, A. *The Intimate Environment.* Boston: Little, Brown, 1978.

SLOCUM, S. "Woman the Gatherer: Male Bias in Anthropology." In R. Reiter (ed.), *Toward an Anthropology of Women.* New York: Monthly Review Press, 1975, 36–50.

SMART, C. *Women, Crime and Criminology: A Feminist Critique.* London: Routledge & Kegan Paul, 1977.

SMEDLEY, A. "Women of Uder: Survival in a Harsh Land." In C. Matthiasson (ed.), *Many Sisters.* New York: Free Press, 1974, 205–228.

SMITH, B. "Notes for Yet Another Paper on Black Feminism, Or Will the Real Enemy Please Stand Up." *Conditions: Five* **2**(Autumn 1979):123–127.

SMITH, D. E. "Women's Perspective As a Radical Critique of Sociology." *Sociological Inquiry,* **44**(1974):7–13.

———— "An Analysis of Ideological Structures and How Women Are Excluded: Considerations for Academic Women." *Canadian Review of Sociology and Anthropology,* **12**(1975):353–369.

———— "Women, the Family, and Corporate Capitalism." *Berkeley Journal of Sociology,* **20**(1975):55–90.

———— "A Sociology for Women." In J. A. Sherman and E. T. Beck (eds.), *The Prism of Sex.* Madison, Wisc.: University of Wisconsin Press, 1979, 135–187.

———— "A Method for a Sociology for Women." Paper presented at the Meeting of the American Sociological Association, Toronto, 1981.

SMITH, L. S. "Sexist Assumptions and Female Delinquency." In C. Smart and B. Smart (eds.), *Women, Sexuality, and Social Control.* London: Routledge & Kegan Paul, 1978, 74–86.

SMITH-ROSENBERG, C. "The Female World of Love and Ritual: Relations Between Women in Nineteenth Century America." *Signs,* **1**(Fall 1975):1–29.

SMUTS, R. W. *Women and Work in America.* New York: Columbia University Press, 1959.

SORENSON, P. *Adolescent Sexuality in Contemporary America.* New York: World, 1973.

SPENCE, J. T., HELMREICH, R., and STAPP, J. "Ratings of Self and Peers on Sex Role Attributes and Their Relation to Self-Esteem and Conceptions of Masculinity and Femininity." *Journal of Personality and Social Psychology,* **32**(1975):29–39.

SPRAFKIN, J., and LIEBERT, R. "Sex-Typing and Children's Television Preferences." In G. Tuchman, A. K. Daniels, and J. Benét (eds.), *Hearth and Home: Images of Women in the Mass Media.* New York: Oxford University Press, 1978, 228–239.

STACK, C. *All Our Kin: Strategies for Survival in a Black Community.* New York: Harper Colophon, 1974.

STAFFORD, R., BACKMAN, E., and DIBONA, P. "The Division of Labor Among Cohabiting and Married Couples." *Journal of Marriage and the Family,* **39**(1977):43–57.

STAINES, G. L., PLECK, J., SHEPARD, L. J., and O'CONNOR, P. "Wives Employment Status and Marital Adjustment: Yet Another Look." In J. Bryson and R. Bryson (eds.), *Dual-Career Couples.* New York: Human Sciences Press, 1978, 90–120.

STAPLES, R. *The Black Family.* Belmont, Calif.: Wadsworth, 1971.

———— "Masculinity and Race: The Dual Dilemma of Black Men." *The Journal of Social Issues,* **34**(Winter 1978):169–183.

STAPLES, R., and MIRANDÉ, A. "Racial and Cultural Variations Among American Families." *Journal of Marriage and the Family,* **42**(1980):887–903.

STEFFENSMEIER, D. "Crime and the Contemporary Woman: An Analysis of Changing Levels of Female Property Crime, 1960–1975." In L. Bowker (ed.), *Women and Crime in America.* New York: Macmillan, 1981a, 39–59.

———— "Patterns of Female Property Crime, 1960–1978: A Postscript." In L. Bowker (ed.), *Women and Crime in America.* New York: Macmillan, 1981, 59–65.

STEIN, D. K. "Women to Burn: Suttee As a Normative Institution." *Signs,* **4**(Winter 1978):253–268.

STELLMAN, J. M. *Women's Work, Women's Health: Myths and Realities.* New York: Pantheon Books, 1977.

STEVENSON, M. H. "Relative Wages and Sex Segregation by Occupation." In C. Lloyd (ed.), *Sex, Discrimination, and the Division of Labor.* New York: Columbia University Press, 1975, 175–200.

———— "Wage Differentials Between Men and Women: Economic Theories." In A. Stromberg and S. Harkess (eds.), *Women Working.* Palo Alto, Calif.: Mayfield, 1978, 89–107.

STIMPSON, C. "Thy Neighbor's Wife, Thy Neighbor's Servants: Women's Liberation and Black Civil Rights." In V. Gornick and B. Moran (eds.), *Woman in Sexist Society.* New York: Basic Books, 1971, 622–657.

STOLL, C. S. *Female and Male.* Dubuque, Iowa: William C. Brown, 1978.

STRAUSS, A. (ed.). *George Herbert Mead: On Social Psychology.* Chicago: University of Chicago Press, 1977.

STRAUSS, M. A., GELLES, R., and STEINMETZ, S. *Behind Closed Doors.* Garden City, N.Y.: Doubleday-Anchor, 1980.

STROMBERG, A. H., and HARKESS, S. (eds.). *Women Working.* Palo Alto, Calif.: Mayfield, 1978.

STROUSE, J. "To Be Minor and Female: The Legal Rights of Women Under 21." *Ms.,* **1**(1972):70ff.

SUTER, L., and MILLER, H. "Income Differences Between Men and Career Women." *American Journal of Sociology,* **78**(1973):962–974.

SWERDLOW, A., BRIDENTHAL, R., KELLY, J. and VINE, P. *Household and Kin.* Old Westbury, N.Y.: Feminist Press, 1980.

TANNER, D. M. *The Lesbian Couple.* Lexington, Mass.: Lexington Books, 1978.

TANNER, N., and ZIHLMAN, A. "Women in Evolution, Part I: Innovation and Selection in Human Origins." *Signs,* **1**:3, Part 1,(Spring 1976):585–608.

TARR-WHELAN, L. "Women Workers and Organized Labor." *Social Policy,* **9**(1978):73–77.

TAVRIS, C., and OFFIR, C. *The Longest War.* New York: Harcourt Brace Jovanovich, 1977.

TAYLOR, V. "Review Essays of Four Books on Lesbianism." *Journal of Marriage and the Family,* **42**(1980):224–228.

TEA, N. T., CASTANIER, M., ROGER, M., and SCHOLLER, R. "Simultaneous Radio-immunoassay of Plasma Progesterone and 17-Hydroxyprogesterone in Men and Women Throughout the Menstrual Cycle and in Early Pregnancy." *Journal of Steroid Biochemistry,* **6**(1975):1509–1516.

THOMAS, W. I. *The Unadjusted Girl.* Boston: Little, Brown 1923.

THOMPSON, E. P. "Time, Work-Discipline and Industrial Capitalism." *Past and Present,* **38**(1967):56–90.

TILLY, L. A., and SCOTT, J. W. *Women, Work, and Family.* New York: Holt, Rinehart & Winston, 1978.

TOLSON, A. *The Limits of Masculinity.* New York: Harper Colophon, 1977.

TOBIAS, S. *Overcoming Math Anxiety.* New York: Norton, 1978.

TREIMAN, D. J., and TERRELL, K. "Sex and the Process of Status Attainment: A Comparison of Working Men and Women." *American Sociological Review,* **40**(1975):174–200.

TUCHMAN, G. "Women's Depiction by the Mass Media." *Signs,* **4**(Spring 1979):528–542.

TUCHMAN, G., DANIELS, A. K., and BENÉT, J. *Hearth and Home: Images of Women in the Mass Media.* New York: Oxford University Press, 1978.

TUCKER, R. (ed.). *The Marx-Engels Reader.* New York: Norton, 1972.

TURKEL, G. "Feminist Theory, the Family, and the State." Paper presented at the Research on Women Series, University of Delaware, 1981.

U.S. Department of Commerce: *Statistical Abstracts of the United States.* Washington, D.C.: U.S. Government Printing Office, 1980.

———— *Population Profile of the U.S.: 1980.* Washington, D.C.: U.S. Government Printing Office.

U.S. Department of Commerce, Bureau of the Census. *Current Population Reports, Household and Family Characteristics: March 1980.* Washington, D.C.: U.S. Government Printing Office, September 1981.

———— *Current Population Reports, Marital Status and Living Arrangements: March 1980.* Washington, D.C.: U.S. Government Printing Office, October 1981.

———— *Current Population Reports, Money Income and Poverty Status of Families and Persons in the United States, 1980.* Washington, D.C.: U.S. Government Printing Office, August 1981.

———— *Current Population Reports, Money Income of Families and Persons in the United States, 1978.* Washington, D.C.: U.S. Government Printing Office, June 1980.

U.S. Department of Labor. *Employment and Earnings.* Washington, D.C.: U.S. Government Printing Office, 1980.

———— *Employment and Earnings.* Washington, D.C.: U.S. Government Printing Office, 1981.

———— *Employment and Earnings.* Washington, D.C.: U.S. Government Printing Office, 1982.

———— *Employment in Perspective: Minority Workers.* Washington, D.C.: U.S. Government Printing Office, May 1980.

U.S. Department of Labor, Women's Bureau. *Minority Women Workers: A Statistical Overview.* Washington, D.C.: U.S. Government Printing Office, 1977.

———— *Employment Goals of the World Plan of Action: Developments and Issues in the U.S.* Washington, D.C.: U.S. Government Printing Office, July 1980.

U.S. Environmental Protection Agency. *First Annual Report to Congress by the Task Force on Environmental Cancer and Heart and Lung Disease.* Washington, D.C.: Printing Management Office, Environmental Protection Agency, August 1978.

U.S. Senate Committee on Labor and Human Resources. *Adolescent Family Life.* 97th Congress, 1st Session, Report No. 97-161, 1981.

VAN DEN DAELE, W. "The Social Construction of Science: Institutionalization and Definition of Positive Science in the Latter Half of the Seventeenth Century." In E. Mendelsohn, P. Weingart, and R. Whitley (eds.), *The Social Production of Scientific Knowledge.* Dordrecht: Riedel, 1977, 27–54.

VANEK, J. A. "Housewives As Workers." In A. H. Stromberg and S. Harkess (eds.), *Women Working*. Palo Alto, Calif.: Mayfield, 1978, 392–414.

VETTER, B. M. "Women Scientists and Engineers: Trends in Participation." *Science,* **214**(1981):1313–1321.

VIDA, G. *Our Right to Love: A Lesbian Resource Book*. Englewood Cliffs, N.J.: Prentice-Hall, 1978.

WALDRON, I., and JOHNSTON, S. "Why Do Women Live Longer Than Men?" *Journal of Human Stress,* **2**, Part II(1976):19–30.

WALKER, K. E. "Time-Use Patterns for Household Work Related to Homemakers' Employment." Paper presented at the National Agricultural Outlook Conference, Washington, D.C., 1970.

WALLEN, J. "Physician Stereotypes About Female Health and Illness." *Women and Health,* **4**(Summer 1979):135–146.

WALLERSTEIN, I. *The Modern World System*. New York: Academic Press, 1976.

WALSH, M. R. *Doctors Wanted: No Women Need Apply*. New Haven, Conn.: Yale University Press, 1977.

WARDLE, R. M. *Mary Wollstonecraft, A Critical Biography*. Lawrence, Kan.: University of Kansas Press, 1951.

WEBER, M. *The Theory of Social and Economic Organization*. New York: Free Press, 1947.

WEBSTER, P. "Matriarchy: A Vision of Power." In R. Reiter (ed.), *Toward an Anthropology of Women*. New York: Monthly Review Press, 1975, 141–157.

WEINSTEIN, F., and PLATT, G. M. *The Wish to be Free; Society, Psyche, and Value Change*. Berkeley, Calif.: University of California Press, 1969.

WEISSMAN, M. M., and PAYKEL, E. S. *The Depressed Woman: A Study of Social Relationships*. Chicago: University of Chicago Press, 1974.

WEISSTEIN, N. "Psychology Constructs the Female, or the Fantasy Life of the Male Psychologist." In M. H. Garskof (ed.), *Roles Women Play: Readings Toward Women's Liberation*. Belmont, Calif.: Brooks/Cole, 1971, 68–83.

WEITZMAN, L. *Sex Role Socialization: A Focus on Women*. Palo Alto, Calif.: Mayfield, 1979.

WEITZMAN, L., EIFLER, D., HOKADA, E., and ROSS, C. "Sex Role Socialization in Picture Books for Preschool Children." *American Journal of Sociology,* **77**(1972):1125–1150.

WELCH, S., and BOOTH, A. "Employment and Health Among Married Women." *Sex Roles,* **3**(1977):385–397.

WERMUTH, L. "Book Review: *The Policing of Families* by Jacques Donzelot." *Contemporary Sociology,* **10**(1981):414–415.

WERTHEIMER, B., and NELSON, A. H. *Trade Union Women*. New York: Praeger, 1975.

WERTZ, R. W., and WERTZ, D. C. *Lying In: A History of Childbirth in America*. New York: Free Press, 1977.

WESTKOTT, M. "Feminist Criticism of the Social Sciences." *Harvard Educational Review,* **49**(1979):422–430.

WESTOFF, C., DEBURG, J., GOLDMAN, N., and FORREST, J. D. "Abortions Preventable by Contraceptive Practice." *Family Planning Perspectives,* **13**(1981):218–223.

WILSON, D. "Sexual Codes and Conduct." In C. Smart and B. Smart (eds.), *Women, Sexuality, and Social Control.* London: Routledge & Kegan Paul, 1978, 65–73.

WILSON, G. L. "The Self/Group Actualization of Black Women." In L. F. Rodgers-Rose (ed.), *The Black Woman.* Beverly Hills, Calif.: Sage, 1980, 301–314.

WILSON, W. J. *The Declining Significance of Race.* Chicago: University of Chicago Press, 1978.

WISEMAN, J., and ARON, M. *Field Projects for Sociology Students.* Cambridge, Mass.: Schenkman, 1970.

WOLCOTT, I. "Women and Psychoactive Drug Use." *Women and Health,* **4**(Summer 1979):199–202.

WOLF, W. C., and FLIGSTEIN, N. D. "Sex and Authority in the Workplace: The Causes of Sexual Inequality." *American Sociological Review,* **44**(1979):235–252.

WOLFGANG, M. *Patterns in Criminal Homicide.* New York: Wiley, 1958.

WOLFGANG, M., and FERACUTI, F. *The Subculture of Violence: Toward an Integrated Theory in Criminology.* London: Tavistock, 1967.

WOLFSON, A. "Caution: Health Care May Be Hazardous to Your Health." *Up from Under,* **1**(1970):7–10.

WOLLSTONECRAFT, M. *A Vindication of the Rights of Woman.* Ed. by C. Poston. New York: Norton, 1975.

Women on Words and Images. "Dick and Jane As Victims: Sex Stereotyping in Children's Readers." Princeton, New Jersey, 1972.

WONG, A. K. "Women in China: Past and Present." In C. Matthiasson (ed.), *Many Sisters.* New York: Free Press, 1974, 220–260.

WOOD, P. L. "The Victim in a Forcible Rape Case: A Feminist View." In L. Bowker (ed.), *Women and Crime in America.* New York, Macmillan, 1981, 190–211.

WRIGHT, M. J. "Reproductive Hazards and 'Protective' Discrimination." *Feminist Studies,* **5**(Summer 1979):302–309.

WRONG, D. "The Oversocialized Conception of Man in Modern Sociology." *American Sociological Review,* **26**(1961):183–193.

YAMAUCHI, J. S. "Asian American Communications: The Women's Self-Concept and Cultural Accomodations." Paper presented at the conference on the Minority Woman in America, San Francisco, 1979.

YBARRA, I. "Conjugal Race Relationships in the Chicano Family." Doctoral dissertation, University of California, Berkeley, 1977.

ZABIN, L. S., and CLARK, S., Jr. "Why They Delay: A Study of Teenage Family Planning Clinic Patients," *Family Planning Perspectives,* **13**(1981):205–217.

ZABIN, L. S., KANTNER, J. F., and ZELNIK, M. "The Risk of Adolescent Pregnancy in the First Months of Intercourse." *Family Planning Perspectives,* **11**(1979):215–226.

ZARETSKY, E. *Capitalism, the Famly, and Personal Life.* New York: Harper & Row, 1976.

ZEITLIN, I. *Ideology and the Development of Sociological Theory.* Englewood Cliffs, N.J.: Prentice-Hall, 1968.

ZELNICK, M., and KANTNER, J. F. "Contraceptive Patterns and Premarital Pregnancy Among Women Aged 15–19 in 1976." *Family Planning Perspectives,* **10**(1978):135–143.

——— "Sexual Activity, Contraceptive Use, and Pregnancy Among Metropolitan Area Teenagers, 1971–1979." *Family Planning Perspectives,* **12**(1980):230–237.

ZELNIK, M., KIM, Y. J., and KANTNER, J. F. "Probabilities of Intercourse and Conception Among U.S. Teenage Women, 1971–1976." *Family Planning Perspectives,* **11**(1979):177–183.

ZIHLMAN, A. L. "Women and Evolution, Part II: Subsistence and Social Orgnization Among Early Hominids." *Signs,* **4**(Autumn 1978):4–20.

INDEX

A

Abortion, 156, 157–60, 192
  in prison, 202
Academic life, *see* Universities
Accidental death rates, women's vs. men's, 41
Adams, Abigail, 241
Adolescent Family Life law, 155–56
Advertisements
  women in, 198, 207–208
  see also Media
Aged people, 41–42
  poverty of, 97, 121
  sex role socialization and, 56–58
  as victims of crime, 194
Aggression
  hormonal differences and, 31–32
  men's, compared to women's, 64
Alcoholism, women's, 151–52
American Women (commission report), 257–58
Analytical ability, girls' vs. boys', 60
"Anatomy as destiny," 22, 30
Androgen, 24
Androgynous gender roles, self-esteem and, 65
Anthony, Susan B., 163, 245, 265
Aries, Philip, 123
Artists, women, 5
Asian-Americans, 64, 84, 140, 215
Australopithecus, 35
Authority
  Wollstonecraft's concern with subservience to, 242–44
  see also Male dominance

B

Bacon, Francis, 37
Baird, Bill, 154, 156
Battered women, *see* Wife-beating

Bauer, Bruno, 267–68
Baxandall, R. F., 128
Behaviorist theory, 67–68
Bellotte v. Baird, 156
Berger, Peter, 62
Bernard, Jessie, 129
BFOQ (bona fide occupational qualification), 149
Biological sex
  behavior and, 28–33
  conservative view of, 239
  definitions of, 25, 49
  gender and, 23–26
  in Marx's theory, 269
  in Thomas's theory, 179
  see also Sex differences
Birth control (contraception), 154–57, 256
Black women, 8, 11
  adolescent, 55
  aging and, 57
  as domestic workers, 78, 82, 90, 107, 139
  as research subjects, 163-164
  history of work by, 104, 105, 138–39
  juvenile-delinquent, 200
  maternal mortality rate of, 147
  sex role socialization of, 64–65
  statistics on work by, 81–82, 92
  sterilization of, 147, 159–60
  as victims of crime, 145, 194, 195
  women's movement and, 290
  work attitudes of, 83, 99
Blacks
  civil rights struggle of, 258–59
  family among, 113, 115, 116, 117, 120, 136–39
  health of, 143, 146–47
  marriage expectations of, 65
  in the media, 215, 221–22
  poverty of, 94–95, 121
  self-esteem of, and "the system," 64